THE ROYAL ABBEY OF READING

BOYDELL STUDIES IN MEDIEVAL ART AND ARCHITECTURE

ISSN 2045–4902
Series Editors
Dr Julian Luxford
Professor Asa Simon Mittman

This series aims to provide a forum for debate on the art and architecture of the Middle Ages. It will cover all media, from manuscript illuminations to maps, tapestries, carvings, wall-paintings and stained glass, and all periods and regions, including Byzantine art. Both traditional and more theoretical approaches to the subject are welcome.

Proposals or queries should be sent in the first instance to the editors or to the publisher, at the addresses given below.

Dr Julian Luxford, School of Art History, University of St Andrews, 79 North Street, St Andrews, Fife KY16 9AL, UK

Professor Asa Simon Mittman, Department of Art and Art History, California State University at Chico, Chico, CA 95929–0820, USA

Boydell & Brewer, PO Box 9, Woodbridge, Suffolk IP12 3DF, UK

Previously published titles in the series are listed at the back of this volume.

THE
ROYAL ABBEY
OF READING

Ron Baxter

THE BOYDELL PRESS

First published 2016
The Boydell Press, Woodbridge

ISBN 978 1 78327 084 2

The Boydell Press is an imprint of Boydell & Brewer Ltd
PO Box 9, Woodbridge, Suffolk, IP12 3DF, UK
and of Boydell & Brewer Inc.
668 Mount Hope Ave, Rochester, NY 14620–2731, USA
website: www.boydellandbrewer.com

The publisher has no responsibility for the continued existence or accuracy of
URLs for external or third-party internet websites referred to in this book, and
does not guarantee that any content on such websites is, or will remain, accurate
or appropriate

A CIP catalogue record for this book is available
from the British Library
This publication is printed on acid-free paper

Printed and bound in Great Britain by
TJ International Ltd, Padstow, Cornwall

CONTENTS

ILLUSTRATIONS

FIGURES

PLATES

TABLES

The author and publishers are grateful to all the institutions and
individuals listed for permission to reproduce the materials in which they
hold copyright. Every effort has been made to trace the copyright holders;
apologies are offered for any omission, and the publishers will be pleased
to add any necessary acknowledgement in subsequent editions.

GLOSSARY OF ARCHITECTURAL TERMS
USED IN THE TEXT

This is by no means intended to be a complete architectural glossary, or even a complete glossary of terms used in medieval architecture. Rather I hope it will serve as a simple guide to technical terms as they are used here, especially in chapters six to eight.

Abacus
The top part of a capital, not to be confused with an **impost**. Both of these terms have their roots in classical architecture. In a classical context the abacus is the upper part of a capital that the entablature rests on, while the impost is a heavy stone supporting an arch. Transferring the terms to medieval buildings has caused endless confusion and heated disagreements. The distinction used here is explained more fully under impost.

Aisle
An area alongside the nave or chancel of a church, parallel to it and separated from it by an arcade.

Ambulatory
A semicircular or polygonal aisle. Often an ambulatory leads around the east end of the choir; separating the choir from apses or chapels.

Arcade, blind arcade
A series of arches supported by piers or columns. When applied to the surface of a wall it is called a blind arcade; when used ornamentally, it is called arcading.

Ashlar
Squared blocks of stone cut to an even face.

Beaker clasp
A geometric form of beakhead, alternately seen as a precursor to beakhead or a variant of it.

Beakhead
An ornament in the form of a bird's head, or a human or beast's head, superimposed on the roll moulding of an arch. Beakhead is predominantly found on doorways as a repeated form but occasionally also on windows and chancel arches and, as a single motif, on corbels.

Billet ornament
An ornament consisting of a band or bands of raised short cylinders (roll billet) or square blocks (square billet) placed at intervals.

Capital, Block capital, Cushion capital, Scallop capital, Trefoil capital
The capital is the architectural member which surmounts a column and supports an arch. It often provides the visual transition between a round column or shaft below and a square impost block above, which in turn supports the springing of the arch.

A **block capital** is the simplest form of capital, in which the top is square and the bottom round. The transition between them is most simply achieved by a gradual change of profile, but there are other options. The surface may be decorated. A **cushion capital** is normally described as a capital formed by the intersection of a cube and a sphere. It has flat semicircular faces below the abacus, and the triangular lower angles of the bell are all that remain of the spherical form. The semicircular faces are called shields. In variations of the cushion capital, the angles may be keeled or tucked. The shields and the bell may be decorated with carving. A **scallop capital** is a development of the cushion capital, where the shields and the bell supporting them are multiplied to form double scallop, triple scallop or multi scallop capitals. Scallop capitals are susceptible to a large number of variations, of which the commonest include recessing the shields, or defining them with a groove; sheathing the cones (into which the bell is divided), and carving wedges, fillets or rolls between the cones. A **trefoil** or **trilobed capital** is a form of cushion capital in which the shield is not semicircular but has three lobes, the central one descending further than those flanking it.

Chancel
The east end of a church where the altar is situated, usually reserved for the use of the clergy and choir. Sometimes known as the presbytery.

Chevron ornament
A form of three-dimensional architectural ornament consisting of zigzags formed by mouldings. The term 'zigzag' is itself reserved for the essentially two-dimensional form.

Chip carving
Simple geometric patterns (often saltire-in-square or star pattern) bevelled into a surface.

Corbel / corbel table
A corbel is a projecting block of stone or timber to support a feature above. A row of corbels, often carved, supporting a parapet, stringcourse or the eaves of a roof is called a **corbel table**.

Crossing
The central space at the junction of the nave, chancel and transepts of a cruciform church.

Crossing pier
One of the four great piers at the angles of the crossing, often supporting the weight of a crossing tower.

Embattled ornament
Also called fret. It consists of horizontal and vertical straight mouldings, repeated to form a band like the battlements of a parapet, and often used in the decoration of arches.

Extrados
The outer edge of an arch (as opposed to the intrados).

Giant order
An order whose columns or pilasters rise through two (or more) storeys. It is sometimes called a colossal order.

Hemicycle
The group of columns, arranged in a semicircular formation, that divide the east end of a choir from the ambulatory.

Impost / impost block
A horizontal block of stone immediately below the springing of an arch, sometimes immediately above the capital, or sometimes used instead of a capital. It should not be confused with an **abacus**. The commonest 12thc. forms have a chamfer below a vertical face, and decoration may be applied to the upright face, or the chamfer, or both.

Intrados
The inner edge of an arch (as opposed to the extrados).

Lavabo
A trough for washing in a monastery. It was usually placed near to the refectory.

Nook-shaft
A shaft set in the angle of a pier or respond, or the jamb of a doorway or window.

Order
One of a series of recessed arches and supports on a doorway, chancel arch etc. More generally a system of supports and the arches they carry.

Respond
A half pier or half column, bonded into a wall and supporting one end of an arch or arcade

Slype
In a greater medieval church, a covered way or passage leading east from the cloisters between transept and chapter house.

Soffit
The underside of an arch.

Springer/springing, Double springer
The first stone of an arch or vaulting rib above the springing point (the level at which an arch or vault rises from its supports). A double springer is a gabled stone from which spring two adjoining arches.

Stringcourse
An horizontal course projecting from a wall, often moulded and at times richly carved.

Stylobate
A low wall that carries an arcade, as in a cloister.

Transept
A rectangular area which cuts across the main axis of a basilica and projects beyond it. In church architecture it is usual to refer to the transept as two separate projections, the north and south transepts, on either side of the crossing.

Voussoir
The blocks forming an arch. They are usually wedge shaped, but can be rectangular with wedge-shaped mortar joints between them. The keystone (at the apex of an arch) and the springers (at its lowest points) are particular types of voussoir.

PREFACE AND ACKNOWLEDGEMENTS

In 1989 I was invited by George Zarnecki, who was in the process of setting up a Corpus of Romanesque Sculpture in Britain and Ireland, to take on the fieldwork in the county of Berkshire. This probably took me longer than it should have done – Berkshire is not a large county, nor is it particularly rich in Romanesque sculpture – but when it was complete I could not leave it alone, and the reason for that lay in Reading. Reading Abbey, I thought, had had a raw deal from the Reformation onwards. In its heyday it had been one of England's largest and most important abbeys: a royal foundation built to be the final resting place of King Henry I on a scale that surpassed most of England's other great churches. Four centuries later its last abbot, Hugh Cook of Faringdon, was executed in a particularly grisly fashion outside his own abbey. The church and most of the monastic buildings were systematically demolished over the next twenty years, and the useable building materials were dispersed.

At the beginning of the English Civil War, Reading's position controlling the crossings of the Thames and the route to the king's Oxford headquarters from the south made of the town an important strategic focus. It was garrisoned by the Royalists and besieged by the Parliamentary forces, and major defensive earthworks were dug across the abbey site. As a consequence of the early demolition and the siege in the Civil War, not even the plan of the church could be accurately determined by the time antiquarians began to take an interest in medieval buildings, although eighteenth-century artists were attracted by the imposing but not especially informative rubble cores still standing on the site. It is not surprising that Reading Abbey was unable to take its rightful place in the chronology of English architecture: a church whose east-end arrangement and elevation were unknown, and whose length was a matter of speculation could hardly be expected to contribute much to the big picture. Reading was an object almost exclusively of local interest until the discoveries of a wealth of spectacular sculpture from its cloister by Charles Keyser and George Zarnecki in the last century forced it on our attention.

This book is an attempt to put Reading Abbey back where it belongs. On the whole it is not concerned with the internal organisation of the monastery, but with its relations with the world outside, and in particular with the world of the court. It draws on the talents and hard work of many colleagues who have generously offered me their help and support over more years than I care to disclose.

I should like first to express my gratitude to The Paul Mellon Centre for Studies in British Art for their generous financial support. The staff of Reading museum have always been unfailingly generous with their support, but I must single out Leslie Cram, Christelle Beaupoux, Jillian Greenaway and Angela Houghton for special thanks. I have also received valuable assistance and local support from that useful source of oral history, the Reading Forum, where Avis Furness was especially helpful to me. Among the staff of libraries and museums who have assisted me with unfailing patience I must express particular gratitude to Nick Millea of the Bodleian Library, Martin Mintz and Jo Dansie from the British Library, Lily Szczygiel of the Osler Library at McGill University, Sarah Blick and Lydia Shan of Kenyon College, Gambier, Ohio and David McKitterick of Trinity College Library, Cambridge.

In writing the book I have been helped by many people, but I would especially like to thank my wife, Kathryn Morrison, for her help and encouragement throughout the research and writing of the book, and for her important contributions to its content. Stuart Harrison and Malcolm Thurlby have been more than generous in contributing their skill in analysing the standing remains, and Stuart drew all the reconstruction drawings and plans in the book. Eric Fernie has also read parts of the text in draft, and offered his unrivalled advice. Many other friends and professional colleagues have answered my calls for assistance, and I cannot hope to list them all, but I must mention Tim Ayers, Christopher Blakeman, Steven Brindle, Emily Cole, Stephen B. Cox, Jon Crump, Alfredo De La Fe, Canon Donald Gray, Canon Antony Griffiths, Edward Impey, Sandy Heslop, Jim King, Matthew Richter, Warwick Rodwell, Mike Vosper and Antony Wilson. I must also thank those photographers who have made their work freely available to me, and who are listed, sometimes pseudonymously, in the illustration credits.

Finally I should like to thank the Boydell Press, and especially Caroline Palmer, Nick Bingham, Rohais Haughton and Robert Kinsey.

INTRODUCTION

A sizeable area in the centre of Reading is occupied by the remains of what was once one of England's greatest Benedictine monasteries (plate 1). The hub of the monastery, around the church and cloister, survives as a collection of rubble walls stripped of their fine ashlar facings. The only standing remains of the church are parts of its south transept with the east end of the south nave aisle wall, including the east doorway into the cloister; rather less of the north transept; and column bases of the south side of the crossing and chancel arcade. However, the line of the south nave aisle wall is continued by a row of nineteenth-century terraced houses on Abbot's Walk (plate 2), while the wall of the Day Nursery, formerly the Roman Catholic school, marks the position of the south chancel arcade. The chapter house is the most complete and identifiable survival, and to the south of it, where the ground falls away to the river Kennet and the Holy Brook, the west wall of the dormitory block still stands (figure 1). The Holy Brook itself, although it is older than the ruins, takes its name from the abbey, for which it served as a drain and a millstream, driving the mill whose remains stand to the south-west (figure 2). The southern boundary of the precinct, or Forbury, is marked by the Kennet and the Holy Brook. To the north it followed the line of the north wall of the Forbury Gardens that runs along North Forbury Road. When the road passes HM Prison Reading it turns south, still following the line of the precinct, until it reaches the Kennet again at Blake's Bridge. None of the original precinct outer gateways survive, but the inner gateway, dividing the monastic area to the south from the more public zone including the church, still stands at the east end of Abbot's Walk, albeit totally rebuilt in 1861–62. Carved stones from the abbey are built into walls around the town, especially around St James's Roman Catholic Church, built to the north of the abbey church's north transept, and replicating its dedication.

As well as the physical remains, street names like Abbey Street, Abbey Square and Forbury Road preserve the memory of the monastery.

Reading Abbey was begun in 1121 by King Henry I and was designed from the outset to be his mausoleum. Henry was buried in the chancel in 1136, not without considerable delay as he had died in France late in the previous year, when channel crossings were hazardous owing to harsh weather conditions, and by 1164 the church was ready for consecration by Archbishop Thomas Becket. Henry's Foundation Charter, dating from 1125, describes the abbey's function as a family memorial, and lists generous gifts of land to support it. It also specifies provision for the accommodation of pilgrims, an important original function of the church reflected in its plan and in the early royal gift of a significant apostolic relic, the hand of St James. But Henry had founded more than a family mausoleum at Reading. The grandeur of the abbey complex, its royal associations, and its strategic position on the roads from Westminster and Windsor to the royal centres in the west like Woodstock, Clarendon and Winchester were to ensure its continued importance to successive monarchs throughout the Middle Ages. One of the major aims of this book is to recreate, in the mind at least, this aspect of Reading.

Royal visits to Reading, and important ceremonies, marriages and burials have been noted before, in an episodic fashion, and largely by the medical practitioner Jamieson Boyd Hurry (1857–1930), who wrote prolifically on the abbey while continuing his general practice in Reading

2 THE ABBEY MILL STRADDLES THE HOLY BROOK BEHIND ABBEY SQUARE.

and publishing the definitive book on woad.[1] To medical historians he is well known for his works on the subject of the vicious circle in individual and social pathology, describing manifestations of the phenomenon in such varied areas as urinary diseases, alcohol abuse, heart disease and dermatology.[2] His devotion to Reading Abbey included the commissioning of a series of ten oil paintings illustrating the history of the abbey from four established artists, and he gave a guided tour of the ruins every Whit Monday at which the townspeople and visitors were treated to a performance of the *Sumer* canon, more familiarly known by its opening phrase, *Sumer is icumen in*. The only surviving medieval version of the canon is in the Reading Abbey manuscript London BL, Harley 978, a mixed volume containing musical, calendrical, medical and literary texts produced between the mid-thirteenth century and the late fourteenth.[3] This transcription of the song dates to the period 1245–65,[4] and is remarkably sophisticated in its polyphony for a work of this date, consisting of a four-part canon carrying the main melody, with two more voices singing a polyphonic bass line.[5] Hurry also installed three relief tablets in the chapter

[1] Hurry (1930)
[2] e.g. Vicious Circles in Disease (1911); Poverty and its Vicious Circles (1917).
[3] Coates (1999), 162–63.
[4] Ibid., 73; Hohler (1978), 6.
[5] The bibliography is extensive, but for a useful introduction see Duffin (1988); Hohler (1978), 6.

3   ON JULY 10 1911 THE CANADIAN PHYSICIAN SIR WILLIAM OSLER UNVEILED THE MEMORIAL TABLETS COMMIS-
SIONED BY JAMIESON HURRY FOR THE WALLS OF THE CHAPTER HOUSE.

house. Two carved by William Silver Frith (1850–1924) depicted the first
and last abbots of Reading, Hugh of Amiens and Hugh Cook Faringdon,
and were unveiled in 1911 by the distinguished Canadian physician Sir
William Osler, who had accepted a Regius Professorship at Oxford after
a busy career teaching in various North American universities (figure 3).
The third tablet, carved by the local architect, antiquarian and freemason
William Ravenscroft (1848–1943), commemorates the *Sumer* canon
(figure 4), and Hurry produced a short work on it to coincide with the
ceremony on 18 June 1913 when it was unveiled by Dr Hugh P. Allen,
a Reading man who became organist of New College Oxford and later
director of the Royal College of Music.[6]

Hurry's 1901 monograph on the abbey has not really been surpassed
as a general overview, although an important study of its architecture had
already been published by Albury in 1881.[7] Since the 1960s Brian Kemp
has produced much important work on the abbey, including articles on
the miracles worked by the hand of St James,[8] and the abbey seals,[9] and
especially an edition of the abbey cartularies that includes a valuable
account of the abbey's foundation.[10] No author, however, has yet produced

[6]   Hurry (1914).
[7]   Albury (1881).
[8]   Kemp (1970).
[9]   Kemp (1988).
[10] Kemp (1986), 13–19.

anything that might be called a continuous narrative history of Reading Abbey, and in chapter four of this book an attempt has been made to do this by establishing a framework of royal involvement with Reading, based largely on royal visits that can be identified from the public record, and setting the more anecdotal evidence from chronicles within it. This approach locates the abbey in a series of royal itineraries, allowing conclusions to be drawn about changing patterns of royal travel in which it was included, and also the personal preferences of individual kings, some of whom, at key points in their reigns, preferred monastic lodgings to any other kind.

When the abbey church was completed, only three churches in the country were longer, Bishop Walkelin's Winchester Cathedral (founded 1079), Abbot Baldwin's Bury St Edmund's (1081) and Bishop Maurice's London cathedral of Old St Paul's (1087), and Reading's chancel was longer than any except Bury's.[11] The elaborate arrangement of eastern chapels, with four on the transept and three on the ambulatory, was paralleled in only two earlier English great churches, Bury St Edmund's and Anselm's 'glorious choir' at Canterbury of 1096, both justly renowned for the pilgrimage implications of these features.[12] Despite these compelling claims to our attention, the abbey church has signally failed to find its rightful place in the discourse of English architectural history.[13]

4   THE *SUMER* TABLET, CARVED BY WILLIAM RAVENSCROFT AND STILL ON DISPLAY IN THE CHAPTER HOUSE, COMMEMORATES THE COMPOSITION OF THE CANON *SUMER IS ICUMEN IN* AT THE ABBEY IN THE MID-THIRTEENTH CENTURY.

[11]   See chapter six. Norwich might have been slightly longer overall, but its chancel was much shorter.

[12]   For Bury, see Whittingham (1951); Gilyard-Beer (1970); Abou-el-Haj (1983). On Anselm's choir at Canterbury, see Willis (1845); Woodman (1981), 23–86.

[13]   Hurry (1901) dealt with the architecture of the church in fewer than four pages. Among the general histories of English Medieval architecture, Rickman (1881) briefly described the state of the ruins and mentioned the excavation of pieces of ornamental stonework, and Parker (1902) noted the abbey in a list of the foundations of Henry I's reign. Later writers have concerned themselves with the plan of the church. Prior (1900) stated that it was 'exactly that of the Royal Westminster of St Edward's building', which he illustrated with an eastern

The reason for this has already been mentioned; practically nothing of the church remains. Even antiquarian drawings, of which a series survives from the eighteenth and nineteenth centuries, can show us little more of its original appearance because demolition began early after the Dissolution and was unusually fast and thorough, owing largely to the convenience of having a source from which high-grade building stone could be quarried right in the centre of a thriving town (see chapter five).

There is no reason to doubt that Reading Abbey was an influential building. This is demonstrable for the surviving cloister sculpture which was copied both locally, e.g. at Avington and Cholsey, and in important buildings at a distance. The beakhead decoration, which was a prominent feature of high-quality buildings during the twelfth century, was widely and inventively used in Reading cloister and is not known earlier in England. It is reasonable to assume, then, that features of the architecture of the church might also have been copied, but apart from the plan, which has only been fully clarified within the last quarter-century, there is no agreement on what the building looked like. Before the present investigation it was not clear how, or even whether, the church was vaulted.[14] To some extent, therefore, the church is an empty vessel which architectural historians have felt free to fill, proposing Reading as the original site of ideas which appeared in a developed form elsewhere. This dustbin effect is one which Reading shares with other lost major buildings. Edward the Confessor's church at Westminster, Lanfranc's Canterbury, Suger's choir at Saint-Denis,[15] and the cathedrals of Arras[16] and Cambrai[17] have all

ambulatory and no ambulatory chapels, but a pair of east chapels on each transept. Bond (1905) agreed on the apse and ambulatory, but was 'uncertain whether there were radiating chapels'. Clapham (1934) accepted the radiating chapels, comparing the plan to Leominster and St Bartholomew's, Smithfield, while Boase (1953) described the plan as following Battle Abbey, Bury St Edmunds and Norwich, and gave measurements of the church (taken from Albury (1881) or Hurry (1901)) without comment. Kidson (1962) made no mention of the plan but devoted a short paragraph to speculating on the role of Reading in the dissemination of sculptural decoration. Webb (1965) noted only the survival of fragments from the cloister. None of these general histories devoted more than a few lines to Reading, and it was not until the publication of Fernie (2000) that the abbey church was placed in its proper context in a major synthesis.

[14]   See chapter six.

[15]   Wilson (1990), 41–43 argued that the choir vault of Saint-Denis was supported by flying buttresses, the earliest in the West.

[16]   For Arras, see Bony (1958).

[17]   Cambrai Cathedral was destroyed following an order of 1796, and is known only through a plan of c. 1800 made when only part of the church was still standing, a photograph of a model made in 1695 but sadly destroyed in 1945, and various drawings and prints of the exterior. Although no image of the interior survives, Cambrai has been given an important role in the development of the four-storey

been credited with important architectural innovations on the flimsiest of evidence.

The feature claimed for Reading is a giant-order elevation in the choir, with columnar piers rising through two storeys to support arches above a gallery, as at Romsey, Jedburgh, Oxford and probably Tewkesbury.[18] This would only be innovative at Reading if, as McAleer has argued, there was no giant order at Tewkesbury, but since his argument relies heavily on the absence of other giant-order elevations in England before *circa* 1140 at Romsey it cannot accommodate a giant order at Reading anyway.[19] For those who propose a giant order at Reading Abbey, its significance is as a major royal site from which Romsey, Jedburgh and St Frideswide's, Oxford took their ideas.[20] The issue is an important one, though ultimately not resolvable with absolute certainty. It will be discussed in more detail in chapter six.

Setting aside these speculations, there is no doubt that the fame of Reading Abbey today largely rests on its cloister sculpture. This did not come to light in any quantity until Charles Keyser's chance discovery of fifteen capitals and two voussoirs lying in the flower beds of Holme Park, Sonning in 1912 (see figure 77).[21] These, he discovered, had been brought to Holme Park from Borough Marsh, and Keyser was also able to trace a group of carved voussoirs and springers which had been ferried across the River Thames from Borough Marsh to Shiplake House and assembled into an arch in 1889. Before Keyser's discoveries, the most significant piece of abbey sculpture known was the so-called 'Reading Abbey stone', a quadruple capital discovered in 1835 among the ruins which was adapted by Augustus Welby Pugin, the architect of St James's Roman Catholic church, for use as a font (see plate XVII).[22] Other fragments of carved stonework were to be seen built into walls around the abbey ruins, or preserved in the town museum, but in accounts of the abbey written before Keyser's discoveries the sculpture received no more than an incidental notice.[23]

Keyser's discoveries were enormously augmented when, in 1948–50, George Zarnecki and a team of staff and students from the Courtauld Institute of Art excavated and removed carved stones from a site in

---

nave elevation, and is the subject of a virtual reconstruction by Matthieu Deltombe. See Héliot (1956), 91–110; Thiébaut (1975).

[18] The giant order reconstruction of the choir at Tewkesbury was first proposed in Clapham (1952). For more recent discussions of the problem, see McAleer (1983); Halsey (1985); Halsey (1990).

[19] McAleer (1983), 556–58.

[20] Halsey (1985), 28.

[21] Keyser (1916).

[22] Albury (1881); Hurry (1901), 147–48.

[23] Albury (1881), 81–82; Hurry (1901), 147–48. Buckler (1823) and Prior and Gardner (1912) do not mention the sculpture at all.

Borough Marsh itself, whence both the Sonning and Shiplake stones had been taken.[24] Zarnecki discovered some fifty more pieces of sculpture, including the Coronation of the Virgin capital which is probably the most celebrated of the Reading Abbey sculptures. Keyser's and Zarnecki's discoveries and the Shiplake stones are all now in Reading Museum along with other carved stones from the abbey. Zarnecki is responsible, more than any other, for putting Reading Abbey on the sculptural map. Between the publication of Keyser's finds in 1916 and Zarnecki's own in 1950–51, the significance of the Reading sculpture remained largely unrecognised.[25] After 1951, however, the Reading cloister sculpture began to occupy its present important place in the chronology of English twelfth-century art.[26]

Inevitably, attention has been concentrated on the foliage decoration of the spectacular capitals, the range of grotesque and fantastic animal carvings on the capitals, springers and voussoirs, and the precocious iconography of the Coronation of the Virgin capital. It was not until the *Corpus of Romanesque Sculpture in Britain and Ireland* (CRSBI) began in 1988 its mammoth task of recording every piece of Romanesque stone sculpture in these islands that the possibility emerged of making some sense of the great quantity of carved abbey stone still surviving in Reading Museum and elsewhere. It was fortunate that around the same time the Corporation of Reading began to carry out their long-envisaged move of material from storehouses around the town into greatly enlarged museum quarters in the Town Hall, so that to some extent the work of recording material for the CRSBI and acquisitioning long-neglected stones for the museum has gone hand in hand, to the benefit of both parties.

As a result of this, there was found to be sufficient material of known provenance in the museum to attempt a reconstruction of the cloister and its decorative scheme (see chapter seven). The significance of this rests in the fact that there are no Benedictine cloisters of this early date surviving *in-situ* in England at all. The oldest genuine survivals, standing as built, are from at least 100 years later, like parts of the Lincoln cloister. Apart from that, we have a few reconstructions of sections of arcade, but these are all either speculative and intended only to give a general impression based on limited material, as at Westminster Abbey and Bridlington Priory, or at least 50 years later than Reading, like the plain Cistercian arcades of Rievaulx and Newminster. The reconstruction of the Reading cloister provides a detailed view of the hub of an English twelfth-century Benedictine abbey of the top rank for the first time.[27]

---

[24]   Zarnecki (1949); Zarnecki (1950b), 1; Baxter and Harrison (2002), 309–11.
[25]   Gardner (1937), 79 illustrates one of Keyser's capitals as 'probably from Reading', remarking on the 'rather crude figure drawing with fine decorative effect'.
[26]   e.g. Boase (1953), 71–77; Stone (1955), 59–61; London (1984), 147, 159, 167–71.
[27]   First published in Baxter and Harrison (2002).

In part this book is an attempt to reinstate Reading into the discourse of architectural history as a rich and functioning building, rather than the home of a collection of high-quality carved fragments. Chapter one offers an account of the foundation of the abbey by Henry I, analysing the reasons for Henry's choice of Reading for his mausoleum, the sources of funding he set up, and the events at the abbey until his death and burial there. Chapters two and three focus on specific aspects of the abbey: its reliance on pilgrimage and relics, and the evidence for burial there. In chapter four the focus returns to the court, and on the way the abbey was used by successive rulers between the twelfth century and the sixteenth as a residence and a royal centre. In 1539 Reading Abbey was dissolved by Henry VIII, and chapter five describes the bloody events of this process and the dispersal and decline of the abbey fabric over five centuries into the ruin that survives today. It also includes an analysis of what we know of the enigmatic Royal Palace, into which the abbey was converted after the monks left.

Chapters six and seven are devoted to aspects of the abbey's architecture: the church, and the lavishly carved cloister. Chapter eight concentrates on the sculptural decoration of Reading Abbey, beginning with a detailed stylistic and iconographic analysis of the cloister sculpture, intended mainly to clarify workshop connections with sculpture produced elsewhere in England and beyond.

This book concentrates on the relationship of Reading Abbey to the world outside, particularly the court. The internal organisation of the abbey, and the personalities of its abbots and other obedientiaries are largely ignored except where they come into this story – that is at the beginning and the end. Like Jamieson Hurry, I have only devoted any significant attention to the first and last abbots.

FOUNDATION: READING ABBEY
AS A ROYAL MAUSOLEUM

1

According to the Annals of Reading, the abbey was founded by King Henry I on 18 June 1121.[1] The 'foundation charter' of 1125 was actually a formal confirmation of the abbey's rights, possessions and responsibilities,[2] in which King Henry set out his motives for building it. He built the abbey for the salvation of his soul, and for those of his dead relatives: his father William the Conqueror (d. 1087), his brother William Rufus (d. 1100), his only legitimate son William Aetheling, who tragically drowned in the wreck of the White Ship off Barfleur in 1120, his mother Matilda (d. 1083) and his first wife, Eadgyth-Matilda (d. 1118).[3] This formula leaves us in no doubt that Henry intended from the start that Reading Abbey was to be a family memorial, and when he died overseas in 1135 his body was brought back to Reading for burial.

The fashion for royal burial in personal or family mausoleums in England was apparently begun by Edward the Confessor. Between the death of Egbert and the accession of the Confessor, English kings were

---

[1] 'Petrus prior et vii cum eo fratres rogatu regis Henrici a Pontio Abbate Cluniacensi missi in Angliam, associatis sibi nonnullis fratribus de monasterio Sanct Pancratii Cluniacensis ordinis observantiam in monasterio Radingensi noviter tunc a rege fundato inchoaverunt 14 kl. Julii.' *Annales Radingensis*, 10.

[2] The original charter does not survive, but the text is given in five cartularies, the earliest, BL Egerton 3031, dating from the 1190s (see Kemp (1986), I, 33–36). Elements of this text are certainly suspicious; for example, it grants the abbey the liberty of *hutfangentheof*, the right to fine thieves taken outside the abbey's jurisdiction, which is not recorded elsewhere before 1135–40. Nevertheless, Kemp is probably right to argue that the text is not a forgery but that the original text was 'improved' for the cartulary, its main provisions remaining unaffected.

[3] 'pro salute anime mee et willelmi regis patris mei et Willelmi regis fratris mei et Willelmi filii mei e Mathildis regine matris mee et Mathildis regine uxoris mee et omnium antecessorum et successorum meorum ... ' Kemp (1986), I, 33.

most commonly buried at Winchester (Egbert d. 839, Æthelwulf d. 856, Alfred d. 899, Edward the Elder d. 924, Eadred d. 955, Eadwig d. 959, Cnut d. 1035, Harthacnut d. 1042),[4] or Glastonbury (Edmund I d. 946, Edgar d. 975, Edmund Ironside d. 1016), although various other sites were also used.[5]

According to his biographer, Edward the Confessor decided on a complete rebuilding of Westminster Abbey as his burial church because of his devotion to St Peter, to whom it was dedicated.[6] The concept of constructing (or reconstructing) his own mausoleum was therefore in Edward's mind from the outset of the rebuilding programme. His successors followed his example for their own burials. Harold II was buried in his own foundation of Waltham, and William the Conqueror lies in the *Abbaye aux Hommes*, which he had built at Caen in Normandy. Given this background, the burial of William Rufus at Winchester requires some examination. Rufus made no provision for his burial during his lifetime; indeed the only building work he can reliably be associated with is the rebuilding of Westminster Hall, under construction by 1096 and officially used for the first time at Pentecost 1099.[7] Westminster Hall was (and is) by any standards a spectacular building. Its lower walls survived the fire of 1834, although they have been refaced, and the hall retains its original dimensions, measuring 73 metres by 21 metres (240 ft by 67 ft 6 in.). This was secular building on a gigantic scale – perhaps the largest in Europe – although, as Fernie points out, its size is unexceptional in comparison with contemporary great churches.[8]

On 2 August 1100, Rufus was killed by an arrow while hunting in the New Forest. This episode, described by Edward Freeman as 'one of those events in English history which are familiar to every memory and come readily to every mouth',[9] was recorded in the major chronicles, and has been analysed by historians ever since.[10] Despite variations in detail, the salient facts are clear enough. The king was shot with an arrow in the chest, probably by Walter Tirel, Lord of Poix, and died immediately. Tirel fled,

---

[4]   For Anglo-Saxon burial at Winchester, see Crook (1994); Biddle (1993); Woodward (1861–69), I, 70–71.

[5]   For Glastonbury, see VCH, Somerset (1911), 82–99. For other sites: Æthelbald (d. 860) and Æthelbert (d. 866) were buried at Sherborne; Æthelred I (d. 871) at Wimborne; Æthelstan (d. 939) at Malmesbury; Edward the Martyr (d. 978) at Shaftesbury; Æthelred II (d.1016) at Old St Paul's; and Harold Harefoot (d. 1040) at St Clement Dane's.

[6]   Barlow (1962), 68–69.

[7]   Anglo-Saxon Chronicle, 234; Henry of Huntingdon, 47, 48.

[8]   Fernie (2000), 84–87.

[9]   Freeman (1882), II, 336.

[10]   Henry of Huntingdon, 48–49; Anglo-Saxon Chronicle, 235–36, William of Malmesbury, 284–85.

as did all the noblemen in the royal party; the one fearing retribution, the others to protect their own interests at a time that was likely to be at best unstable. Rufus's body was loaded onto a cart by some of his attendants and taken to Winchester cathedral priory, less than twenty miles distant.

Rufus's youngest brother acted swiftly. By the following day Henry had arrived at Winchester to take possession of the Royal Treasury, along with sufficient of the nobility to have him declared king by acclamation. Rufus was buried there the next morning in what was effectively the nearest suitable place, given that Rufus had given no instructions for his burial. Henry could easily have pointed out that Winchester more than any other cathedral had a tradition of royal burials, and technically it is arguable that Rufus was ultimately responsible for Bishop Walkelin's rebuilding, since it took place in his reign. If Christopher Brooke was correct in his view that Walkelin built the church on such an enormous scale because he envisaged it as the resting place of generations of kings to come, these arguments might be expected to carry a good deal of weight.[11] But Walkelin had died in 1098 and was buried in his newly-built cathedral alongside the steps in front of the pulpitum, and since his death, Rufus had kept the see of Winchester vacant; a policy that did not endear him to the chapter there. Henry's first act after his acclamation as king was to appoint William Giffard to the see, which was at least an excellent piece of public relations and looks suspiciously like a bribe. It was important for Henry to get Rufus under the ground and himself crowned as quickly as possible to consolidate his claim to the throne before his elder brother Robert arrived home from the Crusades.[12] In the event Rufus was the last king to be buried at Winchester, and the collapse of the tower on his tomb in 1107 was read, according to William of Malmesbury at least, as a judgement on him.[13] Apart from the odd case of William Rufus, then, Henry's decision to build his own foundation as a personal mausoleum simply followed late Anglo-Saxon and Norman tradition.

WHY READING?

As for the site chosen by Henry for his personal foundation, William of Malmesbury stressed the importance of Reading's position,

[11] Brooke (1993), 5.
[12] William of Malmesbury, 344.
[13] William of Malmesbury, 285. William has the fall of the tower taking place in the year after William's burial beneath it.

between the rivers Kennet and Thames in a place calculated for the reception of almost all who might have occasion to travel to the more populous cities of England.[14]

The description of Reading in the Domesday Survey gives some idea of its size and complexion.[15] It was one of three boroughs in Berkshire, and probably the second in size after Wallingford. Reading is mentioned in two Domesday entries; in the lands of the king and those of Battle Abbey. The king's holdings included both agricultural land and property in the town. The former consisted of enough land for 40 plough-teams, woodland for 100 pigs and 150 acres of meadow. There was also pasture valued at 16s 6d, four mills yielding 35s and three fisheries yielding 14s 6d. This land was worked by eighty men.[16] Within the borough there were 29 properties belonging to the king and another held by Henry of Ferrers.[17] The Abbot of Battle had a church in the town (St Mary's) held before the Conquest by Abbess Leofgifu (see below) to which belonged an estate with land for 7 plough-teams, 12 acres of meadow and woodland for 5 pigs. This was worked by a further 17 labourers,[18] and the holding also included another 2 mills and 2½ fisheries. The abbot also had 29 properties in the borough.[19] There was therefore a strong agricultural element to the town, but a recorded population of 161, usually taken to mean heads of households, implied a total figure of around 800 – nowhere near as large as Wallingford's 2–3,000 but bigger than Windsor's 500, and very much larger than the 'little hamlet of some thirty one-storied chimneyless hovels' imagined by Hurry.[20] The earliest street plan of the town is John Speed's map of 1610, but if we ignore the abbey (in the NE corner) we can get a good idea of the Domesday town (figure 5).[21] The plan is dominated by the river Kennet, running diagonally from the south-west to the north-east. Most of the town is on the north bank of the river, which has had a network of looping

---

[14]   William of Malmesbury, 358.

[15]   Domesday Survey, 140, 146.

[16]   Fifty-five villans, or villagers, and thirty bordars, or smallholders. Both classes were technically free but economically dependent on wealthier landowners for subsistence; bordars more so than villans. See Stenton (1951), 138–39.

[17]   All thirty were described as hagae. The terms *hagae* and *masurae* are both used for dwellings in the Domesday Survey. *Hagae* are sometimes translated as 'closes', or groups of dwellings of an indeterminate size. *Masurae* are sometimes taken to mean single dwellings, but in many cases it is assumed that the terms are interchangeable. Most authorities simply fail to translate these terms.

[18]   Nine villans and eight bordars.

[19]   Described as *masurae*, see note 17.

[20]   Hurry (1906a), 2–3.

[21]   Speed (1610). The plan of Reading is included as an inset to the map of Buckinghamshire: 'For that Barkshire cold not contain place for this Towne I have here inserted it, as one of ye most ancient and cheifest in ye Countye.'

channels cut to form streams for the mills mentioned in the Domesday Survey. The longest of these is the Holy or Hallowed Brook, which leaves the river some five miles upstream of Reading at Theale, and runs roughly parallel to the river on its north side.[22] At some time it was directed into channels dug to serve the abbey mill (see figure 2). Today it runs in tunnels for most of its course through the town, going underground at Mallard Row, behind Castle Street, and emerging at Abbey Square. It continues eastward past the site of the Abbey Mill, which it once powered, and rejoins the Kennet where it passes the rere-dorter of the abbey (plate III). Returning to Speed's map, the river was crossed by two major roads, both running approximately south-east to north-west. London Street was the eastern road, running from the junction with the main road to London to cross the Kennet at High Bridge. Once over the bridge it became Shoemaker's Row, one of a cluster of trade streets grouped around the old market at St Mary's Butts.[23] The second major road, to the west of London Street, was St Giles Street. It crossed the Kennet at Seven Bridges – corresponding to the multiple streams at that point – and turned into Old Street. At the north of the town ran Broad street, connecting the two main roads from the south, and in the rectangle between this and the river were all the main trading and residential streets of medieval Reading, including Gutter Lane, Fish Street and Butchers' Row. Minster Street, linking London Street and St Giles Street immediately north of their river crossings, was named from the minster church of the Anglo-Saxon nunnery whose possessions helped to fund Henry I's abbey. Although the layout of the streets remains broadly the same as it was in the seventeenth century, most of the street names have been changed or lost. London Street remains, along with Broad Street and Minster Street, but of the former trade streets we have only part of Hosier Lane – now renamed Hosier Street – facing the west end of St Mary's Butts.[24]

Henry I's new foundation was built on open ground on the eastern outskirts of the town, bounded by the river Kennet to the south. Speed's map clearly shows the position of the church at the north of the monastery and the ruined buildings around the cloister running down to the river. The precinct called the Forbury forms an outer courtyard at the north-west, and the church of St Laurence stands between the town and the abbey, alongside the west entrance to the Forbury. Excavations carried out between 1971 and 1973 have uncovered some evidence of occupation of this area before the abbey was built. An inconclusive scatter of Bronze Age and Romano-British sherds was found in disturbed strata around the area of the ambulatory, but a foundation trench that was earlier than the

---

[22] Dormer (1937).
[23] For the rules of the various trade guilds, see Man (1816), 347–53.
[24] I am grateful to Avis Furness at Reading Forum for this information.

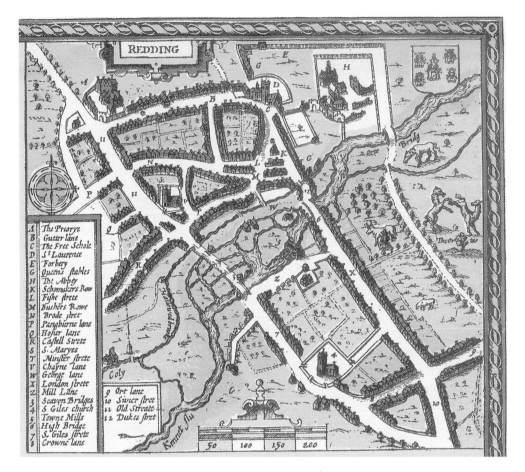

A	The Priorye
B	Gutter lane
C	The Free Schole
D	St Laurence
E	Forbery
G	Queens stables
H	The Abbey
K	Schomakers Row
L	Fyshe strete
M	Buchers Rowe
N	Brode stret
P	Pangbirne lane
Q	Hoser lane
R	Castell Strete
S	S. Maryes
T	Minster strete
V	Chayne lane
W	George lane
X	London strete
Z	Mill Lane
3	Seaven Bridges
4	S Giles church
5	Towne Mills
6	High Bridge
7	S. Giles strete
8	Crowne lane

9	Ort lane
10	Swier stret
11	Old Streate
12	Dukes stret

5   THE TOWN PLAN OF READING IN 1610, PUBLISHED IN JOHN SPEED'S *THE THEATRE OF THE EMPIRE OF GREAT BRITAINE*, SHOWS THE MAIN COMMERCIAL STREETS AT THE NW AND THE ABBEY PRECINCT AT THE NE.

abbey along with Anglo-Saxon pottery and a small knife blade of the fifth to eighth century were found *in situ* in that area, suggesting to the excavator that a late-Saxon building had been present on the site.[25]

FOUNDATION FROM CLUNY

The foundation date of 18 June 1121 coincides with the arrival in Reading of seven monks from Cluny led by a prior, Peter, who were sent in response to King Henry's request to Abbot Pons. They were soon joined by

---

[25] Slade (1975–76), 44–45. The lack of any signs of occupation pointed to an ecclesiastical rather than a residential building.

other monks from the Cluniac priory of Lewes in Sussex.[26] Cluny at this time was the largest and most powerful abbey in Europe. By harnessing his new foundation to Cluny, Henry was associating it with a tradition of splendour in architecture and decoration, with an elaborate liturgy en-livened by music, and with a foundation that had been at the forefront of the reform movement for over a century. There was usually a price to pay for association with Cluny, and that price was autonomy. Under Odilo, Abbot of Cluny from 994–1049, Cluny began to turn abbeys over which it had reforming power, or which wanted to adopt Cluniac customs, into dependencies. By the beginning of the twelfth century, the subservience of Cluniac houses to the mother house was such that all monks in Cluniac houses were, in theory at least, monks of Cluny and subject to its abbot. They were supposed to profess their vows to the Abbot of Cluny himself, either by going to the mother house or at a visitation. Their own houses were therefore priories rather than abbeys, headed by a prior (normally the second-in-command of a Benedictine abbey), rather than an abbot.

Reading was in this position for only two years. In 1123 Prior Peter returned to Cluny and Hugh of Amiens left Lewes, where he had been prior, to take up the new position of Abbot of Reading.[27] Reading was the first Cluniac house in England to achieve independent abbey status, and how this was accomplished we have no idea, but by some means Henry and his new abbot managed to create a house with all the benefits of Cluniac observance and none of the disadvantages of dependence on Cluny.[28] In this respect Reading had much in common with Fécamp, the site of the Palace of the Dukes of Normandy and the abbey where Dukes Richard I and Richard II were buried. Richard II, Henry's great-grandfather, invited the Cluniac William of Volpiano to reform the Abbey of Fécamp in 1001, and it seems impossible that Henry did not have this example in mind when he called on Abbot Pons.

Hugh of Amiens was one of the leading churchmen of his day. He was born of the noble family of de Boves, Counts of Amiens, studied at the School of Laon, and became a monk of Cluny. In 1115 he was appointed Prior of Saint-Martial de Limoges, and later the same year he was ap-pointed to the same position at Lewes Priory, Sussex. While he was Abbot of Reading he wrote the *Dialogi de Summo Bono*, otherwise known as

---

[26] Annales Radingensis, 10.
[27] Annales Radingensis, 10. See also Flor. Hist., II, 49, a compilation partly by Matthew Paris that relies upon a lost chronicle of Reading. Such a work (though not necessarily the same one) is noted in the late twelfth-century Reading booklist (see Barfield (1888), 119; Coates (1999), 28).
[28] Henry's nephew and successor, Stephen, founded his own burial church of Faversham along much the same lines in 1148, taking monks from the Cluniac house of Bermondsey and setting up Prior Clarembald of Bermondsey as the first abbot.

6   THE FIRST ABBOT, HUGH OF AMIENS, LEFT READING IN 1130 TO TAKE UP THE POST OF ARCHBISHOP OF
ROUEN, WHICH HE HELD UNTIL HIS DEATH IN 1164. HIS TOMB, SHOWN HERE, IS IN ROUEN CATHEDRAL.

his Dialogues, his best known work and one that has been described as
'the first comprehensive text of systematic theology'. He might also have
written the *Reprehensio* at this time, a polemical response to Bernard of
Clairvaux's *Apologia ad Guillelmum* (discussed more fully in chapter eight
below).[29] It was probably his scholastic writings that brought him to the
attention of Pope Honorius II, who summoned him to Rome, and ultimately led to his appointment as Archbishop of Rouen in 1130 (figure
6). King Henry stoutly opposed Hugh's removal from Reading, as did the
monks, but to no avail – the pope wanted him in a more active role.[30]
Although Reading was no longer strictly a Cluniac house after 1123, the
influence of Cluny remained strong throughout the twelfth century. As
well as Abbot Hugh I (1123–30), his successors Anscher (1130–35) and
Hugh II (1186–99) had all been Priors of Lewes before coming to Reading,

[29] Freeburn (2011), 2.
[30] Regesta Regum, 2, 218; Freeburn (2011), 9–10.

and in 1199 Hugh II was elevated from the Abbacy of Reading to that of Cluny.[31]

Independence for his foundation was very important to the king. The foundation charter includes an elaborate grant of immunities for the abbey which effectively freed it from all lay control, even during abbatial vacancies.[32] This was important. Such vacancies were often artificially extended at other abbeys by manufactured disputes over elections, because where estates were held in tenure to a lay landlord, rents would go to the landlord-in-chief, usually the king, while there was no abbot.[33] The foundation charter also includes strictures forbidding nepotism and child oblation, and expressly states that the resources are to be devoted to the relief of the poor and reception of pilgrims and guests. As Brian Kemp has noted, it 'reads like a programme of contemporary monastic reform in a Black Monk context'.[34]

CHARITY AT READING ABBEY

Two hospitals were founded following the stated commitment to charity: the Leper Hospital of St Mary Magdalene within the abbey precinct, and the Hospital of St John the Baptist, outside its walls.

HOSPITAL OF ST MARY MAGDALENE

The leper house was founded by Abbot Anscher (1130–35), the abbey's second abbot, according to a memorandum in the abbey cartulary.[35] The text of the memorandum states that the abbot founded the hospital out of his own piety, within the abbey confines, and that it was called the Hospital of St Mary Magdalene. It housed twelve lepers supervised by their own chaplain. Each inmate was given a daily allowance of half a loaf of bread and half a gallon of middling beer (*servisie mediocris*), and also 5d. every month for buying meat. In Lent the bread was to be of barley. The lepers also had a generous clothing allowance: each one was supplied with hood, tunic and cloak, and with two woollen vests and under-linen. The hood or cape was to contain three ells of cloth, the tunic three, and the cloak

---

[31] Kemp (1968), 511.

[32] 'Statuimus autem tam ecclestiastice quam et regie prospectu potestatis ut decedente abbate Radingensi omnis possessio monasterii ubicumque fuerit remaneat integra et libera cum omni iure et consuetudine sua in manu et dispositione prioris et monachorum capituli Radingensis.' Kemp (1986), 34.

[33] As apparently happened at Bury St Edmunds for thirteen years between 1102 and 1121; see Abou-el-Haj (1983), 5. The case of the Cathedral Priory of Winchester after the death of Bishop Walkelin, described above, is a similar one.

[34] Kemp (1986), I, 18.

[35] Kemp (1986), I, 183.

two and a quarter, and these garments were supplied as often as required. Each inmate also received ten yards of linen a year, and one yard of serge for shoes.

The chaplain was supplied with six ells of russet and ten yards of linen every Michaelmas; he also received all oblations made by the brethren of the house, but other offerings he divided with the brethren. The almoner of the monastery was to undertake any new building or repairs that might be required. The clothes-mender (*sartuarius*) of the monastery was to supply them with leather girdles at Michaelmas and with shoes at Easter. Their carter was to receive bread daily from the granarian and 32d. a year from the almoner. The woman servant was to be supplied with bread and 2s. a year in like fashion. The chamberlain was to supply the hospital with provender for a horse, with four loads of hay, and with the milk of four cows.

The rules of the house were strict. For incontinence or striking a brother the punishment was expulsion; for defamation or disobedience to the master, fasting on bread and water in the midst of the hall, the culprit's portion of meat and drink being placed on the table and distributed by the master. No one was allowed to leave the house or stand at the gate without a companion. Anyone desirous of leave of absence for one, two, or three nights had to obtain permission of the master and of the whole convent, but if for longer the master's consent was necessary, and then only with a companion. The brothers were to prepare to rise at the first ringing of the bell, and when it rang for the third time to enter the church. If anyone found anything on the premises it was not to be concealed, but shown to the brethren and placed in the common fund; but if it was found outside it might be considered the finder's if he so willed. Alms given by anyone to an inmate on the roadside for infirmity were to go to the common purse. No one was to enter the wash-house without a companion, nor was anyone to send the servant of the house any long distance without leave.[36] At first it was simply paid for out of the general abbey fund, but by the fifteenth century it had its own endowment of lands at Arley Whiteknights and Spitalfields. As time passed leprosy grew less common, and the profile of the inmates began to change. In 1414, King Henry V made a grant for life to William Bruer, a servant and carter of his grandfather the Duke of Lancaster, who had become blind and unable to look after himself in his old age. Bruer was given a chamber within the Hospital of St Mary Magdalen by Reading. He was fed from the kitchen of the abbey every day, and given two loaves of bread a day, one white and the other called copyn, presumably a lower grade of loaf, along with a gallon of ale. Every year he was to receive two cartloads of wood for fuel. Later in the century the house fell into disrepair, and in 1479 an enquiry by Edward IV revealed

[36] VCH Berkshire 2 (1907), 98–99.

that it had been taken down by the abbot, who had also appropriated its lands.[37]

HOSPITAL OF ST JOHN THE BAPTIST

This was founded by Abbot Hugh II (1186–99) at a date between 1189 and 1193, and supported by a grant in free alms of the church of St Laurence, Reading. The hospital was founded to supply food, clothing and accommodation to thirteen local poor persons, and to needy wayfarers. As the parish church was involved, Bishop Hubert Walter (1189–93) was necessarily concerned with the establishment of the hospital. He provided a perpetual vicar for St Laurence's, whose duties also included acting as chaplain to the paupers.[38] The hospital buildings were to the north of the church, and the north aisle of the chancel was set aside for the use of the inmates. It is usually assumed that the long-term residents were both men and women, and that the women at least were widows of former town officials who had fallen into poverty. The inmates led a semi-religious life. They were admitted by a religious formulary, were clothed as monks and nuns, and took vows of celibacy. At some time in the fifteenth century the charitable purposes of the hospital were abandoned: the income passed to the almoner's general fund and the chambers were simply rented out. The hospital was suppressed after a royal visit in 1479, when it was reported that, while in the past the inhabitants had been chaste women praying night and day for the King, and for their founders,

> now ther ys nother Goddservyce nor prayour, nor creature alyve to kepe hyt. But thabbot takethe the profytts ther of and dothe no suche almes nor good deds ther wyth.[39]

When King Henry VII visited Reading for the appointment of Abbot Thorne II in 1486, he asked the new abbot to convert the suppressed hospital to a pious use, and it was subsequently adapted for use as a Grammar School (see figure 22, chapter four).

FUNDING THE ABBEY: RENTS

The abbey was to be funded from three main sources; rent, relics and coinage. The first, and most important, was rent. The foundation charter opens by noting that three abbeys, Reading, Cholsey and Leominster, had been dissolved on account of their sins and that their confiscated prop-

---

[37] Ibid., 99.
[38] Ibid., 97.
[39] Bruce (1841), 60.

erties were in the hands of laymen.[40] The new monastery would receive these properties, and thus the charter would remove church lands from lay hands and restore them to their rightful owners according to strict reforming principles. The endowment was, by any standards, a generous one. The estates of the earlier nunnery at Reading included the town and the central estate, but also the nearby manors of Tilehurst, Beenham and Sulhamstead Abbots, while Leominster had 27 ancient holdings that were still more or less intact at the time of the Domesday Survey, as well as the income from more than 40 parish churches.[41] In order to endow his new abbey in these terms, Henry needed to tidy up a tangle of existing post-Conquest endowments. The earlier Reading nunnery's holdings had been granted by his father to Battle Abbey as a foundation gift, and so Henry had to compensate Battle for taking them back with a grant of lands in Sussex. Tutbury Priory had also received land in Reading, needed for the new abbey's endowment, and it was given the unidentified manor of Brincheale in exchange. Cholsey church had been awarded to Mont St Michel, and that Norman abbey was compensated with land at Budleigh (Devon).

We might think that all this reshuffling of holdings was simply aimed at providing Reading Abbey with a large, local economic base were it not for Leominster, almost a hundred miles away in the Welsh Marches. Leominster's holdings have been analysed by Joe Hillaby, who noted that they 'formed a remarkably compact unit, occupying most of the lowland basin of what is now north Herefordshire, except for a segment represented by the parishes of Kingsland, Monkland, Eardisland and Pembridge'.[42] This was a massive endowment, large enough on its own to support a respectable abbey, and apparently unconnected with Reading in any way. Proximity, therefore, was not the only consideration in Henry's mind, and the foundation charter itself offers two other clues.

First is the reforming aim of returning to the church lands that had passed into lay ownership.[43] In all three cases the lay ownership into which they had passed was royal, and Henry was thus righting the wrongs of his predecessors in a very direct way. Associated with this is the second consideration, that all three houses had, according to the charter, been destroyed on account of their sins.[44] The historical record does not entirely support this claim, and it is worth examining it a little more closely.

There is no direct record of the destruction of the earlier abbeys of Cholsey and Reading, and it has often been assumed that both were

---

[40]   Kemp (1986), I, 33.
[41]   Kemp (1986), I, 287–88 (document 354).
[42]   Hillaby (1995), 5.
[43]   *Quas manus laica diu possedit earumque terras et possessions alienando distraxit.*
[44]   *Sciatis quia tres abbatie in regno Anglie peccatis exigentibus olim destructe sunt.*

destroyed by the Danes in 1006 when, according to the Abingdon and Worcester texts of the Anglo-Saxon Chronicle,

> at Christmas they proceeded out through Hampshire into Berkshire, to their well-stocked food depot at Reading, and as usual kindled their war signals as they went. They went to Wallingford, and burned it to the ground, and spent one night at Cholsey, and proceeded along the Berkshire Downs to Cuckhamsley Knob.[45]

The destruction of the two abbeys is not specified, but the presence of the Danes in inflammatory mood certainly is. Cholsey is said to have been founded by the dowager queen Ælfthryth on land given by her son Æthelred the Unready about 986 in atonement for their part in the murder of Æthelred's half-brother King Edward the Martyr at Corfe Castle in 978. The fullest contemporary account of Edward's death is in the Anglo-Saxon Chronicle, but its author does not even speculate on the identity of the murderers:

> No worse deed for the English was ever done than this was,
> since they first came to the land of Britain.
> Men murdered him, but God exalted him;
> in life he was an earthly king,
> But after death he is now a heavenly saint.[46]

The notion that Edward was killed by his half-brother's advisors appears slightly later, in the Life of St Oswald, written soon after Oswald's death in 992.[47] Twelfth-century chronicles place the blame squarely on Queen Ælfthryth, the second wife of Edward's father, King Edgar and the archetypal wicked stepmother. In Henry of Huntingdon's version, she stabbed him with a dagger while she was offering him a cup to drink.[48] The traditional foundation date of 986 must be incorrect, as Æthelred did not obtain land in Cholsey until 996, when he received it in an exchange with his mother Ælfthryth.[49] The story of its foundation and the appointment of Germanus of Fleury as its abbot is given in the Chronicle of John of Wallingford, a late twelfth-century writer relying on early sources no longer available to us.[50] Land was left to Cholsey Minster by Ælfric, Archbishop of Canterbury, in his will of 1002–05,[51] and while Germanus continued to witness charters until 1013–16 and 1019, there is no evidence that he

[45]   Anglo-Saxon Chronicle, 136–37.
[46]   Ibid., 123.
[47]   *Vita Oswaldi, 448–52.*
[48]   Forester (1853), 177; see also the version in John of Worcester.
[49]   Sawyer (1968), Charter S877.
[50]   John of Wallingford, 555–58.
[51]   Sawyer (1968), Charter S1488.

7   READING ABBEY'S GREAT BARN AT CHOLSEY WAS DESTROYED IN 1815 AND ITS FABRIC
USED AS BUILDING MATERIAL. THIS PRINT BY J. C. BUCKLER WAS PUBLISHED IN *THE
GENTLEMAN'S MAGAZINE* IN THE FOLLOWING YEAR.

was still Abbot of Cholsey at those dates. The Domesday Survey makes
no mention of Cholsey abbey, but records that the manor was in royal
hands, before and after the Conquest, and that a church there was held by
the Norman abbey of Mont St Michel in 1086. There is evidence of Reading Abbey's later activities at Cholsey in the form of the great barn that
was there until 1815, when it was demolished and its fabric sold off for
building material (figure 7).[52] Before its demolition it was surveyed by J. C.
Buckler, who produced a plan, two sections and a perspective view, now
held in the British Library.[53] The barn that Buckler recorded was divided
into a nave and two aisles by a two rows of seventeen rubble piers with
quoined and chamfered angles.[54] These rose to a height of 31 feet (9.5 m)
and supported a queen post roof. The barn was 303 feet (92.4 m) long, 54
feet (16.5 m) wide and 51 feet (15.5 m) high at the apex of its roof, giving
a footprint of 1,520 square metres. This does not, as Horn thought, make
it the longest medieval barn recorded in England, let alone Europe.[55] Minster Court Thanet (Kent), a grange and manor-house of St Augustine's Abbey Canterbury, was longer but slightly narrower at 352 feet (107.3 m) by

52   The Gentleman's Magazine, 86 (1816), 105.
53   British Library, MS Add. 36436, nos. 574, 680 and 681.
54   Horn (1963), 14–15 reproduces three of Buckler's drawings and provides his
     measurements.
55   Ibid., 15.

47 feet (14.3 m) with a footprint of 1,537 square metres.[56] In the absence of documentary evidence it is very difficult to date a barn. A construction date in the fourteenth century was suggested by Walter Horn based on the use of arched braces, but he did not rule out a thirteenth-century date.[57]

The second of the houses said to have been dissolved on account of their sins was in Reading itself, and if anything the situation here is even more complex than at Cholsey. Like Cholsey, the nunnery at Reading was said to have been founded as an act of atonement for the murder of King Edward the Martyr by his stepmother Queen Ælfthryth. Its abbess, Leofrun was mentioned in the New Minster *Liber Vitae*, either in the late 980s or around 1000. An abbess of the same name was present at Canterbury in 1011 when it was captured by the Danes, but she might not have been the Abbess of Reading. The real confusion begins in the Domesday record. The borough of Reading was held by the king, before and after the Conquest, but a church in Reading was held by the Abbot of Battle – presented to him as part of the foundation endowment of his new monastery.[58] Before the Conquest this church was held from Edward the Confessor by Abbess Leofgifu. The Leofgifu we know about is the Abbess of Shaftesbury, and if she is meant there is a link to the foundation myth of the nunnery through Edward the Martyr who was buried after his murder at Wareham but was soon translated to Shaftesbury, a royal abbey endowed by Alfred the Great, and the place where Edward and Ethelred's grandmother Queen Ælfgifu had spent her last years. In 1001 Edward's remains were translated again, to a more prominent place at Shaftesbury. It has also been suggested, however, that the Abbess Leofgifu who held a church in Reading under Edward the Confessor was an Abbess of Reading, and that the nunnery was still in existence just before the Conquest.[59] In any case, the endowment included the nunnery's ancient minster church of St Mary, from which Minster Street takes its name. The church of St Mary Butts, at the west end of Minster Street, stands on the site of the minster church.[60]

While Anglo-Saxon Reading and Cholsey were recent foundations that might not have existed for more than a decade or two in all, Leominster (figure 8) was an ancient house dating back to the seventh century and the beginnings of Christianity in western Mercia.[61] Like the other two it was royally endowed (by Merewalh, king of the Magonsaete – a sub-kingdom of Mercia). By the beginning of the eleventh century it was either

---

[56] Hasted (1797–1801), 10, 278. I am grateful to Edward Impey for this information.
[57] Horn (1963), 17–19.
[58] Domesday Survey, 140, 146; VCH Sussex 2 (1907), 52.
[59] Stafford (2000), 8–9.
[60] VCH (Berks), 3 (1923), 367–78.
[61] What follows is based largely on the account by Hillaby (1995), 4–5.

8   LEOMINSTER PRIORY WAS REFOUNDED AS A POSSESSION OF READING ABBEY IN THE FOUNDATION
CHARTER. THE NORMAN NAVE, SHOWN HERE, IS THE EARLIEST PART OF THE PRESENT BUILDING.

a nunnery or a mixed house. At any rate it had an abbess, Eadgifu, in 1046, and it was the scandal surrounding her abduction by Earl Swein Godwinson, the eldest son of Earl Godwin of Wessex and brother of Harold Godwinson, later Harold II, that probably led to its closure.[62] The episode is described in the Anglo-Saxon Chronicle, which simply states that Swein had the abbess of Leominster fetched to him and kept her as long as he pleased, and then let her go home.[63] That this resulted in the dissolution of the abbey is suggested by the fact that immediately before the Conquest of 1066 Leominster was held by Edward the Confessor's queen, Edith. It passed from her into William the Conqueror's hands, and the lengthy description of the manor in 1086 makes no mention of an abbey. It does, however, mention an abbess who held Fencote, a possession of Leominster, both before the Conquest and in 1086, and it further records that the manor of Leominster was at farm in 1086 for £60 besides the

[62]   Ibid., 9.
[63]   Anglo-Saxon Chronicle, 164.

sustenance of the nuns. Nuns and an abbess were still in Leominster in 1086, therefore, although their house might have been dissolved.[64]

Recent analyses of this frustratingly incomplete information have tended towards the conclusion that while Leominster may have been destroyed on account of its sins, as the foundation charter states, Cholsey and Reading were more probably destroyed by the Danes. This could scarcely be viewed as the retribution of an avenging God, if that is indeed what happened. But it is equally surprising that the Anglo-Saxon Chronicle failed to record these events, in a passage which appears to show detailed knowledge of the actions and motives of the invaders. Instead, all we are told of Reading is that the Danes had a food-store there, and of Cholsey that they spent the night. This is not sufficient evidence to discredit Henry I's assertion, or at least his honesty, and once we accept this it fits well with his reforming aims, and above all with the decision to impose discipline from Cluny.

All the lands held by these three destroyed monasteries were given to the new foundation at Reading, together with the manor of Thatcham and the church of Wargrave. More gifts followed soon afterwards: Hanborough church in 1130–33,[65] and probably the manors of Bucklebury and Pangbourne.[66] This was an extremely generous endowment – more than had been necessary at an earlier date to support three monasteries.

FUNDING THE ABBEY: RELICS

The second source of income was pilgrimage. Pilgrims would bring gifts to the shrine and trade to the region. Reading was never important on an international scale, like Becket's shrine at Canterbury, or the shrine of the Virgin at Walsingham, but King Henry took care to set up the abbey with a respectable relic which would command veneration. This was the hand of St James, first recorded at the abbey in a charter dateable to 1126 which, in its present form, is either corrupt or forged.[67] The complex of issues associated with this relic will be examined in more detail in chapter two, but for the moment it is worth noting that while the hand was the abbey's most important and celebrated relic, at least in the early years, it was by no means Reading's only relic. By the end of the twelfth century, when an inventory was made, the stock had grown into an impressive collection of

[64] Stafford (2000), suggests that the nunnery was still in existence as a community in 1066.
[65] Kemp (1986), 1, 376.
[66] In 1212 Bucklebury and Pangbourne were stated to have been given to Reading Abbey by Henry I, although there is no contemporary charter evidence. See Kemp (1986), 1, 16 n. 2.
[67] Kemp (1986), 1, 39–40.

relics: 234 of them including Christ's foreskin (one of at least nine scattered around Europe), blood and water which flowed from his side at the Crucifixion, some of the Virgin's hair, parts of the rods of Moses and Aaron and a tooth of St Luke, as well as the hand of St James.[68] In spite of the lavish provision of relics, it seems unlikely that any great income was forthcoming from this source. Some estimate of the profitability of a shrine can be gauged from the survival of the pilgrim badges and ampullae which were popular souvenirs from the beginning of the fourteenth century onwards. No such souvenir certainly from Reading Abbey is known to survive, although it may well be that some of the scallop shell badges and ampullae commonly found in England and assumed to originate in Santiago de Compostella had their origin there (figure 9).

9   SCALLOP-SHELL PILGRIMS' BADGES ARE GENERALLY ASSUMED TO COME FROM SANTIAGO DE COMPOSTELLA, BUT SOME, LIKE THIS EXAMPLE OF ENGLISH ORIGIN, MIGHT WELL HAVE BEEN SOLD IN READING.

FUNDING THE ABBEY: COINAGE

Henry I's establishment of an abbey mint and moneyer might have been more lucrative,[69] but it was not usually a reliable source of wealth. New dies had to be purchased every time the design of the currency was changed, and dues (usually of 20 shillings) were payable to the king at the same time.[70] Changes of coin types were thus a useful source of royal income, and Henry changed the design of the penny fifteen times during his reign, and probably four times in the ten years between the foundation charter and his death. A mint did not buy bullion or issue coin to the public. These functions were performed by the exchange (*cambium*), which was normally in the king's hands. The income derived by the mint was

[68]   See chapter two and Appendix A.
[69]   Brooke (1976), 75 records Anglo-Saxon moneyers at Reading in the reigns of Aethelred II and Edward the Confessor, but the old mint was not maintained by the first Norman kings.
[70]   Ibid., 79–80.

simply whatever profit could be gleaned on sale of coin to the exchange after paying the necessary production costs. There was therefore always a temptation to defraud the exchange by debasing the metal or issuing coins of low weight, and these practices were so common in Henry's reign that on one notorious occasion in 1125 all the moneyers in the country were accused, and in the graphic words of the Peterborough continuator of the Anglo-Saxon Chronicle,

> Bishop Roger of Salisbury sent all over England, and commanded them all to assemble at Winchester. When they came thither they were then taken one by one, and each deprived of the right hand and the testicles below.[71]

The arrangements for the Reading moneyer were exceptional in two ways. Although the foundation charter referred to a mint at Reading (*apud Rad-ingiam*), in the event, by an act of Roger, Bishop of Salisbury, the abbey moneyer Aedgar was installed in London.[72] Nevertheless, he was to be in the possession of the abbot and monks as if he dwelt at Reading, as were his successors, who were to be appointed by the abbot and monks. More significantly Aedgar was also to hold an exchange in London on behalf of the abbey, which was a much more profitable activity. Furthermore, the dues payable by the mint for the purchase of new dies were to go to the abbey rather than the king. A few late coins of Henry I (type xv), mint-ed in London and marked with the name of Aedgar, survive, and these are presumably the products of the Reading Abbey mint (figure 10). No Reading coins were minted after the death of Henry I, either in London or Reading, until the Reading Abbey mint was re-established by Edward III in 1338 (see chapter four).

THE BUILDING OF THE ABBEY AND THE DEATH OF HENRY I

Contemporary records of the building progress are scanty. The campaign began in 1121, and in 1123 Prior Peter returned to Cluny and Hugh of Amiens was installed as Reading's first abbot. It is difficult to imagine what the Cluniacs could have achieved in these two years: presumably no more than the laying out of the plan on the ground and the establishment of Cluniac customs in temporary buildings. The foundation charter is dated 1125, and it has sometimes been assumed from this that the monastic buildings were completed in the four years between 1121 and 1125,[73] sim-ply because in the charter Henry states that he has built (*edificavi*) the

---

[71] Anglo-Saxon Chronicle, 255.
[72] Kemp (1986), I, 145.
[73] Hurry (1901), 26; Scantlebury (1943), 4.

10   HENRY I SILVER PENNIES LIKE THIS ONE, MARKED
WITH THE NAME OF AEDGAR, WERE STRUCK IN LONDON FOR
READING ABBEY.

monastery. This charter is certainly spurious as it stands, however, and probably represents an improved version of the original.[74] Even if it were reliable it would be a mistake to read it quite as literally as this. Henry's contribution to the building process extended only as far as the gifts described above, and once these were made he could reasonably claim to have done his share of the building. In any case, Henry left England in 1123 to deal with a rebellion in Normandy, and did not return until the autumn of 1126, so he could have had no first-hand knowledge of the progress of the building.[75]

The gift of the hand of St James, recorded in a charter dateable to 1126–27, might be thought to imply that building was sufficiently advanced for the relic to be suitably housed in the choir. This charter too is demonstrably unreliable,[76] but if we accept the statement in the *Flores Historiarum* that the hand was given by Henry in 1133, we must also assume that the choir was substantially complete by that date.[77] In any event we can be certain that the choir was complete by January 1136, when Henry I was buried there.[78] The *Annales de Waverleia* imply rather more than this, stating that Henry built the church from its foundations and enriched it with ornaments and lands.[79] Henry's death was described in some detail by Ordericus Vitalis.[80] The king arrived at the castle of Lyons-la-Forêt, some 20 miles east of Rouen, on Monday 25 November 1135, and prepared to go hunting on the following day. During the night he fell ill, and died at nightfall on the following Sunday. In the meantime he confessed his sins to his chaplains. He took spiritual counsel from Hugh of Amiens, now the Archbishop of Rouen, and on Hugh's advice he revoked

---

[74] Kemp (1986), I, 35–36. Kemp suggests that the improvements to the text were made between 1189 and 1193, but that the list of signatories, which includes the abbots of Bec, Sées, and Mont-Saint-Michel, the Archbishop of Rouen, and the bishops of Lisieux, Evreux and Avranches, implies an original document drafted in Normandy.

[75] Anglo-Saxon Chronicle, 253–56; Green (1986), 45.

[76] Kemp (1986), I, 40.

[77] Flowers of History, II, 42.

[78] Annales Radingenses, 11; Winchcombe Annals, 127; Henry of Huntingdon, 67.

[79] Annales de Waverleia, 225.

[80] Ordericus Vitalis, VI, 449–51.

all sentences of forfeiture, allowed the disinherited to recover their ancestral inheritances and freed exiles to return home. He arranged for the
payment of wages to his household and army, and gave instructions that
his body should be taken to Reading 'where he had founded a monastery
of two hundred monks'.[81] After receiving penance and absolution from the
priests he was anointed with holy oil, took communion, commended his
soul to God, and died.

Henry was attended on his deathbed by his illegitimate son Robert
de Caen, Earl of Gloucester; William of Warenne, Earl of Surrey; Rotrou
of Mortagne, Count of Perche and husband of his illegitimate daughter
Maud; the twin brothers Waleran, Count of Meulun and Robert, Earl
of Leicester, as well as Archbishop Hugh of Rouen and Bishop Audoin
of Evreux, and the five nobles agreed to escort the body to the coast for
shipping to England. They set off on the next day (Monday 2 December)
for Rouen along with 20,000 men, and the body was taken to the cathedral. That night it was opened by a skilled embalmer and the entrails were
removed and taken for burial to the priory church of Notre-Dame-du-Pré
in the Rouen suburb of Émendreville, while the body cavity was filled with
fragrant balsam. The king's body was then escorted to Caen, where it was
placed in the choir of the Conqueror's church of Saint-Étienne to await a
suitable wind for the channel crossing. This wait stretched to four weeks,
and it was not until after Christmas that it was placed on a ship with an
escort of monks from Saint-Étienne and conveyed to Reading for burial.

What is striking about this more or less conventional account of the
funeral arrangements is the long period that elapsed between Henry's
death and his burial. Henry of Huntingdon's version of the same events
takes much more account of this.[82] After the removal of the dead king's
entrails, brain and eyes for burial together, the corpse was cut all over with
knives, sprinkled with a great quantity of salt and wrapped in ox hides.
This was normal procedure for preserving meat on a sea voyage, but in
this case the chronicler records that it was done

> to stop the strong, pervasive stench which was already causing the deaths of
> those who watched over it. It even killed the man who had been hired for a
> great fee to cut off the head with an axe and extract the stinking brain, al-
> though he had wrapped himself in linen cloths around his head: so he was
> badly rewarded by his fee.[83]

---

[81] Ordericus here states that the monastery was founded in honour of the Holy
     Trinity; this is an error, repeated in Knowles and Hadcock (1971), 74. The original
     dedication was to the Virgin and St John the Evangelist.
[82] Henry of Huntingdon, 66–67.
[83] Ibid., 67.

While the body was lying at Saint-Étienne de Caen a fearful black fluid began to run out of it, leaking through the hides and being collected in vessels for disposal.

Henry had died on 2 December 1135 and was buried on 3 January 1136, and in this crucial month the events took place that led to a civil war over the succession lasting almost twenty years. The strongest candidate would seem to have been the Empress Matilda, King Henry's daughter by his first wife, Matilda of Scotland. When the king died, his daughter was 33 years old. She had been married in 1114, aged 12, to the Holy Roman Emperor Henry V, 15 years her senior, and after his death in 1125 she was recalled to England by her father, retaining the title of Empress which she continued to use. King Henry named her as his successor in a very public ceremony at the 1126–27 Christmas court that began in Windsor and travelled down the Thames to London.[84] According to William of Malmesbury,

> After deliberating long and deeply on this matter he then, at this same council, bound the nobles of all England, also the bishops and abbots, by the obligation of an oath that, if he himself died without a male heir, they would immediately and without hesitation, accept his daughter Matilda, formerly empress, as their lady.[85]

The oath was then sworn, first by the clergy, beginning with William of Corbeil, Archbishop of Canterbury and followed by the other bishops and abbots, then by the laity, beginning with King David of Scotland, Matilda's maternal uncle, then by Stephen of Mortain, the king's nephew by his sister Adela, then Robert, Earl of Gloucester, King Henry's oldest illegitimate son. Malmesbury commented on a dispute that arose between Robert and Stephen about who should swear first 'the one claiming the prerogative of a son; the other the rank of a nephew.'[86] In this version both seem eager to swear first, but John of Worcester gave a rather different account, in which Robert of Salisbury, acting as the king's master of ceremonies, called first for Earl Robert to take the oath, but Robert did not move. 'Get up,' cried the bishop, 'get up and take the oath as the king requires it of you!' Robert refused, saying that as the elder Stephen should swear first, and this was done.[87] This curious incident could simply reflect the reticence of an illegitimate child to precede a senior legitimate relative, but there might be more significance to it. Edmund King conjures up the image of two possible successors sitting on their hands; reluctant to swear but unable

---

[84]   William of Malmesbury HN, 6–9; AS Chron. 1127; John of Worcester III, 166–67. King 2000, 288–90 provides a useful summary of events based on these sources.
[85]   William of Malmesbury HN, 6–7.
[86]   Ibid., 9.
[87]   John of Worcester, 3, 178–79.

to refuse the king's direct command.[88] It is worth noting, however, that in his preliminary explanation for choosing Matilda as his successor, King Henry dwelt at some length on her descent from the Anglo-Saxon kings from Egbert to Edward the Confessor on her mother's side. This line distinguishes her from both Robert and Stephen (and from the other possible candidate, William Clito, son of Henry's elder brother Robert Curthose) and taking the oath could be seen as an implicit acceptance of the importance of her maternal descent.

In the following year, now 26 years old, Matilda embarked on a second political marriage; to the 15-year old Geoffrey Plantagenet, Count of Maine and heir to the County of Anjou, to which he succeeded when his father died shortly afterwards. The alliance was intended to cement relations between Normandy and Anjou; in fact it was to found a new dynasty of Angevin or Plantagenet kings of England, that began with Matilda and Geoffrey's son Henry, born in 1133. Those who had sworn the oath in 1127 might well have considered, however, that they had been tricked into accepting a succession that would lead to England being ruled by an enemy of Normandy, and felt justified in considering it invalid. It was perhaps for this reason that Henry insisted on a further swearing ceremony at a full meeting of the nobility in 1131 when, according to William of Malmesbury, the oath of fidelity to Matilda was renewed by all who had already sworn, and was also taken by those who hitherto had not.[89] There can have been no doubt in the king's mind, then, that the matter of the succession was settled, and the fact that the same council sent her back to her husband strongly suggests that they were expected to make a start on founding a new dynasty.[90]

In the face of all this, it might seem surprising that the old king's death prompted a feverish bout of action, discussion and negotiation about his successor. Matilda, the nominated heir, was in Anjou with Geoffrey. She had no chance of reaching England to claim the throne in person, and doubtless little hope that her father's magnates would seek her out to offer her the crown in fulfilment of the oaths they had sworn. The pair therefore sought to consolidate Matilda's position in Normandy by occupying the border castles she had received as her dowry, she at least probably remaining in this area until she set out for England in 1139.[91]

Henry's closest retainers, who had been at his side when he died, had sworn to stay with the body until it was taken to Reading for burial, which entailed a delay of four weeks at Caen while they awaited a favourable wind. They took advantage of the wait to discuss the succession, and had

[88]   King (2000), 289.
[89]   William of Malmesbury HN, 20–21.
[90]   Henry of Huntingdon, 63.
[91]   Chibnall (1991), 66–67.

decided to offer the Duchy of Normandy to Theobald of Blois, Henry's senior nephew by his sister Adela, when the news reached them that they had been pre-empted by Theobald's younger brother Stephen. Stephen was in his county of Boulogne when Henry was taken ill, and responded to the news by preparing for a channel crossing, rather than by hurrying the relatively short distance to his uncle's bedside. Certainly the *Gesta Stephani* records that he crossed to England as soon as he received definite news of Henry's death, and this early start allowed him to avoid the bad weather that was to delay any possible rival candidate.

> So this great man, as soon as he heard by report that King Henry had breathed his last, forming a mighty design like the famous Saul, made for the coast, since he was on the other side of the Channel, and happening to gain a favourable wind turned his mind and his ship towards England.[92]

Once in England, Stephen made his way to London where he was acclaimed as king by the city magnates.[93] His next move, to Winchester, was the key to ensuring the necessary coronation and anointing. His brother Henry of Blois, Bishop of Winchester, and Bishop Roger of Salisbury were certainly the two most powerful English bishops. As Henry I's treasurer, Roger had control over the exchequer and the treasury; the civil service and the money, while Henry of Blois was influential at Rome and Cluny, and importantly for Stephen represented a family endorsement for the snub delivered to Theobald. William of Malmesbury's view was that it was Henry's endorsement that persuaded the Archbishop of Canterbury, William of Corbeil to set aside his oath to support Matilda and officiate at the coronation of Stephen. This event took place on 22 December 1135, while the old king's body still lay at Caen, guarded by the great men of the realm. Stephen had important churchmen on his side, but he had little lay support, and certainly nothing that could be called a court.[94] He was attended at the coronation by Hugh Bigod, Earl of Norfolk, and William Martel, King Henry's butler, who had been with the king in Normandy but had not stayed with his body. A party of monks from Bath Abbey also turned up to take advantage of the air of festivity by persuading the new king to confirm a charter in their favour. It is interesting to find that the only witnesses to it were the clerics William of Corbeil, Roger of Salisbury and Henry of Blois.[95]

Given the scant lay support that Stephen had around him at his coronation, the return of the old king's body and his funeral at Reading

---

[92] Gesta Stephani, 5.
[93] Ibid., 5–6.
[94] William of Malmesbury made the point that at his coronation there were only three bishops, no abbots and scarcely any of the nobility.
[95] Crouch 2000, 38; Regesta III, 16.

assumed great significance for the new king, who did his best to ensure that it represented a passing of power from King Henry to his legitimate successor. It must have been around this time that a story began to go the rounds that Henry had changed his mind about the succession on his deathbed and nominated Stephen. It appears in the *Liber Eliensis* and later in John of Salisbury's *Historia Pontificalis* where it is attributed to Hugh Bigod.[96] As Edmund King has it, 'that it represents what actually happened on Henry's death-bed can be safely discounted: this would have been not just a change of mind but a change of policy.'[97] No, the *Liber Eliensis* account was no less than the official version of events put forward by Stephen's party to justify his usurpation. Stephen had every reason to be grateful that Henry had provided Reading as a spectacular stage on which to act out the drama of the passing of power from one king to his successor. In the confirmation of the abbey's rights, probably issued at the time of the burial, the new king stated,

> however general is my obligation to safeguard royal alms, it is more pressing and particular towards the abbey of Reading, for good and sufficient reason.[98]

The longest account of the burial is given by John of Worcester, and it is worth examining closely.[99] The new king accompanied by a large body of nobles went to meet the cortege when it arrived from Normandy, and he and some of his barons carried the bier on their shoulders to the burial place at Reading. The Archbishop of Canterbury was present at the burial, when masses were sung, rich offerings made, and alms distributed to the poor. Others present were not named by John of Worcester, but the witnesses to two royal charters in favour of Miles of Gloucester, Earl of Hereford, signed at Reading on the day of the burial must have been there.[100] These included William de Corbeil, Archbishop of Canterbury; Henry of Blois, Bishop of Winchester; Bishop Roger of Salisbury; Hugh Bigod; Ingelram de Say, a Shropshire baron who was later captured with King Stephen at the battle of Lincoln; William Pont de l'Arche, sheriff of Hampshire; and Baldwin FitzGilbert de Clare, lord of Bourne (Lincs).[101] The dead king's effigy was exposed to view on a hearse, and his body was deposited in a tomb before the High Altar of the abbey church (plate IV) while Stephen sat enthroned overlooking the ritual. From the information available, therefore, all we can say is that despite Stephen's attempts to put

---

[96]   John of Salisbury, 84; Liber Eliensis, 285; Crouch 2000, 36–37.
[97]   King (2000), 293.
[98]   Regesta Regum III, 249–50.
[99]   John of Worcester, 3, 215–17.
[100] Regesta Regum, III, 148–49.
[101] The complete list also includes Roberto filio Ricardi, Pagano filio Johannis, Walter filius Ricardi, and Roberto de Ferrariis.

on a noble show, the burial attracted no more genuine magnates than the coronation had. Nevertheless, he could justifiably claim that he had carried out his duty to his uncle by ensuring his burial in the correct place. The same chronicler made the point that this church, dedicated to the most blessed and glorious Virgin Mary, had been endowed by Henry himself with lands, woods, meadows and pastures, and enriched with many ornaments, for the good of his soul:

> *Rex hic Heinricus terrenis rebus opimus; Eruptus poenis, coeli potiatur amoenis.*[102]

In other words, he would escape the tortures of hell because of his generosity in endowing the church. This explains his determination to build the church in the first place, and to insist on burial there, despite the practical difficulties involved. On the day of his resurrection, the evidence of his piety would be all around to speak for him at the Last Judgement.

Henry's widow and second queen Adeliza hosted a gathering of bishops and abbots at Reading on the first anniversary of his death. She granted land in her manor of Stanton Harcourt (Oxfordshire) to fund the convent and the religious people attending the ceremony, and to provide lights that would burn continuously before the Holy Sacrament and before Henry's tomb at Reading.[103] That this was to be an annual event is made clear from this, and from the gift of 100 shillings annually from a hithe, or small port, that she held in London.[104] At the same time as she made this gift, she presented her manor of Aston in Hertfordshire to the abbey in commemoration of the anniversary of Henry's death, and it is notable that this charter, signed by the bishops of Salisbury and Winchester and the abbots of Abingdon, Eynsham and Mont Saint Michel is very sumptuous, and bears a fine and almost complete impression of Adeliza's seal in white wax on a leather tag.[105] Adeliza remarried after Henry's death, bearing at least seven children by her second husband, William d'Aubigny, who had been one of Henry's advisors and was created Earl of Arundel and Earl of Lincoln by King Stephen. She died in 1151 and was buried alongside King Henry according to the evidence of a charter issued by her brother Jocelin of Louvain, that states that he gave land in Petworth (Sussex) including a piggery of ten sows and one boar to Reading Abbey, specifically noting that he presented the gift to the abbey while he was there for his sister's burial.[106] A marginal note in the Reading Abbey manuscript Lambeth

---

[102]   John of Worcester, 3, 217. McGurk translates the couplet, 'May this king so rich in earthly goods; Rejoice in heaven freed from pains.'
[103]   Kemp 1, 403–05 (charters 534, 535).
[104]   Ibid., 353 (charter 459).
[105]   Ibid., 301–02 (charter 370).
[106]   Ibid., 416–17 (charters 550, 551).

Palace 371 confirms that she was indeed buried in the presbytery, but not alongside Henry. Because she had married again she was buried apart from her royal husband, between two of the piers on the north side of the choir.[107] This apparently impeccable version of events is disputed in the annals of Margam, where it is claimed that she was buried in Afflighem (Flanders), but it is more likely that the Flemish house, site of her father's tomb, received some of her internal organs at her death.[108]

THE FATE OF HENRY I'S TOMB

John of Worcester's Chronicle described the founder's tomb as 'made according to custom', which might imply a relatively plain affair, certainly without an effigy.[109] Sometime afterwards this simple tomb was replaced with a grander monument with a life-sized effigy that had fallen into disrepair by 1397–98, and was repaired by the order of Richard II, who was so concerned that this should be done that he withheld some of the abbey's privileges until it was completed.[110] Although the main dismantling of the abbey did not take place until 1549, George Hynde's accounts of the sale of fabric in that year make no mention of the tomb,[111] and it may be that it was broken up immediately after the Dissolution. A tradition that the king's body lay in a coffin of solid silver could well have hastened this.[112] No more was heard of it until 1784, when a foundation was being dug for a new County Gaol on the abbey site and human remains were found. An account of the discovery was published in the following year:

> Divers bones were thrown up: this being the burial-place of Henry I. each bone was seized as a kind of treasure, contemplating it as one of the king's, till at length a vault was discovered, the only one there, and which was of curious workmanship: in the vault was a leaden coffin almost devoured by time. A perfect skeleton was contained therein, and which undoubtedly was the king's.[113]

---

[107]   London, Lambeth Palace MS 371, f. 1v. The relevant text reads: 'Willelmus comes lincolnie desponsavit Adelizam Reginam fundatoris nostril uxorem ut patet in carta et confirmacione eiusdem Willelmi. Et ideo consilium regium noluit permittere eam iacere cum eo in medio presbiterii ante altare. Illa tamen iacet sepulta in boreali parte chori inter duas columnas seorsum a rege henrico primo fundatore nostro et marito eiusdem, quorum animabus propicietur deus. Amen.' See also James (1932), 503.

[108]   Thompson (2002), 63 n. 57.

[109]   John of Worcester, III, 216–17.

[110]   Kemp (1986), I, 107

[111]   Preston (1935).

[112]   Guilding (1891), 98.

[113]   Pigott (1785), 881.

The author, F. Pigott, added that the coffin contained fragments of rotten leather, and took this to be the remains of the ox-hides in which the king's body had been wrapped, and further confirmation of the identity of the occupant. He then went on to describe what happened to the remains.

> The bones were divided among the spectators; but the coffin was sold to a plumber. The under jaw-bone has been sent to me, and a small piece of the leaden coffin. The jaw contains sixteen teeth perfect and sound, even the enamel of them is preserved.[114]

In the following year Pigott's assumption that the grave was Henry's was disputed by a correspondent calling himself Juvenis, who asserted that the discovery was made outside the walls of the church, in which the king was known to have been buried; that in fact no vault was discovered; that the plumber gave it as his opinion that the lead coffin was a relatively modern casting, and the supposed ox-hide fragments were 'the remnants of an old slipper'. Furthermore the skull had been examined by a distinguished local surgeon, who gave it as his opinion that it was from a young person under thirty years of age.[115] The dispute continued for more than a year in the pages of the *Gentleman's Magazine*, but in the absence of any fresh evidence no satisfactory conclusion could be reached about the identity of the skeleton.[116]

In 1815 two large fragments of stone making up the base of a sarcophagus were discovered buried three feet underground in the area of the High Altar.[117] Archdeacon Nares, who published the discovery, failed to provide an illustration, but gave a detailed description. The discovery consisted of the entire base of the sarcophagus, which was 7ft long and 2ft 6in wide at the head, tapering to 2ft at the foot. Although it included nothing of the sides or ends, it was 7½in thick and carved with a moulding and the bases of a series of attached shafts which ran all round the tomb chest. There were fifty attached columns in all, eighteen along each long side, eight at the head end and six at the foot.[118] The column bases had enough of their shafts still in place to show that they were alternately half-round and half-hexagonal. Nares described the object as 'elegantly carved', but in his estimate of its date he called it Saxon and pre-Gothic, and took the view that it was probably a fragment of the tomb of Henry I.[119]

After their discovery the two pieces were placed in the Boys' Schoolroom in the Forbury, where they could be viewed by application

---

[114] Ibid.
[115] Juvenis (1786), 11–13.
[116] *The Gentleman's Magazine*, LVI (1786), 105–06; 393–94
[117] Nares (1817), 272; Guilding (1891), 95.
[118] Ibid., 273.
[119] Ibid., 273–74.

to the Headmaster. In the succeeding years they progressively deteriorated owing to the desire of visitors to take home a souvenir of the founder's tomb. At length every bit of the ornament had been chipped off.[120] When the abbey ruins came into the possession of Reading Corporation it was decided to restore the pieces as a single slab and set it up in the ruins. After the restoration, the slab was some two feet shorter than before, and it was installed at the foot of the inner wall of one of the south transept chapels. After the demolition of the old gaol in 1843, a Tudor fireplace was removed and set up over the slab as a fitting canopy for Henry's tomb.[121] This horrific arrangement can be seen in early twentieth-century photographs and postcards (figure 11). Of course it is unlikely that the tomb was Henry's. The only evidence is that it was found in approximately the place he was buried, but as neither the burial site nor the find site is accurately known, this constitutes no kind of proof, especially as it seems certain that the tomb was not unearthed at its original location.

With the burial of Henry and Adeliza, Reading's first purpose was achieved. Henry I's mausoleum now housed the bodies of the founder and his queen, embalmed in their tombs, prepared for their ultimate reward when the Day of Judgement should come. But the church itself remained incomplete, both architecturally and in the fulfilment of its purposes as a pilgrimage site, a burial place for those who wished it, and a royal destination for almost 400 years to come.

11   THE MUTILATED REMAINS OF A SARCOPHAGUS, FOUND ON THE ABBEY SITE AND SUPPOSED TO BE THAT OF HENRY I, WERE RESTORED AND SET UP IN THE FOUNDER'S CHAPEL, AND AFTER 1843 A TUDOR FIREPLACE FROM THE OLD GAOL WAS SET UP OVER THE TOMB CHEST AS A FITTING CANOPY.

[120]   Guilding (1891), 95.
[121]   Ibid., 96.

PILGRIMAGE AND RELICS 2

The foundation charter of Reading Abbey implied that pilgrims would visit, urging future abbots not to misuse alms, but to use them for the care of the poor, and pilgrims and guests.[1] The plan of the abbey church, as we shall see in chapter six, was designed from the outset with the circulation of pilgrims in mind, allowing them to follow designated routes around the building, visiting each altar in turn and venerating the holy relics housed in their costly and evocative shrines. In a sense Reading started at a disadvantage, owing to its relatively late foundation, but by the end of the twelfth century it had built up an assemblage that rivalled any other church in the land, and its royal status was an important factor in the growth of the collection.

THE TWELFTH-CENTURY RELIC LIST

The Reading Abbey manuscript, British Library Egerton 3031, is largely a collection of the abbey's charters, but it also includes a book-list, a list of vestments and a list of relics.[2] This last, occupying folios 6v to 8r of the cartulary (see Appendix A), has the power to mystify, to fascinate and to repel the modern reader in equal measure. Although its importance has long been recognised, no edition has been published until now.[3] The list is written in a neat late twelfth-century book-hand, with rubrics in red and capitals in red or blue marking the start of each item.

The relics it describes are categorised in groups rubricated as follows:

---

[1] Kemp (1986), I, 34.
[2] British Library Manuscript Catalogue, Egerton 3031.
[3] It has been discussed by Barfield (1888), 115–16, Kemp (1986), I, 187, and in most detail by Bethell (1972), who recorded his attempt to produce such an edition.

Relics of the Tree of the Lord
Relics of Our Lady St Mary
Of the prophets and patriarchs
Of the apostles
Of the martyrs
Of the confessors
Of the virgins.

This is broadly an inventory arranged in order of importance of the holy figures it contained, but the relics themselves also had an intrinsic importance depending on how intimately they were connected to the holy person. According to the Catholic church, first-class relics are items associated with the events of Christ's life (the Cross, crib, or foreskin for example), or parts of the body of a saint; second-class relics are items worn by a saint in his lifetime, or important in his life or martyrdom; third-class relics are things placed in contact with first- or second-class relics – called *brandea* – usually pieces of cloth or oil. Despite the careful layout and taxonomy, it is by no means clear exactly how many relics there were. There are 230 separate items in the list, numbered in this edition for reference purposes but not in the manuscript itself. Some items, however, consist of more than one relic, like item 3, which includes wood from the True Cross and frankincense offered to the baby Jesus; or item 121 which contains six different relics of St Thomas Becket. Confusingly too, many of the items are described as being in several places (e.g. item 34, which has relics of St Mary's tomb *in viii locis*).[4] Whatever the precise numbers involved, it cannot be denied that the collection was made very rapidly indeed, beginning no earlier than 1121 and almost complete by around 1190 when the list was made.[5] The only addition to the list of relics records the gift of the head of St Philip by King John described below, although at the end of the list is an added note in a later hand recording the gift of the statue of a child by the Duke of Aquitaine, which will also be discussed separately. A list like this one can simply be read as a curiosity, prompting reflections on the outlandishness of medieval people and their religion, their ghoulish tastes and above all their gullibility, but as historians we must assess their actions on their own terms rather than ours. This might lead to an acceptance that these grisly and evocative objects were spiritually important, and that the questions we should be asking are: where did they come from, and how were they displayed?

[4] Hence Barfield (1888), 115 records that there are 234 entries, while Bethell (1972), 61 writes that it lists 242 relics. Readers might like to make their own estimates.
[5] Dating evidence is available for the booklist that follows the relic list in the manuscript. Kemp suggested a date of c.1191–93 (Kemp (1986), I, 3), while Coates argued for a date range of 1180–91 (Coates (1999), 20).

In many cases we cannot know where they came from, but a few sources are obvious, either because they are mentioned in the text or in other texts, or because they could only have come from one place.

RELICS FROM KING HENRY I – RELICS FROM CONSTANTINOPLE

As the founder of the abbey it would be surprising if King Henry did not endow it with as many relics as he could; the more pilgrims it attracted the more his own soul would benefit in the afterlife. The most famous of the relics, the hand of St James (item 56), was brought to England by the Empress Matilda after her first husband's death, and given to Reading by her father, Henry I, at her request. This history must be shared by items 57 and 58, two pieces of cloth in which it was wrapped. The relic list does not provide any evidence about its provenance at all: this comes from various charters and from the chronicler Matthew Paris, and will be presented when the relic is discussed below. Another relic provided by the founder was the foreskin (or possibly the umbilical cord) that was sent to him by the Emperor of Constantinople along with wood from the True Cross (item 7). This will also be discussed in its own section below, but Denis Bethell, whose major article on the relic-list was published in 1972, has suggested that both it and item 1 might have been among the relics obtained by an embassy that the King sent to Constantinople in 1118 for the specific purpose of collecting them.[6] If this is so, it suggests that he was collecting suitable relics at least three years before the foundation date. Other relics that could only have come from Constantinople include the bone of Constantine (item 135), the collarbone of the enigmatic St Fredmundus (117) and the relics of St John the Almsgiver, St Auxentius, St Mardarius and St Cyril of Alexandria (items 171 to 174 – listed in sequence). Bethell also suggested that the Salonika relics of St Demetrius (and presumably his brother Dionysius, items 103–104), St Nestor (128) and St Irene (226) could well have been obtained by this embassy.[7]

Constantinople must also have been the ultimate sources of those relics that Bethell called 'highly improbable'.[8] Many might feel that this epithet could be applied to most things in the list, but Bethell singled out Christ's sandal (item 8); swaddling clothes; blood and water from Christ's side (21); bread from the feeding of the five thousand (19), and from the Last Supper (18); the Vernicle (22); the shroud (25); Our Lady's hair (29), bed (32) and belt (33); the rods of Moses and Aaron (38 and 39); and the

---

6   Bethell (1972), 69.
7   Ibid.
8   Ibid., 67.

relics of St John the Baptist (43 and 44), St Anne (47 and 48) and Simeon (52 and 53). To these might be added the fragments of the Magi's gifts (1 and 3); the water in which the infant Christ was bathed (12); the Mosaic relics of the Burning Bush and the manna that fell from heaven (41 and 42); and the relics of the prophets Daniel, Elijah and Zechariah (45 and 46).

SOUVENIRS OF THE HOLY LAND

Another group of relics from the East are the Holy Land souvenirs – earth, rocks and vegetation from places mentioned in the Bible that would routinely be pointed out to tourists. This category would include items 8, 13, 17, 20, 23, 27 and 30: all taken from sites associated with Christ or the Virgin, but none claiming any specific content or contact with either of them.

LEOMINSTER RELICS

This group must be treated separately on account of the complex relationship between Reading and Leominster. The Reading foundation charter, it will be remembered, opens by referring to the former houses of Reading, Cholsey and Leominster which had been dissolved on account of their sins, stating that their confiscated properties would be given to the new abbey. In the case of Leominster it is almost certain that the pre-Conquest nunnery was dissolved by Edward the Confessor on account of the scandalous liaison between its Abbess, Eadgifu, and Earl Swein Godwinson. The nunnery and its possessions passed to the crown, and were held by William the Conqueror in 1086. Anglo-Saxon Leominster was not just a nunnery, however. It is clear that from its foundation in the seventh century onwards the nuns were supported by a college of secular or semi-monastic clergy, who were initially also charged with the evangelizing of the region. There followed the usual problems with the Danes, but it is safe to say that when the nunnery was dissolved and its lands confiscated, the college of priests continued to exist, under royal ownership.[9] The Leominster relic list, in its surviving copy of 1286, would therefore include relics that were held by the college before the Conquest, and the description of its contents as relics that were held *ab antiquo* can be accepted at face value.[10]

Leominster Priory was refounded as a daughter house shortly after Reading's foundation, and Reading immediately profited by acquiring

---

[9] Kemp (1968), 505–07; Hillaby (1995).

[10] The relic list is in the Herefordshire Record Office, copied into the Register of Richard Swinfield in 1286 (ref. Diocesan Records, Reg. Swinfield, f. 36 verso). A printed copy is available in Capes (1909) and a translation in Doble (1947).

relics from Leominster. It was clearly not a one-way street, however, especially after the acquisition of fresh relics by Reading gathered speed; the compiler of the Reading list notes under item 66 that the missing tooth of St Luke might be at Leominster, so some exchange of relics was clearly normal. It is thus reasonable to assume, with Bethell, that saints appearing in both the Reading and Leominster relic lists came to Reading from Leominster, in the form of detached fragments or objects placed in contact with the relic. Relics obtained from Leominster certainly include items 183 and 184, parts of St Hemma, first Abbot of Leominster, and might well also include the fragments of King Edward the Martyr (95 to 97), that Leominster must have obtained from Shaftesbury where he was buried. Both Reading's list and Leominster's include holdings of Irish, and Breton, saints, which Bethell reasonably suggests went to Leominster from King Athelstan's collection in the tenth century, and from Leominster to Reading in the twelfth.[11] The Bretons include St Malo (138), St Branwalator (142), St Samson of Dol (147) and St Columba (213).

GIFTS FROM ENGLISH HOUSES

Many of the relics in the Egerton list can only have come from the English or Welsh houses that held the body of the saint, and Bethell's conclusion that 'it is clear from Reading's list that at its foundation or during the century a number of older houses were persuaded to give relics to the new community' must be correct.[12] Relics of almost thirty saints fall into this category, but there might be more or fewer than this, depending on whether the English relics arrived via Leominster. From Winchester there were relics of St Swithun himself, and the less distinguished figures of St Machutus, St Birstan, St Birinus and St Hedda (items 138 and 155 to 159). The relics of St Cuthbert and St Oswald (items 178 and 94) must have arrived from Durham – clearly, in Cuthbert's case, accompanied as it is by a documentary explanation that has been copied into the list. The long entry explains that the two fragments of the vestments of St Cuthbert had been in the tomb, in contact with the dead saint's body, for different lengths of time. The larger was there for ten years, while the smaller had been there for 418 and was removed at a translation. This fits closely enough with information from Bede that St Cuthbert's tomb was opened eleven years after his death in 687, when he was found to be incorrupt. It was opened again in 1104 and the contents translated to a new shrine in Durham Cathedral. The small cloth must therefore have been removed at that time, and the larger one at the time of the first opening, making the

[11]　Bethell (1972), 63–64.
[12]　Ibid., 66.

smaller and less beautiful scrap of fabric more valuable as a relic because it had been in contact with the saint for longer. In spite of all this, they were after all only second-class relics, and in spiritual terms St Alban's Abbey was far more generous. They provided two bones of their titular saint as well as part of the cloak that his severed head was wrapped in after his martyrdom (91 to 92), and the little finger of St Amphibalus (127); the priest who converted Alban to Christianity and whom Alban died to protect (plate V). The presence of Amphibalus in the list is a valuable indicator of its date, since the saint's remains were not discovered until 1178, at Redbourn a few miles north of St Albans, and his body was installed in the abbey.[13] It is worth noting that St Alban himself was transferred to a new shrine, completed by order of Abbot Simon (1166–83) at around the same time.[14] From Bury St Edmunds came part of St Edmund's cloak (93), and a cloth stained with the blood of St Robert – a boy murdered in 1181 whose death was blamed on the Jews. St William of Norwich was a similar case – he was killed in 1144 and his body found in woodland just outside the town (plate VI).[15] Again the Jews were blamed, and again Reading obtained its relics – a blood-stained shoe and part of the tree from which he was hanged (126). Canterbury supplied relics of St Alphege, St Lanfranc and St Dunstan (125, 165, 177), in addition to a spectacular collection of Becket relics (119 to 124), studied separately later in this chapter.[16] Becket, of course, had a special importance for Reading since he consecrated the Abbey church in 1164. He was murdered in 1170 and canonised only three years later. The acquisition of Becket's relics, like those of Amphibalus, and the boy-saints Robert of Bury and William of Norwich, is evidence that Reading's abbots were quick to move in this period, obtaining newsworthy saints while they were still in the public consciousness in order to attract pilgrim revenue.

ROMAN RELICS

Relics of saints martyred in Roman Imperial persecutions, especially those of Septimius Severus, Decius, Valerian and Diocletian, are extremely common from an early date, and were traded and forged copiously.[17] Like most houses, Reading possessed a strong collection of relics of around

---

[13] Chron. Maj. 2, 301–08; McCulloch (1981), 767–68.

[14] Gesta Abbatum S. Albani, 2, 189–90.

[15] St William never received papal canonisation, although Bishop William de Turbeville (1146–74) campaigned vigorously for it.

[16] The Dunstan relic could have come from Glastonbury, which also claimed to have his body.

[17] See Geary (1978), 45–49 for an account of the Italian relic trade in the ninth century.

twenty Roman martyrs, the most famous being St Peter and wood from his cross (54), and St Lawrence, who came complete with coals from the gridiron on which he was roasted (70).

FRENCH RELICS

The relics of French saints, like the Romans, were both numerous and common, and many came to England in the tenth century, in response to King Athelstan's well-known thirst for the relics of saints.[18] The Reading list includes at least twelve relics whose myths if not their bones must have originated in France. A famous case involving French saints is represented in items 115 and 116 of the Reading collection. The bodies of the two brothers, Bishop Maximus of Evreux and Deacon Venerandus, who were beheaded by pagans c. 384 were said to have been stolen by a relic dealer (who left the heads behind) from the church at Acquigny (Eure) in the tenth century. He was apprehended after the relics miraculously caused him to behave drunkenly while trying to board a ship to England, and was taken to the nearby abbey of Fontenelle, where the Duke of Normandy, called to give a ruling, decided that the relics should remain.[19] There can be no doubt that this story was an invention of the monks of Fontenelle, in justification of their possession of relics to which they had no title. The implication was that the saints themselves engineered the theft. They were dissatisfied with the veneration they received at Acquigny, and arranged a series of miracles that would take them to a house where they knew they would be properly appreciated. Tales like this one – including elements of theft, alienation, and the division of relics – raised doubts about the precise location of the saints that could easily be exploited by hustlers with a few bones and a silver tongue. And Athelstan appears to have been the perfect mark: desperate for relics and ready to believe a good story.

RELICS AND SHRINES

The proper veneration of the relics of saints began with the provision of a suitable home. For a whole body this would be a shrine, covered in precious metal and perhaps decorated with enamel and gemstones. Reading had nothing this large, but some of its smaller relics were afforded similarly rich settings, appropriate to their spiritual value. None survives, of course, but we have a description among a list of treasures given on loan

---

[18] William of Malmesbury GP, 398.
[19] Geary (1978), 50–52.

to Edward III by the Abbot of Reading 'for the furtherance of the king's affairs' on 4 June 1338.[20]

> *Unum Scrinium auri, ad modum parvi Feretri, Garnitum de Saphiris, Perlis Orientalibus, Camahut, Rubinis, Balamitibus, & aliis diversis Petraris, pro Reliquiis imponendis, Ponderis Viginti Librarum, Novem Solidorum, & Octo Denariorum, & Pretii, per aestimationem, Ducenarum Librarum.*

> (A gold reliquary in the form of a little shrine, garnished with sapphires, oriental pearls, cameos, rubies, balas rubies and other diverse stones, to hold relics, weighing twenty pounds, nine ounces and eight pennyweights, with an estimated value of two hundred pounds).[21]

Although it is described as a gold reliquary, the gold can only have been a thin sheet, or coating or the box would have been much more valuable. (The price of gold stood at approximately £1.33 per ounce in 1343 (when the gold florin was introduced), so a solid gold reliquary of the weight given would have been worth £330 for scrap, plus the value of the precious stones). The present-day value of the reliquary loaned to Edward III must be in the region of £150,000 using gold prices as a measure.[22]

A reliquary casket like this would be suitable for all manner of relics, but reliquaries were sometimes designed to suit the relic they housed, so that fragments of the True Cross were often set into crosses, while parts of hands, arms or heads often took the shape of the body-part they protected. These body-part reliquaries are sometimes known as 'speaking reliquaries', and two of the best known, one holding a nail from the crucifixion and the other the sandal of the apostle Andrew, are in Trier Cathedral Treasury.[23] The nail and the sandal had special significance for Archbishop Egbert (977–93), who commissioned their bejewelled reliquaries, because they were said to have been brought from the Holy Land by the Empress Helena (d. 330), the mother of Constantine the Great. Several of the Reading relics in the Egerton list clearly merited special veneration too, and five have been selected for a more detailed analysis.

THE HAND OF ST JAMES

The first mention of the hand of St James (item 56) in connection with Reading Abbey is in a charter dateable to 1126 which, as noted in the

---

[20]   Rymer, 2, pt 4, 22.
[21]   I suggest balas rubies, the older name for spinels, for balamitibus. The Black Prince's ruby was such a stone.
[22]   Based on a current gold price of £1,040 per ounce, and estimating the £200 value of the shrine to be equivalent to the value of the gold in 1338.
[23]   On speaking reliquaries, see Hahn (1997).

previous chapter, is either corrupt or a forgery.[24] The charter states that King Henry gave the hand to Reading at the request of his daughter Matilda, who brought it from Germany, but it is witnessed by Roger Bigod, Henry's steward, who had been dead for nineteen years in 1126. Nevertheless, it is reasonable to suppose that the hand was given to Reading by Henry, because Matthew Paris records that it was sent there from Normandy by the King in 1133.[25] Hallam takes the view that this, and not 1126, was the original date of the gift,[26] and perhaps the original dedication of the church, recorded in the 1125 charter, to the Virgin and St John the Evangelist, implies that the gift of the hand of St James was not foreseen from the outset. The hand was borrowed by Henry of Blois, Bishop of Winchester, in 1136 and not returned until 1155.[27] It was certainly back in Reading before 1161, since a grant of forty days' indulgence to all who visit the abbey on the feast of St James (25 July) by Theobald, Archbishop of Canterbury (d. 1161) refers to the hand as being there.[28] There is also evidence that it was present in the abbey church at some time in the episcopacy of Gilbert Foliot, Bishop of London from 1163 to 1187, who translated the relic to a new reliquary on St James's Day of some unspecified year. The bishop 'went up on to the screen, and as he transferred the hand of the most holy apostle from the old reliquary to a new one, he blessed the people with it.'[29]

The old reliquary, we must presume, was that in which it was housed during its alienation by Henry of Blois, and the new one in some sense a gift to celebrate its return, albeit surprisingly delayed. The form of neither is known for sure, but it is probable that both imitated the form of the relic it enclosed, like the late thirteenth-century reliquary containing a bone from the arm of St Pantaleon in the Walters Art Museum, or those from the Guelph Treasure now in the Cleveland Museum of Art and the Staatliche Museen, Berlin (plate VII).[30] The later Reading reliquary was certainly valuable enough for King Richard I to remove it to use the gold to finance his crusade in 1189, but the hand was not left naked for long.[31] His brother John, Count of Mortain, provided a third reliquary, and

---

[24] Kemp (1986), I, 39–40.
[25] Chron. Maj. 2, 159.
[26] Hallam (1981), 44.
[27] Kemp (1970), 2–3.
[28] Kemp (1986), I, 148.
[29] Kemp (1970), 14; Yarrow (2006), 198.
[30] For body-part reliquaries in general, see Bynum and Gerson (1997); Boehm (1997); Hahn (1997). On the Guelph treasure see Lasko (1972), 205; Swarzenski (1954), 42. It is worth noting, however, that the hand of St Stephen is preserved in a house shrine in St Stephen's, Budapest.
[31] Landon (1935), 10.

supplied one mark of gold every year for its maintenance as early as 1192, confirming the annual gift in 1200 as king.[32]

It might be assumed that if St James's left hand was at Reading Abbey, it would be missing from the body at Santiago de Compostella, but matters are not quite as simple as this, and to understand the complexity it is necessary to go right back to the original martyrdom. James, son of Zebedee was executed with the sword by King Herod Agrippa I (10 BC–44 AD), probably in 42 AD.[33] The legend that St James had preached in Spain at one period of his life can be dated as early as the seventh century, in the *Breviarium Apostolorum*,[34] but the story of his burial in Spain first appears rather later, in the *Martyrology* of Usuard of Saint-Germain-des-Prés, dating from c. 865.[35] This followed the discovery of two graves c. 814, one containing a man's bones and the other the bones of two men, assumed to be St James and the two disciples who transported his corpse to Compostella.[36] The truth of the burial legend is impossible to verify, and has generated a great deal of controversy.[37] St James was certainly executed and buried in Jerusalem, so if he ended up in Spain it was the result of a translation after his death. In their attempts to trace the course of this translation, various writers have suggested staging points along the way, including St Catherine's in Sinai, Zaragosa and Lugo; or Mérida; or the Mennas monastery near Alexandria and Iria Flavia.[38] The version that was generally accepted around the time of the foundation of Reading, however, was that given in the *Historia Compostellana,* an account written by an author in the circle of Diego Gelmirez of Compostela (Bishop 1100–20, then Archbishop from 1120–40), and centred on Gelmirez's deeds and on the status of Compostela and its connection with St James. It was therefore the official propaganda version, and according to this, after James's martyrdom his body was taken by sea to Spain by two of his disciples, Athanasius and Theodore, landing at Padrón on the Galician coast. It was then taken inland to Compostella, and all three men were buried close together in the graves discovered in the early ninth century.[39]

When we come to examine how the Reading hand fits into this history we find that it does not, but relies on an entirely different account from

[32] Kemp (1986), 1, 68, 71–72.
[33] Acts 12, 1–2; Taylor (1997), 97.
[34] Quoted in Herwaarden (1980), 3.
[35] Ibid., 18–20.
[36] Taylor (1997), 97
[37] Ibid., 23–30.
[38] Ibid. See also Gams (1956), 2, 363ff; Navascués (1948), 349–50; Hell & Hell (1966), 31–36.
[39] Historia Compostellana, 5–7; Fletcher (1984), 53.

the official version.⁴⁰ In this account St James's body was still in Jerusalem in the late fourth century, when Bishop Heliodorus of Altino visited his grave and took away an arm. From Altino, near Venice, the arm was taken in 640 to the island of Torcello to protect it from Lombard raiders, and there it stayed until the Roman expedition of 1046/47 when the hand (not the whole arm) was surrendered by Bishop Vitalis of Torcello to Adalbert, Archbishop of Hamburg-Bremen. At Adalbert's death in 1072 nothing was found in his treasury except books, vestments and relics, and these were seized by the Emperor Henry IV and inherited by his son Henry V, who married Matilda, the daughter of Henry I of England. When, on Henry V's death in 1125, Matilda was recalled to England by her father, she brought the hand with her.⁴¹ It is also clear, as Leyser has demonstrated, that the Emperor Frederick Barbarossa tried to persuade Henry II to give it back to the imperial chapel, and that Henry refused.⁴²

This was the hand that was presented to Reading Abbey, and it is worth reviewing the situation with regard to relics of St James the Great in the mid-twelfth century. Compostela claimed to have his entire body except for two pieces. An arm had been given by the King of Navarre to the Bishop of Tongres and Liège in modern Belgium, and permission was granted for a lock of hair to be taken by the deacon of the Bishop of Pistoia in 1144. He took bone along with the hair, but was allowed to keep it. Meanwhile another arm was still in Torcello cathedral but the hand removed from it was at Reading, and remained there until the dissolution of the house in 1539. It was noted among the list of the abbey's relics recorded by the king's commissioner, John London, Warden of New College Oxford, in his report to Thomas Cromwell dated 18 September 1538.⁴³

It is at this point that the Reading hand disappears from the historical record, but it might have survived the Dissolution. In October 1786 workmen digging the foundations for Reading Gaol discovered a left hand in a wall at the east end of the abbey church. Interestingly, although nowhere in the medieval accounts of the hand is it stated whether it was a left or a right hand, the image on the abbey seal in use in 1239 clearly shows a left hand raised in benediction, accompanied by the words ORA PRO NOBIS SANCTE IACOBE, which would be unusual unless this represented the reliquary itself. The newly rediscovered hand was given to one Dr Blenkinsop and passed from him to Dr Hooper, who gave it around 1801 to the Athenaeum, the museum of the Reading Philosophical Institute,

---

⁴⁰ The definitive account is in Leyser (1975), but Taylor (1997) provides a useful summary.

⁴¹ Leyser (1975), 491. The account of Matilda's removal of the relic is found in the Annals of Disibodenberg; MGH (SS), 17, 23.

⁴² Leyser (1975), passim, esp. 499.

⁴³ Wright (1843), 225.

where it was displayed for some years. When this closed down in 1853 the relic was returned to Dr Hooper's executors, who sold it to the Roman Catholic Lewis Mackenzie in 1855. Mackenzie died the following year,[44] and his heir sold the hand to Charles Robert Scott-Murray (1818–82) for fifty guineas. Scott-Murray had converted to the Catholic faith in 1844, and he engaged the architect Augustus Welby Pugin to build a catholic church dedicated to St Peter in Marlow-on-Thames, and a private chapel at Danesfield, his own house nearby. The hand was kept in Danesfield chapel until the house was sold out of the family to Robert William Hudson, heir of the Sunlight soap magnate Robert Spear Hudson, in 1897. Hudson rebuilt the house and demolished the chapel, and the hand was given to St Peter's Marlow, where it is still preserved (plate VIII).[45]

What the Catholic Church felt and feels about this situation is diffi-cult to imagine. The Santiago authorities claimed proprietary rights over St James the Great, and were clearly embarrassed when in 1852 Father Morris, parish priest of Marlow, wrote to ask Archbishop Miguel Garcia Cuesta of Compostela whether the apostle's body had a hand missing.[46] The Archbishop replied that the tomb was not accessible, because the shrine had been dismantled at the time of Sir Francis Drake's attack on nearby Corunna in 1597, and the saint's body was then hidden below the sanctu-ary and walled in.[47] This situation could not be allowed to continue, and in 1878 Cardinal Miguel Paya y Rico, the new Archbishop of Compostela, authorised a search for the apostle's bones to be performed by Canon Antonio López Ferreiro, the historian of the church, and another canon. They ultimately announced their success, having found a chest of brick and stone under the floor behind the altar. It proved to contain the bones of three men, one of whose skull had damage consistent with a decapita-tion. When the relic of bone and hair at Pistoia was remembered, it was sent for and proved to fit the skull, and this was taken as confirmation that this was indeed St James, accompanied by his two disciples; a judgment approved by Pope Leo X in his bull *Deus Omnipotens* of 1884.[48]

Obviously this judgment had implications for the other alleged relics, and when Brian Taylor asked whether the state of the bones identified as the apostle's was consistent with the claims of Torcello, Liège and Marlow he received the reply, 'Parece que si' – apparently yes – for Liège; 'No

---

[44] Accidentally killed by his cook who mistakenly used aconite root to make horseradish sauce.

[45] Hurry (1915); Taylor (1997). A plan to install the hand in the new Westminster Cathedral was reported in *The Times* of 30 July 1901, 11, but this was not carried out. I am grateful to Canon Antony Griffiths of St Peter's Church, Marlow, who allowed me to examine and photograph it.

[46] Taylor (1997), 99–100, 102 n. 23.

[47] Ibid.

[48] Beani (1885), 112–21.

consta' – no clear evidence – for Torcello; and 'Parece que no' – apparently not – for Marlow.[49]

The power of relics does not depend on their authenticity, however, but on what people believe about them, and the hand given by Henry I and his daughter to Reading Abbey was demonstrably effective. An account of miracles worked by the hand is preserved in a manuscript of c. 1200 in Gloucester Cathedral Library.[50] The *Miracles of the Hand of St James* contains descriptions of twenty-eight miracles, thirteen of which include internal evidence of a date before c. 1190, and one of which is precisely dated to 1127. While this apparently proves that the hand was at Reading in 1127, rather than being a gift of 1133 as stated by Matthew Paris and argued above, two points count against it. First, it is the only miracle to be precisely dated, and that to the year after the date given for the gift in the demonstrably corrupt charter that records it.[51] Second, despite being the earliest in date it appears last in the manuscript, and might well have been an addition to the original manuscript. All but two of the miracles are cures, many worked by drinking or bathing in water in which the reliquary had been immersed, the so-called 'water of St James'. In a few cases, the mere sight of the reliquary was enough to work the cure, and in two instances, even this was not needed, the cure following a visit to the abbey or else a promise to visit. Of the two non-medical miracles, one involved the movement of heavy timber and the other the death of a man who failed to observe James's feast day with the proper reverence. St James's power did not generally extend very far: eleven of the twenty-eight miracles involved Berkshire people and in most other cases the beneficiary came from the south of England. The two exceptions to this are a keeper of hounds from some unspecified location in the north and a young man accompanying Prince John to Ireland in 1185. A flavour of the text may be gained from Miracle XIX, the account of the healing of Abbot Osbert of Notley (Bucks), dateable before his death in 1189.

> There was a man of a venerable way of life named Osbert, Abbot of Notley, famous for his integrity and laudable in religion, who began to languish in the grip of a most grievous affliction of the eyes. Having tried ointments and several medicines, he not only received no cure, but seemed rather to have grown very much worse and incurred great expense. He suffered more intense pain and more acute torment. If, for example, he happened to look at a ray of the sun or at any lamp, it seemed as if his head was suddenly being pierced and his eyeballs darkened. He spent sleepless nights and ever wakeful days. When he had been for some time in this pain and could find no rest for his head nor sleep for his eyes, on the advice of one of his canons he vowed to go to Reading and honour St James with his service. And no sooner had he

[49] Taylor (1997), 100.
[50] Gloucester Cathedral Library MS 1. See Kemp (1970), Yarrow (2006).
[51] Kemp (1986), 1, 39–40.

uttered this vow with his mouth than his anguish started to ease and the pain began to go down, so that within three days he was able to sing mass, and so came to Reading as he had vowed fit and well. He presented a tall candle to the blessed apostle in fulfilment of his vow, light for light and praise for so speedy a dispensation.[52]

The *Miracles* also includes an anecdotal confirmation of King Henry II's veneration of the Reading relic. Miracle XXVI describes the agonising and debilitating illness of one Roger Hosatus, a canon of Merton Priory with a swollen tumour. By chance, two monks of Reading who were carrying the hand back to the abbey, after the king had sent for it to pray for a safe channel crossing, turned aside at Merton to ask for a night's lodging. The sick canon was immediately cured by a taste of the miraculous water of St James: he vomited up the poison that had settled in a lump on his chest and heart, and by judicious doses of the water on the next two days he was restored to perfect health.[53] The key feature of the story is the presence in it of the king, who considered the hand to be not merely an effective relic but (on account of its provenance) a royal one, available to him and his successors on demand. It has been argued that this political dimension is an important feature of the power of St James, and that the apostle and his relic were used to add support to the Angevin dynasty.[54] A key miracle here is XXV, which as it stands seems irrelevant to the relic.[55] It tells the story of Matthew, Count of Boulogne, a supporter of Henry II in the revolt of 1173–74, who led an attack on the castle of Driencourt on St James's day 1173, against the wishes of the king. For this rash act he was struck in the knee by a small barbed arrow, wounding him mortally. What is surprisingly omitted from the account in the *Miracles* is any mention of the hand of St James, but the missing element is supplied by the account of Ralph of Diceto, whose version emphasised that Count Matthew had previously sworn an oath of loyalty to the king, while touching the hand of St James placed before him.[56]

Incidental features mentioned in the *Miracles* give further information about the way the relic was displayed. We have seen that it was normally housed high up on a screen, which the Bishop of London had to climb in order to translate it to a new reliquary.[57] Elsewhere are references to its being carried in processions.[58] St James also had his own altar in the

---

[52] Kemp (1970), 14.
[53] Ibid., 18.
[54] Yarrow (2006), passim, esp. 211.
[55] Kemp (1970), 17.
[56] Ralph of Diceto, 1, 373.
[57] Kemp (1970), 14.
[58] Kemp (1970), 8, 11.

church, with a picture of St James painted above it, and this too was credited with healing powers.[59]

It can be useful for the modern reader to view the contract entered into by the pilgrim and the saint as an economic one.[60] Thus a man might benefit from a miraculous intervention on credit, which left him with an obligation that he must fulfil to avoid retribution from the saint: what Bell and Dale call 'penal miracles.' They give an example from the Reading collection, in which a young man attending Prince John on a visit to Ireland broke his arm, and it would not heal. At length he vowed to St James that he would visit his shrine at Reading if he might be healed, and the saint immediately mended the arm. The young man, however, failed to keep his side of the bargain, and was punished by having his other arm broken in a similar accident: an action, they point out, that is not far removed from the behaviour of modern debt collectors.[61]

It is possible that Reading presented itself as a local alternative to Santiago de Compostella itself. It is certainly true that identification with St James was important enough for his scallop shell badge to be used to distinguish coins minted at Reading in the reign of Edward III (see chapter four). It was also incorporated into the abbey's arms, *azure three escallops or*, but although Hurry credits Henry I with the grant of arms,[62] their earliest definite appearance is in an early sixteenth-century armorial in the College of Arms where they appear twice; once alone and once impaled with the arms of the last Abbot, Hugh Cooke.[63] The latter miniature depicts a procession of four abbots, led by the Abbot of Reading who is followed by his colleagues of St Mary's York, Ramsey and Peterborough (figure 12). Two centuries earlier, the arms appeared in a fourteenth-century book of decretals and associated commentaries in the British Library, leading to a queried attribution of the book to Reading Abbey by Ker.[64] Here the shield appears, painted, gilded and suspended on a *trompe l'oeil* hook, at the foot of the painted frame of folio 1, and it must be part of the original decoration of the book. Some estimate of the profitability of a shrine can be gauged from the survival of the pilgrim badges and ampullae which were popular souvenirs from the beginning of the fourteenth century onwards.[65] No such souvenir certainly from Reading

---

[59] Kemp (1970), 11.
[60] Perhaps the clearest explanation of this approach from the economic historian's viewpoint is found in Bell and Dale (2011).
[61] Ibid., 604–05; Kemp (1970), 16.
[62] Hurry (1901), 93.
[63] London, College of Arms L10, fols 65v., 74r. For a description of the manuscript, see Campbell & Steer (1988), 46–49.
[64] The book is BL Royal 9 F.V, f. 1r; see Ker (1964), 156.
[65] London (1987), 218–19.

12   THIS ILLUSTRATION OF THE PROCESSION OF THE ABBOTS OF READING, ST MARY'S
YORK, RAMSEY AND PETERBOROUGH TO PARLIAMENT, FROM A MANUSCRIPT OF C. 1520
(LONDON, COLLEGE OF ARMS L10, F.74R.) IS THE EARLIEST DEFINITE OCCURRENCE OF
THE SCALLOP SHELL ARMS OF THE ABBEY.

Abbey is known to survive,[66] although it may well be that some of the

---

[66]   Private correspondence from Brian Spencer.

scallop shell badges and ampullae commonly found in the UK had their origin there (see figure 9, chapter one).[67]

THE HEAD OF ST PHILIP

We have seen that King John was concerned to make good the vandalism of his brother, Richard, in stripping the relic of St James of its precious housing to finance his crusade. John later gave the abbey a head reliquary, allegedly containing part of the skull of the apostle Philip (item 61). This relic was brought to the west with many others after the sacking of Constantinople in 1204.[68] It appears in the relic-list as an addition to the original text, with the explanation a few lines below:

> Iohannis rex Angliae dedit nobis caput Philippi apostoli venerandum. Et nobis nundinas ipso die concedit habere.[69]

The gift is recorded in rather more detail on a flyleaf of a book of chronicles now in Lambeth Palace library (MS 371) in the following words:

> Johannes Rex angliae dedit nobis capud s.philippi ap. venerandum quod nobis misit cum maxima episcoporum et procerum reverencia et venerantibus illud ab episcopis indulgencies impetravit. Et ipso die nobis nundinas habere concessit. Cuius anime propicietur deus. Amen.[70]

The fair (*nundinae*) associated with the gift was also separately granted to Abbot Elias and his successors and the monks of Reading in a document of 1 May 1205, which specified that it should be held on the vigil and feast of St Philip and St James (1 May) and the two days following. It should be noted that Philip shares his feast day with St James the Less, not St James the Great whose hand was the abbey's major relic, and it seems likely that the association of the two at Reading was no more than a happy coincidence. The annual fair was one of three known to have been held at the abbey. Henry I also granted a fair on the feast of St Laurence (10 August) and the next three days; and Henry II a fair on the feast of St James (25 July) and the three following days (possibly a confirmation of a grant by Henry

---

[67] Scallop shell badges and ampullae, such as would be expected from Reading Abbey, are extremely common survivals but are usually assumed to have come from the more popular pilgrimage to Santiago de Compostella. The possibility that some were from Reading is accepted by Spencer (1990), 62, 91.

[68] Bethell (1972), 64 and n. 1.

[69] King John of England gave us the venerated head of Philip the apostle, and granted us a fair on the same day.

[70] James and Jenkins (1932), 503. See also Bethell (1972), 64 and n1; Coates (1999), 156.

I).[71] All were still held at the time of the dissolution of the abbey except St Laurence's fair, which had fallen into disuse by the mid-fifteenth century.[72] What must not be overlooked is the intimate relationship between fairs and shrines. By accompanying his gift of the relic of St Philip with a fair on that saint's feast day, King John ensured the presence of a large number of people at the abbey with money to spend and an obligation to venerate the apostle. This is simple economics, but commentators still criticised the link between saints and trade. As William of Malmesbury remarked of St Aldhelm's fair in Malmesbury, it was established,

> so that those who were not lured by the sanctity of the confessor might be attracted by the desire for goods.[73]

THE CROSS OF HENRY THE LION

Item 5 in the Egerton list is described as:

> *de ligno domini crux que fuit de capella ducis saxonie.*

The circumstances of this gift from Henry the Lion, Duke of Saxony and Bavaria of a piece of the True Cross are not known, but might be clarified by a chain of indirect evidence. It must first be remembered that Henry the Lion was King Henry II of England's son-in-law, having married Princess Matilda in 1168. This dynastic union was to prove useful to Duke Henry when he was later banished from Germany for failing to support Emperor Frederick Barbarossa's expedition to Lombardy in 1174. Before that incident, however, Duke Henry undertook a pilgrimage to Jerusalem in 1172, visiting the Byzantine court of Emperor Manuel I Komnenos on both the outward and return journeys, and making gifts to the church of the Holy Sepulchre.[74] Each of his visits to the Byzantine court was accompanied by exchanges of gifts. For the most part these were the usual rich fabrics, furs, horses, weapons and saddles, but the account of Arnold of Lübeck makes it clear that Henry asked for, and was eventually given, many precious saintly relics, turning down a counter-offer of fourteen mules loaded with gold, silver and silken garments.[75] It follows from this

---

[71]   Kemp (1986), I, 40–41; 56–57.

[72]   GMF, Reading, Berkshire, 15 July 2010.

[73]   Quoted in Webb (2000), 42; William of Malmesbury GP, 428.

[74]   Arnold of Lübeck, Chronica, 18–30. See also Joranson (1938) for a full account of the pilgrimage as recorded by Arnold of Lübeck; and Klein (2004), 284–86.

[75]   Ibid., 30. Qui [i.e. Manuel I] multum letatus est reditu eius, et cum henestissime detinuisset eum per aliquot dies, dedit ei quattuordecim mulos, oneratus auro et argento et sericis vestibus. Dux vera immensas gratias agens, noluit accipere, dicens ad eum: 'Habeo plurima, domne mi, inveniam tantum gratiam in oculis

account that both Duke Henry and the Byzantine Emperor prized the relics more highly than gold, but that the Emperor felt obliged by his duty of hospitality to accede to the Duke's specific request.

After Duke Henry's downfall at the hands of Barbarossa in 1180–81, he was banished from Germany for three years, and went to England with his wife and children, to stay with his father-in-law Henry II. It is hard to believe that a man who valued saintly relics as Henry the Lion did would fail to pay a visit to the hand of St James – especially as Barbarossa had tried and failed to secure its return to Germany in 1157, and the most likely time for his gift to Reading of the fragment of the True Cross must be between 1181 and the Duke's return from banishment in late 1184. In that period there was one occasion when we know for certain that he was at the abbey. He had returned to Germany temporarily for the general assembly held in Mainz, and landed in Dover on his return in July 1184. From here he went to Winchester, where the king met him on 25 July, and the two went to Reading together for the council held there on 5 August to try to decide on a successor as Archbishop of Canterbury to Richard of Dover who had died earlier that year.[76]

The setting of the true cross relic might well have been a cross, and as it came from Constantinople, a Byzantine cross seems likeliest, but we know from Arnold of Lübeck that Duke Henry gave the relics he had acquired new settings of gold and silver and precious stones on his return,[77] so that the old settings could have been incorporated into a new Western frame, as in the Stavelot triptych (New York, Morgan Library and Museum), or a totally new setting might have been produced, as is the case with Henry's own reliquary cross in Hildesheim Cathedral treasury.

THE HOLY PREPUCE

Christ's foreskin, otherwise the Holy Prepuce (item 7), was one of the very few of Christ's body parts that he left on earth after his death. Bodily fluids like blood, sweat and water associated with the Passion were available as relics (see items 17, 20, 21, 22). The foreskin, however, had a special resonance since it was both part of the living flesh of Christ, and associated with a scriptural event.[78] This should, of course, be a unique relic but many foreskins were available for veneration in Europe at various times during

---

tuis.' Cumque nimis cogeret eum, et ille nulla ratione consentiret accipere, dedit sanctorum reliquias ei multas et preciosas, quas postulaverat.

[76]   Eyton (1878), 256–57.

[77]   Arnold of Lübeck, Chronica, 30. *Ditavit domum Dei reliquiis sanctorum, quas secum attulerat, vestiens eas auro et argento et lapidibus pretiosis.*

[78]   For the Circumcision, see Luke 2. 21. For a useful discussion of the unique status of the foreskin, see Shell (1996), 345–47.

the Middle Ages, and there are interesting issues of display which should at least be addressed.

Possession of Christ's foreskin was claimed by at least seventeen churches during the Middle Ages, although there probably were not this many foreskins. The Emperor Charlemagne (768–814) gave away at least two. He gave the first to Pope Leo III at his coronation in Rome on Christmas Day 800, and the pope placed it in the *Sancta Sanctorum* of the basilica of St John Lateran, where it was described in a relic list of c. 1100. Charlemagne had probably received it as a wedding gift from the Byzantine Empress Irene, although according to a more picturesque report he received it from an angel while he was praying at the Holy Sepulchre. It was looted from the Lateran basilica by a German soldier engaged in the Sack of Rome in 1527. He was captured in Calcata, a village some 40km north of Rome, and apparently hid the relic in his cell, where it was discovered again thirty years later. It remained in the parish church, and from then until 1856 it was accepted by the Catholic Church as a first-class relic, but in that year another foreskin was rediscovered at the abbey of Charroux. This had also been given to the monks by the Emperor Charlemagne. In the twelfth century it was taken to Pope Innocent III in Rome for a ruling on its authenticity (he refused to rule). At some time it went missing until it was rediscovered by workmen repairing a wall in the abbey in 1856. At that point there were heated arguments between Charroux and Calcata about the authenticity of the two relics, which was resolved by the church issuing a ruling in 1900 that anyone speaking or writing about them would be excommunicated. The villagers of Calcata, however, continued to hold an annual procession of the relic until 1983, when the parish priest announced that it had been stolen from the shoebox he kept it in, in his wardrobe (he could not keep it in the church owing to the official censure). This gave rise to the conspiracy theories described in Farley (2009).

The entry in the Egerton list makes it clear that what Reading had might have been part of the umbilical cord rather than the foreskin – a piece of tissue that looked very similar – and that the group also included a piece of the True Cross. While the foreskin would be a relic of Christ alone, the umbilical cord was shared by Christ and the Virgin, and was arguably less valuable.[79] It is interesting too that this precise combination of relics – the foreskin, umbilical cord and cross – were contained in the Lateran's own cross reliquary according to a description written between 1073 and 1118:

---

[79]   Shell (1996), 345–46.

Crux de auro purissimo adornata gemmis et lapidibus pretiosis, id est hya-cintis et smaragdis et prasinis. In media cruce est (umbilicus et) preputium Circumcisionis Domini nostri Jesu Christi.[80]

(A cross of the purest gold adorned with gems and precious stones, that is, sapphires and two kinds of emerald. In the centre of the cross are the umbilical cord and the foreskin of our Lord Jesus Christ).

The iconographic link between the Circumcision and the Crucifixion was well-established as early as the fourth century when Jerome made the connection between the blood shed by Christ as a child, and that he would shed as an adult.[81] Thus both the combination of the relics and the form of the reliquary were entirely appropriate in the Lateran cross, although this is not the only possible form that the Reading reliquary could have taken. The so-called Reliquary of Pepin at Conques was assumed to contain Christ's foreskin for much of its history, presumably because it was given to the abbey by Charlemagne who was known to possess the foreskin, and while this is not a cross but a small casket, it does have crucifixion imagery.[82]

RELICS OF ST THOMAS BECKET

The Egerton list includes six items associated with Archbishop Becket, and at least twice as many distinct pieces (items 119 to 124). Becket had dedicated the abbey church on 19 April 1164 in the presence of King Henry II, but within a few months he had fled the country in fear of his life. He returned in November 1170, having negotiated a settlement with the king, and was assassinated in his own cathedral on 29 December that year. The earliest miraculous cure took place on 4 January 1171 and by Easter people were queuing at his tomb for healing. The Pope quickly decided to regularise the situation by canonising him, and this was done on 21 February 1173. Meanwhile, the Canterbury cathedral authorities moved to protect his body from possible attempts at theft while ensuring access for pilgrims and the availability of saleable relics to maximise revenue. The body was contained in a stone sarcophagus, covered with a stone box pierced by oval portholes through which pilgrims could see and touch the sarcophagus. A guardian of the shrine was appointed, to watch over it and keep a record of the miracles that took place. Relics were made available for purchase, the most popular being the 'water of St Thomas', which was

---

[80] *Descriptio sanctuarii Lateranensis ecclesie*, quoted in Grisar (1908), 59. Smaragdus is the normal word for an emerald; prasinum is an alternative, sometimes used to mean a green stone like an emerald.
[81] See Remensnyder (1996), 895–96.
[82] Remensnyder (1996), 893–95; Taralon (1989).

holy water that had been in contact with either the saint's body, or his tomb, or his blood, and was supplied in tin or lead phials or ampullae filled from a jug and sold for a farthing each.[83] Higher grade relics were also available, but a glance at the Egerton list will show that while they were evocative, the only bodily remains available were blood, brains and hair. These are assumed to have been spilled during his martyrdom, but could equally well be by-products of the normal embalming process.

Apart from the ampullae, the normal form of reliquary was a casket or *chasse* made of Limoges enamel panels depicting scenes of Becket's martyrdom, burial and apotheosis. More than fifty of these survive in various collections, including two in the Musée national du Moyen Âge in Paris.[84] The Metropolitan Museum in New York is fortunate to possess two rather earlier and more unusual Becket reliquaries. The first is a silver *chasse* set with eight enamel plaques that form four sides of a rectangular box with a pyramidal lid. Stylistically it appears to be of Rhenish manufacture and to date from the 1170s. The interior was originally divided into two compartments, suggesting that separate relics were kept within, one of which, according to an inscription of the exterior, could have been blood.[85] The second reliquary is a personal object: a gold reliquary pendant made for Bishop Reginald of Bath as a gift to Queen Margaret of Sicily before 1177, and a scene of the presentation of the gift is engraved on the back.[86] In its original state a window of crystal or horn on the front of the pendant would have allowed the relics to be seen, but this is now lost, along with the relics. Fortunately, however, they are listed on an inscription, which reads:

DE SANGUINE SCI THOME MRIS. DE VESTIBUS SVIS SANGVINE SVO TINTIS. DE PELLICIA. DE CILITIO. DE CVCVLLA. DE CALCIAMENTO. ET CAMISIA.

(Of the blood of St Thomas martyr. Of his vestments stained with his blood. Of the cloak, the hair shirt, the cowl, the shoe, the shirt).

This is a similar collection to those held by Reading Abbey, and although the relics are no longer in the pendant it is instructive to reflect that these seven fragments could be contained within an enclosure that measured only 49 mm by 31 mm by 7 mm thick. The Bishop of Bath must have detached them from relics held at his cathedral priory for incorporation in the gift, and as such they can be taken as representative of relics held at Bath.

---

[83]   F. Barlow, 'Becket, Thomas', Oxford DNB.
[84]   Accession numbers Cl.22596 and Cl.23296.
[85]   Accession number 17.190.520. See London (1984), 282; Breck (1918).
[86]   Accession number 63.160. See London (1984), 283; Hoving (1965).

THE FATE OF THE RELICS

A second relic list was made in 1538, by Dr John London, the royal agent responsible for the suppression of monasteries in Oxford, Reading, Warwickshire, and Northamptonshire. In a letter to his superior, Thomas Cromwell, on 18 September 1538 he wrote,

> I have required of my lord abbott the relykes of hys howse, wich he shewyd unto me with gudde will. I have taken an inventory of them, and have lokkyd them upp behind ther high awlter, and have the key in my keeping, and they be always redy at your lordships commaundement.[87]

His list is also reproduced in Appendix A and it contains just twenty-three items, although some are grouped together, as in 'Item, bones off saynt Leodigarye and of S. Herenei'. The order of the list suggests that he recorded those deemed most important, or those in the grandest reliquaries, first – although the list makes no mention of any actual reliquaries, which would surely have been of interest to Cromwell had they existed at that date. He began with 'peces of the holy crosse' and continued with the famous relics of the hand of St James and the head of St Philip. A note at the end reported that

> ther be a multitude of small bonys, laces, stonys, and ermys, wiche wolde occupie iiij schetes of papyr to make particularly an inventory of every part therof,[88]

which implies that each relic was labelled (although not especially clearly – the hand of St Anastasia (item 189 in the Egerton list) has now become that of St Anastasius). A comparison of the two lists that satisfies even the most generous criteria of statistical validity would be impossible, but one thing that does stand out is that the sixteenth-century list apparently includes only one relic that was not in the twelfth-century list. This is the bone of St Osmund, who was not canonised until 1456 (despite having died in 1099). This suggests, though it does not prove, that Reading had already collected the bulk of its relics by c. 1190. In fact we know of another gift of relics that was made between the compilation of the two lists, and it does not stand out because the saint concerned was already represented in the collection when the gift was made. The saint was Mary Magdalene, and the gift was made in 1386, but because it was the gift of an image that contained relics it will be described in the next section, where similar objects are treated.

[87]   Wright (1843), 225–27.
[88]   Ibid.

OTHER PILGRIMAGE ATTRACTIONS

The reason the relics of the saints were housed in precious and beautiful shrines was not merely that they deserved a splendid home on account of their holiness. Just as important was the effect on the visiting pilgrims. The notion that the saint deserved gold and precious stones could remind the wealthy pilgrim that such gifts were expected,[89] and an impressive reliquary was an attraction in its own right. We know something of several objects that were not strictly relics, or at least not primarily seen as relics, yet were the object of pilgrimage-like visits. None of these enigmatic attractions survives, but we have enough evidence for some enjoyable speculation.

THE CHILD OF GRACE

At the very end of the Egerton relic list is added the record of the gift of an image of a child that was given to Henry I by the Duke of Aquitaine (see Appendix A). More information about this gift is to be found in the Reading manuscript, Lambeth Palace 371:

> Mem. quod in prima creacione monasterii Rading' dedit dux aquitannie Regi henrico fundatori eiusdem quendam puerum ad ecclesie sue temporibus successivis magnum relevamen. coram quo in omni tribulacione sua in capella propria procumbens per dei graciam sue pie peticionis semper sortitus est effectum.[90]

> (Memorandum that at the first foundation of the monastery at Reading the Duke of Aquitaine gave to Henry, the founder of that same (monastery), a certain child for the great solace of the Church in times to come. He who comes prostrate in the presence of that child, in his own chapel, in every time of trouble, through the grace of God, has always received the granting of his pious request).

We learn from this that the Child of Grace had its own chapel in the abbey church, and that its power to grant the requests of humble supplicants was already established at the time it was given by the Duke of Aquitaine, Duke William X (1126–37), better known as the father of Eleanor of Aquitaine, later Queen of Henry II. It was in all likelihood an ancient statue, therefore.

Elsewhere in the Lambeth Palace manuscript is a six-line verse, or exasticon, referring to the same image:

---

[89] Sainte-Foi at Conques is probably the best example of an acquisitive saint. For her love of jewellery, see Robertini (1994) or the English translation in Sheingorn (1995).

[90] London, Lambeth Palace Library MS 371, f. 1v; James and Jenkins (1932), 503. I am indebted to Dr Christopher Blakeman for the translation.

Ad puerum gracie Exasticon
Nunc veluti faciem geniti sub ymagine mira
Dum colimus pulcram criste benigne tuam
Poscimus arturi memoreris criste Britanni
Principis et puerum dilige sancte puer
Fac modo virtutes imitetur et ille paternas
Et regat hoc regnum cum seniore senex.[91]

(An Exasticon to the Child of Grace
Now, O kindly Christ while we worship your beauteous form
in the wondrous statue of you as you were born;
we ask that you, O Christ, be mindful of Arthur, Prince of Britain
and show favour to the boy, O holy child.
Let it now come to pass that he may match his father's virtues
and may he rule this kingdom as an old man with one even older.)

This is precisely the kind of pious request mentioned in the record of the gift, and the fact that it is made on behalf of Prince Arthur (1486–1502), Henry VII's eldest son and the heir to the throne, provides a fairly close date range for the verse. The content suggests that it was composed either soon after Arthur's birth, or in the spring of 1502, when he suddenly fell prey to a mysterious and rapidly fatal illness. The curious phrasing of the final couplet, especially the phrase *et regat hoc regnum cum seniore senex*, is a borrowing from an epigram of Martial, written in anticipation of the birth of a son to the Emperor Domitian.[92] The notion that Arthur might rule the kingdom when he was an old man, alongside his even older father, Henry VII, could reflect the king's own ambitions – he certainly expended a good deal of trouble ensuring that Arthur was properly trained to fulfil his royal role when the time came, and Arthur himself would have learned to appreciate the erudite allusion to Martial even if his father did not.[93]

In March 1502 the Queen, Elizabeth of York, paid for a costly proxy pilgrimage which must have been prompted by her son's illness, and it is possible that the composition of the exasticon accompanied that. She sent the priest William Barton on a twenty-seven day journey in March 1502 to make offerings at shrines on her behalf. Her Privy Purse expenses list seventeen shrines including the Child of Grace at Reading, each of which received a sum between 20d and 6s 8d (the Child of Grace received 2s 6d). Barton disbursed a total of 48s 4d in offerings, and was paid 22s 6d for his efforts.[94] Although the miraculous image had failed to save Arthur,

---

[91] London, Lambeth Palace Libray MS 371, f. 122v; James and Jenkins (1932), 511. Again I am grateful to Dr Blakeman for the translation.

[92] Epigrams Book 6, epigram 3. I am grateful to Dr Blakeman for this information. The relevant line of Martial's epigram reads, *quique regas orbem cum seniore senex.*

[93] For a useful summary of the prince's education, see Gunn (2009), 7–19.

[94] Elizabeth of York Privy Purse Expenses, Entry 2. Barton visited the shrines of Our Lady and St George, the Holy Cross and the shrine of King Henry (VI) at Windsor;

his mother apparently bore it no ill will, since in September of the same year she paid for a 'plyte of lawnde' to make a shirt for the Child of Grace, which cost her 5s for the cloth and 4d for the labour.[95] At around the same period Edward Stafford, 3rd Duke of Buckingham also displayed a special devotion to the Child of Grace, which he treated with the same kind of generosity as the Shrine of Our Lady at Walsingham and the Shrine of the Holy Blood at Hailes. He visited the image twice, in January 1508 and in April 1521, leaving oblations of 3s 4d and 6s 8d.[96] The second of these visits gains an extra resonance from the circumstances under which it was made. As a direct descendant of Thomas of Woodstock, son of Edward III, Stafford could be seen as having a claim to the throne himself, and Henry VIII was certainly persuaded that he represented a threat, especially in view of the fact that he himself had no male heir. A case was prepared against him, and he was summoned to Windsor on 8 April 1521 from his castle of Thornbury (Bucks), still under construction and destined not to be completed. The journey took him through Reading and to Windsor and Eton, all of which had shrines that he gave money to. He was intercepted by Wolsey's orders and taken to the Tower of London on 16 April, charged with imagining and compassing the death of the king, and was executed a month later on Tower Hill after a trial at which he was not allowed to cross-examine his accusers. It has usually been assumed that Buckingham obeyed the king's summons innocent of what might happen to him, but the offerings to three shrines on his journey suggests that he had an inkling that he would need some divine help.

To visualise the Child of Grace we must first remember that it was already established as a miraculous statue between 1126 and 1137 when it was presented by the Duke of Aquitaine. This suggests something akin to the golden statue of Sainte-Foi at Conques, made in the tenth century to house her relics.[97]

Our Lady at Eton; the Child of Grace at Reading; Our Lady of Caversham; Our Lady of Cokethorp; the Holy Blood of Hayles; Prince Edward's shrine; Our Lady of Worcester; the Holy Rood and Our Lady of Grace at Northampton; Our Lady of Walsingham; Our Lady of Sudbury; Our Lady of Wolpitte; Our Lady of Ipswich and Our Lady of Stokeclare.

[95] Ibid., entry 26.
[96] L. and P. Henry VIII, vol. 3, pt 1, pp.498, 501.
[97] On Sainte-Foi, see Robertini (1994). For the popularity of this kind of figural reliquary in the early eleventh century, see Bernard of Angers' account of a synod held at Rodez, described in Lasko (1972, 104–05).

ST MARY MAGDALENE RELIQUARY

In 1386 the Countess of Pembroke presented the monastery with an image of St Mary Magdalene, described in the following terms:

Mem. quod cometissa de penbrok dedit monasterio Rading. in die S. Margarete ymaginem Marie Magdalene argenteam et deauratum refertam reliquiis eisdem maries temp Regis Ricardi secundi post conq. anno iiij. Et a.d. mill. cccmo lxxxvj.

(Memorandum that the Countess of Pembroke gave to the Monastery of Reading a silver gilt image of St Mary Magdalene filled with her relics on St Margaret's day (20 July) in the time of King Richard II in the fourth year after the conquest and 1386 AD.)[98]

The Countess of Pembroke in question was Lady Philippa Mortimer, daughter of Edmund Mortimer, 3rd Earl of March and Philippa of Clarence, a granddaughter of King Edward III. Her devotion to Reading was unsurprising as her parents were formally betrothed there in 1368 (see chapter four). Around 1385–86, aged ten, she married John Hastings, 3rd Earl of Pembroke. It was his second marriage despite the fact that he was only sixteen, as his slightly older first wife, Elizabeth of Lancaster, had apparently grown tired of waiting for him to reach puberty and obtained an annulment. The Earl of Hastings lived to enjoy only three years of marriage to Philippa before he was killed in a jousting accident in 1389. There is no record of where their marriage was solemnised, and as the gift of the reliquary statue dates from around the time of the marriage, it might seem reasonable to assume that they married at Reading, like Philippa's parents. But the record of the gift does not say this and it is unwise to leap to conclusions.

There is no chance that a silver gilt reliquary such as this would have survived the English Reformation, even if the religious foundation it adorned had not itself been dissolved. A type of reliquary-statue that has survived in France, however, consists of a standing figure holding a reliquary that contains the relic: an elegant conceit executed in an elegant late-Gothic style between c. 1300 and 1400. Early examples are a Parisian female saint of c. 1300 in the Bargello in Florence, a silver-gilt statue of St Blaise in Namur, and an enamelled tooth-reliquary of St James in Santiago de Compostella, made in Paris before the 1320s.[99] That this kind of thing was still being made in the early fifteenth century is demonstrated by the similar reliquaries of St Andrew in Reims Cathedral Treasury and St

---

[98]   London, Lambeth Palace Library MS 371, f. 1v; James and Jenkins (1932), 503. The dating by the reign of Richard II is totally mystifying, as M. R. James implied by a bracketed exclamation mark in his catalogue entry.

[99]   Paris (1998), catalogue entries 123, 148–50.

Barbara in the Walters Art Museum (plate IX).[100] While no metalwork of this type survives in England, the high-quality alabaster figures from Flawford church (Notts) are broadly similar to the Continental work, and serve to demonstrate that English craftsmen were working in what is very much a Parisian style around this time.[101]

STATUE OF OUR LADY

The Bohemian traveller Leo of Rozmital travelled through Europe, including England, between 1465 and 1467. He paid a visit to Reading Abbey where he noted just one item that interested him: not the hand of St James – he planned to visit the main shrine in Santiago later in his journey – nor the Child of Grace, but a statue of the Virgin.[102]

> *In eo templo, tabula arae praefixa, et imago Gentricis Dei admodum visitur, ita ut opiner, me neque conspexisse, nec unquam ei conferendam conspecturum esse, etamsi ad extremos mundi terminos progrediar. Nihil enim ea formosius et venustius effingi potest.[103]*

> (In that temple the altars were fixed tables, and I saw such an image of the Mother of God as I shall never see again, even if I travel to the ends of the earth. Nothing more beautiful or more graceful could ever be made.)

No more clues about the form of the figure are given, and no other traveller described it.

IMAGES OF PROPHETS AND APOSTLES

Somewhere in the abbey, perhaps on a screen or a retable or a stained glass window, was a set of images of Old and New Testament figures with inscriptions. The evidence for their existence is clear, but frustratingly incomplete. Written in the same Reading Abbey manuscript that recorded the gifts of the Child of Grace, the Head of St Philip and the relic of St Mary Magdalene is a set of rhymed couplets in a thirteenth-century hand, which is transcribed in Appendix B.[104] The manuscript supplies no indication of where the verses came from. There are twenty-four lines in all, each labelled with the name of an Old Testament figure or an apostle in a red

---

[100]   For the St Andrew reliquary see Paris (1981), catalogue entry 225. St Barbara (Acc. No. 57.694) is a Netherlandish work of c. 1420–40.
[101]   London (1987), catalogue entries 699–701.
[102]   His itinerary is given in Leo de Rozmital, 197–99.
[103]   Leo de Rozmital, 45.
[104]   London, Lambeth Palace MS 371, f. 6v. See James and Jenkins (1932), 506–07.

rubric added at the end of each line. In general the prophets' verses refer to specific prophecies without following the Vulgate text particularly closely: indeed M. R. James, who catalogued the manuscript and who should have known better than anyone, had not come across them anywhere else.[105] Thus David's verse,

> Rex ueniet fortis qui soluet uincula mortis

is the second part of Psalm 106, 14 (Vulgate) turned into rhyme

> Et eduxit eos de tenebris, et umbra mortis: et vincula eorum disrupit.

Both versions mean more or less the same, but the composer of the Reading verses has taken little interest in reproducing the actual words of the Bible text.[106] All of the prophetic inscriptions concern the Incarnation of Christ, and while some of the prophets did utter slick sound bites on the subject, like Isaiah's

> *Ecce virgo concipiet, et pariet filium* (Is. 7, 14),

which here becomes

> *Uirgo deum pariet: mater sine semine fiet,*

others merely referred to the Messiah obliquely and over entire chapters. Hosea's Reading verse,

> *Missus de celis Christus uenit esto fidelis,*

is essentially the message of chapter 13, but bears no resemblance to any particular verse.

Towards the end of the prophets' verses there might be some confusion, although the connections between the verses attributed to Hosea, Amos and Habakkuk and their actual texts is so tenuous that it is hard to tell. The most worrying is Amos, whose verse,

> *De celis numen ueniet de lumine lumen,*
>
> (from heaven will come the divine; light from light),

---

[105] Ibid., 507.

[106] The commonest source of prophetic inscriptions must be the Pseudo-Augustinian *Contra Judaeos, Paganos et Arianos de Symbolo*, on which see Glass (1987). This is the sixth-century source of the Vulgate inscriptions on prophet figures at Salisbury, the pulpit at Sessa Aurunca, and on the facades of Cremona, Ferrara and Notre-Dame-la-Grande in Poitiers.

reflects, more or less, the sentiments of chapter 5, but is much closer to Habakkuk 3, 4:

Splendor eius ut lux erit

(his brightness was like the light).

If there was a mistake in transcription by the thirteenth-century scribe of the manuscript, it could explain a mismatch in the numbers of prophets and apostles. Even if we count the Baptist among the prophets, as we surely must, they number only eleven.[107] The apostles, in contrast, number thirteen, including both Paul and Judas Iscariot's replacement Matthias, but not Iscariot himself.[108] However, the *et* between the names of Jude and Simon the Zealot suggests that the two were linked together, as they often were. There is every reason to expect that twelve prophets would be matched by twelve apostles. Christ himself selected twelve men, and after the betrayal and death of Judas Iscariot, the first act of the remaining eleven was to find a twelfth to replace him. It is fair to assume, therefore, that a minor prophet has been missed. This issue becomes even more important if images are involved, as here. The evidence for this is apparent from the verses, which time and again imply an address from a speaking figure, thus:

Petrus ego celi portas reserabo fideli

(I am Peter who opens the gates of heaven to the faithful)

or Paul's:

Qui fueram saulus modo dicor nomine Paulus

(I had the name of Saul who now am called Paul)

or Bartholomew's:

Terre prostratus uiuus sum decoriatus

(Prostrate on the ground I was flayed alive).

Sometimes the inscriptions provide clues to the images they accompanied. Peter's refers directly to the keys of heaven that he carried, and Paul may have been shown falling from his horse on the road to Damascus. Those of Andrew, James the Greater, Bartholomew and Matthias all refer to their martyrdoms and it can be deduced, therefore, that they were

---

[107] Moses, David, the four major prophets, four of the minor prophets and John the Baptist.

[108] Acts 1, 23–26. The Judas rubric refers to Judas Thaddeus, normally called St Jude.

depicted either being executed or holding the instruments involved. This might well be true of the others too, since all except John were martyred according to tradition. The Old Testament figures could simply have been shown as standing types of the apostles, with inscriptions on scrolls, although in a few cases other imagery is suggested. Jonah's verse,

Ex utero matris nascetur gloria patris,

refers not to his preaching, which was vengeful rather than prophetic, but to his adventure with the great fish – more usually used as a metaphor for the Resurrection, but here related to the Virgin birth of Christ.[109]

When we come to consider what kind of images the verses were attached to, we have a wide variety of possibilities with little to help us choose between them. At one extreme are the life-sized limestone statues from St Mary's Abbey, York. These date from the 1180s, and although only eleven survive it seems clear that initially there were probably twelve apostles and twelve Old Testament figures.[110] Christopher Wilson argued that the statues were originally arranged in two tiers inside the chapter house, with the prophets supporting the apostles (as on the Fürstenportal at Bamberg), but this interpretation depended upon features of the figures and the site that were peculiar to St Mary's abbey, and early suggestions that the figures could have come from a French-style portal or a screen or been set against the piers of the nave, as at Bruges, would not be inherently improbable at another site.[111]

Another possible site for the images with their verses is a reliquary, like the Three Kings Shrine in Cologne, decorated with silver gilt figures of apostles and evangelists on the upper level and Old Testament figures below. Rather less spectacular but still based on the same typological scheme are the domed tabernacle from Cologne in the Victoria and Albert Museum, London, and its smaller sister object from the Guelph Treasure in Berlin, both of c. 1180.[112] These two reliquaries are in the form of buildings with a Greek cross plan with a dome over the crossing. They are of

---

[109] Jonah is a type of the Resurrection on the Klosterneuburg altar of 1181, and on the English cycles in Eton College MS 177, the Worcester verses (Worcester Cathedral Library MS F81), the Warwick Ciborium in the V&A Museum, and the late-twelfth-century windows in Canterbury Cathedral. See Röhrig (1955) for the Klosterneuburg altar and most conveniently Henry (1990) for the English objects.

[110] Wilson (1983); London (1984), 204–06.

[111] Wilson (1983), 102–14.

[112] The V&A reliquary (7650–1861) was formerly known as the Hochelten (or Eltenberg) reliquary after the nunnery of that name, whence the dealer from whom it was bought claimed it came. Recent research suggests that it was in fact from a Cologne church, probably St Pantaleon. The Berlin reliquary is accessioned as Staatliche Kunstgewerbemuseum Museen zu Berlin W. 15.

gilt and enamelled copper over an oak core, with ivory figures of prophets around the lower level and apostles around the drum of the dome. Both prophets and apostles carry scrolls with inscriptions, but they are not close to the Reading verses.[113]

Parallels from stained glass can also be cited, and the most striking is in the choir clerestory of Bourges cathedral (Cher) dateable c. 1220–25. Here the apostles are in pairs on the south side and the prophets on the north, but the only texts are those at the foot of each light identifying the figures. In England, Lincoln might offer the closest parallel, but the thirteenth-century glass has been moved around, and only Nigel Morgan's reconstruction of the original glazing allows us to identify that there were once standing figures of the prophets and New Testament figures, including apostles.[114] In other media, vault paintings are known from Salisbury Cathedral and choir stalls painted with prophets and apostles carrying scrolls with credal inscriptions survive, for example at St Mary's, Astley (Warwicks).[115]

CONCLUSION

The medieval pilgrim visiting Reading Abbey received a spiritual reward in the form of the gratitude of the saints he could venerate and who would return his veneration with their own intercession for his eternal soul. More than this, however, he could feast his eyes on the rich and beautiful shrines that formed a suitable home for their evocative contents, and on the Child of Grace, the speaking figures of apostles and prophets, and the figures of Our Lady and St Mary Magdalene whose power came from their appearance, their reputation and the richness of their materials.

---

[113] The prophets' inscriptions are from the Vulgate, while the apostles' are taken from Matthew 16. 14 and 16.

[114] Bennett et al. (2012), 22, 30–33.

[115] For Salisbury, see Reeve (2008), 85–87, 136–38. The prophets bore inscriptions from the *Contra Judaeos*, but the apostles had no inscriptions except their names. For Astley, see Tracy (2009), 88–124.

DEATH AND BURIAL AT READING ABBEY 3

THE DEATH OF A MONK

The choice of a burial place in the Middle Ages was more than a matter of life and death: it could affect your soul for eternity. For monks the decision to remain in the abbey after death was an easy choice. They could rely on their present and future brethren to pray for their souls and for the resurrection of their bodies on Judgement Day – in the place where they had served God through the *opus Dei* during their lifetimes, in the hope that this would act as a reminder to their divine judge of the service they had offered him. The precise formula to be followed when a monk died varied from house to house, but it always included both liturgical elements in the form of masses and psalms, and charitable ones in the form of alms. Masses and psalms were said or sung on the day of death and the anniversary, and often once a week for the year after the brother's death. A system of almsgiving on behalf of the deceased monk was also carried out, and could be expected to secure some divine credit. The paupers who relied on hand-outs from the monastery, administered by the almoner, were entitled as a matter of course to the leftovers from the monks' table. When a monk died his place in the refectory was set and his food served to the empty place for a period, depending on the monastery, between thirty days and a year after his death for an ordinary brother, and for at least a year and sometimes in perpetuity for a deceased abbot. All this food, known as corrodies, went to the almonry for distribution to the poor. In some houses too, every anniversary of a monk's death was marked by a corrody.[1]

In the older and larger houses, where the deceased brethren far outnumbered the living, this practice became very costly as the years passed.

---

[1] Harvey (1993), 13–16.

A case in point is Cluny itself, founded in the tenth century and always very large, where in the 1140s Abbot Peter the Venerable was obliged to limit the number of daily portions distributed to the poor to fifty to ease the burden on the abbey's finances.[2] Similarly at Ramsey Abbey distributions to the poor on the anniversary of every dead monk was replaced in the early thirteenth century by an annual distribution to one hundred poor people – a much more economical practice. Customaries were the books in which the minutiae of all monastic procedures, including this one, were recorded, but Reading's does not survive, although several others do from English Benedictine houses.[3] We are fortunate, however, to have some information about practices associated with the death of Reading monks from an unusual source: a letter dateable to the abbacy of Roger (1158–65) assuring Queen Eleanor of Aquitaine, consort of Henry II, that at her death all should be done for her as was customarily done for a professed monk of Reading at his decease.[4]

The letter therefore supplies that portion of the customary relating to the liturgical and charitable consequences of the death of a monk of Reading. Since the full text has already been published there is nothing to be gained by repeating it here,[5] but it included masses and the readings of psalms on the day of death; servings from the refectory for thirteen paupers and a hundred loaves of bread for the poor in the hostel; and a weekly mass and a daily serving from the refectory for the hostel. This culminated in a repetition of the masses and pittances on the anniversary of the death, to be repeated each year thereafter. The letter refers to a book in which the names of dead monks and patrons were recorded but, as Cheney noted, by the time of Eleanor's death the abbey apparently had no record of the agreement, and in all likelihood it was never observed. The abbey did not, of course, expect to have burial rights over her body, and in fact she was buried at Fontevraud alongside her husband in 1204.

MONASTIC AND LAY BURIALS

Even in the democracy of death there were gradations of status. Most of the brethren were buried in the monks' cemetery east of the chapter house. Abbots and important obedientiaries would expect a better location. We have no direct evidence for Reading, but at many houses, abbots who died in office were buried in the chapter house, as at St Albans where

[2]   Ibid., 14.
[3]   See, e.g., Thompson (1902) for St Augustine's Canterbury and Westminster Abbey; Gransden (1973) for Bury St Edmunds.
[4]   Salisbury Muniments of the Dean and Chapter, Liber Evidentiarum C. 290, 213–14.
[5]   Cheney (1936), 492–93.

we have a fifteenth-century account to tell us that eleven abbots were buried in this location: Paul of Caen (d. 1093), his nine immediate successors ending with John of Hertford (d. 1263), and John de la Moote (d. 1401).[6] In fact the first four of the series were exhumed by Abbot Robert de Gorham (1151–66) expressly so that they could be buried in his new chapter house.[7]

For laymen matters were not quite this simple. Founders would certainly expect to be buried within the abbey church; this, after all, was the reason for the foundation as we saw with Henry I, and more famously in the cases of Edward the Confessor and Henry III at Westminster Abbey. Major donors would expect similar treatment, and in this case burial could be seen as the culmination of a lifetime of support. For those of lower rank (and lesser wealth) the choice was between burial at parochial churches, where the laity would include family and friends who would remember them and pray for them regularly, and burial at a monastery, where the monks devoted their lives to prayer, but would remember them (if it all) only as donors. Ultimately the parochial option was to gain the day, but the monastic option was popular for a period between the early twelfth century and the end of the thirteenth, peaking in the early thirteenth century.[8]

Table 1 shows the twenty-four known Reading lay burials, and the first thing to be addressed is the big gap between the burial of Isabella of Cornwall in 1234, and that of Constance Plantagenet in 1416, the next known burial. In part this could reflect the decline in popularity of monastic burials after the mid-thirteenth century, but the cut-off point happens precisely where we would expect a gradual decline to begin, and in any case this should apply only to lesser burials. No, the chief cause of this hiatus must reflect nothing more or less than the absence of evidence for a period of almost 200 years. Most of the evidence comes from the three general cartularies of the abbey, labelled A, B and C by Kemp, as follows:

A. British Library Egerton 3031 (begun 1190s)
B. British Library Harley 1708 (begun 1250s)
C. British Library Cotton Vespasian E xxv (begun 1340s)[9]

The two later cartularies (B and C) generally contained only the records of burials copied into them from A, and no new ones. Burials that took place after A went out of use in the 1250s were not recorded in the cartularies, and we only know about a few of them from other sources. The slight evidence of later burials available to us indicates that Reading was still considered a suitable place to bury the highest aristocracy, with close royal links, as late as the fifteenth century.

---

[6] Biddle and Kjølbe-Biddle (1980), 22.
[7] Stratford (1978), 54.
[8] Postles (1996) gives a clear account of this issue.
[9] Kemp (1986), I, 1–13.

TABLE 1   LAY BURIALS IN READING ABBEY, 1136–1502

Date	Name	Details
1136	Henry I	Founder
1151	Adeliza of Louvain	Queen of Henry I
1156	William of Poitiers	1153–56. First child and heir apparent to Henry II
1175	Reginald de Dunstanville	Illegitimate son of Henry I and Earl of Cornwall
1170–81	Hugh de Mortimer	Son and heir of Hugh (II) de Mortimer, Lord of Wigmore, who predeceased his father
1174–75	Henry FitzGerold	Royal Chamberlain
1193	John of Kington	Of Bearley, Warwickshire
Pre 1194	Simon son of Robert	First husband of Isabel de Sifrewas of Purley, Berks
1194–1217	Michael de Baseville	Second husband of Isabel de Sifrewas of Purley, Berks
c. 1206–20	Hugh de Strepini	Tenant of John de Préaux, Lord of Great Tew, Oxon
Pre 1214	John Grey	Of Rotherfield Greys, Oxon. Father of Archbishop Walter de Grey
1216	Warin FitzGerold	Royal Chamberlain, pilgrim, crusader and literary patron
Post 1221	Richard Morin	A knight of Newnham, Berks. He entered a monastery, presumably Reading, before 1221
c. 1220–41	Peter of Rotherwick	Landlord in Reading
Pre 1231	Henry FitzGerold	In service of William Marshal, Earl of Pembroke
1226–27	Hugh III de Mortimer (heart)	Lord of Wigmore. His body was buried in Wigmore Abbey, Herefs
Post 1231–32	Robert Pincent	Landowner in Sulhamstead Abbots, Berks
1233	John of Cornwall	1232–33. Infant son of Richard of Cornwall and nephew of Henry III
1234	Isabella of Cornwall	1233–34. Infant daughter of Richard of Cornwall and niece of Henry III

1416	Constance Plantagenet	1374–1416. Daughter of Edmund of Langley, Duke of York, and thus granddaughter of Edward III
1449	Anne Beauchamp	Countess of Warwick, died aged 6
c. 1470	Thomas Prowt	High Sheriff of Berks in 1469
1502	Thomas Wode	Chief Justice of the Common Pleas

ROYAL BURIALS

Seven of the known burials are of royalty. As well as Henry I himself and his queen Adeliza of Louvain, described in chapter one, Reading Abbey was to be the burial place of William of Poitiers (1156), Reginald de Dunstanville (1175), John of Cornwall (1233) and his sister Isabella (1234), and Constance Plantagenet (1416), all described below.

WILLIAM OF POITIERS

When his eldest son William of Poitiers died of a seizure aged only two years in April 1156 at Wallingford Castle, Henry II was engaged in besieging the castles of Chinon, Mirebeau and Loudun, held against him by his younger brother Geoffrey of Nantes who claimed that they had been bequeathed to him by their father. Queen Eleanor of Aquitaine had remained in England and was presumably present at the young prince's burial in Reading Abbey church, at the feet of his great grandfather.[10] Reading was convenient, being only a dozen miles away, but a more important consideration was that the burial of the heir to the throne in Henry I's abbey church associated the new king with the stable period before the horrors of the Civil War and insisted upon a legitimate continuity that had been interrupted by Stephen's reign.[11]

REGINALD DE DUNSTANVILLE

Henry I's illegitimate son Reginald (or Rainald) de Dunstanville (born c. 1110), Earl of Cornwall was buried alongside his father in 1175.[12] His tomb was still visible when the abbey was visited by Thomas Benolte, Clarenceaux King of Arms, in 1532. Benolte recorded that Henry I was

---

[10] Annales de Waverleia, II, 237.
[11] Flowers of History II, 55.
[12] Flowers of History II, 65.

'buryed in the myddest of the high Quyer', and 'On the right hand of him liethe buryed Ranawd Le fitz parys.'[13]

Earl Reginald's mother was traditionally thought to be Sybil Corbet.[14] Henry I's prodigious output of illegitimate children is well-known; he is thought to have fathered more than twenty, with at least seven known mistresses. William of Newburgh's conclusion, that he was a man adorned with many princely virtues, though he obscured them greatly by his con-cupiscence, in imitation of the lustfulness of Solomon,[15] rings truer to the modern reader than William of Malmesbury's more charitable assertion that the king was

> altogether free of lewd desires, for, as we have learned from those who know the matter well, he cast himself into the embraces of women not for the grat-ification of carnal pleasure but to beget offspring, nor did he assent to sexual intercourse except when it could bring about the spreading of the royal seed. He was thus the master of his libido, not its servant.[16]

It is true that he made good political and diplomatic use of the male and female bastards that he fathered, but it is harder to believe that he gained no pleasure, however fleeting, from fathering them. Searle's iden-tification of the political advantages he gained from his illegitimate sons and daughters is convincing; she argues that Henry's liaisons before his brother William Rufus's death, when his position was not strong, were intended to produce children whose marriages would be useful supposing better days were on the way. When Rufus died, Henry 'already had a quiv-erful of potential barons, earls, heiresses and queens for his nobility and neighbours – and loyal supporters for their legitimate siblings. And not a one carrying dangerous claims to the crown'.[17] Reginald de Dunstanville was a good example. Robert de Torigni described him as 'a young man without any property' in the late 1130s, from which a birth date in the late 1110s or early 1120s has been assumed.[18] This suggests a liaison after the death of Henry's first wife Matilda in 1118 but before his marriage to

13   Barron (1898), 3.
14   The parentage of Henry I's illegitimate children was illuminated by Geoffrey White in Appendix D to volume 11 of G. E. C. (1910–59). In White's account, the mother of Reginald and his full siblings was named as Sybil Corbet, but investigations in Thompson (2003) raise the possibility that it was Sybil de Dunstanville, whose mother Adeliza remarried after the death of her father Reginald of that name. Robert fitzCorbet was the name of her second husband, and of Sybil's half-siblings.
15   William of Newburgh, 1, 30.
16   William of Malmesbury GR, 2, 488.
17   Searle (1980), 37.
18   Gesta Normannorum Ducum, 248–49.

Adeliza in 1121.[19] At the outbreak of the civil war that followed Henry's death, Reginald can only have been in his mid-teens, but he was a firm supporter of his half-sister in her campaign against his cousin. He headed a successful rising against Stephen in the West Country, and for this he was rewarded by Matilda with the earldom of Cornwall in 1141. In the previous year he had married Beatrice, daughter and heiress of William FitzRichard, a major Cornish landowner, and the earldom served to legitimise his powerbase. His support for Matilda, and for her son Henry II when he came to the throne in 1154, put him in a very strong position, and he virtually ruled the county directly, free of control from the exchequer, until his death without a male heir in 1175.[20] According to William of Canterbury, Reginald was one of the two most powerful magnates in England in the 1150s and 1160s (the other being Robert II of Beaumont, Earl of Leicester). His power stemmed from his royal kinship (as the king's uncle he was the senior ranking male member of the royal house), and from the wealth of his barony,[21] as well as the fact that his guardianship of his grandson Baldwin II of Redvers, the infant Earl of Devon, from 1162 until 1175 gave him effective control over the entire south-western peninsula.[22]

At his death in 1175, the earldom and estates were appropriated by King Henry II, who awarded them to his son John. In 1225 John's son and successor Henry III awarded the title and lands to his younger brother Richard (1209–72), as a sixteenth birthday present. The title and lands thus remained closely tied to the ruling house, and this has always been the case with the Earldom of Cornwall. In 1337 Edward III formalised the arrangement when he established the Duchy of Cornwall, one of only two English royal duchies (the other being Lancaster), from the former earldom, and gave it to his eldest son, Edward the Black Prince.[23] Since then the title has automatically passed to the reigning monarch's eldest son at the time of his birth, and the revenue from the Duchy provides a private income for the Prince of Wales.

JOHN AND ISABELLA OF CORNWALL

The Earl Richard of Cornwall noted above as Henry III's younger brother was thus the great great grandson of the founder of Reading Abbey.

---

[19]   Thompson (2003), 135 also raises the possibility that the king was anxious to demonstrate his continued fecundity in the face the continuing childlessness of this second marriage.
[20]   Given-Wilson and Curteis (1984), 65; Keefe (1981), 195.
[21]   Keefe (1981), 193–95 and table 1 provides a useful analysis.
[22]   Ibid., 195.
[23]   The other is the Duchy of Lancaster, also created by Edward III for his son John of Gaunt.

He is probably best known for his adventures in Germany, where he was crowned King of the Romans in 1257, but never managed to obtain sufficient support to succeed in his campaign to be elected Holy Roman Emperor, the only Englishman to lay claim to the title. In 1231 he married Isabella Marshal, sister of the powerful baron William Marshal, Earl of Pembroke, and the widow of Gilbert de Clare, 4th Earl of Hertford and 1st Earl of Gloucester. The king was opposed to the marriage; he was looking for a more politically advantageous foreign match for his brother, rather than the baronial power bloc that the alliance with the Marshals seemed to threaten. In addition, since Henry himself was childless at that time, his brother was the heir to the throne and any children of the alliance would become heirs in succession. For Richard, Isabella may have seemed a good choice for the same reasons. She had proven childbearing ability, having had six children including three sons with her first husband. In the event she was to bear four children with Richard, including three sons, one of whom, Henry of Almain (1235–71), survived into adulthood. The first child, John, was born at Marlow and died there at an age of 20 months in September 1233, just a fortnight after the birth of his sister Isabella of Cornwall. Isabella was just 13 months old when she died, also at Marlow, and both were buried at Reading Abbey.[24] The last child, Nicholas, died on the day of his birth, 17 January 1240, at Berkhamsted Castle along with his mother who died of jaundice in childbirth at the age of 39. In the account of Matthew Paris,

> The noble Lady Isabella, countess of Gloucester and Cornwall, was taken dangerously ill of the yellow jaundice, and brought to the point of death, and when her time for lying-in arrived (for she was pregnant and very near child-birth) she became senseless, and after having had the ample tresses of her flaxen hair cut off, and made a full confession of her sins, she departed to the Lord, together with a boy, to which she had given birth, and which, not being likely to live, had been baptized and received the name of Nicholas. When Earl Richard, who had gone to Cornwall at that time, heard of this event, he broke out into the most sorrowful lamentations, and mourned inconsolably; he, however, returned with all haste, and caused the respected body of his wife to be buried with honour at Beaulieu, a house which King John had founded and built, and appropriated to the Cistercian order.[25]

The choice of Reading Abbey for the burials of the two firstborn children may have been partly governed by convenience; it was only twelve miles away and as an established royal burial site was certainly suitable. On the other hand, Earl Richard had a longstanding association with Reading, having been created High Sheriff of Berkshire in 1217 when he was only eight years old. Earl Richard gave copes to the abbey when his children

---

24   Annales Monastici 1, 89, 93.
25   Chron. Maj. 4, 2. Translation from Giles (1889), 1, 255.

were buried, two to commemorate John's death and a third to mark young Isabella's, and these are described in an inventory in the cartulary as

> *Cappe due coloribus indicis de panno serico qui venit cum corpore filii Ricardi comitis. Item cappa una de baldekino purpureo qui venit cum corpore filie pre-dicti comitis.*[26]

CONSTANCE PLANTAGENET

Constance Plantagenet (1374–1416) was the daughter of Edmund of Langley Duke of York, 4th son of Edward III, and Isabella of Castile. The Yorkist kings Edward IV and Richard III were her great nephews. Constance was married to Thomas le Despenser (1373–1400), a supporter of the deposed Richard II against Henry Bolingbroke, who was beheaded by a mob of pro-Lancaster townspeople in Bristol in January 1400. His head was sent to the king in London, his body buried in Tewkesbury Abbey, where the family had a tradition of burial (figure 13), and £30 in gold and silver that was found on his person was sent to his new widow.[27] She did not remarry (although she had an illegitimate daughter with Edmund Holland, 4th Earl of Kent); neither did she follow the Despenser tradition of burial in Tewkesbury Abbey. Instead, Constance was buried at Reading,[28] a decision convincingly connected to her royal lineage.[29]

ARISTOCRATIC BURIALS

MORTIMER FAMILY BURIALS

In the Domesday Survey, Ralph de Mortimer (fl. c. 1080–1104) was an important landowner, with holdings in 269 places. Most of his land was in Shropshire and Herefordshire, centred on Wigmore Castle, which he gained after Roger of Breteuil, Earl of Hereford, joined an ill-planned and unsuccessful revolt against William the Conqueror in 1075. Ralph de Mortimer also had substantial holdings in Lincolnshire and East Yorkshire, and in a band running south from Berkshire to the Hampshire coast. In Berkshire his main residence seems to have been Stradfeld, later called Stratfield Mortimer, just six miles south of Reading. Ralph was succeeded by his son Hugh I (d. c. 1148–50), who was in turn succeeded by his eldest son Roger, who was dead by 1153. Roger was succeeded by his brother Hugh II (d. 1181), who had four sons, Hugh, Roger, Ralph and William. The eldest of these, Hugh, would have inherited had he not

---

[26]　Barfield (1888), 117; Kemp (1986) I, 187.
[27]　G. E. C. (1910–59), 4, 280.
[28]　Tewkesbury Chronicle, 62–63. See also Oxford Bodl. Top. Glouc. d.2, fols 27r-v.
[29]　Lawrence (2008), 92.

13   THE DESPENSER TOMBS ARE ARRANGED AROUND THE HIGH ALTAR OF TEWKESBURY ABBEY CHURCH. ON
THE LEFT ARE HUGH LE DESPENSER (D. 1349) AND HIS WIFE ELIZABETH MONTACUTE, AND ON THE RIGHT
IS THE MAGNIFICENT CHANTRY OF THOMAS'S FATHER LORD EDWARD LE DESPENSER (D. 1375). THE FORMER
POSITION OF THOMAS'S OWN TOMB IS NOW MARKED BY A BRASS SET IN THE PAVEMENT. DESPITE THIS
STRONG TEWKESBURY CONNECTION, THOMAS'S WIDOW CONSTANCE WAS BURIED IN READING ABBEY.

died sometime between 1170 and his father's death in 1181, killed in a
tournament at Worcester.[30] This Hugh gave his body to Reading Abbey,
with lands in Stratfield Mortimer only six miles south of the abbey, his
share of a mill in Worthy (Hants) and all his rents from properties in Winchester.[31] His father was thus succeeded in his title and possessions by his
second son Roger (II) de Mortimer (d. 1214), and Roger by his son Hugh
(III) de Mortimer (d. 1227). Hugh (III) was a loyal servant of King John,
and the young Henry III, spending a good deal of his time campaigning
on the Welsh borders against Llywelyn ab Iorwerth, Prince of Gwynedd.
In 1225, Hugh III and Abbot Simon of Reading resolved a dispute in the
royal court at Westminster concerning 5½ virgates of land and a meadow

[30]   Dugdale Monasticon, 4 pt 1, 349. Barker (1986), 8, places Hugh's death in King
       Stephen's reign, awarding him the distinction of being the earliest known fatal
       casualty at an English tournament, but Kemp's later dating seems incontestable.
[31]   Kemp (1986), II, 233–34.

called Red Meade in Stratfield Mortimer, six miles south of Reading.[32] The
Abbot conceded that the land was Hugh's, while Hugh responded by giving the Abbot other lands in the same parish, and it is of interest that this
gift in free alms was made for the souls of Hugh's father and mother, Roger
and Isabel.[33] Just before his death, Hugh restored to the abbey the original
disputed lands, including Red Meade, and this gift was accompanied by
Hugh's own heart and viscera for burial in the abbey. His body was buried
in Wigmore Abbey, founded by his Domesday ancestor Ralph de Mortimer, but a marginal note in the abbey cartulary records that his heart and
viscera were indeed buried in Reading Abbey church, 'between the tombs
before the altar of the Virgin'.[34]

ANNE BEAUCHAMP

Anne Beauchamp (1443–49) was the only child of Henry de Beauchamp,
14th Earl of Warwick, and Cecily Neville. She died in infancy at Ewelme,
and was buried in Reading Abbey church.[35] Her grandfather Richard, the
13th Earl had been entrusted by Henry V in his will with the education
of Henry VI who was only 9 months old when his father died in 1422.
Hence the young king and Warwick's young son Henry, who was four
years his junior, grew up together, and when he reached maturity Henry
de Beauchamp was loaded with honours by his childhood friend. He married Cecily Neville in 1434, and their only child Anne was born almost
ten years later. The earldom of Warwick (which Henry inherited on his
father's death in 1439) was designated the premier earldom of the kingdom in 1444, and a year later he was created 1st Duke of Warwick, second only in ceremonial status to the Duke of Norfolk. Henry died in 1446
leaving Anne as his only heir. She could not inherit the dukedom, but she
did receive the earldom at the age of two, becoming the 15th Countess.
Reading may well have been chosen as her burial site because her great
grandmother Constance Plantagenet had been buried there thirty-three
years before.

OTHER LAY BURIALS

The pros and cons associated with monastic burial for lay people have
been discussed above, but if a layman became a monk near the time of
his death, or was conferred with confraternity, his connection to the

[32]   Ibid., II, 234.
[33]   Ibid., II, 234–35.
[34]   BL Egerton 3031, fol. 82r: *Nota de corde Hugonis Mortemer sepulto inter tumbas
       ante altare beate Marie.* Kemp (1986), II, 235.
[35]   Tewkesbury Chronicle, 64; Hicks (2002), 37 n. 31.

monastery would be that much closer. Further, if the layman was a tenant or liegeman of the monastery he might offer a *legitim*, which was a substantial bequest normally amounting to one-third part of his estate at his death. Both of these conditions operated in the sad case of Robert Pincent of Sulhamstead Abbots (Berkshire). At the end of the twelfth century, and before 1213 at the latest, Robert Pincent entered into an arrangement with the abbey whereby he gave a small meadow and the abbey received him into confraternity, so that at his death he would be given the monastic habit and would convey to the abbey, with his body, one third of his moveable and immoveable goods, grain and land.[36] This was merely the first in a series of transactions that chart the increasing financial troubles of Robert and his family.[37] Over the next two decades or more he sold off his meadows to the abbey in exchange for money and grain for himself, his wife Agnes and his heir William. Finally in a deed dated to 1231 he gave the abbey all their remaining lands and tenants in Sulhamstead Abbots, reserving to the heir, William, only the demesne with two parcels of meadow for which he had to pay rent to the abbey. In exchange the abbey granted the family,

> in their great and pressing need, food and clothing for life, and has remitted to them certain arrears of rent in money and oats to the value of 20s.[38]

Such arrangements were fortunately rare. The more usual formula for burials below the aristocratic level takes the form of a gift of land, goods or rent made for the health of the soul of the donor and members of his or her family, living and dead, to be accompanied by the donor's body at his or her death. A typical example is that of John of Kington, who gave a parcel of land called Bearley, apparently in Preston Bagot, Warwickshire, to the abbey. The precise wording is:

> *ego Iohannes de Kintona, pro salute anime mee et uxoris mee et pro anima patris et matris mee et pro animabus omnium antecessorum meorum et successorum, dedi cum corpore meo et concessi et hac carta mea confirmavi deo et sancte Marie de Rading(ia) et monachis ibidem deo servientibus Burgelaiam ... ..[39]*

The case of Henry FitzGerold and his two sons was unusual in that several members of the same family seem to have entered into a

---

36   Kemp (1986), II, 242, Postles (1996), 629.
37   Ibid., II, 241–48.
38   Ibid., II, 245.
39   Ibid., I, 435. I John de Kington for the health of my soul and of my wife's and for the souls of my mother and father and for the souls of all my ancestors and descendants give, with my body and this charter confirms it, to God and St Mary's Reading and the monks there serving God, Bearley ...

joint arrangement.[40] Henry FitzGerold gave a deathbed gift of land in Sawbridgeworth (Herts) and was buried in the abbey. His sons Warin (d. 1216) and Henry (d. 1217–31) were buried side by side at the feet of their father, and each gave gifts to the abbey for the privilege. The younger Henry, the last of the three to die, gave his gift for the health of his soul, and all those of his ancestors and successors, and his lord William Marshal.[41] The three FitzGerolds were not aristocrats, but they were closely connected to the court. In 1154 or 1155 Henry Fitzgerold the elder was serving as the steward of Geoffrey de Mandeville, son of Earl Geoffrey, and between 1157 and 1160 was in receipt of fifty pounds a year from the royal manor of Sutton Courtenay, Berkshire. He continued in royal service from 1154 until his death, being active at the king's chamber as early as 1157–58, appearing with the title of chamberlain in the year 1159–60, and in possession of the chamberlain serjeanty at Sevenhampton from 1160 onwards. He witnessed numerous royal charters in both England and France, and is said to have officiated as constable of Wallingford shortly after 1154. Between 1164 and 1171 he accounted as farmer for the royal manor of Wycombe in Buckinghamshire, and between 1166 and 1168, during the exile of Archbishop Becket, he acted as paymaster to the king's knights in Kent. In 1168–69 he served as royal justice there, levying fines.

Henry Fitzgerold was dead by the exchequer year 1173–74, when his lands at Sevenhampton and Sparsholt were accounted to his son. He was buried at Reading Abbey, to which he had earlier granted land at Sawbridgeworth. He also granted an annual measure of corn to Southwark Priory and land to the monks of Rochester, for the soul of his brother Warin. With his wife, Matilda de Chesny, heir to major estates in Oxfordshire and elsewhere, Henry had at least two sons: Warin Fitzgerold the younger (c. 1167–1215/16), a minor at the time of Henry's death, and Henry Fitzgerold the younger (c. 1173-c. 1231) who entered the service of William (I) Marshal, Earl of Pembroke (d. 1219). The Fitzgerald chamberlainship of the exchequer passed from Henry the elder to Warin Fitzgerald the younger, married to Alice de Courcy, a major heiress in England and Normandy.

The family's wealth was in the sub-manor of Pishobury (Herts), originally seventy-four *librates* of land carved out of the manor of Sawbridgeworth and given to the brothers by Geoffrey de Mandeville, Earl of Essex (d. 1144).[42] We know most about Warin Fitzgerold, who had been both a crusader and a pilgrim to Compostella by the time he commissioned an Anglo-Norman translation of the pseudo-Turpin, a Latin reworking of the

[40] Postles (1996), 633.
[41] Kemp (1986), I. 244–45, 314–15, 319.
[42] VCH Hertfordshire 3 (1912), 332–47.

Song of Roland.[43] He has been described as a member of an aristocratic social circle including crusaders who also commissioned literary works inspired by the crusades and containing many of the greatest soldiers of the period; Robert de Beaumont Earl of Leicester, Robert de Neubourg, Roger de Harcourt and Roger de Tosny.[44]

Another family affair of a rather different kind is represented by the burials of the two husbands of Isabel de Sifrewast. At some time between 1194 and the early years of the thirteenth century, she gave the abbey a gift of land in Purley Parva, Berkshire, for the souls of herself, her father Robert de Sifrewast, her mother Emma and her husbands buried at Reading Abbey. The terms of the gift have been written into the history of English slavery.[45] Isabel gave

> the half-virgate of land in Purley which Osbert son of Godwin the fisherman holds in villeinage with all its appurtenances forever in pure and perpetual alms, free and quit from all secular service. And so that the abbot and convent of Reading may turn the said Osbert and his offspring either to the work of villeinage or to an annual rent.

In effect she was exchanging the labour of an unwitting villein, Osbert, for the souls of her dead relatives. The two husbands can be identified, although little is known of their lives. The second was Michael de Baseville, who had himself given land in Lashbrook (Berkshire) to the abbey at some time between 1156 and 1189, and at the time of this gift he was married to Isabel, who witnessed the deed.[46] Then after 1194 he and Isabel brought an action against Richard de Sifrewast in Dorset about the dower given her by her former husband, named as Simon son of Robert.[47]

One of the most distinguished clerics to make a gift related to a burial was Walter de Grey (d. 1255), best known as the Archbishop of York, during whose period of office the magnificent Early English transept was built, the oldest part of York Minster surviving above the ground. There, in St Michael's Chapel on the east side of the south transept arm, stands his tomb (figure 14).[48] Before his elevation to York in 1216, de Grey had been Bishop of Worcester for a brief time in 1214–15, and it was as Bishop of Worcester that he gave the church at Rowington (Warwickshire) partly for the soul of his father buried in Reading Abbey (*pro anima patris nostril*

---

[43]   Mason (1988), 86; Short (1973), 1–6.
[44]   Mason (1988), 86–87.
[45]   Stenton (1951), 145–46.
[46]   Kemp (1986), I, 379.
[47]   Rot. Cur. Reg., 1, 81–82.
[48]   For the rebuilding at York Minster see Brown (2003), 11–45, and for the tomb, ibid., 39–40 and Ramm *et.al* (1977).

14   THE TOMB
OF ARCHBISHOP
WALTER DE GREY,
SEEN HERE, IS IN
YORK MINSTER
WHILE HIS FATHER
JOHN DE GREY
WAS BURIED IN
READING ABBEY.

cuius penes ipsos corpus requiescat).[49] Walter's father was John de Grey of
Rotherfield Greys near Henley in Oxfordshire, less than six miles from the
abbey, and Walter also had an uncle called John de Grey who was Bishop
of Norwich (1200–14).[50] Of John de Grey the father, buried at Reading, we
know that he married Hawisia, who was freed from various feudal obliga-
tions to the abbey in 1232.[51]

Another charter, dating from 1219, was apparently intended to ensure
the donor's salvation while simultaneously clearing up a dispute over
fishing rights in the Thames. One Richard Morin of Newnham gave the
abbey his body for burial and land in Newnham Murren, along with a

[49]   Kemp (1986), I, 465–66.
[50]   Greenaway (1971), 56.
[51]   CPR Henry III, 3, 454.

fishing right in the Thames between Mongewell and Wallingford Bridge, over which he had been in dispute with the abbey.[52] Sometime before 25 May 1221, the king was told that he had entered a monastery, and that his land was therefore to be granted to his son William. Whether this was simply a misunderstanding or whether he subsequently left the monastery, he was restored to his lands on 23 June 1222, on payment of a fine of twenty marks.[53]

Sometime between 1206 and 1220, Hugh de Strepini gave his body for burial along with twelve acres of meadow between Little Tew and Showell near Chipping Norton in Oxfordshire. This represented a gift made to Hugh by his lord, John de Préaux, who was lord of Great Tew in the early part of the thirteenth century, and it seems likely that the gift was intended for the purpose of ensuring Hugh's burial in the abbey.[54]

Perhaps surprisingly only one known lay burial concerns a burgher of Reading. This was Peter de Rotherwick who, in a gift dateable between 1220 and 1241, gave the rents from six dwellings and a stall held by William the Cordwainer, to a value of almost one pound a year, and a plot of land on the main road to Pangbourne. This would not merely secure burial at the abbey, but would also provide a pittance on his anniversary, thus ensuring that his name would be remembered, and that he would receive prayers at least once a year.[55]

BURIAL SITES

What is not clear from these documents is just where in the monastery the donors were buried. In most cases they would use a plot in the lay cemetery, within the precinct but separate from the monks who had their own cemetery. The more distinguished burials would be in the church, near to the founder's own tomb. The evidence from a Visitation by Thomas Benolte, Clarenceaux, King of Arms, in 1532, is useful but only covers four tombs, as follows:

> King Henry the first iijd sonne to Wm Conqueror and first founder of the Abbaye of Redding ys buryed in the myddest of the high Quyer w'in the sayd place afore rehursyd.
> On the right hand of him lieth buryed Ranawd Le Fitz Parys.
> Before our Ladye Chappell lyeth buryed Thomas Wood knight sometime Justice of the Comune place.

---

[52]   Kemp (1986), I, 382–83.
[53]   CFR , 1220–21, 176; 1221–22, 210.
[54]   Kemp (1986), I, 400.
[55]   Ibid., II, 177–78.

> In the bodye of the Church in our Ladye Chappell lyeth buryed Thomas Prowt.[56]

We have seen that Ranawd Le Fitz Parys was Henry I's illegitimate son, Reginald de Dunstanville, Earl of Cornwall. Thomas Wood, or Wode, is easily identified with the Chief Justice of the Common Pleas who died at nearby Childrey. Wode has been labelled 'perhaps the most obscure chief justice in the Tudor period'.[57] His birthplace is not known with any certainty, and as he was described as a 'gentleman of London' in 1473 he is assumed to have been born in the 1450s or earlier. In 1478 he became a Justice of the Peace for Berkshire, and MP for Wallingford. He became a Justice in the court of Common Pleas in 1495, and Chief Justice in that court in 1500. He died at his estate in Childrey on 31 August 1502, having made his last will just three days earlier, and in this he asked to be buried near the Lady Chapel at Reading Abbey.[58] He shared the Lady Chapel with Thomas Prowt, the High Sheriff of Berkshire in 1469.[59]

CONCLUSIONS

We have nowhere near a complete record of the burials in Reading Abbey, nor is there much information about the tombs erected over them, but we do know that a group of royal tombs were clustered around the founder's grave before the high altar, including Reginald de Dunstanville, and William of Poitiers, the infant son of Henry II and Eleanor of Aquitaine. The later tombs of John and Isabella of Cornwall and Constance Plantagenet and her great granddaughter Anne Beauchamp might also have been in this area. We know that Henry I's queen Adeliza was buried at a distance from her husband, on account of her second marriage. The Mortimer tombs were presumably grouped together and the record of Hugh III's 1227 heart burial *inter tumbas ante altare beate Marie* suggests a location – perhaps the axial ambulatory chapel later replaced by a large Lady Chapel. Certainly their connection with Reading remained important to the Mortimers: as we shall see in the next chapter, six generations after Hugh III, in 1368 Edmund Mortimer, 3rd Earl of March, was married in the abbey church. The gap in the record between the early thirteenth century and the early fifteenth would certainly have included significant aristocratic burials (and probably more Mortimers) whose traces, for the moment, remain lost to us.

---

[56] Rylands (1907), 1, 1–2. Copied from London, BL, Add. 12479.
[57] J. H. Baker, 'Wode, Sir Thomas', in Oxford DNB.
[58] Ives (1983), 479.
[59] Clarke (1824), 49.

THE ABBEY AND THE COURT

4

The aim of this chapter is to explore the place of Reading Abbey in royal affairs between the death of its founder and the events leading to the Dissolution. It is well known that the life of a medieval monarch was spent on the move, but setting aside necessary trips for military and diplomatic purposes, how much the king moved around and which stations he tended to favour varied greatly from reign to reign. The ease or difficulty of tracking the movements of the king and his household depend very much upon the period involved. In the first years of King John's reign, his chancellor, Hubert Walter, was responsible for a system of enrolling copies of royal letters – the charter, close and patent rolls – that served the government as an official register, was available for the settlement of disputes, and remains as an archive of inestimable value to the historian.[1] This situation endured throughout the thirteenth century, so that while the itineraries of Henry I, Stephen and Henry II and Richard I are at best patchy, those of John, Henry III and to some extent Edward I are clear and more or less comprehensive. After this it once again begins to be difficult to be sure just where the king was at any given time, and the reason concerns the growth of the royal bureaucracy. In Henry III's reign all letters issued under the Great Seal bore the place and date of the king himself. King John introduced a Privy Seal for more private correspondence, which always accompanied him, held by the Keeper of the Wardrobe, which was the personal part of the king's government, able to appropriate large sums from the exchequer for the king's own use. Later, in Edward II's reign, another seal, the Secret Seal, was introduced for royal letters that were even more private. By this time, therefore, letters could be sealed with any one of three different seals, and very often the evidence of place and date

---

[1] Clanchy (1979), 48–53.

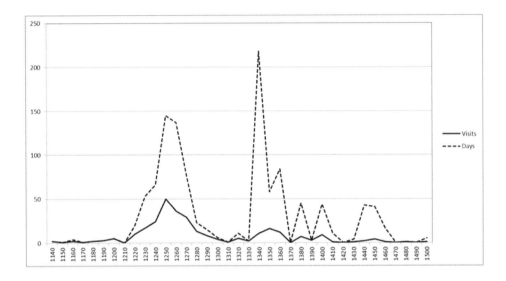

15   THE DISTRIBUTION OF ROYAL VISITS TO READING ABBEY, BETWEEN 1140 AND 1509, SHOWS THE ESTEEM
IN WHICH IT WAS HELD BY SUCCESSIVE MEDIEVAL KINGS. HENRY III AND EDWARD III WERE ESPECIALLY
FREQUENT VISITORS.

they provide is conflicting. Unless there is other evidence of the king's
whereabouts from chronicle sources, there is no way to know whether the
king was present when a letter was sealed or not.[2] In the view of Elizabeth
Hallam the most reliable indicator is the location of the wardrobe, but
evidence for this is nowhere near complete. In a sense it does not really
matter, because it is clear from the itinerary of Edward II that Hallam
established that the seals generally followed similar itineraries, sometimes
diverging slightly with one seal preceding or lagging behind. Thus even if
the king was not present at a location when a letter was sealed, the presence of the seal itself implies that a large part of the royal household was
there, and the king was either expected or had just left.

Figure 15 gives the best estimates, taking into account the reservations
expressed above, of the numbers of visits and days spent at Reading Abbey
by the reigning monarch for the entire period between 1140 and the accession of Henry VIII in 1509, arranged by decade. This presents a general
picture of fluctuating popularity and changing patterns of royal travel that
will be examined in closer detail in the course of this chapter.

---

2   Hallam (1984), 6–7.

READING DURING THE ANARCHY (1135–54)

During the war for succession that followed the death of King Henry I, both Stephen and Matilda actively supported the abbey through the issuing of grants, confirmations, exemptions etc. Twenty-two such are known in Stephen's name and another fourteen in Matilda's or the young Duke Henry's.[3] After Henry's burial in 1136 Stephen visited the abbey rarely, if at all. According to John of Worcester he held a council at the abbey in January 1140, shortly after the death of Bishop Roger of Salisbury, when the main business described was the appointment of abbots to the houses of Malmesbury and Abbotsbury that Bishop Roger had kept in his own hands.[4] John of Worcester's account, however, differs from the versions of William of Malmesbury and the *Gesta Stephani,* neither of which mentions Reading as the location of the council.[5]

Matilda visited the abbey in March 1141, just after the defeat and capture of Stephen at the battle of Lincoln. While there she found that her father's former Master of the Writing Chamber, Robert de Sigillo, was numbered among the monks, having retired to his dead king's foundation when he was replaced in his old post by Stephen.[6] She restored him to public life by appointing him Bishop of London, an appointment accepted by his abbot, Edward, as well as the Archbishop of Canterbury and Henry of Blois, the Bishop of Winchester and Stephen's brother.[7] The appointment was later to anger Stephen, who tried to have him excluded from his see, but Robert's reputation was sufficient to attract the support of Bernard of Clairvaux, and later Pope Eugenius III.

Between March and July of 1141 Matilda issued five charters in favour of the abbey. Many are simply confirmations of rights or gifts originally granted by King Henry or Queen Adeliza, and in many cases too the same confirmations were made by both Matilda and Stephen. An interesting case is that of the royal manor of Blewbury (Berkshire), given to the abbey by Stephen for the good of his soul and the souls of his wife, his son Eustace and his other sons, and his uncle King Henry, in a grant issued in London, probably at Christmas 1146 or 1147.[8] The Empress, however, had already made the same gift, probably as early as 1144, in a grant issued in Devizes, but in her document the souls to benefit were her father and mother, the king and queen, and all her royal predecessors, and the gift was made for the love and lawful service of her supporter Brian fitzCount, the castellan

[3]   Regesta Regum, 3, 249–62.
[4]   John of Worcester III, 279–80.
[5]   William of Malmesbury HN 66–69; Gesta Stephani 96–98.
[6]   Regesta Regum, 3, x–xi; John of Hexham in Symeonis Monachi Opera, 2, 309.
[7]   For refs, see Chibnall (1991), 137.
[8]   Kemp (1986) II, 6 (charter 669).

of Wallingford, and presumably at his request.[9] Brian apparently assumed a close, quasi-patronal relationship with the abbey in the 1140s, according to Kemp, who gives this as the reason for his inclusion, along with the Abbot of Reading, in the address of a gift of the vill of Rhynd (Perthshire) to the abbey by King David I of Scotland.[10]

In 1147 Stephen founded the abbey of Faversham, Kent, in imitation of Reading Abbey. Just as Henry had done before him he donated the land and staffed it with Cluniac monks, not from the mother house but from the priory of Bermondsey, one of whom, Clarembold, became its first abbot in 1148. There are no standing remains of the abbey church, but elements of the plan, notably the paired chapels off each transept, show a debt to Reading. Stephen's queen, Matilda of Boulogne, was buried there in 1153, followed in rapid succession by his son Eustace in 1153 and Stephen himself in 1154.[11] The new king, the Empress Matilda's eldest son Henry II, was now 21, but he continued to use and value his mother's diplomatic skills in the early years of his reign. These were mostly employed in Normandy, but in the later 1150s, probably in 1159, she issued a writ concerning the hamlet of Broadward in Herefordshire that had been given to Reading Abbey by Roger, Earl of Hereford in 1154–55.[12] Her writ was addressed to Maurice of Hereford, the sheriff, ordering him on her own authority and that of her son, King Henry, to ensure that the monks of Reading were not troubled with court actions over their chattels and lands in Broadward.[13] Chibnall speculates that the original gift was made by Roger when he retired to the monastery at Gloucester in July 1155 to compensate the Berkshire house for the damage done by the earl and his men during the war.[14] He was certainly winding his affairs up at this time, having handed the earldom to his brother Walter at the same time, and the fact that he died three months later suggests that he might have been mortally wounded while fighting in the royal war against Hugh Mortimer of Wigmore earlier that year. Matilda's personal interest in this matter must be related to her continuing identification with her father's burial church.

HENRY II (1154–89)

During Henry II's 34-year reign, he was recorded at Reading ten times, all in different years. It is fair to assume, however, that he was there much

[9]   Ibid., II, 5 (charter 667).
[10] Ibid., II, 345 (charter 1276).
[11] On the abbey church, see Fernie (2000),178–79; Philp (1968).
[12] See Kemp (1986), I, 263–64 (charters 327–330).
[13] Ibid., I, 264 (charter 331).
[14] Chibnall (1991), 160.

more often than that, and that the low figure simply represents a lack of evidence. After all, Eyton's itinerary, assembled from a wide variety of sources, could only locate the king on an average of twenty-eight days for each year he spent wholly or largely in England.[15] Even on those occasions, the date was often guesswork and the location often vague. Nevertheless, it is fair to conclude that Reading was favoured by Henry II for official occasions, and doubtless he took the opportunity to visit the tombs of his grandfather and his eldest son while he was there. Apart from the events described below, he held the Whitsun court there in 1175,[16] and was there on Palm Sunday 1177 which might have been the occasion of the issuing of a charter to Mellifont Abbey in Ireland.[17] He was also recorded there in August 1178, in April 1180 and in August 1184.[18]

In 1163 Reading was the site of a uniquely well-recorded example of a medieval trial by combat. It concerned Henry of Essex, King Henry's standard-bearer who was accused of treacherously abandoning the king's standard during the ambush at Coleshill in the Welsh campaign of 1157. Essex shouted that the king was dead, and doubtless he would have been in grave danger had the Earl of Clare not rallied the king's troops again by raising the standard himself. He did not deny the accusation but justified his action on the grounds that he genuinely believed the king had fallen, and the king seems to have believed his account, because he subsequently employed him on his expedition to Toulouse in 1159. Retribution was delayed until 1163, when Robert de Montfort, a kinsman of Henry of Essex, pressed for a trial by battle. The combat took place at Reading, on an island in the Thames near the north gate of the precinct known as De Montfort Island or Fry's Island, probably sometime in April of that year. The account of it comes indirectly from Henry of Essex himself, who told the story to a group of monks from Bury St Edmunds, including Abbot Samson and his almoner and chronicler Jocelin of Brakelond who were visitors to Reading Abbey. According to Essex, he was already getting the worst of the encounter when he looked around and saw a vision in the sky of St Edmund in armour, accompanied by another knight he recognised as Gilbert de Cereville, both of them turning indignant, angry eyes on him. This Gilbert had been unjustly accused by Henry's wife of pestering her with demands for her favours, and Essex had taken his wife's side and tortured him to death. Essex struck out ever more frantically, but was soon overcome by Robert, fell and was left for dead. His kinsmen pleaded that the monks of Reading should be allowed to bury him, and their wish was

---

[15] Eyton (1878).
[16] Ibid., 191.
[17] Ibid., 212; TNA C47/9/15/1.
[18] Ibid., 223, 231, 257.

granted, but Henry was not dead. He soon recovered from his wounds and joined the monastery himself to gain remission from his sins.[19]

This scene was selected by Hurry to be one of the ten paintings illustrating the history of the abbey that he commissioned (plate X). Harry Morley's painting of 1918 shows the moment when Henry of Essex has seen the vision of St Edmund and Gilbert de Cereville, and fallen to the ground stretching his hand towards them to ward them off. Robert stands leaning on his sword and the field of combat is surrounded by a wooden palisade to keep back the crowds, with a raised box for the king who sits under a canopy alongside the abbot. The abbey church is shown from the north-west in the left background. None of the sources mentions that the king was present, but it seems reasonable to assume that he would attend an affair of honour involving his own constable, and his itinerary places him at Windsor immediately before the combat and at Wallingford thereafter.[20]

On 19 April of the following year the abbey church was dedicated by Archbishop Becket, accompanied by ten suffragan bishops, in the presence of Henry II.[21] The dedication was accompanied by the grant of a fair by the king, and by a series of episcopal indulgences varying from 10 days to 25 days offered by Becket and by thirteen bishops in the province of Canterbury to anyone who visited Reading Abbey on the feast of St James (25 July), or within the eight days following it, and made a gift.[22] Presumably such a pilgrim would qualify for all the indulgences on offer: a total of 260 days. It is clear from the charters granting these indulgences that the scheme was organised by Jocelin de Bohun, Bishop of Salisbury, in whose diocese the abbey stands. Bishop Jocelin offered the largest indulgence of 25 days, along with an extra one of 20 days to pilgrims who visited on the anniversary of the dedication and made a gift to the building.[23] He also wrote to all the bishops who participated in the scheme thanking them.[24] It must be significant that Henry of Blois, almost alone among the Canterbury suffragans, failed to offer an indulgence – a clear sign that the enforced return of the hand of St James that he borrowed in

[19]   Jocelin of Brakelond, 68–71; Hurry (1919), passim.
[20]   Eyton (1878), 61–62.
[21]   Annales Radingenses Posteriores, 400; Annales Bermundeseia, 441–42, Chron. Maj, 2, 227.
[22]   Kemp (1986), I, 56–57; 149–55. The bishops involved were Robert of Bath, Hilary of Chichester, Richard Peche of Coventry, Hugh de Puiset of Durham, Nigel of Ely, Bartholomew of Exeter, Robert Chesney of Lincoln, Nicholas ap Gwrgant of Llandaff, Gilbert Foliot of London, William Turbe of Norwich, Godfrey of St Asaph, David Fitz Gerald of St David's and Jocelin de Bohun of Salisbury.
[23]   Ibid., I, 155–56.
[24]   Ibid., I, 155.

1136 and did not give back until 1155 still rankled.[25] There is no detailed contemporary description of the consecration, but it formed the subject of another of the paintings commissioned by Hurry (plate XI), from Stephen Reid.

A visit recorded in August 1184 was significant for the presence of the king's son-in-law, Henry the Lion, Duke of Saxony, who was staying in England while under sentence of banishment from Germany, and could well have been the occasion of the duke's gift of a relic of the True Cross.[26] In February 1185 the king was in Nottingham on his way to York when he received news that Heraclius, Patriarch of Jerusalem, and Roger de Moulins, Master of the Hospitallers, had arrived in England from the Holy Land. He hastened to meet them at Reading, the meeting taking place on 17 March (plate XII). We are indebted to Benedict of Peterborough for an account of the meeting. Benedict reports the Patriarch's speech as if verbatim, and it is a desperate plea for aid against Saladin, who had caused unheard of desolation in the Holy Land, which reduced those listening to tears. Heraclius also brought gifts of relics of the Nativity and Passion of the Resurrection of Christ, and the keys of the Tower of David and of the Holy Sepulchre. Henry's initial response was encouraging, but he promised nothing specific until he should have consulted his bishops and the lords of his kingdom, arranging a council in London.[27] After taking advice, his response was that for him to accept the Kingdom of Jerusalem which they offered to him and to go there and desert the Kingdom of England and expose it to its hostile neighbours would not be acceptable to God, since this kingdom was as pleasing to God and as devout as the other. The king took ship with Heraclius at Dover, landing at Witsand (now Wissant, Pas-de-Calais), and they met King Philip of France at Vaudreuil on 1 May. Here both kings confirmed that they would not accompany Heraclius to the Holy Land, but promised subsidies of men and money. The unsuccessful delegation returned to the Holy Land, reaching Jerusalem by 1 August.[28]

Reading also formed the backdrop to a scene in the tragic life of Henry II's grand-daughter Eleanor, the 'Fair Maid of Brittany'. Eleanor was born in 1184, the eldest child of Geoffrey Plantagenet, King Henry's fourth son, and his wife Constance, Duchess of Brittany. When Geoffrey was killed on 19 or 21 August 1186, probably trampled to death at a tournament in Paris, Eleanor immediately became a political pawn.[29] King Philip II of France demanded her wardship, while Henry II was not prepared to give

[25] Leyser (1975), 497–98.
[26] See chapter two.
[27] Benedict of Peterborough, 1, 335–36; Eyton (1878), 261; Flowers of History 2, 73.
[28] Flowers of History, 2, 73; Eyton 1878, 263–64.
[29] Flowers of History 2, 74; Chron. Maj., 2I, 325.

her up. Henry sent three high-powered ambassadors to France to pacify Philip: his Chief Justiciar, Ranulf Glanvill; William de Mandeville, Earl of Essex and Albemarle; and Walter, Archbishop of Rouen. They set off in early October, returning to meet Henry at Reading on 9 October. They had negotiated a truce with the French king until the feast of St Hilary (13 January 1187), which was later extended.[30] As for young Eleanor, her position appeared to become stronger after the death of Henry II in 1189. As the new king Richard, her guardian, was childless, her younger brother Arthur was heir presumptive to the throne of England and she was a great dynastic prize. Successive attempts to marry her to Frederick, son of Duke Leopold of Austria, to Louis, son of Philip II of France, and to Duke Odo of Burgundy all came to nothing, however, and when Richard I died in 1199 she was caught up in a battle for the throne between her brother Arthur and her father's younger brother John. The position was by no means clear-cut; Norman precedent would favour John as the only surviving son of Henry II, while Angevin precedent preferred Arthur as the heir of Henry's elder son. The only solution was to get the swords out, and the decisive battle took place at Mirebeau (Vienne) on 31 July 1202, when John's sudden attack took Arthur's forces by surprise, and both he and his sister were captured and imprisoned. Arthur was taken to Falaise, and thence to Rouen, and he disappeared mysteriously in April 1203, undoubtedly murdered. Eleanor meanwhile was confined by her uncle in some comfort in the gloriette of Corfe Castle, Dorset.[31] After John's death in 1216 she was arguably a stronger claimant to the throne than Henry III, and she was never released from her confinement, although she was apparently moved between Corfe, Bristol and Gloucester, dying either at Corfe or at Bristol in 1241 at the age of 57, having spent thirty-nine years in captivity.

RICHARD I (1189–99)

King Richard I, as is well known, spent only six months or thereabouts in England during his ten-year reign, and a large part of that was between his coronation at Westminster on 3 September 1189 and his departure for Jerusalem after the feast of the nativity of St John the Baptist following (24 June 1190).[32] He spent much of this time collecting money for his crusade.

---

[30]   Eyton (1878), 274.

[31]   The most recent study of Eleanor's imprisonment is in Seabourne (2007).

[32]   Landon (1935); Flowers of History 2, 78 – 81. According to Landon's itinerary, King Richard was in England only between 13 August 1189 and 12 December 1189, and again from 13 March 1194 to 12 May 1194, a total of 183 days, although since his coronation did not take place until 3 September 1189 he was only in the country as king for 172 days.

A tenth part of all movables was granted and collected throughout England for this purpose, and among the loot was the reliquary that housed the hand of St James (see chapter two). No royal visit to Reading was noted in any contemporary record, and no charters were sealed by Richard at Reading, but Landon suggests that the reliquary was taken on a visit made while Richard was travelling from Woodstock to Westminster.[33] It has also been contended that Richard held a Great Council of the Realm at the abbey in 1191, but as the king was not in England at any time that year this would be impossible.[34]

JOHN (1199–1216)

From the beginning of John's reign, as we have seen, it became easier to trace royal movements, thanks to the efforts of the Chancellor, Archbishop Hubert Walter (c. 1160–1205), who was largely responsible for setting up systems whereby copies of royal charters, letters and writs (usually marked with the place and date of production) were kept in various series of rolls. The series of Charter Rolls begins in 1199, the Patent Rolls in 1201 and the Close Rolls in 1205. The earliest of the Fine Rolls is that of 1199–1200, but the sequence is patchy in John's reign and only becomes continuous after 1215. The Liberate Rolls proper do not really begin until 11 Henry III, which is October 1226, although a broken series of rolls that are called Liberate, but are actually Close Rolls begins in 1200.[35] King John's itinerary, based on the Patent Rolls, has been usefully plotted on an online map by the Itinerary of King John Project, instigated by Jon Crump at the University of Washington in Seattle, and it is easy to trace a pattern of travel, after 1204, that is mostly centred on south-east England with occasional trips to France, Ireland or the north of England.[36] The king paid 22 visits to Reading and spent a total of 61 days there during a reign of over seventeen years.[37] A glance at figure 16 will show that his visits to Reading were very unevenly distributed throughout his reign, concentrated in the years 1204–05 and after 1212. This is hardly surprising; in the four-and-a-half years between his accession on 27 May 1199 and December 1203, he spent a total of ten months in England, most of the remaining time being spent campaigning in Normandy against King Philip II of France, who had designs on the Duchy, and initially against his rival for the throne, his

---

[33] Landon (1935), 10. The king was recorded at Woodstock on 30 September 1189 and at Westminster on 6 October.

[34] Hurry (1901), 31; Coates (1802), 252; Cooper King (1887), 179.

[35] See CLR Henry III, 1, v-vi.

[36] Crump.

[37] Rot. Litt. Patt. King John. The most convenient way to consult this material is through Crump.

nephew Arthur of Brittany. The battle for the succession was won at the Battle of Mirebeau on 31 July 1202, when John captured Arthur and his commanders, subsequently imprisoning his rival at Rouen castle and having him murdered, probably in April of the following year. John still faced the threat from King Philip, however, and in December 1203 he returned to England, effectively abandoning his claim to Normandy. He spent little time at Reading between 1206 and 1212 when his main preoccupations were with defending his lands in Aquitaine, which were vulnerable after the death of his mother Eleanor, and with preparations for an attempt to recapture Normandy. He also spent a good deal of this time reinforcing his power in Scotland, Ireland and Wales.

There is plenty of evidence, however, that John had strong feelings for Reading Abbey. As we have seen, he took care to compensate the abbey for the damage caused to the hand reliquary by his brother, supplying gold for its maintenance and to make a new cover for it as early as 1192, when he was still Count of Mortain, and confirming the annual gift as king in 1200.[38] To accompany the hand reliquary, John gave a head reliquary allegedly containing part of the skull of the Apostle Philip (see chapter two).

John was in Reading from 18 to 21 December 1204, and on the 18th he received two visitors from the London Knights Templar: their Preceptor Alan Marcell and the almoner Brother Roger, who brought him a large quantity of jewellery and elaborate clothing and accessories from the Royal Treasury, then housed in the Temple (see Appendix C).[39] The list includes a gold crown, made for him in London; clothing, sandals, socks, gloves, belts and combs, many of the garments of samite bordered with orphreys, and all ornamented with precious stones, enamels or cameos; no less than thirteen buckles (*firmacula*) set with emeralds, sapphires, rubies, pearls, turquoises, diamonds and topazes; and seven sceptres (*bacula*) similarly ornamented. Each piece is carefully described to avoid confusion, and in a couple of entries there is evidence that the king himself was checking that everything was as it should be. One buckle is described as

> *unum firmaculum cum smaragdinibus et rubis quod Episcopus Norewic' dedit nobis*

> (a buckle with emeralds and rubies that the Bishop of Norwich gave to us),

while another is

> *unum firmaculum cum saphiris quod camerarius nobis dedit*

> (a buckle with sapphires that the chamberlain gave to us).

---

[38] Kemp (1986), I, 68, 69, 71–72.

[39] Rot. Litt. Pat. King John, 54–55; see also the expanded edition of the list in Bayley (1830), 182–83.

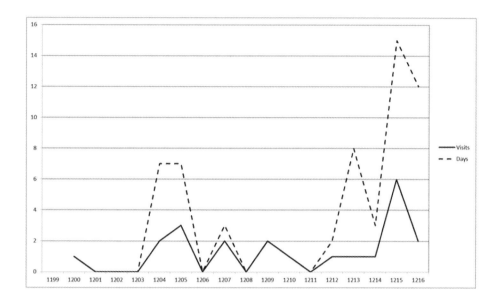

16   THE PATTERN OF VISITS OF KING JOHN TO READING ABBEY INDICATES THE IMPORTANCE OF
THE ABBEY TO THE KING.

Perhaps the most surprising thing about this collection is the number
of ceremonial items included. The crown is the most obvious, but there is
also a square silk cloth for the king's throne, and the sword made for his
coronation with a scabbard with orphreys. The clothing too is more than
usually ceremonial: a mantle of vermillion embroidered samite with sapphires and cameos and pearls, and its own separate buckle; a dalmatic of
the same samite bordered with orphreys and precious stones; sandals and
socks of the same samite, likewise bordered with orphreys; a baldric or
belt of the same samite with cameos and other stones, and a pair of white
gloves with a sapphire and an amethyst. Bayley suggested that the king
needed this regalia in Reading because he was spending Christmas there,[40]
but in fact he left Reading only three days later and spent Christmas at
Marlborough or Tewkesbury.

In 1206 Reading was the scene of a council called by John of Ferentum,
legate of Pope Innocent III. The event is known only from the account in
the *Flores Historiarum*, which is not particularly informative, but which
gives the information that the legate traversed England collecting a great
deal of money, and at last held a council at Reading on the day after the
feast of St Luke (18 October), whose only purpose was to make it appear

[40]   Bayley (1830), 182–83.

that something had been achieved.[41] He then went home, having, as the account has it, filled his baggage. King John was not personally involved; indeed he was not in England at this time.[42] It is hard to imagine that the legate's visit was not in some way connected with the fiercely contested election of a new Archbishop of Canterbury to succeed Hubert Walter, who had died on 13 July 1205.[43] The dispute over his successor involved King John, the Pope and the suffragan bishops of Canterbury diocese, and eventually resulted in the election of Stephen Langton on 17 June 1207, followed rapidly by the expulsion of the monks of Christ Church Canterbury by the king on 15 July 1207, the placing of England under an interdict by the pope, and eventually the excommunication of the king, which was not lifted until 1213.

John and Abbot Elias of Reading (1199–1213) shared an interest in books, which they often exchanged. On 29 March 1208 the king acknowledged the receipt of six theological works from the abbot while he was at Aldingbourne (Sussex) and the return of his own copy of Pliny that he received from Simon his chamberlain while he was at Waverly.[44]

On 12 March 1209 the church was struck by lightning but there is no mention of any damage or rebuilding as a result of this.[45] Towards the end of John's reign his visits to Reading became longer and more frequent, and he found time to spend Ascension Day there in 1215 and the whole of Easter week in 1216. Shortly afterwards Prince Louis, son of King Philippe-Auguste of France, had entered England at the invitation of the rebel barons, taking London on 2 June 1216 and moving west. John returned to Reading with an army for a few days in September, feigning an offensive to relieve the pressure on Windsor, under Louis's control, before setting off on his final and fatal trip north to relieve Lincoln from the siege of his rebellious barons. The story of his return via King's Lynn, where he fell prey to dysentery, and his loss of part of his baggage train as he crossed the tidal estuaries that flow into the Wash is probably all that most people know of King John. Traditionally the Crown Jewels were lost, and if they included the objects brought to him by the Templars at Reading it was a grievous loss indeed. Contemporary chroniclers are divided on this issue. According to Matthew Paris he lost everything; the Flores Historiarum says he lost his carriages and much of his baggage.[46]

---

[41]   Flowers of History, 2, 105.
[42]   He was recorded at Niort (Deux-Sevres) on 13 October and was still in the same part of France at La Rochelle (Charente-Maritime) on 25 October.
[43]   Knowles (1938), 211–20.
[44]   Excerpta Historica, 309.
[45]   Annales Radingenses Posteriores, 401.
[46]   Chron. Maj. 2, 667; Flowers of History 2, 128.

HENRY III (1216–72)

Henry III was only nine when he ascended the throne, and the posts of protector of the infant king and regent of England were bestowed on the ageing William Marshal, Earl of Pembroke, by the dead king's council on the day of his burial. Marshal was around 70 years old at the time, but prosecuted the war against Prince Louis and the rebel barons with such vigour that they withdrew from the struggle after his victory at the Battle of Lincoln on 20 May 1217. Two years later, his health failing, Marshal retired to his estate at Caversham near Reading. Early in 1219 he resigned his regency at a council of prelates and magnates held at Reading Abbey and presided over by the papal legate Pandulf, and he died at Caversham on 14 May of that year.[47] His son William commissioned a biography of his celebrated father in French verse, *L'Histoire de Guillaume le Marechal Comte de Striguil et de Pembroke*, and the description of his death and burial provides interesting information about Reading Abbey.[48] Since the beginning of his last illness, Marshal had confessed his sins every eight days. Absolution was pronounced by Abbot Simon of Reading (1213–26), assisted by the Abbot of Nutley. After his death his body was carried with the ceremony befitting such a man, and placed in the rich chapel founded by Marshal in the abbey church.

> *Ainz que del porpris eissist fors,*
> *Li dist la messe a la chapele*
> *Qu'il fist molt gloriose et bele.*[49]

(Before the body was taken from the precinct
Mass was said in the chapel
That he himself had made, glorious and beautiful.)

His wife and her son gave 100 sous to Reading Abbey while his body still lay there; then it was taken to Staines and from there to Westminster and its final resting place in the Temple Church in London (figure 17).

After the accession of Henry III a good deal more information becomes available about the king's activities, and this is largely because the series of Fine Rolls is unbroken from the start of Henry's reign. Figure 18 is a graphic summary of the number of visits the king made to Reading in each year of his reign, and the number of days he spent there. The information was taken from the Calendars of Close Rolls, Patent Rolls, Fine Rolls and Liberate Rolls.[50] Reading was an important destination and

---

[47]   Meyer (1891), 2, 284–85, 3, 253–55.
[48]   Ibid., 3, 265–66.
[49]   Ibid., 2, 323.
[50]   Craib (1923) was made available later, and was used to check the data. I am grateful to Steven Brindle for this.

17   WILLIAM MARSHAL WAS REGENT OF ENGLAND IN THE FIRST THREE YEARS OF THE INFANT HENRY III'S
REIGN. HE FOUNDED A CHAPEL AT READING ABBEY, WHERE A MASS WAS SAID FOR HIM AT HIS DEATH BEFORE
HIS BODY WAS ENTOMBED IN THE TEMPLE CHURCH, LONDON.

stopping-off point in the royal itinerary, especially between 1227 (when Henry declared himself of age) and around 1255, when his ill-considered designs on Sicily led to his effective removal from power by Simon de Montfort's party in 1258, culminating in his and Prince Edward's capture and detention following the battle of Lewes in 1264. Despite the downfall of de Montfort in 1265, Henry never really regained his power, and spent more and more of his time at Westminster, where he was personally concerned with the Cosmati paving of the Confessor's chapel, the translation of Edward the Confessor's body into his incomplete tomb in 1269, and the continuation of work on the tomb.[51]

David Carpenter and Julie Kanter of King's College London have analysed Henry III's most favoured locations during that period of his personal rule (1234–58) when he was most in England, i.e. the seventeen years from 1234 to 1241 and 1244 to 1252.[52] Unsurprisingly, Westminster comes out on top of the list, but Reading is sixth, with a respectable 238 days, headed only by Windsor, Woodstock, Clarendon and Marlborough.

[51]   Binski (1995), 93–104.
[52]   Carpenter and Kanter (2009).

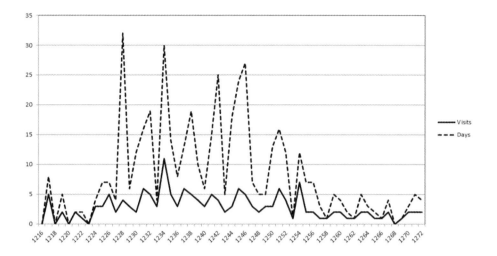

18   HENRY III PAID VISITS TO READING ABBEY THROUGHOUT HIS MAJORITY, OFTEN SPENDING MAJOR FEASTS THERE.

Again and again during his long reign, Henry travelled back and forth along two favoured routes: from Westminster to Windsor, then Reading, Winchester, Clarendon and Marlborough; or Westminster, Windsor, Reading, Wallingford and Woodstock. Even when he deviated from these well-worn trails, westward journeys from Westminster almost always began and ended with visits to Windsor and Reading. Most of the places he stayed at were royal residences; as well as those mentioned above he was a frequent visitor to Gloucester, Guildford, Kempton and Ludgershall. Of all the monasteries he frequented, Reading was by far the most used, although he stayed at Chertsey during his minority and also at Abingdon, Bisham and Sandleford.[53]

He stayed at Reading for many important Christian feasts: Easter of 1222, 1225, 1228, 1230, 1235 and 1242; Christmas 1226; Trinity of 1239; Ascension Day of 1244, 1247, 1251 and 1255 and Pentecost of 1226. He was also present on 19 April in 1236 and 1242 for the anniversary of the consecration of the abbey church in 1164. The feasts of Christmas, Easter and Pentecost, or Whitsun were both important and impressive, because on these occasions the King wore his crown.[54]

[53]   An invaluable analysis of Henry III's favoured residences is given by Brindle in Craib (1923), 4–5.
[54]   Brindle in Craib (1923), 4; Biddle (1985), 54–55.

The Liberate Rolls provide a good deal of information about Henry's visits to Reading. They begin at the end of October 1226, just in time to record some of the preparations for Christmas. On 10 December he sent a writ to the Sheriff of Gloucester to buy 40 salmon and as many lampreys as he could find, and send them to Reading by Tuesday or Wednesday (22 or 23 Dec), in good time for Christmas.[55] On the 18th he ordered the sheriff of Oxford to send the venison of boars, and also the king's own venison from St Briavel's in the New Forest, to Reading by the Wednesday before Christmas.[56] He cannot have stayed very long on this occasion; he was recorded at Reading on Christmas Day, but was in Westminster on 22 December and had moved on to Wallingford by the 27th. There is no record of wine for this particular feast, but it is obvious from the Liberate Rolls that he maintained a cellar at Reading for his own use, replenishing it when stocks fell low. Throughout the reign there are regular writs addressed to the bailiffs of Southampton to send wine to important royal stations in the south, most often Winchester, Guildford, Clarendon, Reading, Oxford, Wallingford and Woodstock. In less than a year, for example, between December 1240 and November 1241 Henry issued five orders for a total of 60 tuns of wine to be sent from Southampton to Reading, and it is worth noting that a tun of wine was not just a vague term for a barrel, but a specific measure of 256 gallons that literally weighed a ton.[57] Each tun of wine would fill 1,272 modern wine bottles. The wine was stored in the abbot's cellar, reserved for the king's use.

At Easter 1228 Henry was treated to a performance of *Christus Vincit* by Walter de Lenches and his fellows, clerks of the King's Chapel, for which Walter received a payment of 25s, and he heard it again at Reading on Trinity Sunday, 1239.[58] The performance of this chant was a regular feature of Henry's itinerary, occurring not only on the major feast days but also on special occasions like the purification of the queen on 31 July 1239, and her confinement on 2 October 1240.[59] For his Easter visit in 1230, Henry had his own chapel furniture carried to Reading,[60] and on Wednesday 4 May 1233 we find him urging the sheriffs of London to cause 13 linen surplices to be made with all speed, so that the king would have them ready in time for his Ascension Day celebrations on the Thursday of the next week.[61] Later that year a great flood, 'such as had not been seen since

---

[55] CLR Henry III, 1, 8; Flowers of History 2, 151.
[56] CLR Henry III, 1, 9.
[57] Ibid., 2; 11, 30, 86, 89. 91.
[58] Ibid., 1; 79, 406; on the Chapel Royal, see Flood (1924), Bent (1963).
[59] The ritual purification (or churching) of women was usually performed on the 40th day after giving birth. In this case the ceremony took place 45 days after the birth of Prince Edward on 17 June 1239.
[60] CLR Henry III, 1, 170.
[61] Ibid., 1, 213.

Noah's flood', was recorded for the feast of the Translation of St Benedict (July 11) 1233, but while this swept away bridges and buildings in the town, it does not seem to have caused any major damage to the abbey.[62]

Many of the Liberate Roll entries point to a degree of uncertainty or flexibility in the king's plans. On 14 November 1241 he sent an order to Walter de Tyre and William de St Ouen from Windsor, for sixty of his bucks that they were keeping for him to be sent to Reading, or to Windsor if they could assure themselves that he was going to stay there.[63] In fact he stayed at Windsor until the 18th of the month and was at Reading by the 20th, but there is no record to tell us where the venison ended up. Likewise, he was due to arrive at Reading on Sunday 8 May 1244 for a stay of a week including Ascension Day, and on Monday 2 May he sent an urgent writ from Westminster to the bailiffs of Southampton ordering 30 tuns of wine to be sent to Reading, 15 of which were to be waiting for him on his arrival and the rest to be delivered as soon as possible thereafter.[64] During this stay the Bishop of Carlisle, William Mauclerk, who was Henry's Lord Treasurer, fell ill at Reading where his brother had been the prior in 1215.[65] The king's party left for Windsor on 15 or 16 May, but the bishop stayed behind, and was consoled by a gift of two roes that Henry arranged to be sent to him from Winchester.[66]

In 1246 he visited Reading five times, spending no less than 27 days there during the year. On 27 March he recorded payments to a goldsmith named Hugh Blund for two silver-gilt chalices for use in the Eucharist, sent to two churches in Marlborough, and a payment of 32 shillings for twenty-four *oboli de Musca*, sent to him at Reading. These were Spanish gold coins, probably Almohade dinars, that were used for ecclesiastical or ceremonial payments or oblations and could be melted down for other uses.[67]

In 1264 a council was held at Reading to resolve the pope's attempt at interference in the Barons' War by excommunicating some of the barons.[68] The papal legate had excommunicated Simon de Montfort and all his adherents on 20 October, and at the council of Reading the English bishops appealed against this action.

[62] Annales Radingenses Posteriores, 402.
[63] CLR Henry III, 2, 89.
[64] Ibid., 2, 231.
[65] Rot. Litt. Patt. King John, 140 mentions 'R. priorem radingem fratrem Walteri Mauclerc'.
[66] CLR Henry III, 2, 236.
[67] See Grierson (1951), passim.
[68] Flowers of History, 2, 421.

EDWARD I (1272–1307)

Before his accession to the throne, Prince Edward had sometimes accompanied his father on his travels around the realm, but had spent increasingly large amounts of his time abroad once he was of an age to travel independently. He was with his father at Reading on 14 March 1254, aged 14, on 29 October 1263 and on 28 Nov 1269. Earlier that year, on 26 October, he had been at Reading without his father.[69]

Henry III died on 16 November 1272 when Prince Edward was crusading in the Holy Land, but Edward did not return to England until 2 August 1274, and was crowned in Westminster Abbey on 19 August. This may well be the first occasion in English history that the heir to the throne felt sufficiently confident of his right to the crown to remain away from London for such a long period before returning to claim his patrimony. Thereafter his itinerary in England can be traced more or less completely from the information in the various chancery rolls.[70] Edward's patterns of movement were completely different from his father's. He spent much of 1282–84 and 1295 campaigning in Wales, and long periods in 1291–92, 1296, 1298 and 1300–01 in Scotland. While Henry had spent the bulk of his time in England moving around the Thames valley and central Wessex, Edward tended to stay in one place for much longer; sometimes several months. Many of his lodging places were familiar – Westminster, the Tower of London, Windsor and Woodstock – but he also spent long periods at the palaces of Kennington and Brill, and the hunting lodges at Geddington and King's Cliffe in Rockingham forest. Unlike his father he tended not to lodge at monasteries; he stayed at Abingdon only twice, and rarely visited Reading Abbey, a favourite haunt of his father's. In the whole of his reign of more than thirty-four years he spent only 8 days there, and never stayed for more than 3 days at a time.

EDWARD II (1307–27)

It was in the reign of Edward II that the problems outlined above in tracing the whereabouts of the king first became acute. The situation is so complex, indeed, that Elizabeth Hallam, to whom we are indebted for tracing the royal itinerary, found it necessary to track the various elements of the royal presence, the privy seal, wardrobe, secret seal, household and, when possible, the king himself separately, presenting them in separate columns.[71] Edward II succeeded to the throne on the death of his father on 7 July 1307, and we first find evidence connecting him with Reading

---

[69]   Information from Studd (2000), 1, 73, 119, 120.
[70]   See Gough (1900) and more recently Safford (1974–77).
[71]   Hallam (1984), passim.

I THE RUINS OF THE ABBEY STAND IN THE CENTRE OF READING. THIS VIEW SHOWS THE SOUTH TRANSEPT AND SLYPE FROM THE EAST.

II THE TERRACE OF HOUSES ON ABBOTS WALK, BUILT IN THE 1840S, AND AT ITS FAR END THE LINE OF THE FACADES IS CONTINUED BY THE REMAINS OF THE SOUTH NAVE AISLE WALL.

III   THE HOLY BROOK HERE REJOINS THE KENNET OPPOSITE THE RERE-DORTER OF
THE MONASTERY.

IV   *THE BURIAL OF HENRY I, 1136* WAS PAINTED BY HARRY MORLEY IN 1916.

V   READING HELD A RELIC OF ST AMPHIBALUS, THE CHRISTIAN PRIEST SHELTERED BY
ST ALBAN DURING DIOCLETIAN'S PERSECUTION. HIS RESTORED SHRINE STANDS IN THE
NORTH CHANCEL AISLE OF ST ALBANS CATHEDRAL.

VI WILLIAM OF NORWICH, A BOY ALLEGEDLY MARTYRED BY JEWS IN 1144, SHOWN
ON THE EARLY SIXTEENTH-CENTURY SCREEN OF HOLY TRINITY, LODDON (NORFOLK).
READING ABBEY POSSESSED HIS BLOODSTAINED SHOE AND PART OF THE TREE FROM
WHICH HE WAS HANGED.

VII THE THIRTEENTH-CENTURY ARM RELIQUARY OF ST PANTALEON IS NOW IN THE
WALTERS ART MUSEUM, BALTIMORE. THE HAND OF ST JAMES MIGHT WELL HAVE BEEN
HOUSED IN A SIMILAR SHRINE.

VIII   THIS DESICCATED HAND PRESERVED IN ST PETER'S RC CHURCH, MARLOW (BUCKS), MIGHT WELL BE
THE ONE VENERATED AS THE HAND OF ST JAMES THROUGHOUT THE LIFE OF THE ABBEY.

IX   A NETHERLANDISH STATUE OF ST BARBARA IN THE WALTERS ART MUSEUM, BALTI-
MORE, HOLDS A RELIQUARY WITH A CRYSTAL WINDOW TO DISPLAY HER OWN RELICS.

X   HARRY MORLEY'S 1918 PAINTING, *TRIAL BY COMBAT, 1163*, SHOWS HENRY OF ESSEX
COLLAPSING TO THE GROUND AS HE SEES A VISION OF THE VENGEFUL ST EDMUND
ACCOMPANIED BY GILBERT DE CEREVILLE. HENRY WAS LEFT FOR DEAD ON THE FIELD,
BUT MADE A SURPRISE RECOVERY AND ENDED HIS DAYS AS A MONK AT READING.

XI   STEPHEN REID'S *CONSECRATION OF THE ABBEY CHURCH, 1164* WAS COMPLETED IN
1920 AND IS DOMINATED BY THE CENTRAL FIGURE OF THE YOUNG ARCHBISHOP BECKET.

XII   STEPHEN REID'S *VISIT OF HERACLIUS, PATRIARCH OF JERUSALEM, 1185* DEPICTS HENRY II ENTHRONED AT READING ABBEY WHERE HE IS HEARING A PLEA FROM THE PATRIARCH AND THE MASTER OF THE KNIGHTS HOSPITALLERS, ROGER DE MOULINS FOR AID AGAINST SALADIN. THE KING EVENTUALLY TURNED DOWN THEIR REQUEST.

XIII   HORACE BOARDMAN WRIGHT'S *THE MARRIAGE OF JOHN OF GAUNT AND BLANCHE OF LANCASTER, 1359* DEPICTS WHAT MUST BE THE MOST SIGNIFICANT DYNASTIC MARRIAGE OF THE LATE MIDDLE AGES IN ENGLAND. THE COUPLE'S UNION FOUNDED THE HOUSE OF LANCASTER AND BROUGHT ABOUT THE WARS OF THE ROSES, AND THEIR SON, GRANDSON AND GREAT GRANDSON WERE ALL KINGS.

XIV   KING EDWARD IV CHOSE THE COUNCIL MEETING HELD AT READING ABBEY IN SEPTEMBER 1464 TO
ANNOUNCE THAT HE HAD SECRETLY MARRIED THE LANCASTRIAN WIDOW ELIZABETH WOODVILLE ON MAY
DAY OF THAT YEAR. ERNEST BOARD'S 1923 PAINTING SHOWS THE KING LEADING HIS WIFE UP THE CHANCEL
STEPS OF THE ABBEY CHURCH.

XV   HARRY MORLEY'S PAINTING, *THE MARTYRDOM OF HUGH FARINGDON, LAST ABBOT OF READING*, SHOWS
THE ABBOT TIED TO A HURDLE WHILE A HORSE IS PREPARED TO DRAG HIM THROUGH THE TOWN. THE EXE-
CUTIONER WAITS ON THE GALLOWS. THE ONE REALISTIC ARCHITECTURAL FEATURE IS THE ABBEY GATEWAY
SHOWN ON THE RIGHT OF THE PAINTING.

XVI ST JAMES'S RC CHURCH, READING, SEEN HERE FROM THE SOUTH-WEST, WAS BUILT BY PUGIN FOR JAMES WHEBLE IN 1837.

XVII THE READING ABBEY STONE, A QUADRUPLE CAPITAL ENRICHED WITH FOLIAGE CARVING, WAS EXCAVATED BY WHEBLE ON THE ABBEY SITE AND CONVERTED FOR USE AS THE FONT OF ST JAMES'S CHURCH, READING.

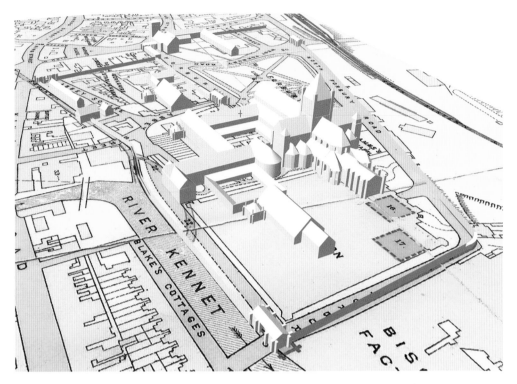

XVIII   THE BUILDINGS OF THE ABBEY CHURCH AND PRECINCT SUPERIMPOSED ON POULTER'S 1901 TOWN
PLAN.

XIX   THE INNER SOUTH TRANSEPT CHAPEL IS BOTH DEEPER AND BETTER PRESERVED THAN THE OUTER,
WHICH IS REDUCED TO LOW STUBS OF WALL. BOTH ARE SEEN HERE FROM THE WEST.

XX THE SOUTH CHANCEL AISLE IS HERE SHOWN LOOKING EAST. ON THE LEFT
(NORTH) THE LINE OF THE SOUTH WALL OF THE FORMER ST JAMES'S RC SCHOOL, NOW
THE FORBURY GARDENS DAY NURSERY, FOLLOWS THE SOUTH CHANCEL ARCADE, THE
SOLE SURVIVING PIER BASE OF WHICH IS VISIBLE BELOW IT. THE CORRESPONDING AISLE
WALL RESPOND BASE IS VISIBLE ON THE RIGHT.

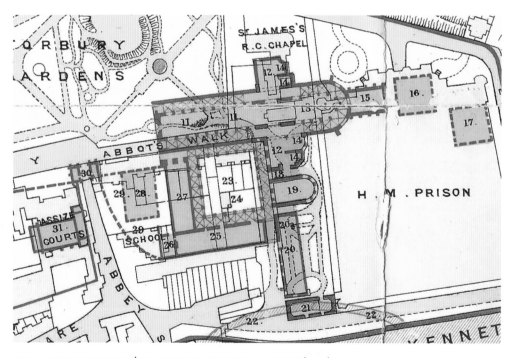

XXI A DETAIL OF POULTER'S PLAN SHOWN, PUBLISHED IN HURRY (1901), SHOWS THE POSITION OF THE
ABBEY BUILDINGS RELATIVE TO THE TOWN.

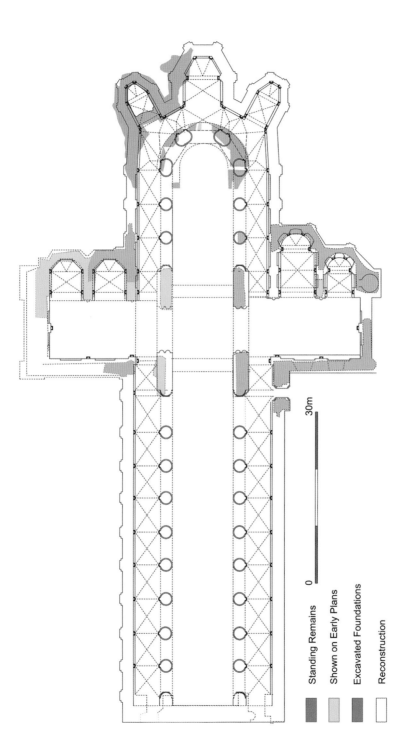

Standing Remains

Shown on Early Plans

Excavated Foundations

Reconstruction

0   30m

XXII   THE PLAN OF READING ABBEY CHURCH BASED ON ANTIQUARIAN AND ARCHAEOLOGICAL DATA.

XXIII MATTHEW PARIS'S *HISTORIA ANGLORUM* OF 1250–59 INCLUDES PORTRAITS OF
WILLIAM I, WILLIAM II, HENRY I AND STEPHEN HOLDING MODELS OF BUILDINGS WITH
WHICH THEY WERE ASSOCIATED. KING HENRY IS SHOWN AT THE LOWER LEFT HOLDING
READING ABBEY CHURCH.

XXIV IN THE *ABBREVIATIO CHRONICORUM ANGLIAE* OF C. 1255–59, THE SAME FOUR
KINGS HOLD SIGNIFICANT OBJECTS. HENRY I CARRIES A SIMPLER MODEL OF READING
ABBEY CHURCH AND STEPHEN A MODEL OF FAVERSHAM, WHILE WILLIAM I HOLDS THE
SHIP IN WHICH HE INVADED ENGLAND AND WILLIAM II THE ARROW WITH WHICH HE
WAS SHOT.

XXV   IN THIS VIEW OF THE INTERIOR OF THE SOUTH TRANSEPT FROM THE NORTH-EAST, THE LINE OF THE
SOUTH NAVE AISLE WALL IS REPRESENTED BY THE HOUSES ON ABBOT'S WALK ON THE EXTREME RIGHT. THE
TWO BAYS OF THE TRANSEPT WEST WALL AND A SHORT SECTION OF THE SOUTH WALL STILL STAND, AND
IN THE DISTANCE IS READING'S TALLEST BUILDING, THE BLADE, DESIGNED BY THE ARCHITECTS SHEPPARD
ROBSON AND COMPLETED IN 2009.

on 2–4 December of that year.[72] During that time the privy seal was certainly at Reading, and there is evidence for the court and household too on the 4th, but while the king himself is not definitely known to be there or anywhere else, the wardrobe was at King's Langley during that period, and given his love for the palace there it is most probable that the king was there too. We are on firmer ground the following year, when the king almost certainly visited Reading three times. Around 27 March the wardrobe and the privy seal were recorded at both Reading and Windsor, and on the next day they were at Wallingford, which suggests a movement from Windsor to Wallingford via Reading.[73] On 16 June the wardrobe was at Reading, and on 17 June the privy seal. Likewise on 7 July the wardrobe was at Reading but on the following day the privy seal had arrived but the wardrobe had moved on to Windsor.[74] These two examples well represent the kind of disjunction mentioned in the preamble to this section as typical of Edward II's itinerary.

After the visits of 1307 and 1308 there is no evidence for the king at Reading for another nine years. The privy seal and the court and household were at Reading on 14 April 1317, but this was presumably a flying visit as they were also recorded at Cookham and Windsor on the same day.[75] The privy seal was there on 3 May 1318, but the secret seal and the wardrobe (and thus probably the king) were at Whitchurch.[76] He was certainly at Reading from 17–19 May 1320, when he celebrated Pentecost at the abbey, and the wardrobe and both the privy seal and the secret seal were recorded there in that period.[77] Finally on 11 and 12 December 1321 the wardrobe and the privy seal were at Reading, while the king was not known to be anywhere else. A footnote to this discussion, which throws some light on the value of Hallam's method of tracing the various elements of the court's trajectory separately, is provided by the records of the king and the wardrobe in the months leading to his deposition. Edward was arrested in November 1326 and held at Kenilworth castle from 5 December to his formal deposition on 21 January 1327. Queen Isabella meanwhile had issued a proclamation at Bristol announcing that Prince Edward was now the Keeper of the Realm. The chancellor, Henry Cliffe, joined the queen and Prince Edward at Woodstock on 4 December, and the party stayed at Reading on 30 December *en route* to Westminster.[78]

John of Towcester was a member of Edward's household for most of his reign. He was appointed keeper of several manors for the king including

---

[72] Ibid., 26.
[73] Ibid., 29.
[74] Ibid., 29–35.
[75] Ibid., 152.
[76] Ibid., 167.
[77] Ibid., 196.
[78] Ibid., 292–93.

Langley Mareys (1312) and Queenhythe (1314).[79] In April 1324 he was put in charge of the manor of Shinfield, confiscated from the Bishop of Hereford, Adam Orleton, after he was charged with conspiring with Roger Mortimer, Earl of March, against the king.[80] John of Towcester retired from public life in November 1325, and King Edward sent him to Reading Abbey to receive maintenance for life.[81] His retirement was interrupted when on 10 October 1326 the king appointed him to 'select all men-at-arms wherever he goes and to lead them to the king as he is instructed'.[82] This muster was to resist his impending capture by Mortimer and Isabella, but it was too late to save the king. John of Towcester presumably returned to Reading Abbey, but is heard of for a final time in 1330, when an order for his arrest was issued in the infant Edward III's name by Mortimer to all the sheriffs of England on the grounds that he was plotting with Edward II's half-brother, Edmund of Woodstock, the Earl of Kent, who believed the old king was still alive and in prison at Corfe, to release him and restore him to the throne.[83] Just over six months later Mortimer was overthrown, and it seems likely, therefore, that John of Towcester's retirement was not interrupted again.

EDWARD III (1327–77)

Prince Edward was crowned at the age of 14 on 1 February 1327, and until his revolt against the increasingly unpopular Roger Mortimer, his mother's lover and the *de facto* ruler of England, his movements were determined more or less by Mortimer's own concern with his ancestral lands in the Welsh marches and the Severn valley.[84] After 1330, however, the young king spent more time in East Anglia and the Midlands, although in the period before 1340 a tendency to explore different areas of the kingdom can be detected. Up to June 1345 Edward III or his household visited Reading 15 times, spending more than 30 days there in all (figure 19). The longest visits were in 1337, when the privy seal was employed there over a period of eleven days in late November and early December. Evidence for the king's own whereabouts is not generally available for this period, but we know that he paid special alms at Reading on his visit of May 1336, the only time he did this.[85] For the rest, the most that can be said is that there

[79]   CFR 1307–19,195; CPR 1307–13, 513.
[80]   CFR 1319–27, 269.
[81]   CCR 1323–1327, 517.
[82]   CPR, 1323–1327, 326.
[83]   CFR 1327–1337, 169.
[84]   Shenton (2007), 8–9.
[85]   Cotton Nero C viii, f. 205r, Ormrod (1989), 859; Webb (2000), 115.

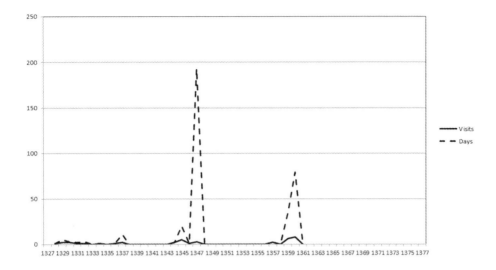

19   EDWARD III VISITED READING ABBEY FREQUENTLY BEFORE 1346, BUT THE LONG VISIT IN 1346–47 WAS
BY HIS SON LIONEL OF ANTWERP, APPOINTED REGENT DURING THE KING'S ABSENCE IN FRANCE. READING
WAS AGAIN CHOSEN AS THE MAIN SITE OF THE REGENT'S COURT DURING THE KING'S CAMPAIGN OF 1359–60,
WHEN HIS SON THOMAS OF WOODSTOCK WAS LEFT IN NOMINAL CHARGE.

is no record of him anywhere else, except for 30 November, when he was
at Westminster.[86]

After Henry I's establishment of a mint and a moneyer at the foundation, the production of coinage at Reading apparently died out until it was
revived by Edward III. In August 1338 he ordered the exchequer to deliver
dies to the abbot and monks of Reading to produce pennies, halfpennies
and farthings. They were sent by the beginning of December, but in the
following February the abbot complained that the halfpenny and farthing
dies had still not arrived and the king was obliged to repeat his order to
the exchequer.[87] The dies eventually did arrive, as is proved by the existence of a few farthings, halfpennies and pennies of Edward III struck at
Reading. In addition to the name of the town these bear the scallop shell
in one of the quadrants of the reverse design, in place of the usual three
pellets (figure 20).[88]

In July 1346 the king set sail for France with an army, taking the
city of Caen on a single day on 26 July and engaging the French army
of Philip VI at Crécy, south of Calais on 26 August. There is no doubt

86   CFR 1327–1337, 170–71.
87   Cal. Close Rolls 1337–39, 450, 577; 1339–41, 20.
88   Allen and Vosper (1999), 214.

20 EDWARD III REVIVED THE READING MINT IN 1338, AND COINS LIKE THIS SILVER PENNY STRUCK THERE WERE MARKED WITH A SCALLOP SHELL IN THE UPPER RIGHT QUADRANT OF THE REVERSE.

that Edward's army was heavily outnumbered, and the victory he gained was an overwhelming one, seen as a vindication of the effectiveness of the English longbow against armoured knights, and proof of the valour of the sixteen-year old Edward of Woodstock, the Black Prince, who led one of his father's three divisions at the battle. King Edward did not return to England until 12 October 1347, and for the 15 months he was away he appointed his second surviving son Lionel to the regency. Lionel of Antwerp was 7 years old when he took on the role, and as usual the civil service was divided. The chancellor, John de Ufford, and the treasurer William Edington remained in London, Ufford using the seal of absence to transact the royal affairs. The head of the council in England was the Archbishop of Canterbury, John de Stratford, while the regent's seal, specially made for him, was held by Simon Islip, a royal clerk who accompanied Lionel.[89] Letters and writs sealed with this seal were dated from Reading between early February and the end of August 1347.[90]

It was in the early morning of Good Friday 1347 (30 March), while Lionel and his brothers and sisters were staying at Reading Abbey, that a band of more than sixty men led by John de Dalton, a Lancashire knight, broke into Beaumes Manor at Swallowfield, just outside the town. The Patent Rolls for the following day contain this account of the raid:

> Inasmuch as a scandalous outcry prevails everywhere among the people and very grievous complaint has been made to the King that John de Dalton, chivaler, … and others by force ravished Margery de la Beche, united in lawful matrimony to Gerard del Isle, on the holy day of Good Friday, before the dawn, at her manor at Beaumes by Redyng, where the king's son Lionel, keeper of England, was then staying, within the verge of the Marchalsea of the household of the said keeper, and abducted her against her will, whither they would, without reverence for God, Holy Church or the king, and to the terror of the said keeper and the rest of the king's children with him there and all in those parts, and are now running to and fro that they may not be brought to justice for the felony; the king has appointed the said Gerard to arrest the said

89   Tout (1920), 3, 165–66. Three of these four men were to serve as Archbishops of Canterbury: Stratford (1333–48), Ufford (1348–49) and Islip (1349–66).

90   CCR 1346–49, passim.

persons and all who shall be indicted of the felony wherever found and bring them before the council, and because Gerard fears bodily harm in the execution of the appointment from the said evil-doers, who are plotting to do him all the evil which they can, he has granted special licence for him and all of his company to go armed for their self-defence.[91]

The sources are positive that Lionel was holding his court in Reading itself, and that Beaumes Manor was within the verge of the Marshalsea of his court, in other words, within his jurisdiction.[92] An order was also issued in Lionel's name, obliging John de Dalton to bring Margery de la Beche before him and the council at Westminster, and when he did not comply the Keeper of the Realm sent out orders to all the sheriffs in England to arrest John de Dalton and take him and his accomplices to the Tower of London to be held until further orders.[93] By then it had become clear that the raiders had attacked the manor by night, ravished Margery and killed her uncle Michael de Ponynges, and Thomas the Clerk of Shipton, and wounded, beaten or mistreated many others so that their lives were despaired of, and carried off goods to the value of £1000. It is also obvious that the authorities had no clear idea of where John de Dalton might be, or who his associates were. They knew, or suspected that he had fled northwards, and on 10 May commissioned Henry Percy and Ralph Nevill to arrest him, providing a list of his associates to be apprehended that included his father Robert, his cousin, another Robert, and his aunt Sarah Baillof.[94]

Dalton had indeed gone north with Margery and many of his companions, and took refuge in various vacant houses on their way, thus bringing under suspicion the unwitting owners of these properties, including the priors of Burscough and Upholland and, notably, Maud (Matilda) de Holland, the widow of Sir Robert de Holland of Upholland in Lancashire, and a substantial heiress in her own right. It was revealed later in 1347 that on the Sunday after Easter (8 April)

> John de Dalton, chivaler, Matthew de Haydok, Thomas D'Ardern, chivaler and others unknown, with Margery, late the wife of Nicholas de la Beche, came to the manor of Holland, then vacant, which is the manor of dame Matilda de Holand, she being ignorant of their coming, and on Monday next following (9 April) the said John de Dalton married the said dame Margery and they dwelt there until Roger le Archer, sergeant at arms, came into Co. Lancashire, bringing the King's writ to the sheriff to take the said John de Dalton and others and proclaiming that nobody should assist the said John under pain of forfeiture to

---

[91] CPR 1345–48, 310–11.
[92] The wording of some of the writs involved has deceived some authors into the belief that the royal household was at Beaumes.
[93] CCR 1346–49, 271.
[94] Ibid.,319–20.

the King, by virtue whereof John Cokayn sheriff and the said Roger le Archer went to the said manor of Holland to take the said John de Dalton; that the said John and others then left Lancashire and went to Yorkshire where they remained some time; they then returned to Lancashire, but afterwards went away in the night into northern parts where they still live, but in what place or county they are is not known.[95]

This curious story has no satisfactory ending. The only person ever punished for the murders, abduction and theft was John de Dalton's father, Robert, who was imprisoned for a time in the Tower of London and released when it was realized that he had played no part in the business.[96] Several of the other accused men received pardons after Henry of Lancaster intervened with the king on their behalf.[97] John de Dalton, the prime mover in the affair, was pardoned two years later on 4 May 1350, in these words:

> Pardon to John de Dalton, knight, for good service and because he has humbly submitted himself to the king's grace, of the king's suit for the ravishment of Margery late the wife of Nicholas de la Beche and other felonies and trespasses in the manor of Beaumes by Redyng, co. Wilts, within the verge of the household of the king's son Lionel, guardian of England, in the absence of the king beyond the seas, whereof he has been indicted with others.[98]

Margery was dead by this time, and may have been a victim of the Black Death that arrived in 1348.

On 15 July 1359, the queen's clerk Thomas de Chynham received a payment of ten pounds for performing three marriages in the same chapel at Reading Abbey.[99] One was in fact a betrothal, between Philippa, the three-year-old daughter of the king's third son Lionel and Edmund Mortimer, the seven-year-old son and heir of the Earl of March. The two were to marry fully in 1368.[100] The second marriage was that of the king's own twelve-year-old daughter Margaret Plantagenet and the eleven-year-old John Hastings, Earl of Pembroke in the Queen's Chapel at Reading Abbey on 13 May 1359.[101] The two events might well have taken place on the same day; in any case the two young brides were decked out in 2,000 pearls for which King Edward paid £216 13s 4d to Simon Bochel.[102]

[95]　Lancs Inquests, III, 166–68.
[96]　CCR 1346–49, 370.
[97]　CPR 1345–48, 543–44.
[98]　CPR 1348–50, 498.
[99]　Devon (1837), 170. For Chynham see Wilkins (1979), 87.
[100]　G.E.C. (1910–59), 5, 243–44.
[101]　Margaret died only two years afterwards; John Hastings remarried in 1368 and died in captivity in 1375 while campaigning with the Black Prince in Spain.
[102]　Devon (1837), 172. Simon Bochel was the London representative of the Lucchese banking house of the Spifame. In 1361 he was described as 'The King's Merchant',

Later that month, on Sunday 19 May 1359, John of Gaunt, fourth son of the king, married Blanche, daughter of Henry of Lancaster.[103] The two were distant cousins, having a common ancestor in King Henry III, and a dispensation was required from Pope Innocent VI to allow them to marry. It was the first marriage for both of them (although John of Gaunt's illegitimate daughter (also Blanche) was born in the same year as his marriage).[104] On their wedding day John was 19 years old and Blanche was 13 or 14, and their marriage was to last until 1369 when Blanche died of the plague at Bolingbroke Castle. This ten-year marriage produced at least seven children including Henry Bolingbroke, later King Henry IV. The ceremony was the subject of another of the paintings that Hurry commissioned. Horace Boardman Wright's *The Marriage of John of Gaunt and Blanche of Lancaster, 1359*, was completed in 1914 (plate XIII).

After the wedding the festivities lasted fourteen days, and the journey back to London after the ceremony was enlivened by jousting, a preliminary to the curious three-day tournament held in the capital from 27 to 29 May, in which the king, his sons Edward, Lionel, John and Edmund, and 19 other noblemen dressed up as the Mayor and his 24 aldermen and defeated all comers in the tilting.[105]

The king clearly considered that his experiment of leaving a young son in nominal charge while he was away on campaign in 1347 had worked well enough, because he did it again in October 1359, when he left again for France, not to return for more than two years. He was accompanied on this campaign by his oldest son Edward the Black Prince, now a veteran of 29, and his three younger brothers, Lionel of Antwerp, John of Gaunt and Edmund of Langley. The boy left behind as regent and Keeper of the Realm was Thomas of Woodstock, aged four. Again the chancery remained in London but the regent's court seems to have moved around a little, favouring Reading above other homes during the early part of his father's campaign. Between the beginning of November 1359 and mid-May 1360 Thomas spent some 114 days at Reading – around 60 per cent of his time, including Christmas 1359, alternating his time with stays at Woodstock and Windsor. Thereafter no writs were dated from Reading at all during the king's absence. As for the king himself, there is little evidence of visits to Reading in the later part of his reign, except for two writs dated there in 1357.[106]

and was granted citizenship of London in consideration of his services to the King and Queen Philippa (CPR 1361–64, 42).

[103] John of Reading, 131.

[104] The illegitimate daughter was the result of an affair between John of Gaunt and Marie de Saint-Hilaire, one of his mother Queen Philippa's maids of honour, according to Froissart, 2, 166.

[105] John of Reading, 131.

106 CFR 1356–68, 25; CCR 1354–60, 316.

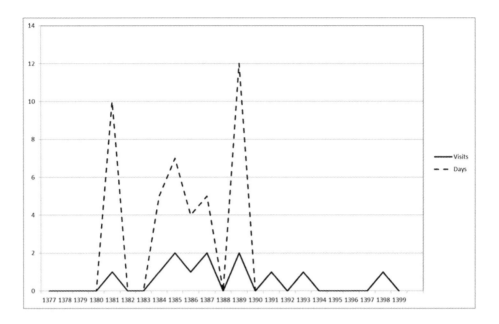

21   KING RICHARD II'S VISITS TO READING ABBEY INCLUDED A LONG COUNCIL MEETING IN 1389, THE YEAR HE
DECLARED HIMSELF OLD ENOUGH TO RULE ALONE. HIS EARLIER VISITS TOOK PLACE DURING HIS MINORITY.

RICHARD II (1377–99)

Richard II reigned for more than twenty-two years and in that time he
stayed at Reading between 10 and 12 times, staying for a total of at least
46 days (see figure 21). This is an average of two days per year, but his
stays were very unevenly distributed through his reign. Most of his time at
Reading was concentrated in three periods; 1381, 1384–87 and 1389, but
even in those years he spent no major feast at Reading.[107] It should be remembered, too, that for the first two of these periods Richard was a minor
(he was born in January 1367), and that since he succeeded to the throne
as a ten-year old, he initially had to exercise his kingship with the aid of a
series of continual councils.

The perceived danger was that John of Gaunt, Duke of Lancaster, who
had effectively ruled England in the name of the ailing Edward III since
the Black Prince's last illness reached its final stages early in 1376, would
usurp the throne, and he was accordingly excluded from the council. The
Reading visit of 5–14 August 1381 included the Great Council called for
10 August. This was a key council, intended to emphasise the restoration

[107]   For Richard's Itinerary, see Saul (1997), 71–92.

of normality after the Peasants' Revolt. New ministers were appointed: Hugh Segrave, previously Steward of the Household, was elevated to the post of Treasurer in place of Sir Robert Hales, who had been beheaded by the rebels on Tower Hill the month before, and Sir John Montague replaced him as Steward. William Courtenay, a younger son of the Earls of Devon, only recently elevated to the see of Canterbury, was made Lord Chancellor.[108] This council also saw the return of John of Gaunt to the main political arena after his mission to conclude a peace treaty with the Scots. The leaders of the Peasants' Revolt had identified the duke as a target for execution, largely because he was responsible for introducing the first Poll Tax in 1376, and they had destroyed Savoy Palace, his great London home. He was thus both angry at the destruction of his property and the slurs cast on his good name, and uncertain of his reception at court, and it took a personal appeal from King Richard to secure his return to the scene of his wedding more than twenty years before. His appointment on 18 August as sole justice of the king to hear and determine all crimes connected with the Revolt must be seen as a move to reassure and placate him.[109] Gaunt's main quarrel was with Henry Percy, Earl of Northumberland, and at the root of it lay Gaunt's commission as the king's lieutenant in the Marches, renewed in May 1381.[110] Percy saw this as an intrusion by the Duke of Lancaster into his own traditional sphere of influence, and the situation was worsened by the duke's strong support for Percy's rivals in the north, the Nevilles. When Gaunt came under threat from the Peasants' Revolt that summer, Percy refused him shelter and he was forced to return to Scotland. The ill-feeling between the two magnates was simmering at the council of Reading, and came to a head at a later council at Berkhamstead in early October, when an argument in the king's presence led to Percy losing his temper and challenging the duke to single combat (a fight that never took place).[111]

In 1384 there was a trial at Reading Abbey involving John Northampton, a draper who had been mayor of London in 1381–83. Northampton's term of office was marked by initiatives intended to alleviate the conditions of the city's poorest citizens, which were strenuously opposed by the better established guilds, notably the victuallers. His public profile brought him to the attention of John of Gaunt, Duke of Lancaster, an occasional but by no means a reliable supporter. Northampton failed in his bid for re-election for a third term in 1383, and was promptly arrested by the successful candidate, the strongly royalist Nicholas Brembre, on grounds

[108] Tout (1920), 3, 377–78; Westminster Chronicle, 18–21.
[109] CPR 1381–85, 77. See also Anon. Chron., 152–54; Chron. Angliae 327–29; Chron. Knighton, 2, 144–49.
[110] See Storey (1957), 595–96.
[111] Tout (1920), 3, 379.

of sedition, and he was brought to trial on this charge before the king at a general council held in Reading in mid- August 1384. The main witness for the prosecution was Thomas Usk, a former copyist and confidential secretary of Northampton's, who had been arrested in July or August and persuaded to testify against his former master. He seems to have done this with enthusiasm, producing a literate *Appeal* (or legal accusation) against Northampton that he read out to the king and council. Northampton's behaviour at his trial was stubborn and disrespectful, which annoyed the king. According to the Westminster Chronicler's account the last straw came when the king, exasperated by the prisoner's behaviour, proposed to proceed to judgement. Northampton's response that this was impossible in the absence of John of Gaunt, provoked Richard to remark that he was competent to sit in judgement on Northampton and on the Duke of Lancaster as well. He sentenced him to be drawn and hanged, and all his goods to be forfeit, but the queen intervened on Northampton's behalf and the sentence was commuted to lifelong imprisonment and he was taken away to Corfe Castle.[112] By the end of October, he and his associates, the mercers Richard Norbury and John More, had been sentenced to death by hanging, but his sentence was reduced to ten years' imprisonment, and he was pardoned in 1386, but still banished from London.[113]

Richard's long stay at Reading in 1389 included a council called for 10 December. That spring Richard had declared himself of an age to rule,[114] and in November John of Gaunt returned from a three-year absence in Spain, where he had been unsuccessfully attempting to claim the throne by right of his marriage in 1371 to Constanza, the exiled elder daughter of the murdered Pedro I of Castile. After landing in Plymouth, the Duke of Lancaster immediately proceeded to the King's council at Reading with a large following. Richard rode out two miles to greet him, and welcomed him courteously with a kiss of peace. This pleasant atmosphere continued at the council, when the duke's first action was to renew his friendship with the Earl of Northumberland.[115] There were 19 council members present at Reading on that day: the four clerics were the Archbishop of York (Thomas Arundel, 1353 – 1414), the bishops of Winchester (William of Wykeham, 1320–1404), and St David's (John Gilbert, d. 1397), and the prior of the Hospital of St John of Jerusalem (John Radington, d. 1406). The three dukes were all children of Edward III: John of Gaunt (1340–99), Duke of Lancaster; Edmund of Langley (1341–1402), Duke of York; and Thomas of Woodstock (1355–97), Duke of Gloucester. There were six earls: Thomas Holland (c. 1350–97), earl of Kent; Richard FitzAlan (1346–97),

---

112   Westminster Chronicle, 90–93; CPR 1381–85, 2, 470.
113   He received a full pardon in 1390 and his citizenship was restored in 1395.
114   This was at the council held at Westminster on 3 May 1389.
115   Westminster Chronicle, 406–09.

earl of Arundel; John Holland (c. 1352–1400), earl of Huntingdon; Henry of Bolingbroke (1366–1413), Earl of Derby; Henry Percy (1341–1408), Earl of Northumberland; and the Earl Marshall, Thomas Mowbray, Earl of Nottingham (1366–99). The barons were represented by John, 4th Baron Beaumont, and John, 5th Baron Lovell. Finally there were four knights: William Neville, Lewis Clifford; Richard Storey and Richard Adderbury.[116]

Even a cursory glance at the list will show that Richard had assembled a group of men whose interests had conflicted, either with his own or among themselves, sometimes violently, in the earlier part of his reign. The longstanding enmity between Lancaster and Northumberland has already been mentioned, and in addition Lancaster had clashed with Wykeham in the last years of Edward III's reign when the bishop was accused of mismanagement of royal policy while he was chancellor and stripped of the temporalities of his see. By the end of the reign he had been restored to favour, and the new king gave him a full pardon, but it is hard to imagine that he and Lancaster were the best of friends. Four council members, Gloucester, Arundel, Bolingbroke and Nottingham, were among the Lords Appellant who had stripped Richard of his friends and advisors in 1387–88, accusing them of treason. The reprisals were bloody, and caused a rift between the Duke of Gloucester and his more tolerant brother of York. Huntingdon was Gaunt's man at this time, accompanying him on his Spanish adventure but returning in 1388. He was approached by the Lords Appellant, who might have wanted to recruit Gaunt through him, but resisted them and was later to be Richard's lieutenant in his revenge against them in 1397. John Gilbert was also a close associate of John of Gaunt throughout his life. William Neville was the younger brother of Alexander, Archbishop of York, a former advisor of Richard who was accused of treason by the Lords Appellant in 1387.

William Neville, Lewis Clifford and Richard Stury were named among the Lollard Knights, a group of influential courtiers who were accused by contemporaries of promoting heretical doctrines based on the writings of the Oxford theologian John Wycliffe.[117] A key feature of Wycliffe's reform movement was criticism of the church and its wealth, a stance that was attractive to many at court, including Richard himself and, initially, John of Gaunt – although the latter changed his views in the face of Wycliffe's stance on the Eucharist (he denied the doctrine of transubstantiation). The Archbishop of Canterbury, William Courtenay, had condemned Lollardy in 1382, and many of Wycliffe's Oxford supporters were arrested and forced to recant. Unsurprisingly the churchmen on the council were opponents of the Lollards, particularly Thomas Arundel.

[116] Privy Council, v.1, 17.
[117] Chron. Knighton, 2, 295; Annales Ricardi secondi, 174. See also McFarlane (1972).

HENRY IV (1399–1413)

The itinerary compiled by Wylie has Henry IV at Reading for just one long visit before his second marriage, from 9 to 20 January 1403.[118] The king's future wife Joanna of Navarre, the widow of John V of Brittany, was collected from Brest by a squadron of twenty large ships that had sailed over from Plymouth for her. She went on board on 13 January, and next morning they set sail for Southampton, but they lost their course, and after five days at sea landed at Falmouth in Cornwall on 19 January 1403. The king meanwhile was on a leisurely progress from Windsor, where he had spent Christmas, to Winchester for the wedding. He slept at Easthampstead on 8 January and arrived at Reading on the following day. Here, on 15 January, he took delivery of a large consignment of rich cloth of gold as a present for his bride-to-be (for which the country had to pay £200). He moved on to Farnham on 20 January, then Clarendon and entered Winchester with Joanna on 4 February. After a lavish feast they were married in Winchester on 7 February.[119]

HENRY V (1413–22)

In Henry V's 3,452-day reign he spent less than half his time in England (1,521 days), and only eleven days in Reading: a single visit between 5 and 15 May 1417.[120] This was the occasion of a council reported in biblical language by Adam Usk, who declared that

> a decree went out from Caesar to compile a record of anyone in the world who had money, and having thus been summoned they emptied their coffers. Then, having first of all banned all Irishmen from the kingdom, the lord king set off with a great army to make war in Normandy, destroying on the way a French fleet which was lying in wait for him.[121]

The wording of this writ allowed a good deal of flexibility to the tax collectors, who were authorised to demand the loans they considered reasonable from whoever they thought could pay.[122]

Despite the king's absence from Reading he was well aware of what the abbey offered. On 20 April 1414, he made a grant for life to William Bruer, a servant and carter of his grandfather the Duke of Lancaster, who had become blind and unable to look after himself in his old age. Bruer was given a chamber within the Hospital of St Mary Magdalene by Reading.

---

[118]   Wylie (1884), 4, 290.
[119]   Ibid., 1., 310; 2., 288 n; 4., 201, 290.
[120]   Mowat (1919), 123, 322.
[121]   Adam Usk, 264–65.
[122]   Rymer, 4 pt2, 199–200; Mowat (1919), 123.

He was fed from the kitchen of the abbey every day, and given two loaves of bread a day, one white and the other called copyn, presumably a lower grade of loaf, along with a gallon of ale. Every year he was to receive two cartloads of wood for fuel.[123]

HENRY VI (1422–61, 1470–71)

When Henry VI came to the throne in 1422 he was just nine months old, and he only took the reins of power in 1437 when he was 15. His first visit to Reading thereafter was in January 1438, and between then and his capture by the earls of Warwick and Salisbury at the battle of Northampton in 1460 he paid six more visits to the abbey, staying for a total of 88 days. The bulk of this time was taken up by two stays of more than a month each. The first was the continuation of a parliament that began in Westminster on 12 November 1439 and was adjourned to Reading on 14 January 1440. The parliament was mostly about money, or the lack of it. There were complaints from royal household staff and from judicial officers that they had not been paid, in some cases since the reign of the king's grandfather. Since he had assumed power himself, Henry's own expenses had rocketed because he had a larger and more active household than ever before. One measure taken to ensure solvency was the assignation of the revenues from the duchies of Lancaster and Cornwall to the treasurer of the household, and another was the imposition of a tax on all non-English (or non-Welsh) residents of the realm; 16d a year for householders and 6d from non-householders.[124] This chimed with a general xenophobia that had followed from the English reverses in France; notably the Congress of Arras and the subsequent Treaty (1435), in which an agreement between France and Burgundy effectively led to England's main ally in the war against France changing sides.[125]

By the time of the second Reading parliament, held in the abbey refectory in March-April 1453, matters were no better but worse.[126] The House of Lancaster was bankrupt, and on the continent only Calais and parts of Gascony remained in English hands. Henry was fortunate that the speaker was the pro-Lancastrian and vastly experienced Thomas Thorp, who presided over a parliament that has been described as 'the most royalist and accommodating parliament with which he had had to deal'.[127] To address the French problem, the Commons authorised a subsidy of a fifteenth of the value of all moveable goods to pay for the enlistment of

[123]   CPR 1413–16, 202.
[124]   Privy Council, 5, 421; Griffiths (1981), 310–11; Chron. London, 153.
[125]   Griffiths (1981), 551.
[126]   Rot. Parl., 5, 227; Parry (1839), 186.
[127]   Griffiths (1981), 699. On Thorp, see Wedgwood and Holt (1936), 849–51.

20,000 archers, and funds to pay them for six months.[128] Further draconi-
an taxes were levied on foreigners whereby alien merchants were assessed
at 40 shillings and travellers visiting for less than six months at 20 shillings. After Easter the parliament moved to Westminster until 2 July, when
it was adjourned again, proposing to resume at Reading on the feast of
St Martin (11 November), but when that day came the chancellor, John
Kemp, recently created Archbishop of Canterbury and Cardinal-Bishop
of Santa Rufina, arrived at the abbey, only to defer the parliament again.[129]
It resumed at Reading on 11 February the next year, and was immediately
moved to Westminster.[130] The king was not there and the Duke of York
presided in his place.[131]

These postponements stemmed directly from the king's sudden onset
of illness in early August 1453. He was at the royal hunting lodge at
Clarendon, when he fell suddenly into a stupor that rendered him unable
to communicate. What brought this on is a matter for speculation but
it has been suggested that the sudden shock of hearing the news of the
destruction in July of an English army at the Battle of Castillon, which
effectively ended the English presence in France, might have been responsible. After this he remained in a totally uncommunicative state for
several months, unable to recognise or respond to visitors or to walk or
even stand unaided. These episodes continued for the rest of his life. He
slept for much of the time and spent his few waking hours in religious
devotion. Between mid-August 1456 until his capture by the Yorkists, he
spent fully one third of his time in monasteries, including Reading, where
he stayed for a short visit in December 1457.[132]

EDWARD IV (1461–70, 1471–83)

Public records point to two visits to Reading by King Edward, corresponding with a council in 1464 and a parliament in 1467. On May Day
1464 Edward IV secretly married Elizabeth Woodville, a famous beauty,
but a widow five years Edward's senior who already had two sons by her
first husband, Sir John Grey of Groby, a distinguished Lancastrian soldier
killed fighting against Edward's forces at the second battle of St Albans in
1461. Edward and Elizabeth kept their marriage secret until September,
when Edward made an announcement at the council meeting at Reading.
Scofield placed the announcement on 14 September 1464, but a date a
week or so later seems more likely in view of the chancery records that

[128]   Benet's Chronicle, 209.
[129]   Ibid., 209–10.
[130]   HBC, 569–70.
[131]   Benet's Chronicle, 211.
[132]   Wolffe (1981), 305 n.

have the king at Reading from 19 September to 4 October.[133] The scene at Reading was the subject of a 1923 painting by Ernest Board, one of those commissioned by Hurry (plate XIV). This shows King Edward leading Elizabeth Woodville up the chancel steps of the abbey church. Her train-bearers are her two sons, Richard and Thomas Grey, while others depicted are Abbot John Thorne I on the extreme left, and (behind the queen) the Earl of Warwick in a green doublet and hose, the Duke of Clarence in red, and Elizabeth's father Richard Woodville in a gold doublet.

The 1467 parliament was called for Westminster on 3 June 1467.[134] On 1 July it was prorogued (or deferred without being dissolved) to Reading by the chancellor, Robert Stillington, Bishop of Bath and Wells on account of the prevalence of the *plagam pestilentiae*. Representatives of the three estates duly assembled at Reading 'in a chamber *infra abbaciam de Redynge*', where the king authorized the chancellor to prorogue the parliament to 5 May of the following year, this time on account of 'the present shortness of the days and the nature of the season'. Parliament assembled again on that date, only to be prorogued again for a week to allow it to be moved back to Westminster.[135]

RICHARD III (1483–85)

Within a fortnight of his coronation on 6 July 1483, Richard set out on a major public progress of his realm. He left London with a large and impressive train including the Duke of Buckingham, five bishops and four earls on a journey that was to take him through Windsor, Reading, Oxford, Gloucester, Worcester, Coventry, Leicester, Nottingham and Pontefract to York, which he reached on 29 August.[136] He arrived at Reading on 21 July, and remained there until 23 July, when he sealed an indenture swearing to Katherine Neville that she would not suffer through the treachery of her late husband, William Hastings, whom Richard had had summarily beheaded after accusing him of conspiring against him with the Woodvilles and his mistress Jane Shore.[137] By the following day he had moved on to Oxford, and he never returned.

---

[133] Scofield (1923), II, 354; CPR 1461–67, 327–83; CCR 1461–68, 216–73.
[134] HBC, 571.
[135] Parry (1839), 191.
[136] Edwards (1983), passim; PRO C81/886/13; Howard Accounts, 411.
[137] Horrox and Hammond (1979–82), 2, 4–5 (Harley 433 f. 108v – 109r).

HENRY VII (1485–1509)

Although there is no direct evidence for this, King Henry VII might have been in Reading in the first year of his reign, when The Royal Grammar School was founded by Abbot Thorne in the refectory of the former Hospitium of St John, which had been suppressed by 1480 (figure 22). According to Leland,

> Henry the vij. cumming to Reading, and asking what old house (i.e. the Hospitium) that was, thabbate told hym and the the king wylid himto convert the house self and the landes *in pios usus*. Wherapon thabbate desirid that it might be made a grammar-schole, and so it was.[138]

The Privy Purse expenses have Henry VII at Reading on 19 August 1494, and on 16 June 1497, and the Patent Rolls record a single stay from 11 to 15 October 1505.[139] There is also some evidence that Prince Arthur stayed at Reading from time to time, presumably while en route from London to his lands in the west.

Arthur was Henry VII's firstborn son, born in 1486 and heir to the throne until his sudden death in 1502. He was prepared from his birth to be an educated Christian king, instilled with knightly virtues. From his infancy he had his own council and household, based from 1493 in Ludlow, intended to teach him how to rule,[140] and as part of this process he travelled around the Welsh Marches learning to administer an itinerant household and to dispense justice in the king's name.[141] This was interrupted in the autumn of 1501 by his marriage to Katherine of Aragon, daughter of Ferdinand of Aragon and Isabella of Castile, a dynastic alliance that Henry VII had been planning since Arthur was two. After two proxy marriages in 1497 and 1500, when Katherine was represented by Dr Rodrigo Gonzales de Puebla, a Jewish diplomat employed by Katherine's parents for the purpose, Katherine herself arrived at Plymouth on 2 October 1501 after a nightmarish journey over land and sea from Granada that took five months in all.[142] Her progress to the capital was a slow and ceremonious one – apparently too slow for Henry who set out from Richmond on 4 November to meet up with the Princess, despite having been told by the Prothonotary of Spain that her parents had forbidden her from conversing with either the King or her husband-to-be before the day of the marriage. The two parties met up at Dogmersfield (Hants), shortly to be joined by

---

[138] Leland Itineraries, 1, 110.
[139] Excerpta Historica, 99, 112; CPR 1494–1509, 444, 452.
[140] Gunn (2009), 7–10.
[141] Ibid., 10–15.
[142] CSP (Spain), 1485–1509, 299–306.

22 THE HOSPITIUM OF ST JOHN, NOW A CHILDREN'S NURSERY, WAS MADE INTO A GRAMMAR SCHOOL ON
THE INSTRUCTIONS OF HENRY VII IN 1485.

Prince Arthur.[143] Arthur's movements are not known in any detail for this
period, but what is known is that he was at Reading Abbey at some time
in October, presumably breaking his journey to London from the West
Country, when a 'riding gowne of cremysyne velwet' was sent to him from
London.[144]

The marriage was solemnized at St Paul's Cathedral on 14 November
when Arthur was just fifteen and Katherine almost sixteen, and the young
couple went to live at Arthur's castle of Ludlow. Within a few months, both
were taken ill, probably with the sweating sickness. Katherine fought it off,
but Arthur died on 2 April 1502. As described in chapter two, Arthur's
mother, Elizabeth of York, the daughter of Edward IV and Elizabeth
Woodville, responded to the news of their sickness by going on a pilgrimage by proxy, including the Child of Grace at Reading in the itinerary.[145]

---

[143] Ibid., 306.
[144] Gunn (2009), 12.
[145] Elizabeth of York Privy Purse Expenses, 3. Barton visited the shrines of Our Lady
and St George, the Holy Cross and the shrine of King Henry (VI) at Windsor;

Another incident involving a stay at Reading took place in the following year and concerned King Philip of Castile and his queen Joanna, daughter of King Ferdinand of Aragon. Under Ferdinand, the kingdoms of Aragon and Castile had been united, but he had governed Castile in right of his wife, Isabella I, and when she died in 1504 that right passed to her daughter Joanna, married to the Habsburg Philip the Handsome, titular Duke of Burgundy. In January 1506, Philip and Joanna set sail from Zeeland bound for their kingdom of Castile, but they hit a storm in the English Channel and were compelled to land in England, either at Falmouth or at Melcombe Regis, near Weymouth.[146] King Philip sent his secretary Anthoine le Flameng to seek out the King of England, tell him what had happened, and ask for permission to visit him. This was given, and the two kings met at Windsor on 31 January. They apparently enjoyed one another's company, and on 9 February Philip was admitted to the Order of the Garter. Meanwhile their respective counsellors had been preparing a peace treaty between their two nations, and this was signed by the kings after mass on the same day.[147] On the following day Queen Joanna arrived at Windsor, but she left shortly afterwards to rejoin her fleet, which was lying at Dartmouth and Plymouth, spending a night at Reading Abbey on the way, where she was received honourably by the abbot, John Thorne II.[148] King Philip meanwhile spent another three weeks in King Henry's company 'in recreation', and apparently largely at Richmond. During their time together, King Philip volunteered, according to the official account, to give up Edmund, Earl of Suffolk, the leading Yorkist claimant to the English throne, who had fled to the continent and taken refuge with Philip's father Maximilian I, the Holy Roman Emperor.

After their stay at Richmond, the two kings parted, Henry to return to Windsor and Philip to rejoin his queen and the fleet. Like Joanna he headed first for Reading, but he was feeling feverish, either on account of the Lenten diet or the bad weather, and spent eight or ten days there recuperating before the journey. While he was at Reading he wrote to his father-in-law, Ferdinand of Aragon, a letter dated 8 March 1506.[149] He rejoined his queen at Exeter, and they continued their journey to Castile.

This Spanish episode was recorded in an anonymous Flemish chronicle, which described the Reading Philip visited as a *bonne ville et grosse*

Our Lady at Eton; the Child of Grace at Reading; Our Lady of Caversham; Our Lady of Cokethorp; the Holy Blood of Hayles; Prince Edward's shrine; Our Lady of Worcester; the Holy Rood and Our Lady of Grace at Northampton; Our Lady of Walsingham; Our Lady of Sudbury; Our Lady of Wolpitte; Our Lady of Ipswich and Our Lady of Stokeclare.

[146] Gachard (1874–82), 1, 407–09, Tighe (1858), 1, 434–44.
[147] CSP (Spain), 1485–1509, 380–81.
[148] Tighe (1858), 1, 443.
[149] Gairdner (1861–63), 2, 365.

abbaye de noirs moinnes et beau parck.[150] The park was the abbey's park at Whitley a few miles to the south of the abbey, established as early as the 1160s by the Abbot of Reading.[151] After the Dissolution, in 1548, the park and manor of Whitley were granted to Edward, Duke of Somerset, and the wording of the grant makes it clear that this was a park for hunting.

> The whole park and liberty of a park in Whitley, Berks, with all the game and deer, male and female; all which belonged to Redying monastery.[152]

It was shown on Pride's map of 1790, but only survives today in scattered patches of woodland in a loop of the M4 south of Reading town centre, and in topographical names in the area.

Henry VII died on 21 April 1509, and the Abbot of Reading, John Thorne II (abbot 1486–1519) played an important role in the ritual surrounding his funeral. The king's body was taken to St Paul's Cathedral on 11 May, where it was received and borne into the church, the ritual conducted by the Bishop of London assisted by the Abbots of Reading and St Albans. On the following day the corpse was solemnly borne back to the chariot and conveyed through Fleet Street and Charing Cross, where the abbots of Westminster, St. Albans, Reading and Winchcombe, revested and mitred, with the whole convent of Westminster, met and accompanied it to the west door of Westminster abbey; and there the Archbishops of Canterbury and York received and censed it. On the third day, three masses were sung, respectively by the Abbot of Westminster, the Bishop of Winchester and the Archbishop of Canterbury. The Abbot of Reading assisted at the second of these.[153]

HENRY VIII (1509–47)

Until Henry VIII had been on the throne for more than twenty years, relations between the abbots and the king continued much as they had before. On 17 July 1509, two months after his father's funeral, the new king wrote to his father-in-law Ferdinand of Aragon a letter in which he outlined his immediate plans. He would not neglect affairs of state, he wrote, but in the meantime he was diverting himself with jousts, birding, hunting and other innocent and honest pastimes, also in visiting different parts of his kingdom.[154] The park at Reading was a familiar hunting ground for him and his father, and Reading was one of the two places

[150] Gachard (1874–82), 1, 429.
[151] Hatherley and Cantor (1980), 78.
[152] CPR 1548–49, 28–29.
[153] L and P Henry VIII 1509–14 (2nd ed.), 10–21.
[154] Cal. State Papers Spain, II, July 1509.

that we know he visited during that first progress, the other being the Old Hall at Gainsborough.[155] This set a pattern of progresses that was to be repeated almost every summer of his reign, and Reading usually featured in these itineraries, both before and after its Dissolution in 1539.[156] In August 1529, for example, he visited with Anne Boleyn, having ordered Queen Katherine to be removed from court. The couple left Greenwich early in the month, going to Reading by way of Barnet and Tittenhanger. He was in Woodstock by 25 August, and stayed there until 12 September, hunting and amusing himself with Anne while leaving Wolsey to look after affairs of state.[157] Henry was also at Reading on 6 July 1535, quite possibly hunting, as Alison Weir suggests, while his former Lord Chancellor was beheaded on Tower Hill.[158] In 1525 the king sent his nine-year old daughter Mary to the Welsh Marches to preside over the council of Wales and the Marches, accompanied by a large entourage headed by Lord Ferrers as Steward and Lord Dudley as Chamberlain, and including Bishop Veysey of Exeter as President of a council of around a dozen distinguished lawyers.[159] On her way west she stayed at Reading for several days in August, receiving a gift of victuals valued at £17 12 0d from the Abbot.[160]

EPIDEMICS

In 1517 the country was hit by a plague of the sweating sickness, a fast-acting disease that could kill within four hours of the first symptoms appearing. Since the first symptom was a slight headache, the country was soon in a state of panic. We have an account of the disease from Francesco Chieregato, Pope Leo X's nuncio in England:

> To some it proved fatal in 12 hours, to others in six, to others in four hours. It was an easy death. Most patients were seized with the disease in a recumbent position, but some even standing, and some walking; some very few persons having taken the disease on horseback. The sweat lasted 24 hours, more or less. During the fit it was fatal to take any cold beverage, or to allow any air to penetrate the garments or bed clothes in which the patient commenced perspiring. It was necessary to have rather more covering than usual, though even in this great caution was needed, as some had been suffocated by a more than requisite amount of covering. The bedchamber should have a moderate fire, so as not to heat the room, but to keep it at a tepid temperature; the arms should

---

155   Weir (2001), 114.
156   Thurley (1991), 240 identifies nine visits before the Dissolution and one afterwards but this must be a minimum estimate.
157   L and P Henry VIII, 1524–30, dviii-dix.
158   L and P Henry VIII Jan – July 1535, 391–92; Weir (2001), 365.
159   Robinson (1998), 236–37.
160   L and P Henry VIII, 1524–30, 707–11; Robinson (1998), 243–50.

THE ABBEY AND THE COURT

be crossed on the patient's breast, and great care be taken lest the least air reach the arm-pits. To neglect these precautions insured immediate death.[161]

The sweating sickness was not always fatal; indeed Cardinal Wolsey seemed to be a frequent sufferer, surviving while his servants died around him.[162] In August 1517 he wrote to the king complaining that he had been 'so vexed with the sweat he dare not yet come to his presence,' and announced his intention of setting off for Walsingham and to Our Lady of Grace in fulfilment of a vow he had taken to ensure his recovery.[163]

Wolsey was well aware of the king's almost paranoid fear of the disease, and after disappearing for the winter it came back with renewed force in the following spring, forcing the King to move his court to Richmond (18 March) then to Reading (24 March) and Abingdon (27 March).[164] The sweating sickness recurred in 1528 and in 1551, after which it apparently disappeared, but it was not the only epidemic the king feared. In 1536 and 1537 he was receiving reports of deaths from the bubonic plague epidemic in those years. One such, a letter from Sir Francis Bryan to Sir Thomas Cromwell dated 17 July 1537, illustrates the difficulties of planning a journey that would avoid exposing the king to infection.

> I hear they die at Reading, and am sure they do at Thame and also within a mile of Mr. Williams' house at Buckingham. The King might come from Est-hampstead to Bishops Owburne, thence to Berkhampstead, 12 miles, thence to Eston, my lady Bray's, 7 miles, for neither my Lord nor my Lady is at home. Then to Whaddon, 7 miles, and thence to Grafton, 7 miles. These houses would be sufficient for the King as the Queen is not coming, 'and, thanked be God, all clerear as yt' (clear air as yet). They die at Tosseter very sore. Orders should be given that none of the King's servants nor of the town 'come there.' Stony Stratford, Northampton, Brickhill, Hanslap, Olney, Newport Panell, Woburn, Dunstable, St. Albans, Ampthill, Hitchin, and Hertford, are as yet clear, Tyddington somewhat infected. If the King please, he may go from Ampthill to Hitchin, and so to Hertford, and on to Hunsdon.[165]

CONCLUSION

We have reached the point beyond which matters would begin to turn sour for Reading and for English monasticism in general. It is clear, however, that between the foundation early in the twelfth century and the early sixteenth, abbeys like Reading had fulfilled a valuable function for the

---

[161] CSP Venice 1509–19, 410–18.
[162] L and P Henry VIIII 1515–18, 1149–50. Giustiniani reports on the 27 August 1517 that the Cardinal is ill with it for the fourth time.
[163] L and P Henry VIII 1515–18, 1538.
[164] L and P Henry VIII, 1515–18, 1243, 1246, 1247–48.
[165] L and P Henry VIII, June–Dec 1537, 115.

monarchy as focusses for devotion, but equally importantly as residences on the royal itinerary, as grand conference and hospitality centres for councils and less formal meetings, and as centres of charity where faithful retainers could be rewarded. The ways in which this situation was to change with shocking rapidity are the matter of the next chapter.

5

DISSOLUTION AND DILAPIDATION

HUGH COOK OF FARINGDON – HIS CAREER AND RELATIONSHIP WITH HENRY VIII

Abbot Thorne, who had assisted at the funeral of Henry VII, died in January 1519 and was succeeded by Thomas Worcester, a Reading monk who was himself dead by 28 July 1520.[1] The former sub-chamberlain of the abbey, Hugh Cook (who took the name of Faringdon, perhaps from his birthplace), was confirmed as the new abbot on 26 September in the presence of the Dean of Windsor, John Clerk, and the Dean of Sarum, John Longland.[2] Two days later the king arrived at Reading Abbey and was presented with a generous gift of fish.[3] He stayed for Michaelmas, and was reported by his secretary Richard Pace to be contented with the new abbot.[4] Abbot Hugh was one of only nine abbots to find his way onto the King's New Year gift lists.[5] These records of gifts exchanged between Henry and his intimates survive for the years 1528, 1532, 1534 and 1539, although the 1528 list is a rough draft only, with no useful details. All the abbots received gilt silverware from the king: generally cruses or cups with covers, made to order by the royal goldsmiths, and carefully weighed. In return they gave him money in a purse. Abbot Hugh gave the king a gift of £20 in each of the three years: in a purse of white leather in 1532; in gold

---

[1] L and P Henry VIII, 1519–23, 342.
[2] Ibid., 370.
[3] Ibid.
[4] Ibid., 368–69.
[5] L and P Henry VIII, 1531–32, 327–29. These lists are most conveniently accessed in Hayward (2005). The other abbots were those of Westminster, Southwark, Glastonbury, Ramsey (Cambs), Peterborough, St Albans, Waltham and Abingdon (Ibid., 147, 165 and notes).

in 1534, and in a purse of crimson velvet in 1539. In return he received, in 1532, a gilt cruse and cover weighing 23¾ oz; in 1534, a gilt cup with a cover weighing 23⅛ oz, and in 1539 a gilt cup with a cover weighing 22¾ oz.

When Henry was seeking to end his marriage to Katherine of Aragon in 1530, Abbot Hugh was among the spiritual lords who petitioned Pope Clement VII on his behalf,[6] and as late as 1536 he supplied men to oppose the great insurrection in northern England. In the following year, on 24 October, Queen Jane Seymour died of postnatal complications a fortnight after giving birth to Henry VIII's only male heir, Edward. She was given an elaborate state funeral, the only one of Henry's queens to be honoured in this way, in which the Abbot of Reading played an important role. Her body lay in the chapel at Hampton Court until 11 November, and from 1 November until then masses were conducted by a series of clerics, including the Abbot of Reading who took the first Sunday mass, on 4 November. On 12 November the body was transported to Windsor for burial, and again Abbot Hugh was among the clergy who assisted the Archbishop of Canterbury in the choir.[7]

In December 1537, Abbot Hugh wrote to Thomas Cromwell, Henry VIII's Chief Minister, to report that 'there is sprung up in our country the most lamentable tidings that ever was, that the king and the Lord Marquis of Exeter are dead'.[8] This disclosure sparked off a witch-hunt carried out by Sir Walter Stoner, Sir William Essex and Thomas Vachell to discover the original source of the false rumour. It was traced to various people, each of whom could point to another from whom they had heard it, until the trail reached one Edward Lyttelworke, a fuller, who could not provide a source for the rumour. For punishment, he was

> set on the pillory there [i.e. at Wallingford] one ower in the myddest of the market day, his years fast nayled, and after to be cut of by the hard hed, and then he to be tyed to a cartys ayrse, and to be strypped naked to the wast of his body, and so to be whypped round aboute the towne; whyche was don on fryday in the myddest of the market then holden at Wallyngford afforeseyd; and from thens the same day the said Edward was delivered to the mayre and officers of Redyng, and ther on Saterday, being market day ther, he was sett on the pyllory by one ower space and then and there whypped round about the same towne, as he was at Wallyngford aforseyd; and at Redyng he remaynyth in gayle styll untyll the Kyng's pleasure be further therein declared.[9]

---

6   L and P Henry VIII, 1524–30, 2929–30.
7   L and P Henry VIII, Jun–Dec 1537, 372–74.
8   Ibid., 423.
9   Ibid., 441.

THE DISSOLUTION OF READING ABBEY AND THE DEATH OF HUGH COOK

In searching for the cause of what appears to be a rapid degeneration in the relationship between the Abbot and the King, that was to lead to the former's gruesome death, it is a mistake to look for personal reasons. While Hugh had no difficulty in acknowledging Henry as his temporal ruler, he could not deny a spiritual duty to Christ and his earthly representative, the Pope. The king, perhaps foreseeing uncomfortable times ahead, placed the execution of his policies firmly in the hands of a series of Chief Ministers: Wolsey, More and, in the key period, Thomas Cromwell. Under Cromwell's direction a series of Acts designed to exclude the papacy and bring the church totally under royal control followed in the next few years. By Acts of 1532 and 1534 payment of annates, or first-fruits, was transferred from the papacy to the Crown. In 1533 appeals from England to Rome were abolished, and in the following year all the other legal rights and duties of the Pope were transferred to the King. In 1534 too the Act of Supremacy declared that the king was the supreme head of the Church in England: this act did not contain the reservation 'as far as the Law of Christ allows' previously inserted by the clergy in Convocation.

With these instruments in place to free him from any possibility of intervention from Rome, Cromwell could turn his attention to the owners of landed wealth, the monasteries. In 1535 he appointed two commissioners, Richard Layton and Thomas Legh, to visit the southern monasteries. Their report, known as the 'Black Book', was presented to Parliament in 1536, and in the same year an act dissolving the smaller monastic houses, those valued at less than £200 per year, was passed. The reason given was the immorality discovered by the two commissioners. The Court of Augmentations, also set up in 1536, administered the transfer of possessions of dissolved monasteries to the Crown, while their inmates were either pensioned off or transferred to larger houses.

Attention now turned to the greater houses. Visitors toured the country persuading the monks to accept the dissolution of their monasteries, and offering pensions. Since it was rumoured that dissolution would soon be compulsory anyway, many of them were easy to persuade, and the first surrenders were as early as November 1537. This had been envisaged in the 1536 Act, and another act of 1539 vested in the crown the possessions of houses that had been surrendered. By and large, surrender was a peaceful affair, but the 1539 Act paved the way for coping with concerted resistance by adding that treason would also result in forfeiture, which meant in effect that an abbey would be forcibly dissolved if its abbot was convicted of treason. Hugh Cook (Faringdon) of Reading, John Beche of Colchester and Richard Whiting of Glastonbury were present in the House of Lords in April 1539 when the act granting to the crown the houses of abbots attainted of treason was passed, and apparently none of them made any objection. Between April and September all three abbots were again asked to surrender their monasteries voluntarily, and their refusal to do so seems to have been interpreted as loyalty to the Holy See, equivalent to High Treason.

The trial of Hugh Cook apparently followed regular precedents.[10] On 27 October a commission was issued to the Sheriff of Berkshire, Sir John Baldewyn, and Sir William Essex and others, authorising them to try cases of treason. This was followed on 3 November by a writ to the Sheriff summoning twenty-four good and lawful men to act as a jury in such cases.[11] The indictment of Hugh Cook states that he clearly asserted and strongly maintained the authority of the Pope, while those of his fellows, John Eynon and John Rugge, indicate that they denied the royal supremacy. In this document Hugh Cook is reported as saying:

> the king is nott supreme hedde of the Churche of Englond. And I trust to see the Pope bere as greate a rule in Englond as ever he dyd shortly. And I wyll saye masses ons every Weke for hym.[12]

Finally the *Inquisicio*, or report of the trial, indicates that all three men pleaded not guilty, but were found guilty and given the appropriate sentence.

> *quod predicti Hugo Abbas monasterii de Readyng predicta Johannes Eynon et Johannes Rugge ducantur per prefatum Vicecomiten usque Gaolam domini Regis ville de Redyng predicta. Et deinde per medium ville de Readyng predicta directe usque ad locum execucionis separatim trahantur et super furcas ibidem suspendantur. Et quilibet eorum vivens ad terram prosternatur et interiora sua extra ventrem suum capiantur ipsisque viventibus comburentur et capita eorum amputentur. Quodque corpus cuiuslibet eorum in quattuor partes dividatur. Ac quod capita et quarteria illa ponantur ubi dominus Rex ea assignare voluerit.*[13]

(that the aforesaid Hugh Abbot of the Monastery of Reading, John Eynon and John Rugge should be taken to the King's gaol of Reading. And they should be separately dragged through the middle of the town of Reading to the place of execution and there hanged on the gallows. And each should be taken down while living and laid on the ground, and their bellies taken out and burned while they are alive, and their heads cut off. And their bodies shall be cut into four parts. And their heads and their quarters shall be placed wherever the lord King should wish.)

---

[10]   Paul (1960), 116.
[11]   TNA, KB 9/548, f. 9, f. 7.
[12]   Ibid, fols 4–6.
[13]   Ibid., f. 1.

Despite the trial papers, it was by no means clear to contemporaries just what these venerable clergymen had done to deserve their punishment. A letter from the French Ambassador Marillac to King Francis I written on 30 November reported that

> two abbots have been lately executed for high treason, one before the gate of his own abbey; they were Abbots of Glastonbury, 50 miles from here and of Reading 120 miles. Could learn no particulars of what they were charged with, except that it was 'les reliques' of the late lord Marquis. They were hanged and their bodies left in chains.[14]

Care was taken to ensure that the trial and sentence were carried out according to proper form, but there is absolutely no doubt that verdict and sentence were foregone conclusions. This is made clear by the 'remembrances' or rough notes kept by Cromwell during his ascendancy and discovered after his downfall. In October 1539 he wrote 'the abbot Redyng to be sent down to be tried and executed at Redyng with his complices. Similarly the abbot of Glaston at Glaston'.[15] A mutilated and virulent diatribe against treason that can only have come from Cromwell's circle gives some flavour of the Chief Minister's state of mind, and might help to explain his actions. In this, dateable to November 1539, shortly after the trial, he writes of the abuse of the mass by the Abbot of Reading, 'who was not ashamed to say that he would pray for the Pope's Holiness as long as he lived and would once a week say mass for him'. This was seen as an act of treacherous ingratitude towards the king, who had raised him from 'the meanest monk in Reading to be a governor of 3,000 marks a year and suffered him to pass the time in his Grace's company at shooting, and used to call him his own abbot'.[16] Eynon, as the abbot's chief councillor, deserved no less than his master, and Rugge was the subject of a series of embarrassing questions complied for use in his interrogation that survives from late September 1539. There he was asked to account for his possession of books written against the king's supremacy and his divorce; to explain why he had asked Thomas Vachell to hide one of them; and to explain his possession of the hand of St Anastasius at Reading, knowing that his Majesty had sent visitors to the abbey to put down such idolatry.[17]

---

[14] L and P Henry VIII, Aug–Dec. 1539, 214. Marillac has clearly transposed the distances to Reading and Glastonbury. The 'late Lord Marquis' was Henry Courtenay, Marquis of Exeter, a staunch catholic and political rival of Cromwell, executed for conspiracy in January 1539.

[15] Ibid., 139.

[16] Ibid., 216–17.

[17] Ibid., 96. This is curious since that relic was among those locked away by Dr London a year before.

Unsurprisingly the execution of the last Abbot of Reading was the subject of the final painting in the series commissioned by Hurry to illustrate the history of the abbey (plate XV). Harry Morley's 1917 painting shows the Abbot tied to a hurdle preparatory to being dragged around the streets of the town by a horse. Behind him the scaffold has been erected for the later stages of his execution, and behind this rises the great mass of the abbey church. The two monks who were executed with him, John Eynon and John Rugge, are shown standing at his feet, and a group in the left foreground includes Thomas Vachell and John Raymond representing Parliament, and the Mayor of Reading, Thomas Mirth.

THE ABBEY IN ROYAL HANDS

Before the shocking events of October and November 1539, Cromwell's agents had been to the abbey to value the contents. The examination of the relics by Dr London in September 1538 was noted in chapter two above. Then on 8 September 1539, the commissioner Thomas Moyle reported to Cromwell that he and Thomas Vachell had arrived at Reading on Saturday (6 September) about 4 p.m.

> We two began to 'peruse' the house, and next day at noon Mr Dean of York came thither. We find all according to the inventory, and certain plate have attained that was conveyed to other houses, and more trust to find. As we were to certify what stuff were meet for the King: there is a chamber hanged with meetly good tapestry, which would hang a mean little chamber in the King's house, and this is all the household stuff meet to be reserved. There is a chamber hung with six pieces of verdure with fountains, but the ends are foul and greasy. The other hangings are of say and other coarse things. There be seven feather beds and four of them furnish four trussing bedsteads hung with silk like bawdekyn. In the church are eight goodly pieces of tapestry, but of no depth, 13 copes of white tissue, and 10 of green, which are meet to be preserved. We guess we shall make, besides the plate in the inventory, 200 marks and more, which will not be enough, by 100 mks., to despatch the house. The debts appear to be over 500l., but we purpose not to meddle much with the payment of them, unless it be small sums to very poor men. 230l. a year will serve for the pensions. We beg to know the King's pleasure soon, for here is a chargeable house with no provision. Meanwhile we will be despatching them as far as our money will extend. Who is to have the custody of the house and reserved goods?[18]

From the same time there survives a summary or breviate of

> such pieces of cloth of gold, tissue, and bawdkyn, as also remnants of the same of divers colours, taken out of the monastery of Reading, to the use of the

---

[18]   Ibid., 40–41.

> King, by Ric. Pollard and John Williams, commissioners, viz., one piece of cloth of gold with 'pyrled pound garnettes', four of tissue, four of bawdkin, and four remnants, all described, followed by a list of vestments also received[19]

and

> the parcels of gold, as well broken as whole, received to the use of the King at the abbey of Reading by John Williams and Ric. Pollard, esqs., appointed by commission for the same, viz., gold plate, silver plate, gilt plate, and white plate. The gold, 89 oz.; the silver, gilt, and not gilt, 2,645¼ oz.[20]

The commissioners took their departure, informing Cromwell that the abbey and its possessions had been committed to the custody of Sir William Penizon, the receiver, and the plate and other valuables had been placed in Vachell's hands. These two men were subsequently to become custodians of the abbey site. Thomas Vachell was a Berkshire man (though a countryman rather than a Reading townsman), and had been a Member of Parliament for Reading since 1529. By 1534 he was carrying out commissions for Cromwell, and his loyalty was rewarded by the grant of the deputy stewardship of Reading Abbey (under Cromwell). Once the abbot was deposed, it was Vachell who took his place for local duties; hence on 9 October 1539, while Abbot Hugh lay in prison awaiting his execution, Vachell administered the oath to the newly-appointed mayor in the Great Hall of the monastery.[21] In February 1540 he was made overseer of the possessions of Reading Abbey and Leominster Priory, and bailiff of the town of Reading at a total salary of 30 marks.[22] Girolamo Penizon was an Italian diplomat who had worked abroad for the King and Cromwell, and was involved in the negotiations with the Pope and King Francis I over Henry's marriage in 1533.[23] He had a position in the royal stables, and was among the gentlemen who received New Year's gifts in 1539 and 1532.[24]

In late August 1540, less than a month after the execution of Cromwell, the King and his Privy Council met at Reading, partly at least to clarify the traditional relationship between the town and the monastery, and to decide what to put in its place.[25] Then on 22 November, Penizon was made chief steward of the borough or lordship of Reading, and the terms of his appointment made it clear that he was looking after the lands formerly held by the abbey, on the king's behalf.

---

[19] Ibid.
[20] Ibid.
[21] Guilding (1892–96), 1, 172.
[22] L and P Henry VIII, Jan-Aug. 1540, 116 (para 115).
[23] Friedmann (1884), I, 253.
[24] Hayward (2005), 150.
[25] L and P Henry VIII, Jan-Aug. 1540, 496–97.

To be chief steward of the borough or lordship of Redyng, Berks, and of all the possessions in said co. which belonged to the said late monastery; bailiff of the hundred of the town of Redyng; keeper of the mansion house or chief mansion of Reading, with all pools, waters, fisheries, &c., belonging to the said manor, and keeper of the house or Mansion called the 'Beare'; keeper or gardener of all the gardens, &c., within the said house called the Beare; and master or keeper of all the waters and fisheries, and of the cygnets and other fowl building nests in the said waters, &c., keeper of the woods and underwoods called Tylehurst and Kentwoode, Berks; and master of the hunt of deer in Whyteley Park belonging to the said late monastery:– which manors, lordships and other premises came to the King's hands by the attainder of Hugh, late abbot of Reading.[26]

The change of ownership of the abbey had little practical consequence for the king. The abbey buildings at Reading still offered suitable royal accommodation, conveniently placed and equipped with an excellent deer park – now all at Henry's disposal. It is unsurprising, therefore, that the king's gestes or planned itineraries invariably continued to include Reading.[27]

KING EDWARD VI AND THE DUKE OF SOMERSET

Henry VIII died on 28 January 1547 and was succeeded by his only surviving legitimate son, Edward VI, son of Jane Seymour. He was only 9 years old, and his father's will provided for a regency council to rule on his behalf until he reached maturity. Within a few days of the old king's death, however, this council chose to invest their power in a single Protector who would rule with all the power of a king, consulting his Privy Council only when he felt the need. This man was Jane Seymour's brother, Edward Earl of Hertford, who promptly took the title of Duke of Somerset. Somerset ruled autocratically, by proclamation. When he was opposed by Henry VIII's former chancellor, Thomas Wriothesley, Earl of Southampton, he simply dismissed him from his office. Somerset's arbitrary and frankly confusing response to popular grievances about the encroachment of landlords onto common grazing lands was to lead to his downfall. By April 1549 the complaints had escalated into armed rebellions in Devon and Cornwall and in Norfolk, for which Somerset was blamed. He panicked and locked himself in Windsor Castle, taking the young king with him. King Edward himself recounted the sequence of events that followed in his journal.

Then begane the Protectour to treat by letters, sending Sir Philip Hobbey, lately cum from his ambassad in Flaundres to see to his famyly, who brought

---

[26] L and P Henry VIII, Sep 1540–Dec 41, 142 (para 54).
[27] L and P Henry VIII, Sep 1540–Dec 41, 322–25.

in his returne a letter to the Protectour very gentle, wich he delivered to hime, another to me, another to my house, to declare his fautes, ambicion, vain glorie, entring into rashe warres in mine youth, negligent loking on Newhaven, enriching of himself of mine treasour, folowing his owne opinion, and doing al by his owne authorities, etc; wich lettres was openly redd, and immediately the lordes came to Windsore, toke him and brought him through Holborn to the Tower.[28]

His period of effective control had extended from 4 February 1547 to his arrest on 11 October 1549. He was released from the Tower and restored to the Council, now led by John Dudley, Earl of Warwick in April 1550, but soon began a series of intrigues against Warwick's government that led to his conviction for the felony of assembling an illegal army, and to his execution on 22 January 1552. According to Edward VI's own account, 'the duke of Somerset had his head cut of apon Towre hill betwene eight and nine a cloke in the morning'.[29]

In July 1548 the Lord Protector had been granted the lordship of Reading, including the lands formerly belonging to the monastery, and the park and manor of Whitley, and the two fairs held in the Forbury.[30] In September of that year, Roger Amyce, who had been the general receiver for Reading and Glastonbury, and was now surveyor in the Court of Augmentations for Berkshire, submitted a report calling attention to valuable material in the form of lead and bells at Abingdon and Reading, and estimating the volume of lead on the roof at 417 fodders (396 tons).[31] This figure is very close to the 420 tons quoted to curious visitors for the roof of Salisbury Cathedral.[32] From the following year we have a set of accounts kept by George Hynde, an official in the service of the Court of Augmentations, giving details of receipts of money from people buying pieces of the abbey fabric, payments to carpenters and labourers who worked in the demolition, and expenditure for such materials as ropes, chisels and crowbars.[33] Paving tiles were sold at a fixed rate of 6s 8d per thousand for the standard size and 5s for the smaller size. William Draper, an ironmonger from London, paid 6s a hundredweight for half a ton of old iron, but while he was there he took the opportunity to buy 'all the olde glasse' for £6 13s 4d, a price high enough to suggest that it might have

[28] Nichols (1857), 2, 238–41.
[29] Nichols (1857), 2, 390.
[30] CPR Edward VI, 1548–49, 28–29.
[31] Exch.K.R. Ch.Gds E117/8/23a. V.C.H. Berkshire 2 (1907), 72. The estimate was of 417 fodders (approximately 396 tons) at 15 ft.sq. to the fodder. It is easy enough to demonstrate that 15 ft.sq. really means what it says (i.e. 225 sq.ft.), and not 15 sq.ft., because in the latter case the lead would be almost 2.5" thick.
[32] See www.salisburycathedral.co.uk/history.facts.php [consulted 4 August 2015].
[33] TNA, Ministers' A/Cs Edw.VI, Divers Counties Bundle 774; Preston (1935), 107–44

been painted, as well as 'all the Images and stones standing at the highe Altare' for 46s 8d. Another ironmonger, Mighell Hopen, the king's smith from Windsor, bought 7 hundredweights of old iron for 42s, the same rate as Draper. In addition to tradesmen, the local parish church benefitted from the demolition of the abbey. The churchwardens of St Mary's, Reading paid 53s 4d for the choirstalls in the abbey church. Thomas Vachell also bought a souvenir, 'a halpasse of waynescott that the Abbott made for a respecte to the Churche'.[34]

Two other entries in Hynde's accounts are relevant to the demolition of the abbey's cloister, and we shall see in chapter eight that they provide valuable evidence for its design. Mr John Sands paid 50s for 'certen stones fallen downe upon two sydes of the Cloyster', and Mayster Greye paid 40s 'for the stone upon two sydes of the Cloyster'.[35] These entries are not un-ambiguous, but it seems likely in view of the fact that they paid similar prices that Messrs Greye and Sands took away the entire cloister arcade between them. Of John Sands nothing more is known, but it has been convincingly suggested that Mayster Greye was William Grey, the King's plumber and occasional balladeer, responsible famously for a hunting song called 'The King's Hunt is Up', regularly performed by scholarly and folk music groups, as a typical Tudor hunting song, often without any at-tribution,[36] and less famously but more interestingly for a ballad written in 1540 called 'The Fantassie of Idolatrie', which is a condemnation of papist practices, most notably the ritual of pilgrimage:

> Ronnyng hyther and thyther,
> We cannot tell whither,
> In offryng candles and pence
> To stones and stockes,
> And to olde rotten blockes,
> That came, we know not from whense.[37]

His local abbey was not left out of the general condemnation:

> To Leymster, to Kyngestone,
> To Yorke, to Donyngton,
> To Redyng, to the chyld of grace;
> To Wynsore, to Waltam,
> To Ely, to Caultam,
> Bare foted and bare legged apace.[38]

---

[34] A high step, or *haut pas*, of oak.
[35] Preston (1935), 120, 122.
[36] Most famously recorded by the Albion Dance Band on their 1977 album, *The Prospect Before Us*.
[37] Foxe, 5, 405; Dormer (1923), 70–75.
[38] Foxe, 5, 405; Dormer (1923), 70–75.

In addition to buying two ranges of the cloister, Grey bought 'xv Jakes stoles', some plaster of Paris from the choir walls, the 'lytle rose standing at the end of the Fratrye', 'a shedde and a wyndowe' and 'certayne stone that wente aboute the southe syde of the Churche under Bartlements'. While the jakes stools and the shed are obviously functional, others suggest an antiquarian or at least an aesthetic interest in the abbey fabric. The cloister stone was richly carved, the two windows were presumably bought for their tracery, and the stone from under the battlements may have been a corbel table. It is tempting too to speculate that the plaster from the choir was bought for its fresco decoration. This was not Grey's only venture into collecting. In the same year he bought various items from St Laurence's Church, Reading: the altar from the Chapel of St John, the Trinity Altar, and the cope chest.[39]

In October 1545 Grey, described as 'William Graye of London, the King's servant', had been granted extensive lands in Reading, including 179 houses, four forges, eight orchards, two inns and three mills, all of which had previously belonged to the abbey.[40] He became the MP Reading in 1547 and worked closely with the Protector Somerset.[41] When Somerset fell from favour in 1549, Grey was among those who were sent with him to the Tower.[42] Somerset was released, but Grey was not, and on 22 February 1550 he was fined the enormous sum of £3,000. He was eventually freed on 27 February, but the goods which had been confiscated on his imprisonment were not returned. As Somerset's influence waxed again, attempts were made to compensate those who, like Grey, had suffered during his fall. He was discharged of his debt of £3,000 on 5 May 1551, but by this time he was dead – killed, according to the epitaph he wrote himself, by the malice of Agnes his wife.

> Loo, here Lyes gray under the grounde,
> Amonge the gredy wormes
> that in his Lyffe-tyme nevar ffounde
> bwtt stryfe and story stormes.
>
> And namely through a wecked wyfe,
> as to the worlde aperes;
> she was the shortynge of his Lyfe
> by many dayes and yeres
>
> he myght have Leved Longe, god watt,
> his yeres were very yonge;

[39] Kerry (1883), 38.
[40] L and P Henry VIII, Aug–Dec 1545, 328–29.
[41] Bindoff (1982), 256–57.
[42] Ibid.

of wecked wyfes this is the lott,
to kell with spytfull tonges.[43]

Shortly after this piecemeal disposal of second-hand building material (but occupying three different reigns), three major building projects bene-fitted from the availability of the abbey fabric. Under Edward VI, between 1550 and 1553 the parish church of St Mary's, Reading was rebuilt, and the churchwardens' accounts reveal that the choir of the abbey church was taken down at this time, piers were removed and reused in St Mary's, timber and lead were stripped from the roofs, and other fabric including a rose window, the cloister door and various loads of stone and tiles were taken away for the rebuilding.[44] Edward's successor, the Catholic Queen Mary, was responsible for the construction of the Poor Knights' Lodging near St George's Chapel, Windsor around 1557. The following extracts from the masons' accounts give some idea of the damage done to the abbey during this campaign:

Reading – The stones for the building were fetched from Redding Abbey
by water,
Reading – Carpenters viewing the Roofes at Reading and Wallingford by
the day   12d
Reading – Masons taking downe the great stones of the dores and
windowes in the Chappell of our Lady there by the day &c.   12d
Reading – Labourers digging stones out of the walls there per diem   7d
Reading – Masons Chusing of stones there per diem   10d
Reading – Labourers digging of Cane Stone out of the windows for ye
Batlements in the New Lodgings per diem   7d

The work was supervised by Richard Woodward and the royal surveyor, Roger Amice, and the master mason in charge of the project was Henry Bullok.[45] It is fair to assume that by the time the work was complete most of the lady chapel had disappeared.[46]

Queen Elizabeth succeeded her sister in 1558, and on 23 September 1560, she gave a new charter to Reading, intended to ameliorate the decayed state of the town that was due, at least in part, to the loss of its abbey. There is no doubt that the charter improved matters for the borough, mainly by granting to the mayor and burgesses the rent on properties that had formerly belonged to the monastery.[47] For the abbey buildings, however, it

---

[43] Dormer (1923).

[44] Garry (1893), 4, 5, 9, 14, 22.

[45] Tighe and Davis (1858), 1, 605–06.

[46] Slade (2001), 29.

[47] Berkshire Record Office Charter R/IC1/8, charter of Elizabeth I dated 23 September. 23 1560. For the full text in translation see Pritchard (1913). Long sections are also reprinted in Doran (1835), 40–42. See also Slade (2001), 29–30.

was just the latest in a series of disasters. At the Dissolution the Crown had inherited the abbey's responsibility for maintaining no less than nineteen bridges within the town, a responsibility that they had neglected, so that the bridges were now 'very ruinous falling and in great decay for default of repairs and amendments'. By her charter, the queen passed the responsibility for their repair to the borough, discharging her own responsibilities by a grant of building materials. The mayor and burgesses were allowed to cut down and remove fifty timber oaks from the royal parks at Whitley and Binfield, and

> to dig take and carry away two hundred loads of stones called Ragged or free Stones in the aforesaid late monastery of Reading.

No record was made of what part of the abbey was demolished for this project, but as I shall discuss further in chapter six, some of this sixteenth-century repair work has been discovered in the covering of the Holy Brook, and the stones used include a large number of vault-rib voussoirs from the abbey church. In 1568 ashlar from Reading Abbey was used in the rebuilding of piers for the King's Bridge at Westminster Palace.[48] A further request was made in June 1577 by the citizens of Reading for stones from the abbey to be used for paving their streets, but no response has survived.[49] During the first period of demolition of the monastery, the royal lodgings into which part of it was converted were constantly being maintained and repaired, and new stables built, often on a grand scale. This work is described in detail below, but it is fair to assume that the derelict buildings alongside were freely quarried by the royal masons over a long period. By the end of the sixteenth century, then, the cloister arcade was gone and the church was roofless and probably lacked most of its choir and lady chapel.

THE ROYAL PALACE

After the Dissolution, part of the monastery was converted into a house for royal use, variously referred to as the King's (or Queen's) Place or House. In a sense, of course, Reading Abbey was already a royal palace. Certainly, as we have seen, successive monarchs from Henry I to Henry VIII treated it as one. It would be a mistake to underestimate the degree of continuity here. While for the abbot and monks, Reading had always been the physical locus of the *opus Dei* – the achievement of salvation through regular prayer, work and reading, and the honouring of God and the saints – for the king and his court it was a convenient lodging, amply

---

[48] Colvin (1963–82), IV, 295; PRO E351/3204.
[49] CSP (Domestic) 1547–80, 548.

supplied with fine rooms, good food and wine, always ready to receive them and supplied with a well-stocked park for hunting.

The fullest description we have of the palace comes from the report of the Parliamentary commissioners, dating from 1650. By this time it was no longer in use as a royal residence, but was held by Richard Knollys. The description is worth repeating at length.

> All that capital messuage, mansion-house or abbey-house, with the appurte-
> nances, called Reading Abbey, consisting of two sellars, two buttries, a hall, a
> parlour, a dineing room, tenne chambers, a garret, with a large gallery, and
> other small roomes, with two court yards, and a large gate house, with several
> rooms adjoining to the said house and a small gardine, with an old small house
> built with stone, thereto adjoining, and a stable with sellars over the same, and
> a small tenement in the South end of the said stable, with a little gardine, and a
> dove-house which said abbey with the scite thereof, is in the occupation of Mr.
> Richard Knollys, and are bounded with the court called the Forbury, North
> and East, Pondhaies South, and the great gardine West, in all by measurements
> two acres, value per annum £15.
>   There is on the East side of the said mansion-house a great old hall, with
> a very large cellar under the said hall, arched and with some other decayed
> roomes between the said hall and the mansion house, with the ruins of an old
> large chappell, a kitchen and several other rooms, fit to be demolished.[50]

This should be read in conjunction with the map showing the siege defences, probably contemporary with the siege of 1643 (figure 23). In this, the complex labelled 'The Abbey' is actually the palace. It is approximately rectangular in plan, with the main facade facing west, possibly flanked by a pair of towers, and is set within a walled enclosure, approximately rectangular (figure 24). From the description it seems likely that the name of Forbury was being used for this enclosure, and not for the much larger abbey precinct (including the later Forbury Gardens) as in former times. The inner gateway of the abbey was retained as an entrance despite the fact that it was aligned at right angles to the north end of the facade. A visitor entering the complex through the gateway would therefore turn immedi-ately left to enter a small entrance court between the towers.

Matching the features of the palace to the former monastic buildings is a straightforward exercise. The square feature at the north east corner of the complex is the cloister, robbed of its walks, and retaining the ruinous chapter house, described as 'the ruins of an old large chappell', built against the eastern wall. This is faintly drawn, probably because it was a ruin scheduled for demolition. The range on the south side of the cloister is the former refectory, and the long range running south from its eastern end is the dormitory, which fits the description of 'a great old hall, with a very large cellar under the said hall'. The range on the west of the cloister

---

[50]   Coates (1802), 267.

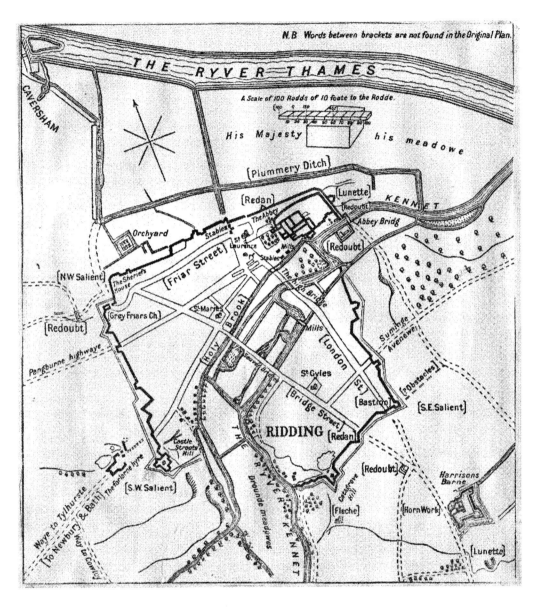

N.B Words between brackets are not found in the Original Plan.

THE RYVER THAMES

A Scale of 100 Rodds of 10 foote to the Rodde.

His Majesty   his meadowe

CAVERSHAM

[Plummery Ditch]

[Redan]   [Lunette]
                 [Redoubt]
         The Abbey   KENNET
                      Abbey Bridg
Orchyard   Stables   St
                      [Redoubt]
            St Laurence
[NW Salient]   Stables
The Sheriefs House   [Friar Street]

[Redoubt]   Grey Friars Ch.   St Maries
                              Holy Brook
Pangbourne highwaye   Mills
                                        [Obstacles]
                   St Gyles   London St
                                            Summinge Avenewe
                              [Bridge Street]   [Bastion]   [S.E.Salient]
RIDDING   [Redan]
         Castle Stroats Hill   [Redoubt]   Harrisons Barne
                                        Craigrove Hill
[S.W. Salient]   [HornWork]
                          THE RYVER KENNET
Waye to Tylhurste   [& Bath] The forlorne hyre   [Fleche]
To Newbury   Way to Conly   [Lunette]

23   THIS COPY OF THE 1643 CIVIL WAR SIEGE MAP IS TAKEN FROM GUILDING (1892–96).

square is the former guest range, while the west front range of the palace may have been the abbot's lodging originally. To complete the picture, the siege map includes the abbey's two recorded stables, one to the north-west on Friar Street and the other to the south-west, alongside the Holy Brook on the street now called Abbey Square.

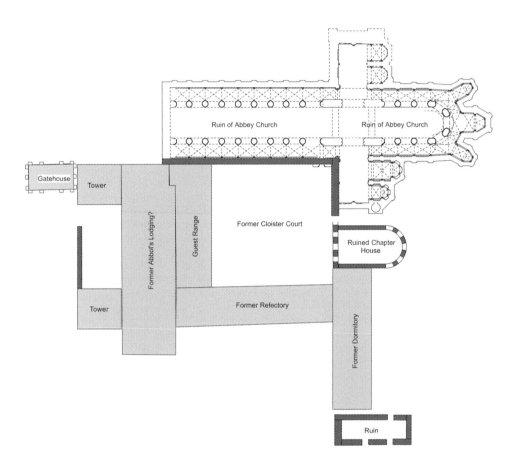

24   THE PLAN OF THE ROYAL PALACE CAN BE RECONSTRUCTED WITH THE AID OF THE SIEGE MAP
AND A DESCRIPTION OF 1650.

READING ROYAL PALACE IN CONTEXT

Maurice Howard has noted that the initial aim of monastic conversions
to secular use was often to recreate the fashionable courtyard houses of
the early Tudor period.[51] Since the courtyard was already present in the
form of the cloister, this would seem at first sight to be relatively straightforward, but the standard monastic layout embodied several problems,
depending on whether the cloister was situated to the north or the south
of the abbey church. In a conventional courtyard house the entrance faced
the great hall across the courtyard. In converting a cloister and its surrounding buildings, the easiest and most logical entrance range was the

[51]   Howard (2003), 221; Howard (1987), 136–62.

west, which was already the guest range and could include the abbot's lodging – domestically the most comfortable and imposing. Unfortunately the facing east range was invariably fragmented, typically including a transept, the slype, the chapter house and often a section of dormitory undercroft that extended well beyond the square of the cloister. Monasteries did have large spaces suitable for use as a great hall. The most obvious was the refectory or frater, which had the advantage of already having a kitchen nearby (usually at the west end). Other possibilities were the nave of the church, if it survived, and the dormitory, which was big enough but in the wrong place relative to the courtyard. Depending on the heights and levels of these buildings, the conversion might involve the introduction of staircases.[52]

The best documented of the monastic conversions is undoubtedly the Premonstratensian abbey of Titchfield (Hants), given to Sir Thomas Wriothesley in December 1537 and turned into his mansion of Place House within a matter of months.[53] A series of letters to Wriothesley from his agents on site reveal that there was a good deal of modification to the original project design.[54] The scheme eventually adopted was to cut through the nave of the church to build a grand four-towered gatehouse as a south entrance to the courtyard (unlike Reading, the cloister was on the north side of the church).[55] The new gateway faced the refectory, which became the great hall, with the high end at the east, and the kitchen at the west. The east range including the north transept, which was divided into three storeys, became lodgings and the chapter house became Wrothesley's chapel. Finally the west range with its undercroft, originally the cellarer's range, became the servants' quarters with its own hall.[56]

The conversion of the former Augustinian priory at Leez (Essex) provides an interesting comparison with Reading.[57] The house was dissolved in 1536 and passed to Sir Richard Rich, Chancellor of the Court of Augmentations and a major beneficiary of the Dissolution of the monasteries. At Leez he built a double courtyard house, using the former cloister as the inner court, containing his main living quarters. This was entered from the west, through an inner gateway cut through the west range of the cloister. As at Titchfield, the cloister of the priory was on the north, and Rich adapted the nave of the church, on the south side of the inner court,

---

[52] Howard (1987), 148–49.
[53] Hare (1999), 17–20 with useful block plans showing the conversion; VCH (Hampshire), 3 (1908), 222–23.
[54] Hope (1906).
[55] This is the most imposing feature of the ruined mansion, now in the care of English Heritage.
[56] VCH (Hampshire), 3 (1908), 222–23; Hope (1906); Hare (1999), 17–20.
[57] For Leez Priory, see Bettley and Pevsner (2007), 531–33; Howard (2003), 223; Howard (1987), 149.

as his great hall. A large outer court was added to the west of the inner
court, entered through a gateway in the south wall. The diapered brick-
work of Rich's new buildings, along with the multi-courtyard plan, has led
writers to compare it with the royal works begun some six years earlier at
Hampton Court, but it is also interesting to compare the winding entrance
route with the system adopted at Reading. Another related conversion was
the Augustinian Priory of Mottisfont (Hants), given to Sir William Sandys
in 1536. As at Reading the cloister was on the south side of the church.
Part of the nave was converted to lodgings, and the frater, on the south
range of the cloister, became the great hall. A second court was built to
the south to provide an entrance court, flanked by towers as was the west
entrance at Reading.

THE CHRONOLOGY OF THE WORK

The Parliamentary Commissioners' Report and the Siege Map provide a
rather blurred snapshot of the Royal Palace around 1650, and this can be
clarified somewhat by some information about the progress of the work in
the previous century. There is no evidence of any building work at the palace between the Dissolution and the accession of Queen Elizabeth in 1558,
except for work on the water supply to the stables in 1549,[58] and repairs to
the King's House in 1550–52, for which the Master Carpenter to the Court
of Augmentations, John Revell, was paid £211.[59] Early in Elizabeth's reign,
in June 1559, a Works official reported that the lodgings were 'very simple for her highness', and that the stables were 'in great decay and lacketh
room'.[60] Substantial repairs were needed for her visits to the palace in 1568
and 1570,[61] under the direction of the Royal Surveyor Lewis Stockett, and
his accounts are useful in mentioning the principal buildings and apartments of the Palace, though not their locations. From this we know that at
this time it included a great gate, hall, great chamber, presence chamber,
privy chamber, bedchamber, raying chamber (dressing room), gallery and
kitchen. This is the standard arrangement for state rooms or royal lodgings in that period. The great chamber was for the guards, the presence
chamber for state occasions, the privy chamber for dining and private re-
ceptions, the bedchamber and raying chamber for sleeping and dressing,
and the gallery (probably a long gallery) a multi-purpose room for enter-
taining, walking and displaying paintings.[62] In 1568 over £300 was spent
on repairs to the fabric: the kitchen roof was retiled; the battlements and

---

[58]   Preston (1935), 137–38.
[59]   TNA, E351/3328; Colvin (1963–82), 4, 221.
[60]   Colvin (1963–82), 4, 221; TNA State Papers Domestic Series SP12/ 4, 57.
[61]   Colvin (1963–82), 4, 221.
[62]   I am grateful to Emily Cole for this clarification.

leads of the gatehouse repaired; and Peter Nicholson, the Queen's Master Glazier, repaired a number of windows and inserted the Queen's arms and badges in those of the great and privy chambers. When the antiquary and Royalist soldier Richard Symonds visited in 1644 he noted and sketched the arms of Queen Elizabeth and of Seymour in the windows of 'a large upper roome, now used as a dyning roome', most likely the Great Chamber.[63]

As part of the same 1568 building campaign, the Queen had repairs carried out in the chancel of St Laurence's church, which stood immediately 'adioyning to the queen's Maiestie's Howse', and for which she was responsible. The walls were roughcast, the roof was tiled, and the glazier Ellis Tomson repaired the glass and marked the Queen's patronage by setting up her arms and badges in the windows.[64] The chancel was again repaired at the queen's expense in 1570.[65]

THE QUEEN'S STABLES

The sorry state of the royal stables has been mentioned before, and in 1569 one hundred oaks were felled at Beenham, near Reading, 'for the Queen's Majesties howse and stables at Reddinge'.[66] In the following year, according to Lewis Stockett's accounts, this timber was used in the building of new stables at a cost of nearly £1,000.[67] Camden found them impressive in 1586; they rate a special mention in his description of Reading Abbey:

> This Monastery wherein that noble King Henry the First was buried is now converted to be the Kings house, which hath adjoining unto it a very goodly stable stored to the full with princelike and most generous steeds.[68]

The stables were surveyed by the officers of the Works in 1607, and they estimated that some £330 needed to be spent on 'the Courser stable' (162 feet long), 'the Barbary stable' (27 ft long), 'the Equirry stable (27 ft long), and the 'fordge shooing place'.[69] These terms need a little explanation. Coursers were the standard medieval warhorses: light, fast and strong and used occasionally for hunting too. This was by far the largest of the stables that needed repair, and must have been used by the court. Barbaries or

---

[63] BL Harley 965, f69. The Seymour arms must relate to the Protector Somerset's brief tenure of the palace in 1547–49.

[64] Colvin (1963–82), 4, 221.

[65] Coates (1802), 163.

[66] Colvin (1963–82), 4, 221.

[67] TNA E351/3204–5.

[68] Camden Britannia, 167. The English is Philemon Holland's 1610 translation of the 1607 edition.

[69] TNA, E178/283.

Barb horses were the favourites of the Muslim rulers of Andalusia, and became popular at the courts of Spain and Italy from the fifteenth century onwards. In appearance they were (and are) heavy-bodied horses with arched necks, luxuriant manes and short legs. Their docile nature and readiness to learn made them ideal for the more affected styles of equitation. Federigo Gonzaga sent Henry VIII a gift of eight Barb mares and a Mantuan Barb stallion to start his own stud: a generous gift which Henry received enthusiastically. Queen Elizabeth's Master of the Horse, the Earl of Leicester, kept up the tradition, obtaining more Barb horses for her stables. Finally the Equirry or Equerry stables were under the control of the Master of the Horse, and were reserved for the Queen's or King's own horses. The site of the stables is clearly marked on the siege map and on Speed's map, on the north side of the Holy Brook, south-west of the main palace complex. This area, now called Abbey Square and extensively redeveloped, was observed in 1974 and excavated in 1976 and 1983.[70] The main excavation, led by John Hawkes, took place in 1983, when a new library was planned for the site, and this revealed two phases of building. The first phase was dated by pottery deposits to the late twelfth or early thirteenth century. This building was apparently gutted by fire, perhaps during the construction of its successor.[71] The second phase was built partly on the foundations of the old stables, and more or less immediately after their demolition, and using at least some of the demolished fabric.[72] The new building was three-aisled, while the original stables had been a two-aisled structure, suggesting a significant enlargement. Both were approximately 10 metres (33 feet) wide between the exterior wall surfaces, with walls 1.2 metres (4 feet) thick, giving an internal width of 25 feet. The second phase was dated by pottery deposits to the fifteenth or sixteenth century, and the presence of decorative stonework from the abbey, including capitals, columns and tracery fragments, and a deliberately mutilated ivory figure, perhaps a Virgin and Child, convinced the archaeologists that this was a post-Dissolution phase, logically Queen Elizabeth's 1570 rebuilding.[73]

The stables were again described in the Parliamentary Survey of 1650, after the description of the palace. What remained then was

a large barn formerly a stable, in length 135 feet, in breadth 30 feet, with a great yard and small garden, bounded by the hollow brook South and the said great garden North.[74]

[70] Hawkes (1991), 67.
[71] Ibid., 70–71.
[72] Ibid., 71.
[73] Ibid.
[74] Coates (1802), 268.

The width and location of the stables matches the excavation well enough, but the length is, according to Hawkes, considerably shorter than the combined lengths of walls excavated or observed, although it is by no means certain that all of these walls belonged to the stables, rather than the abbey mill to the east. In any case, the figure of 162 feet (49.4 metres) given for the Courser Stable by the Office of Works in 1607 is probably the most reliable guide to the scale of the building.

THE QUEEN'S STABLES IN CONTEXT

Both Henry VIII and Queen Elizabeth spent lavishly on stables, but the only major royal stable to survive from this period is Henry VIII's Royal Mews at Hampton Court – a quadrangular, two-storey building with garrets in the roof, built in 1537–38. The quadrangular design was uncommon at this date except for a few royal stables.[75] It is clear from the maps and descriptions we have that the Queen's Stables at Reading were not built around a courtyard, but formed a single range, and there is one outstanding comparison that must be made, at Kenilworth castle (figure 25).

The Queen's Master of the Horse from the very beginning of her reign was her favourite Robert Dudley (1532–88), Earl of Leicester from 1564, who was restored to the ownership of the former royal residence of Kenilworth in 1563. The castle had been formally granted to his father, John Dudley, Duke of Northumberland, by Edward VI in 1553, but within months of the formal grant, King Edward was dead and so was Northumberland, executed by Queen Mary for treason. When Elizabeth succeeded her sister on the throne, the Earl of Leicester returned to royal favour and entertained her at Kenilworth several times, spending lavishly to impress her. As her Master of the Horse he was involved in the building of the new stables at Reading, and he had a model to hand in the new stables built by his father at Kenilworth in 1553.[76] The Kenilworth stables were originally 180 feet by 21 feet (54.9m by 6.4m) internally, although they are now rather shorter, having been shortened at their north end to 156 feet (47.5m).[77] The measurements are not precisely the same as Reading's, but they are very close, and contained stalls for 30 great horses

---

[75] Worsley (2004), 21–23. Greenwich, St James's Palace and Charing Cross had quadrangular plans.

[76] Molyneux (2008), 51; Morris (2009), 242. The attribution to Northumberland rather than his son is based on Molyneux's examination of a survey of the castle made in 1563 (Aberystwyth, National Library of Wales, Chirk Castle MSS F13310). Earlier writers had assumed that Leicester had rebuilt the stables as part of his widespread rebuilding programme (see e.g. Worsley (2004), 23–25).

[77] Molyneux (2008), 51; Worsley (2004), 25.

25   THE STABLES AT KENILWORTH CASTLE, WARWICKSHIRE, WERE BUILT IN 1553 BY JOHN DUDLEY, DUKE OF
NORTHUMBERLAND.

and 20 geldings, which must approximate to the capacity of the Queen's
stables.

ROYAL VISITS TO THE PALACE AFTER 1547

As far as we know, Edward VI and Mary visited their palace at Reading
only once each. The fourteen-year-old Edward VI's visit of September
1552 was briefly noted in his Journal, and in a letter to his friend Barnaby
FitzPatrick, dated from Windsor on 24 September,[78] but a fuller description of his reception appears in the municipal records.

> The xiijth day of Septembre, in the yere aboveseid, the Kynges Majestie in
> th'end of his progresse came to Redyng, at the whiche tyme Thomas Alde-
> worth, Mayour, accompanyed with the substaunce of th'enhabitantes of the
> seid towne, aswell Burgeses as others, in ther best apparelles, receyved his
> Grace at Colley Crosse, all beyng on fote, wher the seid Mayour on his knee
> humblie welcummyd his Grace and kissed the mase and delyvered it unto his
> Grace, who most gentilly stayed his hors and received it, and immediatly de-
> lyvered agayn the mase unto the seid Mayour. And also his Majestie ferther
> stayed his hors untill the seid Mayour had taken his hors and then the seid
> Mayour appoynted by a gentilman hussher rode before the Kynges Majestie
> thorough the towne into the Kynges place. At the whiche tyme forasmuche as
> it was the first tyme of his Graces cummyng, the seid Mayour presented and

---

[78] Nichols (1857), 1, 87; 2, 453.

gave unto his Majestie ij yokes of oxon, which cost xvli, the charges wherof was borne by th'enhabitantes of the seid towne, aswell by the Burgeses as others.

Also at the same tyme, beyng his Grace's first cumyng, certayn Officers ther demaunded certayn dewties, as they call hit, whiche were payed until them at the costes and charges of the seyd Mayour and Burgeses, as herafter followith,

Inprimis to the Harroldes	xxs
To the Serjauntes at Armis	xiijs. iiijd.
To the Trumpetters	xs.
To the Kynges Cuppberer	vjs. viijd.
To the Fotemen	xs.
To the Clark of the Markett	vjs. viijd.
To the Marshall	iijs. iiijd.[79]

Within two years, when Reading received another royal visit, Edward was dead and his elder sister Mary was on the throne. She arrived on 2 August 1554 with her new husband, Prince Philip of Spain, who had been given the Kingdom of Naples by his father to make his rank equivalent to Mary's. The king and queen were received at Reading by Mayor Robert Bowyer and the burgesses and other inhabitants, all dressed in their best clothes. The reception committee met the royal couple at the upper end of Siveiar Strete (now Silver Street), where the mayor kneeled to welcome them, and kissed the mace before presenting it to the queen. She immediately gave it back to the mayor and asked him to give it to the king. He in his turn received it from the mayor and gave it back again. The mayor then rode before the king and queen into the town, holding the mace, leading the procession to the King's Place. When they arrived the mayor presented them with a gift of four great fat oxen that had cost the townspeople £16.[80] Mary retained the abbey in crown possession from the beginning of her reign, and in late 1553 appointed the Roman Catholic Sir Francis Englefield as its bailiff and as chief steward of the borough, manor and lordship of Reading and Theale, and of all lands and liberties in Berkshire that had previously belonged to the monastery. The grants also specified that he was allowed to appoint his own choice of under-bailiff and under-steward.[81] Sir Francis thus combined the positions of Thomas Vachell (who had died that summer) and William Penizon. The grants were for life, but on the accession of Queen Elizabeth in 1559 Englefield, fearing persecution for his Catholicism, fled to Spain where he remained until his death in 1605.

Queen Elizabeth I was well aware of the sufferings caused to the town by the loss of its abbey, and we have already seen that she attempted to rectify the problem by granting a new charter, and by allowing the use of

[79] Guilding (1892–96), 1, 228–29.
[80] Ibid., 1, 240.
[81] CPR 1553–54, 57, 173.

abbey stones for municipal repairs. She also repaired and extended the palace, to accommodate the court on the visits she made throughout her reign. Visits are known to have taken place in 1568, when she sealed a safe-conduct there for the Earl of Murray,[82] 1570,[83] 1572,[84] 1574,[85] 1575,[86] 1580,[87] 1592,[88] 1601, 1602 and 1603.[89] In September 1601 she also dined with Sir William Knollys, Comptroller of her Household, at his nearby residence of Caversham Park, where she 'made great cheer with devices of singing, dancing, playing, wrestlers &c.' and knighted Sir Francis Goodwin, Sir Edmund Fettiplace and Sir Richard Ward.[90] In 1602 the bell-ringers of St Laurence's church greeted her arrival with a peal.[91]

THE END OF THE PALACE

Elizabeth's successor James I settled the palace on his Queen, Anne of Denmark, and after her death in 1619 it passed to their son Charles, the Prince of Wales.[92] In 1603 it was intended to keep the Michaelmas term (October to December) at Reading, but by 17 October the venue had been changed to Winchester, because Reading was 'much infected with the Sicknes'.[93] There is only one record of James I actually visiting Reading. On 20 July 1611 the ringers of St Mary's were paid 7 shillings for ringing when the king passed through the town.[94] Despite Anne's ownership of the site, on the occasion she is known to have visited the town – on her way to take the waters in Bath in 1614 – she stayed at the Friars Minor, part of which had been granted to Robert Stanshawe, a Groom of the King's Chamber at the Dissolution, and had passed to one John Carleton by 1614.[95] After his accession, Charles I kept the Michaelmas term in the town in 1625 to es-

[82] CSP (Scotland) 1563–69, 816; Nichols (1823), 1, 599.
[83] CSP(Domestic) 1547–80, 393; CSP(Scotland) 1569–71, 352–53. 359–60.
[84] Nichols (1823), 1, 599.
[85] See CSP (Scotland) 1574–81, 155, where the Queen was said to be at Reading 'about Midsummer 1574'.
[86] Nichols (1823), 1, 199. She visited Reading after a visit to Woodstock in September of that year.
[87] CSP (Domestic) 1547–80, 676; CSP (Domestic) Addenda 1580–1625, 21–25.
[88] Nichols (1823), 1, 199.
[89] For the visits of 1572, 1575, 1592, 1602 and 1603, see Coates (1802), 20.
[90] CSP (Domestic) 1601–03, 93–106; Nichols (1823), 3, 567.
[91] Nichols (1823), 1, 199.
[92] Coates (1802), 266.
[93] Nichols (1828), 1, 290.
[94] Garry (1893),113. Nichols (1828), 2, 451 erroneously places this payment in 1612, arguing that the visit could not have taken place since the king was en route from Theobalds to St Albans at the time.
[95] Guilding (1892–96), 2, 64; Coates (1802), 306; Man (1816), 294.

cape the plague raging in London.[96] The choice of Reading seems a strange one, since in July of that year there was evidence of the plague there too, a child being dead 'full of blue spots'.[97] As a precaution against infection spreading from London the king forbade the purchase of goods from London or Westminster, or anywhere else that had recently been infected. The various offices of the Court were housed as follows:

> The high court of Chancery, the courts of King's Bench, Common-Pleas, Wards, and Liveries, and the court of Requests, weare all holden and kept in the great hall and other places of the decayed abbey or monasterie of Readinge. The court of Exchequer was holden in the town-hall and chamber there, and the Augmentation-court in the school-house.[98]

The latest court letter from Reading in that year is dated to the 27 November. A second visit was planned in 1629, when the Corporation resolved to present a gilt cup, of £20 value at least, to Prince Charles, and another to the queen, but it seems not to have taken place.[99] When Charles I was in Reading during the Civil War he preferred to stay at Coley Park or with Lord Craven at Caversham. Thereafter, in view of the dilapidations caused by the plundering of the site and its bombardment during the siege of 1642–43 (described below), the palace was uninhabitable by any but the least fastidious.

THE SIEGE OF READING

In 1642–43 Reading was the site of an action in the Civil War which had further serious effects on the abbey. The outbreak of the Civil War is normally dated to 25 August 1642, when King Charles I raised his standard at Nottingham, and around the same time the corporation of Reading was arranging for posts and chains to be set up in the streets for defensive purposes, and for scouts to ride out on the lookout for approaching troops.[100] After the inconclusive battle at Edge Hill (Warwicks) on 23 October, the King rode to Oxford with his army, and on 3 November sent an order to the local council in Reading to strengthen Caversham Bridge in preparation for his arrival with his troops. He stayed in the town for almost a month, ordering the tailors of Reading to make a thousand uniforms for his men. He then retreated to his headquarters in Oxford, leaving Reading as an outpost garrisoned by a force of 2000 infantry and a regiment of

96 CSP (Domestic) 1625–26, 122, 147–60.
97 Reading Corp. MSS, 183.
98 Coates (1802), 21–22.
99 Reading Corp. MSS, 184.
100 Guilding (1892–96), 3, 49–51.

cavalry under the governorship of Sir Arthur Aston, who twice borrowed from the townsmen, at the rate of £500 a week for a month, a total loan of £4,000.[101] By the following April the number of foot-soldiers had grown to nearly 3,000, and the cavalry to 300. On 15 April, the entire Parliamentary army of 16,000 foot and more than 3,000 horse led by the Earl of Essex marched from Windsor and encamped outside Reading. The town was well supplied with food, but otherwise was not equipped to endure a siege, having very little ammunition, 'not forty barrels of powder; which would not have held a brisk and daring enemy four hours'.[102] Only two injuries were reported to men of note among the defenders, both involving elements of whimsy, although the besieging force suffered considerable losses. First was 'lieutenant colonel D'Ews, a young man of notable courage and vivacity, who had his leg shot off by a cannon bullet, of which he speedily and very cheerfully died'.[103] Then, within a week of the start of the siege (on 17 April), Sir Arthur Aston himself was hit on the head by a roof-tile dislodged by a cannon shot, and 'his senses shortly failed him, so that he was not only disabled afterwards from executing in his own person, but incompetent for counsel or direction; so that the chief command was devolved to colonel Richard Fielding, who was the eldest colonel of the garrison'.[104] The position was hopeless for the defenders, and Fielding did well to negotiate a treaty with Essex whereby he would surrender the town but withdraw the garrison without molestation and with flying colours, although he did not escape charges of complicity with the Parliamentarians.[105]

In the course of the defence, Aston had raised defensive works consisting of a rampart with a ditch running across the cloister from south to north, terminating in a hornwork which occupied a large part of the nave of the church.[106] These works are shown in Englefield's survey of 1779 and in the siege map (figures 23 and 39).[107] Stone for the construction of the rampart came, of course, from the abbey, and further damage was caused during the ten days of bombardment necessary to obtain the surrender of the town.

Following the Royalists' withdrawal, the town was occupied by Essex's Parliamentary forces, but he withdrew his garrison to London after the first battle of Newbury on 20 September 1643, and the Royalists returned, refurbishing the fortifications against further attack. When the king came back on 14 May 1644 he decided to abandon the town, removing its

[101] Ibid., 3, 62–63, 70–71;, 187–88.
[102] Clarendon (1717), 4, 23.
[103] Ibid., 27.
[104] Ibid., 28.
[105] Ibid., 37–47.
[106] Englefield (1782), 65; Buckler (1823) f.2r.
[107] The siege map is shown in Guilding (1892–96), 4, 73.

defences lest the Parliamentarians came back. 'We are slighting the works here with all speed that may be according to the materials that we have, and by Thursday night we shall make them unserviceable for the enemy if he should settle himself here', noted the Earl of Forth at the time.[108]

The state of the ruins in 1650 was the subject of a Parliamentary survey that was chiefly concerned with occupied, or at least useable, buildings. It reported the presence of 'the ruins of an old large chappell' within the complex, identified by Cecil Slade as the remains of the abbey church,[109] but which it cannot be. Taking the Survey in conjunction with the more-or-less contemporary siege map confirms that this structure was the chapter house – easily misread as a chapel (figure 23) – and that no part of the church still stood in a useable condition at that date. The corporation had by this time assumed proprietary rights over the Forbury, justified perhaps by the administration of the four annual fairs held there which they had inherited from the abbey. Although the defensive works had been slighted, the ditch and bank were clearly still an inconvenience, and in 1652 the Corporation agreed to assist in levelling the Forbury so that the fairs could be held there.[110]

Royal interest in Reading as a palace, or even a place to stay, was never really renewed after the restoration of the monarchy in 1660. The new king, Charles II, spent £517 19s on the repair of the stables in 1662, and took over five small houses in the Forbury for the use of his grooms and equerries, but he leased the abbey site to Sir Thomas Clarges, a diplomat and MP, 'with the manor house belonging thereto, excepting the stables &c., which are reserved for the king's use'.[111] Clarges assumed that the houses were included in the lease, while the king took the view that they belonged with the stables, but to the latter's annoyance Clarges was judged to be in the right, and he received an annual rent of £30 and back rent for what had not been paid. This arrangement continued only until the early 1670s, when the king appears to have given up all interest in the site. Clarges himself did not live in the palace: his constituencies were in London, then Christchurch (Hants) and Oxford University. He had a town house on Piccadilly, and a country seat in Stoke Poges (Bucks) was less than twenty-five miles away.[112] His name appears in the Corporation records only once, when in 1684 he managed to annoy the Corporation by encroaching on the Forbury, and was threatened with the law if he failed to remove the (unspecified) intrusions.[113] He eventually sold the

---

[108] CSP (Domestic) 1644, 163. Sir Patrick Ruthven, Earl of Forth was the general-in-chief of the king's army at this time.

[109] Slade (2001), 35.

[110] Guilding (1892–96), 4, 450.

[111] CSP (Domestic) 1660–61, 578.

[112] Oxford DNB.

[113] Reading Corp. MSS, 198–99.

26   THE GREAT ARCH AT PARK PLACE, SHOWN IN THIS ENGRAVING, WAS BUILT BY GENERAL CONWAY FROM
READING ABBEY STONES. IT NOW CARRIES THE A321 HENLEY TO WARGRAVE ROAD.

site to John Dalby and Anthony Blagrave, both shares passing down their respective lines until Dalby's heirs sold their share to Henry Vansittart (1732–70), one-time Governor of Bengal.

In 1752 General the Hon. Henry Seymour Conway purchased Park Place, Remenham, an estate on the outskirts of Henley (Berks). Park Place became a rendezvous for members of the circle around Horace Walpole, who encouraged Conway in the kind of landscape gardening associated with the Gothick style. There was a Grecian Temple and a bridge crossing the valley carrying the road from Henley to Wargrave, both constructed using stones brought from Reading Abbey (figure 26), and he later added a Druid's Temple from St Helier, presented to him by the inhabitants of Jersey where he served as Governor from 1772.[114] In a letter of 1763 to George Montagu, Walpole wrote that

> The Works of Park-place go on bravely; the cottage will be very pretty, and the bridge sublime, composed of loose rocks, that will appear to have been tumbled together there from the very wreck of the deluge. One stone is of fourteen hundred weight. It will be worth a hundred of Palladio's bridges, that are only fit to be used in an opera.[115]

[114]   Walpole letters, 9, 142, 145.
[115]   Walpole letters, 4, 115 (3 October 1763).

NINETEENTH-CENTURY WORKS

By the early nineteenth century, the problems associated with having a ruinous dissolved monastery in the middle of a large town were becoming acute, especially in view of the fragmented and sometimes disputed ownership of the site.[116] John Man remarked on the state of the site, which was

> 'now reduced to a mass of ruins, and involved in so much confusion, by the broken fragments which have fallen in almost all directions, as almost to preclude the possibility of tracing an outline of the original building, or the boundaries of its enclosure,'[117]

and he published his own sketch-map based on Englefield's 1789 survey.

He also described the National School for 300 to 400 children, set up inside the chapter house by a group of subscribers at a meeting held on 18 April 1812.[118] Two spacious rooms were erected within the walls, with apartments at the east end for the residence of the master and mistress. Man recognised that 'antiquaries may regret this disfigurement of the finest and most perfect remains of this once beautiful abbey', but excused it on the grounds that 'it could not have been employed to a better purpose'.[119] This intrusion was only possible because the ruins were in private hands, and the owners were at liberty to use them as they wished. Man also noted a cottage built by Lord Fane (MP for Reading from 1754–61) against the north chancel aisle wall, visible in several of the antiquarian views of the ruins, including Tomkins's *North View of the Ruins* of 1791 and Page's *Reading Abbey, in Berkshire Plate 2* (figures 27 and 28).[120]

In 1831 a building scheme was proposed which would have caused great damage to the ruins. It will be remembered that part of the site had been purchased by Henry Vansittart. He died in 1769–70 when the HMS Aurora on which he was sailing to India disappeared without trace, apparently shipwrecked. His share in the abbey site passed to his youngest son Nicholas, who became Chancellor of the Exchequer from 1812–23 in Lord Liverpool's government. His policies were so unpopular that he was forced to resign in 1823, accepting the sinecure of Chancellor of the Duchy of Lancaster and the title of Baron Bexley. He resigned from the Duchy five years later, effectively stepping down from public life, and when he died in 1851 his obituarist remarked that

> A whole generation has passed away from this world since the noble Lord just dead ceased to participate in the active affairs of life, and those who belong to

---

[116] See Slade (2001), 54–93.
[117] Man (1816), 248.
[118] Ibid., 218.
[119] Ibid.
[120] Ibid., 252.

27   C. TOMKINS'S *NORTH VIEW OF THE RUINS* (1791), A POPULAR VIEWPOINT FOR ANTIQUARIAN DRAWINGS, SHOWS THE COTTAGE BUILT BY LORD FANE AGAINST THE NORTH CHANCEL AISLE WALL.

the present age may well inquire what title he has established to the respect of posterity.[121]

Bexley owned a good deal of the abbey site, and planned to demolish part of the ruins to construct a road and buildings. The scheme was rejected by the town council, and a public subscription was raised to buy this remaining part of the site for the town, for a sum of £500, the sale being completed in 1835. This did not put an end to the destruction, however. Bexley also held more than an acre of land extending south from the Abbey Gateway and including the cloisters and the refectory. By the end of 1832 he had cleared more of this part of the site, including parts of the walls of the abbey and the arches at the end of the refectory, shown in drawings by Grimm (1778) and Tomkins (published in Coates (1802), figure 29).

By September 1834, however, Bexley had sold out to James Wheble of Woodley Lodge, a Fellow of the Society of Antiquaries who organised an excavation in the chancel, and discovered, on 24 January 1835, an elaborately carved quadruple capital which he christened the 'Reading Abbey

---

[121]   *The Times*, 12 February 1851, 5.

28   PAGE'S *READING ABBEY IN BERKSHIRE PLATE 2*, PUBLISHED BY ALEXANDER HOGG, IN *PICTURESQUE VIEWS OF THE ANTIQUITIES OF ENGLAND & WALES* (PUBLISHED IN 1786) SHOWS A SIMILAR VIEW.

Stone', and which he removed to his home, presumably to measure and study at his leisure for the article he wrote on it for the *Reading Mercury*.[122] This and other carved stones he later gave to St James's Roman Catholic church, which he founded in 1837 in the area of the north transept of the abbey church (plate XVI). The architect was A. W. N. Pugin, and the Reading Abbey Stone was adapted for use as a font (figure plate XVII), while other carved stones found around the abbey site were set into the standing fabric of the north transept and the adjacent Priest's House (figure 30).

The church was opened for use on 5 August 1840, but Wheble had died a fortnight earlier, leaving his remaining holdings in the grounds to his son James Joseph, who sold a strip on the west of the site that contained the east part of the Abbey Gateway to John Weedon, a solicitor, in 1843–44. This strip of land became Abbots Walk, with twelve superior houses built over the south aisle wall of the church and the N range of the cloister (see plate II).[123] At the east end of the church, the building of a new County Gaol in 1843 involved the demolition of the apse and the

122   Later published as an Appendix to Albury (1881), 88–90.
123   English Heritage Listed Building report 38740.

29   C. TOMKINS'S *SAXON ARCHES IN MRS CLEMENT'S GARDEN* IS AN ENGRAVED VIEW OF THE INTERIOR EAST
WALL OF THE REFECTORY PUBLISHED IN COATES (1802).

30   STONES FOUND ON THE ABBEY SITE DURING THE BUILDING OF ST JAMES'S WERE
RESET IN THE WALLS OF THE NEW COMPLEX, INCLUDING THE PRIEST HOUSE.

31   IN THIS LATE NINETEENTH-CENTURY PHOTOGRAPH OF THE FORBURY ARCH, THE
NEW GAOL IS SEEN BEYOND THE ABBEY RUINS IN THE BACKGROUND.

Lady Chapel, clearly shown in Englefield's 1789 plan (see figure 39) and
in Blackamore's 1759 engraving of the east view of the ruins (figure 41).

The next stage in the cleaning up of the abbey site came during the
construction of the Forbury Pleasure Gardens, between 1854 and 1873.
In November 1854 James Joseph Wheble, owner of Forbury Hill and the
eastern section of the present gardens, sold them to the town for £1,200, of
which he supplied £400 himself, being anxious to rid himself of what had
become something of a liability.[124] Work on the Pleasure Gardens began
in the following year, and they were officially opened on Easter Sunday
(23 March) 1856, providing the town centre with a pleasant and attractive space containing shrubs and trees planted under the supervision of
Sutton's Seeds, whose headquarters were nearby, as well as a fountain and
a summer house, adorned grotto-like with carved stones from the abbey

[124]   Slade (2001), 85–89.

32   THE ABBEY GATEWAY WAS ANOTHER POPULAR SUBJECT FOR ARTISTS. THIS NORTH VIEW WAS PUBLISHED
BY HOOPER, 24 MAY 1784.

ruins.[125] A short tunnel was also built to link the Pleasure Gardens and
the abbey, planned as early as 1855 and completed by May 1859.[126] While
digging out the tunnel a good deal of carved stone and flint was unearthed,
and in this period too a large team of labourers was employed to excavate
the ruins to a depth of two to five feet, the soil being used to build an embankment to Blake's Bridge, which crosses the Kennet a short distance east
of the abbey.[127] The loose bases, capitals and voussoirs unearthed during
these works were either placed about the ruins or worked in amongst the
material used in the construction of the arch over the new tunnel (figure
31). Also in 1859 the town council obtained the southernmost part of the
ruins, buying the area between the chapter house and the river, including
the dormitory and the rere-dorter, as well as the north bank of the river
as far east as Blake's Bridge from the heirs of Richard Buncombe, a timber
merchant.

The final consideration was the abbey gateway, whose ownership was
divided until the 1850s (figure 32). While the eastern half was Wheble

[125]   Abbey Quarter, 13.
[126]   Slade (2001), 60–61.
[127]   Taylor (1890), 156–60.

33   THE COLLAPSE OF THE ABBEY GATEWAY AFTER A STORM IN FEBRUARY 1861 LED TO ITS REBUILDING BY
SCOTT, WHICH WAS COMPLETED IN THE FOLLOWING YEAR.

34   IN THE RESTORATION WORK CARRIED OUT IN 2003–
05 IT WAS CONSIDERED NECESSARY TO CONSOLIDATE THE
CLOISTER DOORWAY BY THE INSTALLATION OF A STONE
ARCH, HERE SEEN FROM THE NORTH.

property that had been sold to John Weedon,
the western part belonged to the Blagrave
estate. By 1860, both parts had been bought by
the Corporation, and plans were afoot to house
the Surveyor of the Board of Health and the
Superintendent of the Pleasure Grounds there.
Meanwhile the gateway was deteriorating, and
by December 1860 it had to be shored up, and
early next year the road under it was closed to
carriages. Parts were falling off, and others were
taken down lest they fell, and in February 1861
a storm precipitated a further collapse (figure
33). Finally, in the following month the money
was released to allow a complete restoration by

35   ATTEMPTS WERE MADE TO PRESERVE THE FORM OF THE NORTH-WEST SHAFT
BASES, NOT ENTIRELY SUCCESSFULLY (SEE FIGURE 69, WHICH SHOWS THE SAME VIEW IN
2003).

the architect George Gilbert Scott and the builders Messrs. Wheeler of Reading. The actual work was completed by the middle of 1862.[128]

The story of the last 150 years has been the usual one of alternating neglect and repair, interspersed by excavations.[129] The ruins were first listed as a scheduled monument in 1915, and they were again listed under Town and Country Planning legislation in 1957.[130] In 1952 an unstable section of the cloister wall, above the slype was taken down, and in 1967 a comprehensive repair programme was begun, intended to be followed up by a system of regular maintenance, but this was discontinued, and in 1982 it was found necessary to close the ruins for safety reasons. Another repair project began in 1985, continuing until 1991 when funding ran out. Planned maintenance was again envisaged, involving repointing work and the resetting of loose flints. In 2003–05 some localised repairs were possible within the framework of a Heritage Lottery funded restoration project centred on Forbury Gardens, and it was in this period that a stone

[128] Slade (2001), 65–70; Abbey Quarter, 14.
[129] For a brief summary, see Abbey Quarter, 15–17.
[130] Scheduled Ancient Monument List entry 1007932, 19 April 1915, amended 29 January 1993.

arch was installed over the doorway linking the south nave aisle and the cloister (figure 34). In installing the arch, an attempt was made to ensure that the in-situ ashlar base socles and plinth courses remained visible, but some loss of evidence was unavoidable (figure 35), and the overall effect is disturbingly out of sympathy with the rest of the site (see figures 67 and 69 which show the doorway in 2003).

English Heritage funding allowed the commissioning of another survey, from Oxley Conservation in Henley, which was published in 2008, and inevitably resulted in the identification of ongoing deterioration that necessitated the closing of the ruins to the public. Meanwhile, support for the conservation of the ruins has been subsumed into a plan to develop the area into a 'historical and cultural destination' to be called the Abbey Quarter. In June 2014 Reading Council secured initial funding from the Heritage Lottery Fund and is now developing more detailed plans for its Reading Abbey Revealed.[131]

---

[131] *Friends of Reading Abbey* Newsletter, Autumn 2014.

6

THE ARCHITECTURE OF
THE ABBEY CHURCH

W hen it was dedicated by Archbishop Becket in 1164, the church of
Reading Abbey was one of the greatest in the kingdom, a building
comparable in size with the abbeys of Ely and Peterborough and encrust-
ed with finely-carved ornament. As we saw in the previous chapter, matters are very different now. Following the dissolution of the abbey in 1539,
the church was gradually stripped of its beautiful ashlar facing and the
lead from its roofs. It fell into a state of disrepair and, as the town of Reading grew in importance, the few surviving fragments of masonry were
forgotten and often swamped by later buildings. The great church built
by Henry I as his mausoleum can only be visualised today with the aid of
careful observation and archive work among the surveys and drawings of
long-dead antiquarians (plate XVIII).

1   THE PLAN

VISIBLE REMAINS

The major part of the abbey church still visible today is the south transept.
Part of its south wall and its entire west wall still stand to a good height
above ground, along with a short section at the east end of the south
nave aisle wall that contains the doorway into the cloister and a window
above it. The line of the aisle wall is now continued by nos. 10–12 Abbot's
Walk, built c. 1840 (see plate II).[1] Of the east side of the transept the entire curved wall of the innermost of the two transept chapels survives,
consolidated at the top, and there are traces of the wall of the polygonal
outer chapel, but they do not rise to any great height (plate XIX). The wall

---

[1]   English Heritage Grade II Listed Buildings, LBS 38740, 38741.

36   THE LARGER
BLOCK OF FALLEN
MASONRY FROM
THE NW ANGLE
OF THE NORTH
TRANSEPT IS NOW
SURROUNDED BY
THE CHURCH OF
ST JAMES (TO THE
LEFT) AND THE
PRIEST'S HOUSE
(BEHIND).

of the school alongside St James's Catholic Church follows the line of the
south chancel arcade, and the remains of the bases of the southern crossing piers and one of the chancel arcade columns can be seen projecting
from it (plate XX). Alongside the Catholic church itself is a large, irregular
block of rubble masonry, representing a fallen section of the north-west
angle of the north transept, and this distinctive block appears regularly on
drawings of the ruins from the eighteenth century onwards (figure 36).
A smaller block represents part of the rubble core of the west wall of this
transept (figure 37), and finally the rubble corework of the inner north
transept chapel where it joins the north presbytery aisle wall still stands
in the tiny back garden of St James's priest house, alongside the Roman
Catholic church (figure 38).

SURVEYS AND EXCAVATIONS

For the plan of the church, therefore, we rely heavily upon early surveys
and excavations. The site has been systematically surveyed on four occasions. By far the most informative of the eighteenth-century antiquarian records is the report of a survey of the site by Sir Henry Englefield,
which was presented to the Society of Antiquaries in 1779, and included
a description of the abbey with a measured plan and two sections.[2] There
were also three nineteenth-century surveys. That by John Chessell Buckler

---

2   Englefield (1782), 61–66.

37   THE
SMALLER
FRAGMENT OF
THE NORTH
TRANSEPT, WEST
WALL IN FRONT OF
ST JAMES'S PRIEST
HOUSE. THE
LARGER BLOCK
SHOWN IN FIGURE
36 IS SEEN IN THE
BACKGROUND.

(1793–1894), eldest son of John Buckler, is substantially work of 1823–24.[3] Towards the end of the century, after the construction of St James's church, the new County Gaol and the Forbury Gardens, the site was surveyed twice more: for the first edition Ordnance Survey that was published in 1879, although the survey was carried out in 1875; and by Frederick Albury, whose results appeared in 1880.[4] As well as these general surveys, more recent excavations by Slade (1964–67 and 1971–73), and Vince, Fasham & Hawkes (1979 and 1981) have

38   THE REMAINS
OF THE INNER
NORTH TRANSEPT
CHAPEL, HERE
SEEN FROM THE
NORTH, STILL
STAND IN THE
BACK GARDEN OF
ST JAMES'S PRIEST
HOUSE.

[3]   Buckler (1823).
[4]   Albury (1881).

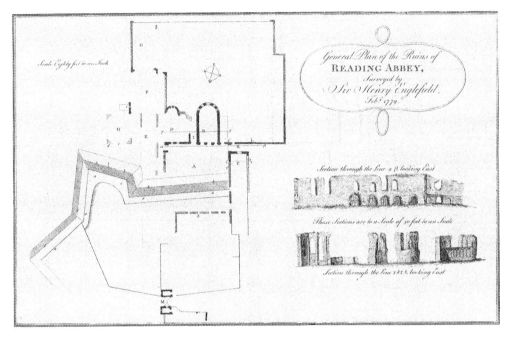

39   SIR HENRY ENGLEFIELD'S *GENERAL PLAN OF THE RUINS*, PUBLISHED IN 1782, SHOWS THE LINE OF THE
CIVIL WAR RAMPART AND DITCH CROSSING THE NAVE AND CLOISTER.

cast some light on specific areas of the complex, notably the east end of the
church and the cloister.

ENGLEFIELD'S SURVEY

The earliest measured plan of the abbey was published by Sir Henry Englefield in 1782 (figure 39). At this time the site was dominated by the great
earthwork erected in 1643 when the town, held for the King by Sir Arthur
Aston, was under seige by Parliamentary forces commanded by the Earl
of Essex. The earthwork ran across the cloisters from south to north, terminating in a bastion towards the west end of the nave, much of which
had been destroyed or buried in its construction, and Englefield could not
precisely locate the west end of the nave.[5] The earthwork can also be seen
in eighteenth-century views of the ruins from the west (figure 40).

The great value of Englefield's survey as far as the church is concerned
is to be found at the east end, where it shows the entire north wall of the
Lady Chapel, which was to be demolished when the new gaol was built in
1843. This wall also appears in Blackamore's 1759 drawing, *The East view
of the Ruins of the Abbey of Reading, Berks* (figure 41). Here a short section
of the wall is shown in the centre foreground, linked by a fence running

5   Englefield (1782), 65.

40   THE CIVIL WAR RAMPART IS CLEARLY SEEN IN THE LEFT FOREGROUND OF GRIMM'S *NORTH WEST VIEW OF THE RUINS*, DATED APRIL 1778.

into the background to a short section of the north chancel aisle wall with a later house built against it (*e* on Englefield's plan). In the background of Blackamore's drawing, just to the right of the south transept chapel, is visible the section of the south nave aisle wall with three windows, immediately to the west of the cloister doorway, which also appears on Englefield's plan.

This section of the nave aisle wall is shown in the centre foreground of Alex Hogg's 1768 view, engraved by Rennoldson, *Reading Abbey in Berkshire. Plate 4* (and in the identical view by Godfrey of 1773), which was published reversed, but is shown corrected in figure 42.[6] To the left of the nave wall can be seen the inner south transept chapel and the Lady Chapel wall, and to the right the triple opening of the chapter house and the north wall of the refectory (now demolished). The dark line in the foreground marks the edge of the Civil War ditch.

[6]   Hogg's print was published in *Picturesque Views of the Antiquities of England & Wales*, 1786.

41   BLACKAMORE'S *EAST VIEW OF THE RUINS OF THE ABBEY OF READING, BERKS* (1759) IS VALUABLE IN SHOWING
THE REMAINS OF THE LADY CHAPEL WHICH WERE STILL STANDING AT THAT DATE.

At the time of Englefield's survey the south transept was much as it is today, while of the north transept only three of the outer angles were visible. No piers are shown on the survey, but parts of the foundations of the crossing piers and the south nave arcade appear.

BUCKLER'S SURVEY

Buckler's survey is contained in manuscript notes and drawings in the British Library. They are bound in two volumes: one (BL, Add. 36400A) contains plans and drawings of Reading Abbey, a plan of Stanton Lacy church, Shropshire and section drawings of the tower of Flempton church, Suffolk. This last is dated 1838. The second volume (Add. 36400B) contains only the written *Notes on the Architecture of Reading Abbey*, covering 50 folios. The Reading Abbey material in Buckler's papers has previously been dated to 1878 on the evidence of a passage from the *Notes on the Architecture of Reading Abbey*:

the writer can state that in the year 1823 the outline of the great apse of the sanctuary, of the choir and of the Transept, indeed of every member of the edifice spared by the Republicans, was distinct and connected throughout. The bases of almost all the pillars retained their positions, but not all an equal amount of their finish. In the course of 55 years which have passed since that

42 HOGG'S *READING ABBEY IN BERKSHIRE. PLATE 4*, ENGRAVED BY RENNOLDSON HAS HERE BEEN REVERSED
TO SHOW THE CORRECT VIEW OF THE RUINS LOOKING SOUTH-EAST. THE NEAREST WALL IS THE SOUTH NAVE
AISLE WALL, WITH THE DOORWAY INTO THE CLOISTER AT THE LEFT END.

date, the quantity and quality of this substantial information have been considerably reduced.[7]

It is clear, however, both from the written text and the drawings that the
survey and most of the observations were actually made in 1823/24, and
indeed it is unlikely that the survey should date from 1878 since Buckler
was 85 years old in that year. We know, for example, from the surveys of
Albury and the Ordnance Survey, that the foundations of the nave were
visible in the late 1850s (see below). Yet when Buckler wrote his description the western parts of the nave were still buried under the earthworks
described by Englefield in 1779:

> but this formidable work [i.e. the construction of the Civil War fortifications]
> could not be effected without the destruction of at least three fourths of the
> length of the Abbey Church. If not uprooted, the lowly walls and pillars still
> repose on their foundations under so vast an amount of soil that with its pres-
> ent occupation all chance is removed of a discovery of these interesting relics.

[7] Buckler (1823), B, f. 2v.

The extent of the nave and the form of the west front are particulars of value not to be ascertained.[8]

This state of affairs is also reflected in Buckler's measured plan of the site (figure 43), which shows the church only as far west as the second bay of the nave.[9] In fact, among the manuscript annotations on this plan is further evidence for the early date of the survey. A note referring to the passage between the chapter house and the dormitory states that

> the arches and groins of the roof of this passage spring from corbels, but they have fallen in and in 1824 nothing more remained of them than the springers on the corbels on each side wall.[10]

The plan of the church on this drawing includes the entire chancel (including the Lady Chapel) and transept, and the two eastern bays of the nave. The chancel is shown with four straight bays and a hemicycle of four piers. There is no indication of the original east chapel arrangement, but Buckler noted in an annotation that the Lady Chapel was an addition to the original fabric:

> there can be no doubt that the Lady Chapel was an addition to the Anglo Norman edifice but nothing more is known of it than can be gathered from the foundation. Its walls were slender compared with any of those in the church and the prominent buttresses indicated a late date.[11]

The transept is shown with a pair of eastern chapels on each arm. Those on the northern arm are of equal size. The inner chapel of the south transept is much deeper, and its companion notably shallower than those on the north. It is to Buckler that we owe the designation of the inner south transept chapel as the Founder's Chapel, on the grounds that it might have been rebuilt in an enlarged form after the burial of King Henry I in 1136.[12] It is hard to credit this, since we know from the Chronicle of John of Worcester that the king was buried before the High Altar, and from the 1532 visitation that he was still there at that date.[13]

THE FIRST EDITION ORDNANCE SURVEY AND ALBURY'S SURVEY

The earliest measured plan showing the entire church appears on the first edition Ordnance Survey (OS), published in 1879 and surveyed four years

---

[8]   Ibid., B, f. 2r.
[9]   Ibid., A, f. 1r.
[10] Ibid.
[11] Buckler (1823), A, f. 1r.
[12] See also Bony (1976), 21, 25 n. 17.
[13] John of Worcester, 3, 214–16; Rylands (1907), 1, 1–2.

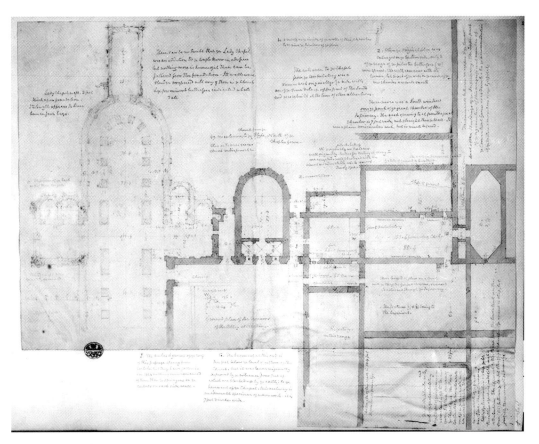

43   J. C. BUCKLER'S PLAN OF THE EAST END OF THE ABBEY CHURCH AND THE MONASTIC BUILDINGS DATES
SUBSTANTIALLY FROM 1823–24 AND IS NOW IN THE BRITISH LIBRARY (ADDITIONAL MS 36400A, F. 1R).

before that (figure 44). This contains far more information that could be
gained by simply surveying the ground and recording the *in-situ* remains
visible at the time. The OS clearly relied to some extent on the plans made
by antiquarian surveyors such as Englefield (1779) and Buckler (1823–24),
but for the positions of the nave piers they must have had access to some
record of their exposure around 1857, when a large team of labourers was
employed to excavate the ruins to a depth of two to five feet, the soil being
used to build an embankment to Blake's Bridge.[14] Loose bases and capitals unearthed during this work were either placed about the ruins or
worked in amongst the material used in the construction of the arch over
the pathway from the ruins to the Forbury Gardens (figure 45). The nave

[14]   Taylor (1890), 156–60; Hurry (1901), 145.

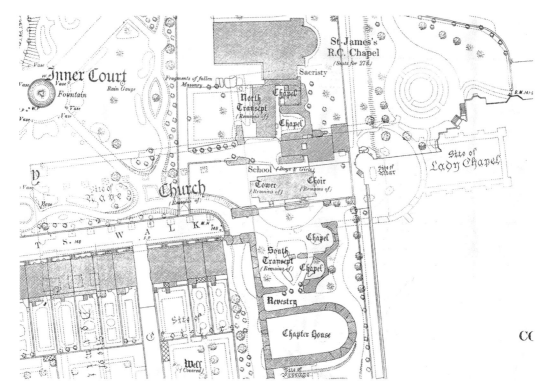

44 THE PLAN OF THE ABBEY CHURCH, WITH THE FOUNDATIONS OF THE NAVE ARCADE PIERS MARKED, IS SHOWN IN THE FIRST EDITION ORDNANCE SURVEY OF 1879.

pier bases were not exposed for very long, for in 1861–62 the Forbury Gardens were laid out with lawns, paths and flower beds covering the site of the nave, and a photograph of about 1875 shows no trace of the foundation walls or pier bases (figure 46). Whence the Ordnance Survey derived their information about the nave piers is not known for certain. They may have actually surveyed the ruins between 1857 and 1861, whilst they were still visible, but it is much more likely that they consulted a local source, and this was almost certainly Frederick Albury. In his article published in the *Transactions of the Berkshire Archaeological and Architectural Society* for 1880–81 he referred to a plan that he had made, and he was careful to emphasise that a good deal of research was involved in its production:

> I must now direct attention to the plan I have prepared with great care and accuracy from actual survey of the existing remains and records of foundations, [which] I have from time to time collected from various sources, as well as from actual discovery, during the carrying out of several works under my direction within the precincts, over a period of 20 years. The plan has been laid down and printed in red on a reduced copy of the recent ordnance survey, so

45   THE FORBURY ARCH WAS CONSTRUCTED FROM CARVED STONES FOUND AMONG THE
RUINS. THIS PHOTOGRAPH DATES FROM MAY 2013, WHEN THE RUINS WERE CLOSED TO
THE PUBLIC FOR SAFETY REASONS.

as to accurately show the relative positions of the ancient buildings with the existing modern ones.[15]

Unfortunately Albury's plan did not find its way into the published journal, but it must have been similar to one prepared for Hurry's 1901 monograph (plate XXI).[16] Hurry's plan can be considered a consensus of received opinion at that time. It shows a cruciform building with an aisled nine-bay nave and an aisled chancel three bays long with an ambulatory with a rectangular Lady Chapel (dateable, despite Buckler's uncertainty, to the abbacy of Nicholas of Whaplode or Quappelade (1305–28) and precisely to 1314), but no radiating chapels.[17] A curious feature that also appears on the OS plan has been retained on Hurry's: a length of wall has been indicated on each side of the external apse wall, leaving it at a right angle just east of the points where the curve of the apse begins. They are certainly too long to be buttresses, and can surely only be the remains of radiating chapels, but Hurry makes no mention of them in his description

[15]   Albury (1881), 83.
[16]   Hurry (1901), facing page 148. This plan and another facing page 6 are signed *Poulter 1901.*
[17]   For the date of the Lady Chapel, see London, British Library Harley 82, fols 1–2 (a fragment of Whaplode's Register).

46   THIS VIEW OF C. 1875 SHOWS THE FORBURY GARDENS LOOKING EASTWARDS TO THE FOUNTAIN, WITH ST.
JAMES'S ROMAN CATHOLIC CHURCH, PRESBYTERY AND SCHOOL IN THE BACKGROUND.

of the church. The transepts have no aisles but two eastern chapels on each
arm, arranged as surveyed by Buckler and Englefield.

THE PLAN IN THE TWENTIETH CENTURY

An arrangement of chapels with four on the transept but none on the
ambulatory was certainly an unusual one, and it is hardly surprising to
find that later many writers were reluctant to accept Hurry's plan.[18] P. H.
Ditchfield and William Page, editors of the relevant volume of the *Victoria County History*, were exceptions; they did not publish their own plan,
but their description of the twelfth-century plan followed Hurry's closely.[19] Sir Alfred Clapham assumed that the ambulatory would have radiating chapels, and that the three radiating chapels of Leominster Priory,
which became a cell of Reading in 1125, had been copied from the example of the mother house.[20] Boase, writing in 1953, followed Clapham's
lead in describing three radiating chapels off the ambulatory, comparing

[18]   It has been assumed that the fourteenth-century Lady Chapel replaced a twelfth-
century eastern chapel, although Hurry did not commit himself to this view.

[19]   VCH Berkshire (1923), 336–42. It is here assumed that there was a twelfth-century
eastern chapel.

[20]   Clapham (1934), 41. Leominster had a single chapel on each transept arm.

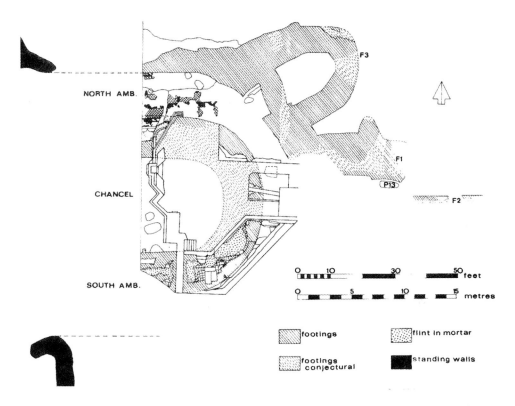

47 IN 1971–73 CECIL SLADE OBTAINED PERMISSION TO EXCAVATE UNDER THE PRISON. THIS PLAN FROM SLADE (1975–76) SHOWS THE FOOTINGS OF THE NORTH AND CENTRAL AMBULATORY CHAPELS.

the plan with those of Battle Abbey, Bury St Edmund's and Norwich.[21] In this assumption Clapham and Boase were anticipating the crucial work of Cecil Slade, who carried out an excavation between 1971 and 1973 at the east end of the ambulatory, within the prison walls.[22] He uncovered the footings of the ambulatory and hemicycle walls on the north side of the apse, including the entire north-east radiating chapel foundation and the northern part of a larger apsidal chapel (figure 48). This important excavation thus completed the picture of the eastern arm, simultaneously providing confirmation that the sections of wall projecting from the apse on the 1875 Ordnance Survey plan did indeed mark the outer walls of the two radiating chapels. The footings, both of the outer walls and the hemicycle, were 12 feet wide and 6 feet deep and made of flints embedded in a yellow mortar. Slade's discoveries at the east end of the church were incorporated into the analysis of the church by Malcolm Thurlby, presented as a paper

21 Boase (1953), 71–77
22 Slade (1975–76), 30–33.

at the British Archaeological Association Conference held at Windsor in 1998,[23] and the most up-to-date plan of the Romanesque church (plate XXII), drawn by Stuart Harrison, based on the first edition Ordnance Survey with Buckler's hemicycle arrangement and incorporating Slade's discoveries at the east end, was published online by the *Corpus of Romanesque Sculpture in Britain & Ireland*.[24]

DIMENSIONS OF THE CHURCH

Englefield, Albury and Buckler all provided measurements in imperial units along with their surveys, and those relating to the church are collected in Table 2, along with figures taken from the Ordnance Survey plan. To judge from the figures, Englefield attempted to measure to the nearest foot, Buckler usually to the nearest inch, or possibly two inches (if he was consistent), and Albury, with one exception, to the nearest five feet. The measurements taken from the OS map are accurate to the nearest half millimetre on the map, which approximates to one foot on the ground. Buckler generally measured internal dimensions, Englefield and Albury external ones. Buckler noted, however, that the walls were 6ft thick, and an appropriate correction has been made to convert his measurements to external ones. The archaeologists also varied in their definitions of some of the dimensions. For the length of the church, for example, Albury and the OS took the distance from the west front to the east wall of the Lady Chapel (i.e. including the Lady Chapel). Englefield's rogue estimate is explained by the fact that he could not locate the west front, as it was still covered by the Civil War earthwork. Buckler was unable to estimate either the total length or the nave length since he did not locate the west front. It is also impossible to know precisely what the three archaeologists meant by the chancel length, since the form of the original east end was not known. Finally the length of the Lady Chapel given in the OS column of the table is the maximum length from the outer face of the east wall to the intersection of the straight side wall and the curving apse. Taking a measurement along the axis from the Lady Chapel east wall to the outer edge of the apse wall gives 75ft, and this may be what Albury has done.

Little can be said about the geometry of the plan, since it is impossible to agree accurate enough measurements. The length of the nave bears a root–2 relationship with the side of the cloister, as was also the case at Norwich, Westminster, Christ Church Canterbury, St Alban's, Winchester, Worcester and Durham.[25] The cloister diagonal measures 62.75m (206ft), and the total length of the nave from the outer face of the west facade

[23]   Thurlby and Baxter (2002).
[24]   R. Baxter, 'Reading Abbey, Berkshire', CRSBI.
[25]   Fernie (1976), 84.

wall to the east face of the transept west wall is exactly the same, according to the Ordnance Survey. The transept measures 62.50m (205ft) between its outer wall faces at the widest part.

Of the 62.75m nave, the west facade wall with its buttresses accounts for 4.7m, leaving 58.5m for the arcade, which was divided into 10 bays.[26] That the same grid was used to lay out the positions of the crossing and chancel piers seems certain from the position of the easternmost piers of the straight section of the chancel, which are 92.74m, or exactly 16 bays from the west responds of the nave. This implies a four-bay chancel and a double-bay crossing. In the transverse direction, the nave width was divided into four units, so that the central vessel was twice the width of each aisle, as at Norwich,[27] but the scheme was not followed with any great precision. The width of the nave measured between the centre lines of the aisle walls is 26.25m, and dividing

48   THE TWELFTH-CENTURY SEAL OF THE ABBEY SHOWS THE VIRGIN HOLDING A MODEL OF THE CHURCH.

this into a 1:2:1 ratio produces notional widths of 6.56m and 13.125m for the aisle and central vessel. The actual measurements are 6.5m and 6.325m for the north and south aisles, and 13.425m for the central vessel, so it is clear that an error was made, either in laying out the line of the south nave arcade or in the 1875 survey.[28] In fact, if the S aisle were as wide as the N, the measurements would be correct to within 0.175m, or 7 inches at 6.5 / 13.25 / 6.5. The puzzling feature of all this is that the units of the grid are significantly bigger in the east-west direction, so that neither the aisle bays nor the double bays of the central vessel are square. It is possible, however, that the discrepancy was a deliberate adjustment made to ensure that the aisle vault bays would be square.[29]

[26]   The eight N arcade bays drawn on the OS map measure 6.0, 5.75, 5.95, 6.0, 5.7, 5.8, 5.35 and 5.8m between pier centres, giving a mean value of 5.79m.

[27]   Fernie (1976), 80.

[28]   Measurements taken between the centres of the aisle walls and the centres of the nave piers.

[29]   Judging from the plan, the aisle vault bays measured 4.1m from east to west and 4.75m from north to south. The vault cells would be square if the transverse arches of the aisle were only 1.1m wide rather than occupying the full width of the piers.

TABLE 2   MEASUREMENTS OF THE ABBEY CHURCH COMPARED

	Englefield	*Albury*	*Buckler*	*O.S.*
Church length	420 ft	450 ft	n/a	450 ft
Chancel width	92 ft		88 ft 4 in	92 ft
Nave width	92 ft	95 ft	90 ft 10 in	92 ft
Clear width (n&c)	34 ft	34 ft	33 ft 4 in	38 ft
Chancel aisle width	19 ft		20 ft	16 ft
Transept length	196 ft	200 ft	182 ft 4 in	205 ft
Transept width	56 ft	75 ft	n/a	71 ft (N)
Chancel length	98 ft	90 ft	100 ft	98 ft
Nave length	215 ft	200 ft	n/a	206 ft
E chapel length	102 ft	75 ft	75 ft	81 ft
E chapel width	55 ft	50 ft	50 ft	48 ft

2   THE EXTERIOR ELEVATION

While the plan of the church can be established with a fair degree of confidence, the same cannot be said of its internal and external elevations.
The demolition of the abbey began very soon after the Dissolution, as we
saw in chapter one, and the only images which might be expected to show
the appearance of the church before that date are on the two abbey seals,
and in the genealogical drawings of English kings by Matthew Paris. The
twelfth-century seal in the British Library shows the Virgin and Child enthroned, with the Virgin carrying a model of a church in her left hand
(figure 48). Little can be deduced from this tiny, worn image except that
the church depicted has a prominent crossing tower. It is not even clear
which aspect of the church is represented on the seal. Of course, there is
no reason to suppose that the church on the seal was intended to represent
Reading Abbey church in any but the most general way. This is truer still
of the image on the seal of 1328, attached to a charter at Hereford Cathedral (figure 49). The reverse of this seal shows Henry I enthroned under a
traceried canopy, flanked by standing figures of St Peter and St Paul, under
similar canopies. In his left hand, Henry holds a model of a church, but it
is a simple gabled box with a central spire, rather like the Sainte-Chapelle
in Paris, and is certainly not intended to resemble the church he actually
founded.

The abbey church is also represented in Matthew Paris's genealo-
gies of the Kings of England in the *Abbreviatio Chronicorum Angliae* of

49 ON THE
SEAL OF 1328
KING HENRY
I IS DEPICTED
HOLDING
THE CHURCH,
FLANKED BY ST
PETER AND ST
PAUL.

c. 1255–59,[30] and the *Historia Anglorum* of 1250–59.[31] Both manuscripts show William I, William II, Henry I and Stephen individually enthroned under arches, each holding objects associated with his reign. In the former, the Conqueror carries a ship in his left hand and a sword in his right; Rufus holds an arrow in his left hand; Henry holds a model of a church and a book; and Stephen a church and a sword. In the more detailed drawings in the *Historia Anglorum*, all four kings carry buildings,[32] and these are identified in the surrounding text (plate XXIII). The Conqueror is shown with Battle Abbey church, Rufus with Westminster Hall, Henry with Reading Abbey church, and Stephen with Faversham. Unfortunately none of these buildings survives in anything like its original state, so the accuracy of the drawings cannot be gauged, but the artist has at least attempted to

---

30 London, BL, Cotton Claudius D. VI, f. 5r.
31 London, BL, Royal 14. C. VII, f. 8v.
32 William I's ship has been retained: he is using it, upturned, as a footstool. Rufus and Stephen hold sceptres.

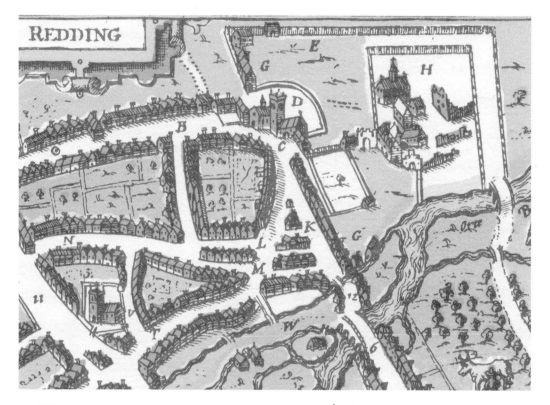

50   THE ABBEY PRECINCT APPEARS AT THE NORTH-EAST OF JOHN SPEED'S 1610 MAP OF READING. THE CHURCH IS TO THE LEFT OF THE LETTER H.

distinguish between them, so that the three churches look very different from one another. Henry's Reading is shown with a pair of towers flanking the west end, no crossing tower and what might be an apsidal chapel at the east end. The western towers are in three stages topped by pointed turrets, and appear to be circular in plan. No other towers are shown, and there is no transept and nothing to mark the division between nave and chancel. Windows are shown along the nave wall and in the top storeys of the towers. Despite the closeness of the two sets of Matthew Paris drawings, the image of Reading Abbey in the *Abbreviatio Chronicorum Angliae* is different again (plate XXIV):[33] the building is shown as a single-celled structure without transepts, but the drawing is much more schematic, with no windows indicated. Twin towers capped with turrets again appear

[33]   Morgan (1982), 142–45 and Ill.306. Morgan argues that the drawings in the Cotton MS were modelled on those in the Royal MS, and attributes differences between them to either hasty execution or the presence of another hand in some or all of the Cotton drawings (144).

at the west end, but they are not articulated into storeys, and appear to be square in plan. A third, taller tower is shown towards the east end of the building.

Similar observations might be made about the models held by other kings in the two series, and it seems to follow that Matthew Paris was interested in showing only generic churches, not particular buildings, and used a stock repertoire of towers and windows to introduce some variety into the images. From the archaeological point of view, the only significant feature of these images is that in the *Historia Anglorum*, Reading is shown as the largest and most elaborate church in the series. Beyond this, none of the medieval images is of much value in gauging the appearance of the abbey church, and with the possible exception of the twelfth-century seal, none of them was intended to be a specific representation.

Our knowledge of the appearance of Henry's church is therefore based largely on antiquarian drawings and descriptions made between the seventeenth century and the nineteenth, and on such remains as survive either on-site or elsewhere. From the seventeenth century, we have a view of the abbey including the church in John Speed's plan of the town, first published in 1610.[34] The church at the top of Speed's plan is shown as a short gabled box with a central tower (figure 50). The roof is shown intact, although it cannot have been in 1610, since the lead and timbers were removed in the sixteenth century. We also know from later drawings that parts of the apsidal east end and the Lady Chapel were standing at this date; furthermore, much of the south transept is still standing today, along with the buildings on the east side of the cloister, which are not shown on Speed's plan at all. These considerations, among others, lead to the inescapable conclusion that as far as the church is concerned, John Speed's representation must be read as conventional too. According to Skelton, Reading was 'not one of the most accurate of Speed's plans',[35] a conclusion he based on irregularities in scale and on inaccuracies in the positions of the rivers. Moreover it is entirely possible that Speed attempted to reconstruct the original appearance of the church, rather than simply drawing what he saw, as he did in representing a castle which was a ruin in his day in his plan of Southampton.[36]

By the eighteenth century, when the ruins became an object of interest to artists and antiquarians, very little more stood of the church than can be seen today. A short description by the antiquary Browne Willis

[34] Speed (1610). The plan of Reading appears as an inset to the Buckinghamshire map, Speed explaining that, 'For that Barkshire cold not contayn place for this Town I have here inserted it, as one of the most ancient and cheifest in the Countye.'
[35] Skelton (1951), 117.
[36] Ibid., 115.

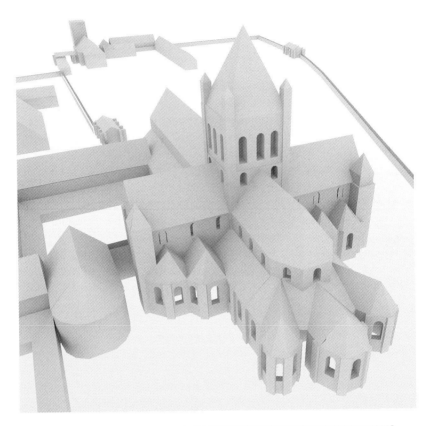

51   READING ABBEY CHURCH: A RECONSTRUCTION DRAWING SHOWING THE MASSING
OF THE ABBEY CHURCH FROM THE EAST.

(1682–1760) is given in Thomas Hearne's edition of Leland's Collectanea of 1774. According to this,

> there is little remaining of this abbey at present, except some rough Walls of the Church, and the Walls of our Ladie's Chapell and of the Refectory, which was a large Room (where was a Parliament held Anno 31. H. VI.) the Cloysters & c. being intirely demolished. The Church seems to have been a spatious Fabrick, and to have been built in the form of a Cross, with a Tower in the middle without Isles.[37]

Two points arise from this: the mention of a tower and the absence of aisles. We know, of course, that the church did have aisles in the nave and the chancel, but even the more careful survey of Englefield, described above, failed to reveal much evidence for them apart from the remains of

[37]   Leland Collectanea 6, 184.

52   THE NAVE OF ELY CATHEDRAL HAS A TALL GALLERY WITH ITS OWN WINDOWS. SUCH AN ARRANGEMENT
IS AN ALTERNATIVE POSSIBILITY FOR READING TOO, WHICH WOULD AFFECT THE GENERAL MASSING OF THE
CHURCH.

the crossing piers and south nave arcade, and it is clear that the latter can
only have been foundations, because they do not appear at all in the contemporary views of Hogg, Grimm and others. It is likely, therefore, that
Willis missed the nave arcade foundations and deduced the tower from
the presence of the crossing arches.

There is no doubt that there was a crossing tower; it would be unthink-
able for a church of this size and grandeur not to have one. As Fernie
remarks, 'almost all churches with transepts have one over the crossing',
and the only English example he finds without one, the eastern crossing
of Anselm's Canterbury Cathedral, is not relevant in this case because it is
not a main crossing.[38] The crossing piers are extremely massive, especially
in the east-west direction, and must have been made so to support the
tower. A general notion of the external massing of the abbey church can
thus be visualised from the plan, and is shown in figure 51. Here the aisle
roofs are shown rising from just above the aisle windows, but the possibility that there were galleries with windows, and that the aisle roofs sprang
from above them, as at Durham, Ely, Winchester and the contemporary

[38]   Fernie (2000), 263.

53   THE ROBBED-
OUT PLINTH
COURSES OF THE
CHANCEL ARE
CLEARLY SEEN ON
THE EXTERIOR
OF THE SOUTH
TRANSEPT INNER
CHAPEL OF
READING ABBEY
CHURCH.

abbey of Peterborough cannot be discounted (figure 52). Similarly we cannot know much about the proportions of the various elements of the elevation, particularly the height of the clerestory.

Little survives in the way of exterior walls of the church that might help us to visualise their articulation, beyond the exterior of the inner south transept chapel, stripped of its ashlar. This chapel retains a deep robbing, nearly a metre high, for a large plinth course and at the base of the windows another robbing representing a lost stringcourse. The surviving robbing of the plinth shows that it was composed of seven courses of stone (figure 53). The buttresses are marked by broad stepped projections in the corework with a narrower angle buttress between the chapel and the south presbytery aisle wall. The surviving window heads and jambs are articulated in stepping for two external nook shafts and arch orders. The extent of the external decoration should also be considered, and in the case of Reading we are entitled to assume that it was extremely elaborate. This conclusion is based partly on the survival of carved stones around the abbey site, many of which are decorated with the chevron and beakhead ornament typical of the period; partly on the knowledge of its status, which would have been expressed in visual grandeur; and partly on what we know of Henry I's other buildings, notably Norwich Castle keep and the churches at Domfront, Lonlay and Goult in Normandy. One certainty is that there was at least one corbel table. Twelfth-century corbels from the abbey church survive in a folly in St Laurence's churchyard made from carved stones found around the site, as well as in the museum and

54 THE FOLLY ERECTED IN ST LAURENCE'S CHURCHYARD, READING, INCORPORATES TWO WORN CORBELS FROM THE ABBEY CHURCH.

in the Forbury arch (figures 54, 55). In the account of the dismantling of the church in 1549, William Grey bought a good deal of carved stone, and among his purchases was 'certayne stone that wente aboute the southe syde of the Churche under Bartlements', for which he paid 13 shillings and 4 pence.[39] In view of his interest in carved stone, evidenced by his purchase of the cloister arcades (see chapter five), we are entitled to assume that this was probably a corbel table.

3   THE INTERIOR ELEVATION

The appearance of the interior of the church is also a matter for speculation and there are very few certainties. Nowhere do the standing ruins rise any higher than the level of the aisle or chapel windows, and even the older antiquarian drawings show little or nothing that is taller than the standing remains. It will be convenient, therefore, to treat separately each part of the church that has some standing remains, either extant or shown in antiquarian views before attempting a synthesis.[40]

[39]   Preston (1935), 122.

[40]   Much of the description and interpretation of the standing walls is taken from a survey carried out by Stuart Harrison, and reported in a private communication to the author.

55   THIS CORBEL,
CARVED WITH A
PAIR OF HEADS, IS
INCORPORATED
IN THE FORBURY
ARCH.

56   THE WEST
WALL OF THE
SOUTH TRANSEPT
RETAINS SOME
OF ITS ASHLAR
FACING AT THE
FOOT.

57   ENGLEFIELD PRODUCED SECTIONS OF THE RUINS IN ADDITION TO HIS PLAN. BOTH ARE VIEWS LOOKING
EAST. THE UPPER SHOWS, FROM LEFT TO RIGHT, THE WEST WALL OF THE SOUTH TRANSEPT, THE SLYPE
ENTRANCE, THE TRIPLE ARCHED CHAPTER HOUSE ENTRANCE AND THE DORMITORY UNDERCROFT. THE
LOWER SHOWS THE SOUTH TRANSEPT CHAPELS, THE INTERIOR EAST WALL OF THE CHAPTER HOUSE AND AT
THE FAR RIGHT THE INTERIOR EAST WALL OF THE REFECTORY (ALSO SHOWN IN FIGURE 29).

58   THE SHAFT
BASES ARE STILL
IN PLACE ON
THE SILL OF THE
NORTH WINDOW
OF THE INTERIOR
WEST WALL OF
THE SOUTH
TRANSEPT.

59   THE STANDING RUBBLE CORES HAVE RETAINED THE IMPRESSION OF THE ROBBED-
OUT SOUTH RESPOND OF THE ARCH BETWEEN THE SOUTH TRANSEPT AND THE SOUTH
NAVE AISLE.

60   IN THIS VIEW OF THE INTERIOR SOUTH WALL OF THE SOUTH TRANSEPT, THE
PROJECTING CORE OF THE RESPOND AT THE FAR LEFT INDICATES THAT IT WAS
ARTICULATED IN THE SAME WAY AS THE WEST WALL.

SOUTH TRANSEPT

The south transept is the most substantial part of the church that has
survived and it retains valuable evidence for the articulation of the walls.
The main surviving elements are a large part of the west wall and part of
the south wall (plate XXV). These walls are massive and impressive but it
should be borne in mind that they have lost at least half of their original
height. The ashlar has largely been stripped, although the lowest courses
remain at the southern end of the west wall, and these show that the ashlar
blocks were precisely cut with fine mortar joints (figure 56). The upper
parts of the standing walls have been consolidated, but in the lower parts,
which have not been conserved, it is possible to read the robbed core and
recover details of the design. The outline of the main ashlar blocks can
easily be observed, to the extent that with a technique such as photogram-
metry it would be possible to recover the precise jointing and even to recognise individual variations that might show building breaks. Looking
first at the west wall, there are two window openings in a flat wall that was
originally articulated with wide vertical responds or pilasters, whose position is clear from the depth of the robbing of the surface ashlar. This shows
that the transept was divided into three bays (plate XXVI), and that the
dividing responds apparently did not support arches enclosing the lower

61   THE ROBBED-OUT ORDERS OF THE SOUTH TRANSEPT INNER
CHAPEL WINDOWS ARE CLEARLY VISIBLE IN THE COREWORK.

windows. This is not absolutely guaranteed, since the window arches have not survived, but it appears certain that their springing points at least are below the top of the surviving wall, and at this high level there is no evidence of arches in the surface robbing. Confirmation of this comes from Englefield's section showing the exterior of this wall in 1779 (figure 57, upper section). In this the northern of the two window arches is almost complete, and yet the height of the wall can be seen by comparison with the west wall of the chapter house to be much as it is today, the only difference being the repairs and consolidation at the top.

This internal arrangement suggests that these recesses formed giant order arches that framed the windows (plate XXVII). The windows themselves employed several orders of shafts and presumably arch mouldings in the heads, but unfortunately, though the remains are very tall, no trace of the arch heads remains. Internally there are small remains of ashlar bases at sill level (figure 58). A horizontal robbing shows that these stood on a stringcourse. The inner, or northern bay, at the extreme northern edge of the standing wall, has a different form of articulation because it adjoined the south nave aisle. Here the south respond of the arch into the nave aisle survives, though robbed, together with the springing of the stilted arch that it carried (figure 59). In the south wall of the transept, the robbed core shows that the bay articulation of the west wall was repeated with a central pilaster and a recess at each side (figure 60). There are no traces of windows because of the three-storey slype to the south, but presumably windows were provided in the lost uppermost part of the wall.

The most impressive remains are of the east wall of this transept, which retains part of the eastern apse of the inner or north chapel together with part of its square forebay, and to the south the low remains of the smaller south chapel. The north chapel apse has two windows, one at the east and

62 THE SOUTH SPRINGING OF THE ENTRANCE ARCH TO THE APSE OF THE INNER SOUTH CHAPEL, RETAINS PART OF THE CUT BACK IMPOST BLOCK.

63 UNLIKE THE INNER CHAPEL, THE SOUTH TRANSEPT OUTER CHAPEL, HERE SHOWN FROM THE WEST, HAS ONLY LOW WALLS REMAINING.

one at the south. The north bay has no space for a window since it is built hard against the south wall of the chancel aisle (plate XXVIII). In this chapel the windows are large and retain stepping for the multiple orders of the jambs and arch heads, suggesting that they were considerably

embellished (figure 61). The remains of the responds at the entrance to the apse show multiple stepping, indicating numerous orders to the shafts. On the east side, some of these are angled to accommodate the curve of the apse wall. The south respond has a cut-back stone at the arch springing which must have been the tail-stone of the capital impost (figure 62). The intermediate responds set around the apse, which must have carried ribs for vaulting, are also of several orders which suggest that the inner wall face was articulated with recessed arches. That this was the case is confirmed by three courses of ashlar vault web above the north respond of

65   BOTH OF
THE SOUTH PIER
SUPPORTS OF THE
CROSSING HAVE
SURVIVED. THIS IS
THE SW BASE.

66   THE SE CROSSING PIER SUPPORT HAS RETAINED NONE OF ITS ASHLAR FACING.

67   IN 2003
SCAFFOLDING
WAS ERECTED IN
PREPARATION FOR
CONSERVATION
WORK ON THE
DOORWAY FROM
THE SOUTH
NAVE AISLE TO
CLOISTER. THE
NAVE AISLE SIDE
IS SHOWN HERE.

67   IN 2003 SCAFFOLDING WAS ERECTED IN PREPARATION FOR CONSERVATION WORK ON THE DOORWAY FROM THE SOUTH NAVE AISLE TO CLOISTER. THE NAVE AISLE SIDE IS SHOWN HERE.

the apse, on its west side (plate XXIX). This is set so far north into the wall that it must have been associated with a deep, arched recess. On the south wall, a small fragment of ashlar retains a curved abutment for the vault on its east side, with two narrow tapered courses of ashlar vault web, and on the west side a curved edge for the abutment to the arched recess.

To the south of this inner chapel are the low remains of another which did not project as far to the east (figure 63, see also plate XXII). There is enough corework remaining on its northern side to show that the apse was divided into three bays like the inner chapel, and that it also featured a deep wall recess. Its south wall has a large squared rubble base for a massive stair turret that gave access to the upper parts of the church and the treasury above the slype.

SOUTH CHANCEL AISLE

The inner south transept chapel adjoins the south aisle of the chancel where the wall retains evidence for the height of the aisle respond piers and the springing for the vaults in the robbed corework (figure 64). To the west side of the remaining vault springing there is a small section of two courses of ashlar walling which abut and retain the curve of the vault web but also another curve on its west edge which indicates that it abutted another arch on that side. This, and the recess in the wall core, suggests that the aisle bays featured large arched recesses that framed the windows. Clearly visible in the rubble core work is the form of a half-cylindrical respond, and

68   THE CLOISTER SIDE OF THE SAME DOORWAY IS SHOWN HERE.

immediately facing this, across the aisle to the north, is the corresponding circular presbytery pier base, now partly covered by a later wall. Only the southern half is visible, clearly showing a half-cylindrical attached shaft towards the aisle. The bases of the SW (figure 65) and SE (figure 66) crossing piers also survive, although in both cases loose capitals found on site have been mortared onto them.

NORTH TRANSEPT

The north transept retains a small section of its west wall and a massive collapsed articulated section of walling at its north-west corner (see figures 36 and 37 above). The former has evidently fallen from the superstructure and lies tilted at an angle. Unfortunately it retains no features that could add to the details of the building. In the back garden of the presbytery of St James's Church, a large section of the north presbytery aisle wall stands to

69   DESPITE THE ROBBED-OUT STATE OF THIS DOORWAY, THE BASES OF THE ORDERS
ARE STILL IN PLACE ON THE NW JAMB. THEY WERE MUCH MORE LEGIBLE BEFORE THE
CONSTRUCTION OF THE REINFORCING ARCH SHORTLY AFTER THIS PHOTOGRAPH WAS
TAKEN (SEE FIGURE 35).

a considerable height (figure 38 above). Though largely robbed of ashlar, it
retains a single base for a semicircular respond shaft on its south side. This
base has angle spurs and stands on a wall bench. The quality of carving is
extremely good and the ashlar joints very fine. North of this is the inner
chapel of the transept and this is of polygonal plan with the lowest courses
of ashlar *in situ*. These indicate the former presence of single shafts at the
angled intersections of the canted walls of the chapel. The deep robbing
above the ashlar strongly indicates the former presence of arched recesses
in the main walls. The adjoining northern chapel has been overbuilt by an
extension to the presbytery.

NAVE

The remains of the nave are restricted to part of the eastern bay of the south
aisle wall and the south-west crossing pier. The aisle wall retains the eastern cloister processional doorway that was an arch of great magnificence,
to judge from the stepped robbing of the jambs and head that were still
present on both sides in 2003 (figures 67 and 68). It is set into a projecting
frame of masonry in order to accommodate the depth of the doorway.
Small sections of ashlar still remained at that time at the bottom, includ-

ing worn bases on the north-west side (figure 69). These have now been partially overbuilt. Above the doorway and set to the east of it is a window that has lost its arch head. It retains worn bases for jamb shafts on the exterior. Its unusual position is related to the internal bay spacing and the vaulting over the first nave aisle bay. The south-west crossing pier is so large that it extends well into the nave and because of this the vaulting had to be adjusted (plate XXX). On its west side it retains the main arcade respond base, which has a semicircular moulded base standing on a tall polygonal sub-base (figure 65). This suggests that like the presbytery piers, those of the nave were also cylindrical. The sheer size of the crossing piers implies that they were intended from the start to carry a substantial high tower, as discussed above. This, following the usual Romanesque pattern, would probably have comprised a large open lantern, to light the monks' choir below and a belfry stage above. The south

70 A VIEW OF THE EAST BAY OF THE SOUTH NAVE AISLE WALL FROM THE NW SHOWS THE CLOISTER DOORWAY AND THE SOUTH JAMB OF THE ARCH FROM THE TRANSEPT TO THE LEFT OF IT.

respond of the arch into the transept from the south nave aisle remains as a robbing with indications of multiple shafts, immediately east of the cloister doorway (figure 70). The capitals were set at the same height as those in the presbytery, six metres high, and indicate that the nave arcades retained the same proportions as the eastern arm. The arch springing above is stilted, showing that it must have been round-headed and on the west side retains the curve of the vault web. This has a distinct flat along its angled face, indicating the former presence of a vault rib.

VAULTING

A large number of vault rib sections have been discovered forming the roof of the Holy Brook conduit, under Courage's brewery site, west of Bridge

71   THE HOLY BROOK IS COVERED WITH STONES TAKEN FROM THE ABBEY RUINS IN THE REIGN OF
ELIZABETH I. THIS VIEW SHOWS REUSED TYPE B VAULT RIBS.

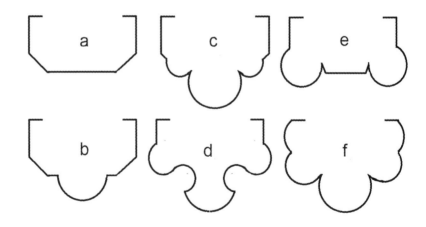

72   SIX DIFFERENT VAULT RIB PROFILES, LABELLED FROM A TO F, HAVE BEEN
IDENTIFIED IN THE HOLY BROOK COVERING. THE SKETCH IS NOT TO SCALE.

Street (figure 71). They were presumably installed there after 1560, when Queen Elizabeth granted the Mayor and Burgesses permission to remove abbey stones to repair ruinous bridges around the town (see chapter five). The ribs are all approximately 10 inches wide and six different profiles have been identified (figure 72), although types c and f are very similar. The commonest profile is type b, represented by some 17 complete arches over the brook. Types a and c each have ten arches and d has three. Types e and f are represented only by occasional voussoirs in other arches. The presence of so many designs suggests that there were rib vaults in various parts of the church – the nave and chancel aisles, certainly, and perhaps the main vessel, at least in the chancel. As was noted in the descriptions of the transept chapels, there is ample evidence for vaulting, including sections of vault webs, still in place.

THE PLACE OF READING ABBEY CHURCH IN CONTEMPORARY ARCHITECTURE

General uncertainty about the original form and scale of the church has prevented it from taking its place in the discourse until now. Three features stand out: the overall scale of the building; the form of the east end; and the presence of enclosing arches in the internal elevation, suggestive of a giant order. These will be looked at in turn, and they are followed by a discussion of the Lady Chapel.

THE SIZE OF THE CHURCH

To obtain some idea of the place of Reading among the English Great Churches of the period, it must first be noted that rebuilding began at practically every cathedral and major abbey church in the country within about thirty years of the Conquest. By 1121, when Reading was begun, this first phase of activity was over, and building was at least well under way at almost every other major site. There is only one contemporary building campaign of comparable status to measure against Reading, and my comparisons will generally be with churches begun at least twenty-five, and in one case as much as seventy-five, years earlier. The single exception is the abbey (now cathedral) of Peterborough, begun in 1118, and the similarity of this cathedral in scale, and indeed in elevation, to the earlier foundations at Ely (begun c. 1081) and Norwich (begun 1096) demonstrates that by and large agreement had been reached on the size of churches of the highest rank.[41] Uncertainties about the original positions of the lost east

---

[41] The original 9-bay nave of Peterborough was 58.4m long (192ft) and the total length of the church was 118.1m (387ft). Figures from Fernie (1984).

73   THE BASE OF PIER 1 OF THE SOUTH CHANCEL ARCADE PROJECTS FROM THE WALL
BETWEEN THE RUINS AND THE FORBURY GARDENS DAY NURSERY.

and west ends of Reading church do not allow absolute confidence about
its length, but if we accept the position of the west end supplied by Albury
and the Ordnance Survey, the length of the nave alone was 62.75m, or
206ft. Likewise we can estimate the length of the original axial chapel at
13m, based on Slade's drawing of this area from his 1971–73 excavation,
which provides a figure for the overall length of Henry I's church in the
region of 127m, or 417ft. Table 3 gives comparative figures for some of the
major Norman Great Churches, including Reading. It will be seen from
this that Reading was comparable with or exceeded in total length any of
the greatest English early-Romanesque churches except Winchester, Bury
St Edmund's and Old St Paul's. Discounting these three, Reading's nave
was shorter than those of Ely and Norwich, but it had a longer eastern arm
than any other church except Bury.

TABLE 3   LENGTHS OF ENGLISH ROMANESQUE GREAT CHURCHES

Church	start date	nave length (ft)	total length (ft)	difference (ft)
Westminster Abbey	c. 1045	c. 203	c. 322	119
Canterbury, Christ Church	c. 1070	c. 185	c. 283	98
Canterbury, St Augustine's	c. 1073	189	324	135
Winchester	1079	266	471	205
Bury St Edmunds	1081	255	c. 500	245
Old St Paul's	1087	260	595	335
Ely	1081	264	410	146
Norwich	1096	254	437	183
Peterborough	1118	192	387	195
Reading	1121	206	417	211

THE EASTERN CHAPELS

There are no precise English precursors for an eastern chapel arrangement like Reading's, with three radiating chapels on the ambulatory and two eastern chapels on each aisleless transept. Several major buildings including St Augustine's, Canterbury (after 1073), Worcester (1084), Gloucester (1089) and Norwich (1096) had three ambulatory chapels and an aisleless transept with a single eastern chapel on each arm. In only two other cases, however, were three ambulatory chapels combined with four on the transept. Baldwin's Bury St Edmunds (1081) was identical in the chapel arrangement, but the transept had an eastern aisle, and in Anselm's re-modelling of Canterbury Cathedral (1096) the old triple-apse east end was replaced with a longer presbytery containing an eastern transept with two chapels on each arm, and an ambulatory with three chapels. As Abou-el-Haj has pointed out, with reference to Bury, this arrangement of seven chapels is a less elaborate version of the European pilgrimage church plan.[42]

---

[42]   Abou-el-Haj (1983), 3. In fact, both Reading and Bury are more elaborate than Sainte-Foi at Conques, which has three radiating chapels but only two chapels on the transept. Saint-Martial at Limoges had five radiating chapels but only two transept chapels, while the pilgrimage churches at Tours, Toulouse and Santiago de Compostella each had five radiating chapels and four transept chapels.

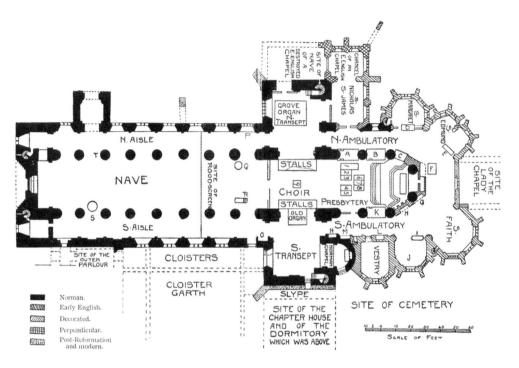

74   THE EAST END OF TEWKESBURY ABBEY CHURCH HAS THE SAME ELONGATED CROSSING PIERS AND
THREE-BAY HEMICYCLE AS READING.

The parallel is an instructive one. The use of aisles in nave, chancel and transept was a feature of all five of the pilgrimage churches to which Abou-el-Haj referred and was intended to allow the circulation of large numbers of pilgrims without hold-ups at the shrines. Bury, with its single transept aisle, and Reading, with no transept aisles at all, clearly envisaged less of a problem. Nevertheless, at Reading, as at Bury, pilgrimage was an essential function of the new church from the start.[43] The abbot's duty to use the alms of the monastery for the care of the poor, of pilgrims and of guests enshrined in the foundation charter has been noted already, and the policy of collecting relics to attract pilgrims has been covered in chapter two.

Another European parallel worth mentioning is Cluny III (begun in 1086), especially since monks from there formed the nucleus of the original community at Reading. Like Canterbury it had a double transept without aisles and a pair of east-facing chapels on the eastern transept, but there were five radiating chapels on the ambulatory. The Cluny plan was

---

[43]   Ibid.

followed much more closely at Lewes Priory where, despite the smaller scale, double transepts and a five-chapel ambulatory were built.

A curious feature of the transept chapels at Reading is that the inner one on the south was deeper than the other three. Buckler's suggestion that this was because it was enlarged in 1135–36 to accept the tomb of Henry I has already been dismissed. A substantial portion of this larger chapel survives (plate XXXI), and although the ashlar facing is lost there is no noticeable discontinuity between its rubble core and that of its neighbour to the south. It is supplied, moreover, with round-headed windows, indicating a twelfth-century date, and no excavation or survey has revealed foundations belonging to an earlier arrangement. We can only conclude that this irregular arrangement was provided from the outset, and that there must have been a liturgical reason for it; possibly it served as the Lady Chapel, as suggested by Hurry.[44] The alternative, that it was built to house the relic of St James, should not be dismissed. While the relic did not arrive in Reading until 1133, and left again three years later when it was borrowed by Henry of Blois, Abbot of Glastonbury, to return in 1155, this is no reason to suggest that the chapel was not built to house it. Henry I may well have intended to present it from the outset.[45]

GIANT ORDER

The evidence of a giant order found in the robbed masonry of the south transept raises the exciting possibility that it might also have been employed in the main elevations. This issue has been raised before, by Richard Halsey in the course of his discussion of the probable giant order in the chancel of Tewkesbury Abbey.[46] But Halsey's argument was based on different observations. First, he noted that the surviving chancel pier bases at Reading indicate that the piers were columnar with attached half-shafts towards the aisle (figure 73). Assuming that the aisles were rib-vaulted, which now seems certain, the half-shafts would carry transverse ribs and the diagonal ribs of the aisle vault would be carried on corbels. This arrangement is characteristic of all the surviving examples of giant order elevations in England. Secondly, many of the dimensions of Reading Abbey church are very close indeed to Tewkesbury, which suggests that other features of the design were also taken up at Reading. In overall scale, of course, Reading was a much larger building, but Halsey points to similarities in the width between the crossing piers, the separation of the chancel piers and the width of the transept.

---

[44] Hurry (1901), 5 n. 2.
[45] Thurlby and Baxter (2002), 295–96.
[46] Halsey (1985), 27–29.

75   THE APSE VAULT AT THE CHURCH OF ST
MARK AND ST LUKE, AVINGTON (BERKS), HAS
RIB VOUSSOIRS OF TYPE E.

The issue of the giant order in England is a complex one. The earliest surviving example is the nave of Romsey, normally dated c. 1140 (plate XXXII). The chancel of Tewkesbury dates from c. 1090–1102, and if the evidence for a giant order there is accepted, it might be expected that the idea would have been taken up before the building of Romsey. Halsey's suggestion that Reading had a giant order was made with a view to filling this awkward gap, and Reading was only one of a number of candidates he put forward for the role with varying degrees of enthusiasm, the others being the nave of Abingdon Abbey, Winchcombe Abbey, St Mary's Priory in Coventry, Exeter Cathedral and Evesham Abbey. All of these buildings had large columnar piers, but the cases for Reading and Evesham are strongest on account of the attached shafts on the aisle side. A later giant order elevation at St Frideswide's Priory, Oxford might be expected to follow a precedent from a larger local abbey, which somewhat strengthens the case for Reading and Abingdon. Finally, it is suggested that a giant order at Reading would be seen as royal iconography, and this would make the adoption of the form at churches with royal connections, like Romsey and Jedburgh, easier to explain.

Ultimately the question has no solution. Even in the earliest of the antiquarian views there is insufficient fabric surviving to indicate the form of the internal elevation, although at first sight Grimm's *NW View of the Ruins of Reading Abbey Berksh.*, dated April 1778, appears to show a giant order arch at the crossing (figure 40). To the left of this view is the fallen stone that still stands outside St James's presbytery, marking the NW angle of the N transept, and alongside it is a standing arch whose piers appear to continue to rise above it, in the manner of a giant order arch. Thurlby has pointed out, however, that in other views – such as Tomkins' *North view of the Ruins* (figure 27) – this arch does not look like a giant order at all, and that even if Grimm's drawing is accurate this must be a pierced SW crossing

76 THE DIAGONAL RIB IN BAY 1 OF THE SOUTH NAVE AISLE AT ROMSEY ABBEY IS
A VARIANT OF TYPE F, AND IS COMPARABLE WITH A DOUBLE-SIZED RIB IN READING
MUSEUM.

pier, and the piercing does not descend to ground level.[47] What we have here, therefore, is an opening through the crossing pier, as in the blocked example at Tewkesbury Abbey.

THE LADY CHAPEL

The addition of an eastern Lady Chapel by Abbot Whaplode around 1314 places Reading firmly within a national trend. An increased devotion to the Virgin can be traced back as far as the 1120s in England, and by the end of the twelfth century a daily mass in her honour was celebrated widely in both secular and monastic communities. The addition of a chapel devoted to her, large enough to house the entire community, was the architectural consequence of this.[48] Such a chapel was constructed in place of the axial chapel of Edward the Confessor's church at Westminster Abbey, beginning in 1220, but this was to be subsumed into Henry III's rebuilding of the entire eastern arm, and was in any case replaced by the chapel of Henry VII, work beginning in 1503. At Winchester a rectangular Lady Chapel was built to replace the main eastern chapel of Walkelin's church, an undertaking begun by Bishop de Lucy (1189–1204) but completed after his death, and normally dated c. 1200–20. De Lucy's Lady Chapel survives but was remodelled in the fifteenth century without significant alteration of its dimensions. At Salisbury the Lady Chapel was part of the original build, dating to c. 1220–30, and follows Winchester in its rectangular form. Hereford Cathedral acquired a rectangular Lady chapel at the east end sometime between 1220 and 1240, probably under Bishop Foliot (1219–34). At Gloucester a new Lady Chapel was built in this position in 1227, but was replaced by the present Perpendicular chapel following the remodelling of the chancel and the installation of the great east window between 1337 and 1367. The Lady Chapel itself was not completed until c. 1500. Where dimensions are known, Reading, at 75 feet by 50 feet, was slightly larger than any of these, all of which were between 30 to 45 feet wide and between 50 and 60 feet long, with the exception of Gloucester which was almost 90 feet long but had a low vestibule at the west end. What seems curious is the late date of Reading's Lady Chapel, but it is not certain that Whaplode's Lady Chapel was the first on the site, or that the foundations recorded by Englefield and the rest were Whaplode's.

SUMMARY

This description of the original form of the abbey church has been hedged about with probabilities and speculation, and while very little in the way

---

[47]   Thurlby and Baxter (2002), 288–91.
[48]   Draper (1987), 86–87.

of absolute certainty has been established, there is enough to provide a synopsis with some confidence. Henry I's church was a cruciform aisled building with a ten-bay nave and four straight chancel bays before a hemicycle with an ambulatory and three radiating chapels. The crossing piers were elongated in the EW direction so that they occupied an entire bay, but some at least were pierced. The transepts were not aisled but each had two eastern chapels with polygonal or semicircular apses and rectangular forebays. The inner chapel of the south transept was deeper than the others, achieved by doubling the forebay into a square plan. The elongated crossing piers served to support a heavy crossing tower. Inside, the church had a three-storey elevation carried on columnar piers that rose in a giant order to enclose the gallery and clerestory. The aisles, chapels and probably the main vessels of nave and chancel were rib-vaulted. Inside and out, the facing was of Taynton stone, finely tooled, and there was lavish decoration of chevron and embattled and billet ornament.

Parallels exist between Reading and various West Country buildings. The most striking and interesting of these is Tewkesbury Abbey (Gloucester) where, as we have seen, there are close correspondences between the measurements.[49] The two churches also shared an unusual hemicycle plan, with three bays carried on regularly-spaced piers (plate XXII, figure 74), and unusually elongated crossing piers. The form of the cylindrical chancel arcade piers with a single half shaft towards the aisle has already been mentioned, in the discussion of the giant order, and the parallels cited there include the churches of Evesham, Tewkesbury and St Frideswide's, Oxford. Romsey Abbey also fits into this group. Reading Abbey church offers little in the way of surviving features suitable for analysis and comparison, but one such is the inner south transept chapel, distinguished by its extra depth, the angled responds that carry its rib vault, and the domical form of the vault itself. The combination of angled responds and domical vaults is unusual in England, but common in Normandy, being found, for example, in the chapter house at Jumièges (Seine-Maritime) and the chancel of the church of Saint-Martin in Verneuil-sur-Seine (Yvelines), the last-named probably taking its design from Henry I's Evreux Cathedral, where excavated diagonal responds in

---

[49] Halsey (1985), 34 n. 86 gives the following comparative figures (Reading first):

Width between E crossing piers	33ft 4in	33ft 4in
Width between choir piers	13ft	12ft 9in
Width of N choir aisle	14ft	13ft 8in
Choir plinth width	7ft 6in	7ft 9in
Width of S transept	32ft	32ft 8in.

His figures are based on Buckler's survey of Reading, and confirmed by personal communications with Richard Emerson, who studied Reading Abbey at the Courtauld Institute in the late 1960s.

the apse imply a similar system.[50] In England, Romsey Abbey (Hants) is relevant in that diagonally set capitals carry the ogives of the aisle ribs in the giant order bay. Finally, the profiles of the six rib types reused in the Holy Brook covering offer some parallels, although many are common types. Type e, with a broad flat soffit flanked by angle rolls, appears in the chancels of St Mark and St Luke, Avington (Berks), and St John, Elkstone (Gloucester), which must succeed Reading in date (figure 75). Type c, with a triple roll, is a common Norman type that is seen, for example, in the west range of Jumièges Abbey and the apse of Saint-Georges-de-Boscherville (Seine-Maritime) at an earlier date. This type is related to type f, and to a double-sized ribstone in Reading Museum with wedges between the three rolls.[51] British examples are probably all later than Reading, but the similar profile found in the S nave aisle of Romsey Abbey (Hants) is again interesting. Here the vault ribs have fillets between the rolls and a hollow outside them (figure 76).

The name of the Master Mason is not known, but there is enough here to demonstrate that his training was probably in the West Country, although he was also familiar with the architecture of Normandy, and was responsible for introducing several Norman features to England. This will become even clearer after the examination of the cloister and its sculpture.

[50]   M. Thurlby, private correspondence; see also Bony (1976), 20–21. Other examples include the crossing at St Denis, Duclair (Seine-Maritime); the chancel and transepts of Saint-Ouen de Léry (Eure); and the chancel of Saint-Germain de Maneglise (Seine-Maritime).
[51]   1998.83. See Thurlby and Baxter (2002), fig. 16.

7

THE ARCHITECTURE OF THE CLOISTER

The cloister, as we have seen, was sited on the south side of the church, its north-east corner lying in the angle of the south wall of the nave aisle and the west wall of the south transept. We have also seen that none of its shaded walks survive above ground, and that even the oldest antiquarian views can tell us little about its structure. And yet the cloister is the part of the complex about which we know the most; so much, in fact, that it merits two chapters to itself.[1]

KEYSER'S DISCOVERIES AT SONNING AND SHIPLAKE

In 1912 Charles Keyser was engaged in excavating the site of the palace of the bishops of Salisbury at Holme Park, Sonning. While the excavations were in progress, Keyser took the opportunity to look around the house (now Reading Blue Coat School) and its gardens about a quarter of a mile away, and he noticed various capitals lying about in the flower-beds. He obtained the owners' consent to remove them, and by 1916 fifteen capitals and two voussoirs from Holme Park had been deposited in Reading Museum (figure 77).[2] Keyser soon discovered that the stones had not been in the gardens at Holme Park for very long, but had come there from an outlying part of the estate called Borough Marsh, some two miles down the Thames. Borough Marsh is effectively an island, cut off from the surrounding lands by the waters of the Thames and the Loddon. At the spot where he was told the stones had come from, Keyser found portions of stone wall and traces of a building, reputedly a chapel. He treated this

---

[1] Much of the material of this chapter was previously published as Baxter and Harrison (2002).
[2] Keyser (1916), 235.

77   THESE CAPITALS AND VOUSSOIRS WERE REMOVED FROM HOLME PARK, SONNING BY CHARLES KEYSER
AND DISPLAYED TO THE FELLOWS AT THE SOCIETY OF ANTIQUARIES.

claim with some scepticism, but was eager to return to the site where he fancied 'some trifling excavations may yield interesting results'.[3] He himself was prevented by the Great War from carrying them out, but his prediction was to be amply fulfilled by George Zarnecki more than thirty years later.

Meanwhile, Keyser had heard another story which dated back to the end of the nineteenth century. Mr Palmer, the owner of the Holme Park estate at the time, had paid a visit to Borough Marsh and interrupted two young men in a punt who were busy removing several carved stones which were in use as steps leading up from a landing place on the island. The young men had come from Shiplake House, which faces Borough Marsh across the Thames, and Mr Palmer gave them permission to carry the stones away on condition that they did not take any more. These stones included twelve voussoirs and fourteen double springers, and in 1889 the Rt. Hon. Sir Walter Phillimore, Bart used them to erect an arch over the path between the house and the church, and a decorative coping on top of the wall to either side (figure 78).

[3]   Ibid., 236.

78   THE CENTRAL
SECTION OF
THE SHIPLAKE
ARCH, WAS BUILT
IN 1889 USING
CARVED STONES
THAT HAD BEEN
REMOVED FROM
THE CLOISTER
OF READING
ABBEY AT THE
DISSOLUTION.

These two groups of carved stones, both taken from Borough Marsh within living memory, were obviously from the same medieval site, and Keyser set about locating it. He dismissed out of hand the suggestion that they were carved for a monastic cell or grange at Borough Marsh itself. For one thing, there is no documentary evidence that such a foundation ever existed, but even if it had, the stones were too numerous and too finely carved for such an unimportant site. He felt, with good reason, that the only reasonable conjecture was that the stones came from Reading Abbey. Transport by water from Reading to Borough Marsh would have been very easy, and he adduced the records of removals of barge-loads of Reading stones down the Thames to Windsor in 1557 to support his argument.

CARVED STONES AT WINDSOR CASTLE

In fact there are a large number of carved stone fragments in the Moat Garden and the so-called Herbarium at Windsor Castle, too – Keyser estimated nearly one hundred – and they have, until recently, been generally attributed to Reading.[4] When Keyser saw them, they were identified by a label describing them as Reading Abbey stones, and he assumed that they came to Windsor along with the stones used to build the Poor Knights' Lodgings in 1557 (figure 79). A moment's reflection, however, will show

---

4   I am grateful to Stephen Brindle for encouraging me to question the Reading provenance of these stones.

79 THESE
ROMANESQUE
CARVED STONES
AT WINDSOR
CASTLE WERE
ILLUSTRATED IN
KEYSER (1916),
FIGURE 15. THE
STONES ARE
STILL THERE,
BUT THE LABEL
IDENTIFYING
THEM AS BEING
FROM READING
HAS GONE.

that this is unlikely in the extreme, because these Windsor stones are Romanesque while those taken from Reading were identified as being from the Lady Chapel, a fourteenth-century building.[5] In fact it is quite possible that they came from Windsor itself; Ambrose Poynter, writing in 1841, illustrated a group of Romanesque carved stones at Windsor which he described as

> a few architectural fragments in the Norman style, brought to light from the excavations during the progress of the late improvements [i.e. Wyatville's 1824–40 restoration], are perhaps the only relics of the palatial edifice of the Twelfth Century.[6]

St John Hope also mentioned the stones in his magisterial work on the castle, but only to alert casual visitors that some of the carved stones they came upon might be from Reading rather than Windsor:

> It is advisable here to add a word of warning concerning the fragments of Norman carved work that are from time to time dug up in the Castle or extracted from later work. Some of these doubtless belong to Windsor, but a large quantity of material was brought here from Reading abbey after its suppression and destruction. Much of this work was also Norman, and it is therefore difficult

---

5   Tighe and Davis (1858), 1, 605–06. See also chapter five above.
6   Wyatvill (1841). See also Stoughton (1862), 6.

80 THIS CHIP-CARVED LOOSE STONE AT WINDSOR CASTLE HERBARIUM IS IDENTICAL IN DESIGN TO CARVED STONES KNOWN TO COME FROM READING ABBEY.

81 A SIMILAR CHIP-CARVED STONE IS SET IN THE EXTERIOR NAVE WALL OF ST JAMES'S RC CHURCH, READING.

to assign to such fragments their proper birthplace. Some carved and moulded Norman fragments, possibly of Henry II's work at Windsor, remain built up as a rude door-jamb in the subterranean postern or outlet into the ditch under the buildings on the south side of the Upper Ward. They have apparently been taken from some important building.[7]

---

[7]   Hope (1913), 1, 22.

82   THIS TREFOIL
CAPITAL FROM A
DOORWAY, NOW
AT WINDSOR
CASTLE, IS
SIMILAR IN
DESIGN TO
CAPITALS FROM
READING ABBEY
CLOISTER.

83   A BLIND
ARCH OR
NICHE HEAD
CARVED WITH
HEAVY BOSSES
STORED IN THE
HERBARIUM AT
WINDSOR CASTLE
IS SIMILAR TO
ONE IN READING
MUSEUM AND
TWO MORE
INCORPORATED IN
THE FOLLY IN THE
CHURCHYARD OF
ST LAURENCE,
READING.

It is well known that Henry I engaged in building work on his father's castle at Windsor, although the precise details of his campaign are unclear. What we know is that the work was carried out between the years 1107 and 1110 (approximately); that it was extensive enough for the castle and town to be renamed New Windsor; and it might have included a chapel.[8]

When we turn to the Windsor stones themselves we find that a few of them are very similar to sculpture that was certainly from Reading. A block in the Herbarium, chip-carved on one face with two elements of a

[8]   Tighe and Davis (1858), 1, 26–27. Henry of Huntingdon, 52 records that in 1110 Henry I held his Whitsun court at 'New Windsor, which he had built himself'. See also Astill (2002), 5. Henry I and Adeliza of Louvain were married at Windsor in 1121 (Symeon of Durham 2, 259).

84   TYPICAL OF
THE READING
CLOISTER
WORKSHOP
IS A FORM OF
BLOSSOM WITH
FIVE ELABORATE
PETALS
RADIATING FROM
A CENTRAL
BOSS, SEEN
HERE ON THE
WEST FACE OF
THE FONT AT ST
JAMES'S CHURCH,
READING.

diaper design of concentric rings intersected by a saltire, can be compared
with one found on the abbey site and reset in the exterior nave wall of St
James's RC church (figures 80, 81). The Herbarium contains a trefoil capital with beaded frames to the shields, too. This is from a doorway, and is a
rather simpler version of several of the Reading cloister capitals, perhaps
significantly not carved with an integral impost block (figure 82, compare
figure 100). There is also a blind arch head carved with heavy bosses, similar (but again not identical) to one in Reading Museum, and two incorporated in the folly erected in St Laurence's churchyard, of approximately
the same dimensions (figure 83).[9]

Whether the Windsor loose stones are similar enough to those that
are undeniably from Reading to prove that they came from the abbey too
must be a matter of opinion. We can say with confidence that the same
sculptural workshop was involved, but that is no great surprise because
we already knew that Henry I's workshop was responsible for sculpture at
both places. On balance, however, the hypothesis that the stones at Windsor were always there, and that they represent an earlier stage in the output
of the royal workshop is more attractive than the notion that they were
salvaged from the Lady Chapel of Reading Abbey, which was built two
centuries later. If they did come from Reading, they could only have been
brought as decorative pieces – a possibility that sits ill with the supposed
date of the transfer and their subsequent burial.

---

9   The museum arch head (1992.53) is more complete but more weathered.

85   A SIMILAR
FORM OF
BLOSSOM TO
THAT SEEN IN
FIGURE 84 IS
FOUND ON ONE
OF THE CAPITALS
EXCAVATED
AT SONNING
BY KEYSER
(NOW READING
MUSEUM
1992.106).

CARVED STONES IN READING

While it now seems doubtful that any of the Windsor carved stones came
from Reading, it is certain that the Borough Marsh and Shiplake ones
did. The clinching evidence comes from Reading itself, because although
practically no twelfth-century sculpture remains in situ on the surviving
buildings of the abbey, there was, and still is, a good deal of material visible around the town. The font in the Roman Catholic church of St James, is
made from a quadruple capital, discovered by James Wheble in 1835 (see
chapter five), hollowed out and set on four short shafts with spurred bases
(see plate XVII). The carving of blossoms on the font bears comparison
with one of the Sonning capitals (Keyser no. 10, now Reading Museum
1992–106, figures 84, 85). The same church also holds a foliage capital of
the same size as those found by Keyser and carved in the same style (compare figures 86 and 87). Most of the material to be seen around the town,
however, is built into walls in and around the Victorian municipal Forbury Gardens (plate 33). Many of the stones are carved and comparisons
between them and sculpture from Borough Marsh are so close as to leave
no doubt of their common origin.

Keyser presented his discoveries to the Society of Antiquaries of
London in 1916, concluding from the form of the Holme Park capitals
that they were from a cloister arcade. His speculations about the double
springers which had been arranged along the top of the wall at Shiplake
House as a kind of battlement (figure 88) were less accurate: he thought

86 THE CAPITAL NOW DISPLAYED IN ST JAMES'S CHURCH, READING, IS IDENTICAL IN SIZE AND FORM TO THOSE IN THE MUSEUM, AND IS CARVED WITH A SIMILAR REPERTOIRE OF MOTIFS.

they 'must have formed portions of a very elaborate corbel table'.[10] This misreading of the function of these stones by a distinguished and experienced archaeologist can only be explained by the fact that there was very little in England to compare them with. There were no twelfth-century cloister arcades standing in England.[11] The misunderstanding was, in fact, cleared up on the spot by the Secretary of the Society, Charles Reed Peers, who was in no doubt that they 'served as skew-backs for a cloister arcade'.[12]

ZARNECKI'S 1948 EXCAVATIONS AND LATER ACQUISITIONS

Charles Keyser died, aged 81, in 1929 without returning to Borough Marsh to carry out the excavations he had envisaged, and the hunt was not

[10] Keyser (1916), 241.
[11] Although it was at precisely this time that the reconstruction of bays of the cloister arcade of Bridlington Priory, was undertaken under the direction of John Bilson (Bilson (1911), 174–75; Bilson (1913), 238–39). Presumably Keyser was unfamiliar with this project.
[12] Keyser (1916), 243.

87   ANOTHER
OF THE CAPITALS
EXCAVATED
BY KEYSER
AT SONNING
(NOW READING
MUSEUM 1992.76)
IS CLOSELY
COMPARABLE TO
THE ST JAMES'S
CHURCH CAPITAL.

resumed for almost twenty more years. Dr Wilfred Bowman, the owner of Barn Acre Cottage, Borough Marsh, had just built himself some new gate-posts using carved stones he had found in his garden (figure 89 a to d), and in 1948 the Eton schoolmaster and lexicographer René Ledesert stumbled upon them by chance. Recognising that the stones were medieval, he told his friend George Zarnecki of the Courtauld Institute of Art about them, and in the autumn of 1948 Zarnecki led a group from the Courtauld Institute to Barn Acre Cottage to carry out the only archaeological dig ever undertaken by that institution (figure 90).

George Zarnecki was a Polish art historian who came to England in 1945 after a distinguished military career. His talents were recognised by Anthony Blunt, then Director of the Courtauld Institute of Art, and he remained at the Courtauld until his retirement in 1980, serving as its Deputy Director for the years between 1961 and 1974.[13] In 1948, however, he was still working on his PhD and simultaneously curating the Conway photographic library, and it is a tribute to the force of his personality that he gathered a team of some fifteen staff and students to carry out the Borough Marsh excavation. Several of the excavators were students who later carved out distinguished careers for themselves; others were members of

---

[13]   See his obituaries in *The Daily Telegraph* September 18th 2008, *The Independent* September 16th 2008, *The Times* September 13th 2008, *The Guardian* September 11th 2008. A memoir by his longtime colleague Professor Peter Kidson provides a more personal glimpse.(http://www.courtauld.ac.uk/alumni/documents/GZobit.doc.)

88   DOUBLE SPRINGERS ARRANGED ALONG THE WALL TO EITHER SIDE OF THE SHIPLAKE ARCH WERE
ILLUSTRATED IN KEYSER (1916), FIGURES 11A AND 11B.

the Institute's staff, such as the librarians Rhoda Welsford and Elizabeth
Edmonds, and Professor Anthony Blunt's secretary Elsa Scheerer (figures
91 and 92). According to Elizabeth Edmonds,

> there were 2 trips; on 24th October 1948 when some of us went down by train
> to Twyford with our spades and shovels, and the second on 14th November
> 1948. This was in a van hired from a George Street greengrocer, and we stayed
> overnight.[14]

[14]   Private correspondence, 18 July 1997.

89 A TO D (THIS PAGE AND OPPOSITE). THE BEAKHEAD VOUSSOIRS NOTICED BY RENÉ LEDESERT IN DR
BOWMAN'S GATEPOSTS LED DIRECTLY TO ZARNECKI'S DECISION TO EXCAVATE THE SITE. PHOTOGRAPHS
TAKEN IN 1948 (A AND C) AND 2005 (B AND D) DEMONSTRATE THE EXTENT OF THE WEATHERING THEY HAVE
SUFFERED IN THEIR EXPOSED POSITION.

What Zarnecki and his team found left him in no doubt that he had found the site that Keyser had hoped to excavate. Dr Bowman's garden was bounded by the River Loddon, and its level had been artificially raised by a sixteenth-century embankment wall to prevent flooding and soil erosion. Some of the material of this wall was reused twelfth-century stone, identifiable by its carved decoration as coming from Reading Abbey. Zarnecki's team also uncovered the foundations of a building complex made of brick reinforced with stone. This excavation brought to light some sixty carved stones, including two of the four great corner springers which marked the angles of the cloister arcade (figures 93 and 94). These were easily the most massive of all the carved stones which made up the cloister arcade, requiring the strength of five men to remove them from the base of the wall where they were set.[15] Their importance for the reconstruction of the cloister is crucial, as we shall see. Zarnecki also unearthed the capital of greatest iconographic interest, carved with the Coronation of the Virgin (plate XXXIV).[16]

The recovered stones were generously given to the Courtauld Institute by Dr Bowman, and after cleaning they were lodged in the Victoria and Albert Museum until such time as they could be accommodated in the Reading Museum. Plans for a new museum building were approved by Reading Corporation in 1973, and in the same year the Courtauld Institute Management Committee accepted Zarnecki's proposal that the stones

[15]   Zarnecki (1949), 524.
[16]   Zarnecki (1950b), 1–12.

90 THE ONLY ARCHAEOLOGICAL EXCAVATION UNDERTAKEN BY THE COURTAULD INSTITUTE OF ART WAS GEORGE ZARNECKI'S 1948 DIG AT BOROUGH MARSH. ZARNECKI IS IN THE CENTRE FOREGROUND, TALKING TO WILFRED BOWMAN (IN THE DARK SUIT).

91 THE COURTAULD EXCAVATORS SET OUT FROM 20 PORTMAN SQUARE ON 14 NOVEMBER 1948 IN A HIRED VAN.

92 THIS PHOTOGRAPH WAS TAKEN TO RECORD THE DISCOVERY OF THE CORONATION OF THE VIRGIN
CAPITAL. IT SHOWS (FROM LEFT TO RIGHT), MME LEDESERT, ROSEMARY CLAY, GEORGE ZARNECKI, DONALD
KING, PETER LASKO AND PETER KELLY.

93   TWO OF THE
CLOISTER CORNER
SPRINGERS WERE
UNEARTHED BY
ZARNECKI AT
BOROUGH MARSH.
THIS, THE BETTER
PRESERVED,
HAS CHEVRON
ORNAMENT AND A
BIRD ON ONE FACE
AND FOLIAGE ON
THE OTHER (SEE
FIGURE 112).

94   THE SECOND CORNER SPRINGER EXCAVATED BY ZARNECKI IS MUCH MORE WORN,
BUT THE BEAKHEAD ORNAMENT IS READILY VISIBLE.

be transferred from the V&A to Reading as a gift to the museum.[17] The
transfer was completed on 16 October 1975, but the stones simply went
from a store at the V&A to another in Reading, where they remained for
almost twenty years, finally being acquisitioned in 1992 and going on display in 1993.

The third batch of Borough Marsh stones, those which had been removed by the two young boatmen in the 1880s and erected at Shiplake
House as an ornamental arch, were eventually purchased by Reading Museum from Colonel Phillimore in 1977.[18] Zarnecki had made an attempt

[17]   The Coronation of the Virgin capital had been given to the V&A, rather than
       loaned, but the Trustees of the V&A felt that it belonged with the other stones in
       Reading, and generously gave it to Reading Museum.
[18]   Reading Museum archives. Phillimore family tradition, reported by Sir Walter's
       grandson, does not support Keyser's story of the boatmen, but asserts instead that
       the stones were brought from Borough Marsh by Sir Walter Phillimore's grandmother
       sometime between 1821, when the family bought Shiplake House, and her death in
       1859 (private communication, Claud Phillimore to G. Zarnecki, 16 April 1949).

in 1949 to persuade the then owner of Shiplake, the Venerable and Honourable Stephen Phillimore, Archdeacon of Middlesex, to dismantle the arch and give the stones to the museum, but the archdeacon was not open to persuasion, giving it as his opinion that the stones were not from Reading at all, but from the 'cell at Borough Marsh', and that in any case he had 'no wish whatsoever to remove them from their present place and put them in a museum, where they will probably not be looked at'.[19]

In addition to these major acquisitions of cloister material from Borough Marsh, the museum has managed to obtain various isolated stones, largely through the efforts of George Zarnecki. A capital at Avebury Manor, Wiltshire carved with men and dragons, which had been taken there from a garden in Reading was first examined by Zarnecki in 1959 and proved to be another cloister capital (figure 95).[20] After lengthy negotiations it was purchased by Reading Museum for the sum of £6,250 in 1971.[21] Three further pieces, a double springer carved with birds, a lion capital and a bird beakhead voussoir, were purchased by Zarnecki from a private collector in Twyford, Berkshire, and have now joined the other fragments in Reading Museum.[22] The final object to be considered was discovered by the Gloucestershire historian David Verey in 1974 in his garden at Barnsley House in Cirencester.[23] Verey reported the stone to George Zarnecki, who identified it as a double springer from Reading Abbey cloister on the basis of a photograph.[24] Between 1975 and 1981 it was in Verey's Arlington Mill Museum in Bibury, Gloucestershire; thereafter it was obtained by Reading Museum and now bears the accession number 1992.75 (figure 96). There is little doubt that it belongs with the other relics of Reading Abbey cloister, but it is difficult to account for its presence

---

[19]   Private communication Stephen Phillimore to G. Zarnecki, 25 May 1949.

[20]   Reading Museum 1977.100 (London (1984), no. 127f).

[21]   National Art Collections Fund 68th Annual Report, 1971, 29. The purchase was made with the aid of a grant of £1,000 from the N.A.C.F.

[22]   Acquisition numbers 1992–70 (lion capital), 1992–81 (bird springer) and 1966–158 (beakhead voussoir). The acquisition date of the voussoir seems to be impossible, in view of the fact that the Twyford stones were not offered to the museum on loan until 2 September 1971, but the balance of probabilities seems to point to a mistake at the museum. The voussoir was photographed by the Conway Library for Zarnecki in 1971 or 1972, along with the very distinctive lion capital (but not the springer), and the photographs were labelled 'Twyford' by Zarnecki at the time. Zarnecki himself remained certain that he still remembered these three stones as the ones he bought in Twyford. The voussoir itself has the acquisition number painted on by the museum, but also painted on it is the word 'Sonning', which could only mean that it was thought to be one of those found by Keyser at Holme Park. This it certainly is not. Keyser (1916) stated that he found only two voussoirs and neither is of the beakhead type.

[23]   Private correspondence, Verey to Zarnecki, 25 May 1974.

[24]   Private correspondence, Zarnecki to Verey, 5 June 1974.

95   THE AVEBURY MANOR DRAGON FIGHT CAPITAL WAS TAKEN TO AVEBURY FROM A GARDEN IN READING
AND LATER PURCHASED FOR READING MUSEUM.

in David Verey's garden unless it was taken there, perhaps by an incum-
bent moving from Reading or Shiplake to Cirencester.

THE CLOISTER PLAN

Englefield, Albury and the Ordnance Survey agreed that the cloister was
a square with a side of approximately 145ft (44.2 m), and this can be confirmed for the east walk by a scar marking the position of the south-eastern
entrance of the cloister that is still visible in the masonry (plate XXXV).
Only Stukeley's and Rennoldson's drawings of the cloister (figure 97) show
significantly more than can be seen today: other artists have paid little attention to this part of the site. The plan of the cloister has been made a little clearer by excavation, although archaeologists who have worked in this
area in recent years are agreed that the cloister has been heavily disturbed
by later activity. Remains of a thirteenth-century tiled floor have been
found in the south and west cloister walks, but nothing of the original

floor has been discovered.[25] The base of a pier discovered by Slade on the line of the arcade of the south walk, opposite the abbey well in the garth, provides evidence of a structure at this point, possibly a lavabo. The remains of the dwarf wall which supported the cloister arcade were discovered in the west walk in 1985–86, which established the width of the tiled cloister walk (i.e. the internal width) as 3.80m, and the total width including the stylobate as approximately 4.60m, which is comparable with equivalent figures of 4.25m to 4.55m given by Fernie for a series of major English eleventh- and twelfth-century abbeys and cathedral priories.[26]

96   THE DOUBLE SPRINGER DISCOVERED AT BARNSLEY HOUSE, CIRENCESTER, WAS IDENTIFIED BY ZARNECKI AS PART OF THE ABBEY CLOISTER.

THE CLOISTER ARCADE

Our only evidence for the appearance of the cloister arcade is provided by the carved fragments housed in the Reading Museum and built into walls and other structures around the town. It is fortunate that these are numerous enough to give a very good idea of what the cloister looked like. The most striking of the fragments are the capitals, which are single and carved on all four sides, implying that the cloister arcade was carried on single rather than paired shafts.

This is confirmed by the carving of the double springers, pentagonal stones which sat on top of the capitals and formed the starting points of the two arches springing from each capital. At Reading the springers are only deep enough for a single capital, and since they are carved on both their front (walk) and back (garth) faces, they must represent the full thickness of the cloister wall (figure 98). They are also carved on their lower side faces, which represent the underside, or soffit, of the arch. The arches themselves were made up of wedge-shaped voussoirs which are also

[25]   Slade (1972), 83, 85–87; Vince, Fasham and Hawkes (1979), 38, 52–53.
[26]   Fasham and Stewart (1991), 91; Fernie (1987), 63–64. Fernie gave 4.55m as the width of the cloister walks at Durham, Ely and Norwich cathedrals.

97   W. STUKELEY'S *RUINS OF REDING ABBY, AUG 14 1721* SHOWS THE CLOISTER ENCLOSURE FROM THE WEST.
THE SOUTH NAVE AISLE WALL AND THE SURVIVING EAST CLOISTER DOORWAY ARE ON THE LEFT; THE REAR,
EAST WALL OF THE CLOISTER WALK IS PIERCED BY THE ARCHES OF THE SLYPE, THE TRIPLE OPENING OF THE
CHAPTER HOUSE, AND THE DORMITORY DOORWAY. THE REFECTORY RANGE IS ON THE RIGHT. THE CLOISTER
HAD ALREADY LOST ITS ARCADES BY THIS DATE.

98   THE BEAKHEAD DOUBLE SPRINGERS HAD THEIR MOST ELABORATE CARVING
ON THE WALK FACE, BUT THE SOFFIT WAS CARVED WITH DAISIES AND ANGLE ROLLS
FLANKED THE PLAIN SIDE THAT FACED THE GARTH.

carved on front, back and soffit (figure 99). The geometry of the voussoirs and springers allows an estimate of the diameter of the arcade arches to be calculated, and this gives us an arcade with column centres 0.98m (38.6") apart, and an inner arch diameter of 0.68m (26.8"). From this it can be calculated that, allowing for the thickness of the mortar beds between the voussoirs, there were in all probability seven voussoirs to each arch, including a keystone for all except the inhabited foliage arches.[27] The latter were made using only five voussoirs including the keystone.[28] These calculations also allow us to estimate that each walk of the cloister had an arcade of 36 arches.[29]

There are 20 capitals in Reading Museum, ten of which are variants of the trefoil type, with octagonal lower faces (figure 100), demonstrating that these capitals stood on octagonal shafts. Two octagonal column bases also survive.[30] The remaining capitals, more elaborately carved with foliage, figures or both, have circular lower faces, implying cylindrical shafts (e.g. figure 87). It is not impossible that the two designs of capital are from different ranges of the cloister, but the likeliest arrangement is an alternating system, with trefoil capitals on octagonal shafts alternating with figural or foliage capitals on round shafts in the same arcade. Such arrangements were common in England in the first half of the twelfth century, a good comparison from *c.* 1100 being the exterior wall arcade of Archbishop Anselm's choir at Canterbury Cathedral, which extended around the choir and transepts and was retained for much of

99   THE UNDERSIDE OF A BEAKHEAD VOUSSOIR IS HERE SHOWN WITH THE ROLL CARRYING THE BEAK AT THE TOP, THE SOFFIT DECORATED WITH A HALF DAISY IN A ROUNDEL, AND THE GARTH-FACING ANGLE ROLL AT THE BOTTOM. THIS VOUSSOIR MATCHES THE SPRINGER IN FIGURE 98.

---

27   Twelve voussoirs, but no springers, were used in the construction of the arch at Shiplake House in 1889. No dimensions for this are available, but photographs show it to be a slightly flattened semicircle. Replacing four of its voussoirs with two springers, and reducing the remaining eight voussoirs by one to give the arch a keystone, would produce a semicircular arch of seven voussoirs.
28   The inhabited foliage voussoirs are both wider and more acutely tapered than the others.
29   For dimensions of all the museum stones, see CRSBI, Berkshire, Reading Museum.
30   The octagonal bases are numbered 1992.69 and 1992.82.

100 A TO J   THE TEN TREFOIL CAPITALS IN READING MUSEUM ARE SIMILAR IN DESIGN BUT NO TWO ARE IDENTICAL. ABOVE LEFT: A. 1992.56. ABOVE RIGHT: B. 1992.57.

ABOVE LEFT: C. 1992.73. ABOVE RIGHT: D. 1992.80. BELOW LEFT: E. 1992.89. BELOW RIGHT: F. 1992.90.

ABOVE LEFT: G. 1992.92. ABOVE RIGHT: H. 1992.100.

ABOVE: I. 1992.107. BELOW: J. 1992.113.

101   W. R. LETHABY, SURVEYOR OF WESTMINSTER ABBEY FROM 1906, USED CARVED
STONES FOUND ON SITE TO GIVE AN IDEA OF THE APPEARANCE OF THE CLOISTER OF
WESTMINSTER ABBEY. HE WAS AT PAINS TO POINT OUT THAT THIS WAS NOT A GENUINE
RECONSTRUCTION.

its length after the 1174 fire (plate XXXVI). Anselm's crypt, likewise, has
a system like Reading's in the main arcades: plain, or only lightly carved
cushion capitals on fluted shafts taking turns with richly carved capitals
of various types on plain shafts.[31] A more relevant comparison might be
with the later cloister at Westminster Abbey, now surviving only in a few
fragments, in which trefoil capitals similar to those from Reading probably alternated with figural capitals (figure 101).

The cloister arcade at Reading was carried entirely on shafts, with no
piers even at the angles. The two corner springers excavated by Zarnecki –
massive blocks carved to provide springing for two arches at right angles
(figures 93 and 94) – originally rested on triple capitals (plate XXXVII)

---

[31]   This explains the unfinished appearance of the capital at the west end of the south
arcade. It stands on a fluted shaft, and should never have been carved at all. Work
on it presumably stopped when it was realised that no more carved capitals were
required.

102   AN ANGLE OF THE CLOISTER HAS BEEN RECONSTRUCTED ON SITE AT RIEVAULX ABBEY (NORTH
YORKSHIRE).

carved to rest on a cluster of three shafts. This arrangement is rather less common than the angle piers found in such French cloisters as Moissac (Tarn-et-Garonne) and Aix-en-Provence (Bouches-du-Rhône), where the flat surface provided a site for relief sculpture, but parallels may be found, for example, in the reconstructed cloister angle at the Cistercian house of Rievaulx (Yorks), re-erected with four shafts at the angle, each with its own capital (figure 102). The arcade at Reading, being carried entirely on slender shafts, was certainly too fragile to support a stone vault, and we must suppose that the walks were roofed with timber.

THE DECORATION OF THE CLOISTER ARCADES

When we come to examine the decoration of the arches, it is obvious from the voussoirs and double springers that while one face of the arcade was elaborately carved, the other was invariably completely plain except for an angle roll. An examination of the two great corner springers shows that it was the cloister walk side that was elaborately carved, while the garth side was left relatively plain. Several French cloisters have a similar arrangement. At Aix-en-Provence, for example, the east walk arches are carved

103   ELABORATE CHEVRON ORNAMENT IS USED TO DECORATE THE WALK FACE OF THE CLOITRE SAINT-
SAUVEUR IN AIX-EN-PROVENCE, WHILE THE GARTH FACE IS LEFT PLAIN.

with a chevron design on the walk side, while the garth side is left plain (figure 103).[32]

Looking more closely at the arch designs reveals a great deal about their original arrangement. The arches were made up of voussoirs carried on the double springers, and between them these voussoirs and springers (59 voussoirs and 26 double springers in the museum alone) carry only four basic designs. Some voussoirs are carved with beakhead, either bird beakhead with the long beak curving over an angle roll (figures 89c, 104), or a type with the rounded head of a beast carved upside-down on the inner angle with a pair of scalloped leaves issuing from its mouth, which I would call beast-head.[33] Further decoration is often carved between the leaves: a pine-cone (figure 105), or sometimes a second head (figure 106). Each beakhead voussoir has a pair of arches carved towards the wider end

[32]   For Aix-en-Provence, see Thirion (1988).
[33]   One beakhead of each types is found on the gateposts of Barn Acre Cottage, Borough Marsh.

of its face, and these would have combined in the arch to form an outer band of cusping. The beakhead voussoirs are also carved on their soffits with a design of roundels, sometimes interlacing. The springers that accompany these voussoirs have two beakheads on each side, and these almost always alternate between the two varieties of beakhead (figure 107), with the beast-head at the bottom. This implies that the voussoirs in the arches also alternated and that, since an odd number of voussoirs must have been used to form the arch, the keystones of these arches were always bird beakheads. Versions of this alternating beakhead arch are not uncommon and may be seen, for example, on the south doorway of St Swithun's, Quenington, Gloucestershire, and the chancel arch at St Mary Magdalene's, Tortington, Sussex (figure 108).

104   ONE OF THE BEST-PRESERVED OF THE BIRD BEAKHEAD VOUSSOIRS.

The second arch design consists of a series of large bulbous projections, carved with intertwining foliage sometimes inhabited by animals or humans, where the carving occupies a large area of the soffit as well as the face of the arch (figure 109). Other peculiarities of these unusual voussoirs will be discussed in chapter eight. A third design consists of a number of voussoirs carved with projecting hemispherical bosses decorated with geometrical designs (figure 110). Finally, one voussoir, one double springer and a corner springer in the museum have beaded chevron on both face and soffit (figures 111, 93).

RECONSTRUCTION OF THE ARCADE DESIGN

The presence of precisely four designs among the voussoirs of the cloister arcades at once raises the possibility that each of the four walks was carved

ABOVE LEFT: 105   READING'S BEAST-HEAD VOUSSOIRS HAVE THE HEAD TOWARDS THE INSIDE OF THE ARCH.
THIS ONE IS ALSO DECORATED WITH A PINE CONE.
ABOVE RIGHT: 106   SEVERAL OF THE BEAST-HEAD VOUSSOIRS HAVE A SECOND HEAD CARVED IN THE
CENTRE.

with a different arcade design, and there is other evidence which appears
to support this hypothesis. Every double springer so far discovered is
carved symmetrically, with the same design on both the arches it carries.
This design, be it beakhead, chevron, bosses or inhabited foliage, would
be continued *via* the voussoirs of the arch to the next springer in the arcade until some break such as an angle or a garth entrance disrupted the
sequence. Something similar occurs at Aix-en-Provence, where the arches
of the east walk are carved with chevron on both face and soffit while the
other three walks have plainer, moulded arches, the design changing at the
angle piers. The east walk of a cloister might be expected to receive special
treatment since it contains the entrance to the chapter house, generally
the most ornately carved feature of any cloister. At Reading it is likeliest
that the arches elaborately carved with inhabited foliage were originally
erected on this walk.

107   THIS BEAKHEAD DOUBLE SPRINGER HAS BEAST-HEADS AT THE BOTTOM AND BIRD
BEAKHEADS ABOVE, INDICATING THAT THE TWO TYPES ALTERNATED IN THE ARCHES.

The pattern of survivals also tends to favour the hypothesis that each walk had its own distinctive arcade design. We have seen that when the cloister was demolished, Mr Sands and Mr Grey each took away stones from two of its walks. The slight ambiguity in the accounts which leaves us uncertain whether they were the same two walks in both cases, or whether the two men bought the entire cloister between them, is irrelevant here: what matters is that in 1549 the cloister was effectively split into two.[34] Carved voussoirs and springers from one of these two batches of stone found their way to Borough Marsh, and thence to the museum, either

[34]   In the likeliest case, Mr Grey bought two walks and Mr Sands the other two, each man taking the stones away to a different destination. The other possibility is that Mr Grey and Mr Sands each took stones from the same two walks, leaving two walks standing on site, which must have been demolished and cleared shortly afterwards. No evidence has yet come to light which connects Mr Grey or Mr Sands or anyone else with the Borough Marsh stones.

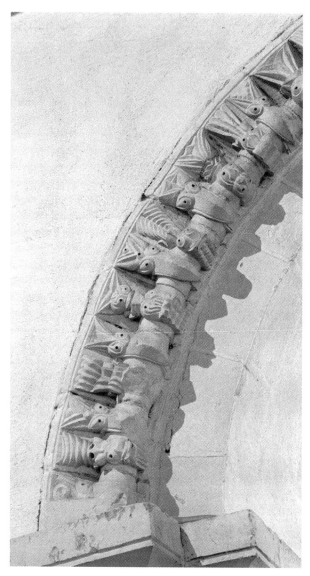

directly (from the Courtauld Institute excavation) or via Shiplake House or Holme Park, Sonning, and most (but not quite all) of these Borough Marsh stones are carved either with beakheads or the inhabited foliage design. It would seem reasonable, therefore, to treat this as further evidence that the four cloister walks had different arch designs.

It is an attractive theory. Unfortunately, however, it is demonstrably wrong. The museum, as we saw, holds two corner springers, both excavated by Zarnecki at Borough Marsh. Each of these enormous stones originally carried two arches at right angles to one another at a corner of the cloister.[35] If the arcade of each walk was carved with a different design, we would expect the two carved faces of each corner springer to be different, and for the better preserved of the two (1992.99) that is indeed the case. One face is carved with interlacing foliage (figure 112); the other is carved with chevron of the same design as the sole chevron voussoir in the museum, and a bird entangled in foliage, biting its own breast (figure 93). The second corner springer is more worn, but not so badly that we can fail to discern a beakhead design on both of its carved faces

108   THE CHANCEL ARCH AT ST MARY MAGDALENE'S IN TORTINGTON (WEST SUSSEX) HAS ALTERNATING BEAKHEAD TYPES.

(figure 94). The theory clearly requires some modification, but perhaps not a great deal.

[35] There is a similar arrangement at Rievaulx, with a corner springer carried on a quadruple capital supported on four shafts. In the standing French cloisters there is generally a pier at the angle rather than a cluster of shafts.

109   THE MOST SPECTACULAR OF THE CLOISTER VOUSSOIRS ARE CARVED WITH FOLIAGE ON A BULBOUS
PROJECTION.

110   SIX OF THE CLOISTER VOUSSOIRS ARE DECORATED WITH ONE OR MORE 'JELLY MOULD' BOSSES.

At least one entrance from the cloister walk to the garth would have
been needed.[36] This could be managed without breaking the rhythm of the
arcade if the spacing between the shafts was wide enough, as in the four
garth entrances at Moissac, by simply leaving a gap in the low wall which
the arcade stands on. In most cloisters, however, the garth entrance is wider than a normal arcade bay and the rhythm is broken. At Reading Abbey

[36]   At most monasteries, including Reading, there was a well in the garth; at St Mary's
Abbey York, there was a herb garden. Even if the cloister garth was entirely grassed
over, access would be needed for mowing.

111   ONLY ONE CHEVRON VOUSSOIR FROM THE CLOISTER HAS FOUND ITS WAY INTO READING MUSEUM.

a gap wider than the standard 0.68m. between columns would certainly have been needed, and in fact we know that there was at least one garth entrance: on the south walk opposite the well in the garth where the base of a compound pier has been excavated.[37]

At this point the reconstruction becomes highly speculative, but one possible arrangement follows if three assumptions are made. First, that the two arcades which provided the bulk of the Borough Marsh stones were adjacent to one another. This is reasonable enough given the evidence of the dispersal of the cloister. Secondly, that there was just one entrance to the garth where the arch design could change, corresponding to a point opposite the well on the south walk. This is the most conjectural of the assumptions. There certainly was a garth entrance at this point, and probably a fountain over the well, but there may well have been others. Thirdly it is assumed that the most elaborate design of arch, the inhabited foliage design, was used in the east walk. If this was the case, then the surviving corner springer with inhabited foliage and chevron could only have occupied the NE angle, and the north walk was therefore decorated with chevron (figure 113). The (lost) SE angle springer must have had inhabited foliage on its east face, and the (lost) NW angle springer would have had chevron on its north face, so the other surviving corner springer, carved with beakhead on both faces, must have occupied the SW angle (figure 114). This means that both the west walk and the south walk west of the

---

[37]   Slade (1972), 85–86 and pls. 20 a, b, c.

112 THIS FACE OF ONE OF THE CORNER SPRINGERS FROM THE CLOISTER IS CARVED
WITH FIGURES IN FOLIAGE. ITS OTHER FACE IS SHOWN IN FIGURE 93.

well were carved with beakhead, while the south walk east of the well had
the bossed arches.

According to this reconstruction, stones from the east and south ranges of the cloister were taken to Borough Marsh. These would include the
inhabited foliage voussoirs and springers of the east range, the beakheads
which took up most of the south range, and the bossed voussoirs from
the short section of the south walk between the SE angle and the garth
entrance. This is precisely what we do find: the museum holds 34 voussoirs and 5 double-springers decorated with beakhead; 12 voussoirs and
5 double-springers with the inhabited foliage decoration; 1 chevron voussoir, and 5 bossed voussoirs. It would not be surprising to find the two
corner springers at Borough Marsh, since they occupied the SW and NE
angles, marking the two ends of the ranges. What we would not expect to

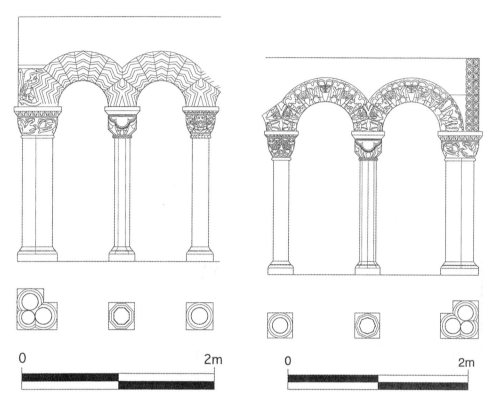

ABOVE LEFT: 113   A RECONSTRUCTION OF THE EAST END OF THE NORTH CLOISTER WALK SHOWS THE
ALTERNATING SHAFT AND CAPITAL FORMS AND THE CHEVRON ARCHES OF THIS RANGE.
ABOVE RIGHT: 114   A RECONSTRUCTION OF THE SOUTH END OF THE WEST CLOISTER WALK SHOWS THE
BEAKHEAD DECORATION OF THE ARCHES.

find would be any of the chevron voussoirs from the north range, and in
fact the single example in the museum is of unknown provenance: it is not
from Sonning, from the Shiplake arch or from the Courtauld excavation.

This reconstruction of the original form of the cloister arcade is necessarily tentative, but even if it errs in some of its details, it must be accurate
in its main outlines. That is to say, it is reasonable to accept that there was
a square cloister with four walks of thirty-six bays each. The arcades were
carried on a low wall, and supported on single shafts, alternately round
and octagonal in section, with a cluster of three shafts at the angles. The
two capital designs alternated along the arcades, with trefoil capitals on
the octagonal shafts and foliage or figural capitals on the round shafts. The
arches of the arcade were richly carved on the side facing the walk, while
the garth face of the arcade was decorated with a simple angle roll. By and

large, each walk had its own arcade design, with the most elaborate design reserved for the east walk.

READING CLOISTER IN ITS ENGLISH CONTEXT

Beginning with the plan, it is obvious at once that for sheer size, Reading was equalled only by the greatest abbeys and cathedral priories in the country. Table 4 summarises the evidence. It is immediately obvious that there is no general trend towards increasing cloister size with time. The largest cloister in the group, Winchester, is also one of the earliest; while the earliest, Edward the Confessor's Westminster is practically the same size as the latest, Reading. In fact, as we have seen in chapter six, the size of the cloister was usually determined by the length of the nave.

No English Romanesque Great Cloister survives *in-situ*, even as a fragment, and although loose twelfth-century cloister stones survive from several foundations, nowhere else has as many as Reading.[38] This house therefore provides our best evidence of the appearance of a twelfth-century Benedictine main cloister of the top rank in England, and the standard against which others of this date must be measured. Sufficient material survives from the Benedictine cloisters at Westminster, Canterbury, Norwich, Hyde Abbey (Winchester), and Glastonbury, and from the Augustinian priory at Bridlington to allow useful comparisons to be made, and these will be passed quickly in review.[39]

1   WESTMINSTER ABBEY

Some time before 1925, a few bays of the Romanesque cloister of Westminster Abbey were reconstructed from fragments and photographed (figure 101).[40] They remained in position in the Undercroft Museum until they were dismantled around 1986.[41] The reconstruction was never intended to be archaeologically accurate, but simply to give an idea of the appearance of a cloister using the stones available. Nevertheless, it demonstrates that the Westminster cloister was very similar to Reading in a few important ways. The arcade is carried on a mixture of cylindrical and filleted shafts, with cushion capitals alternately of trefoil and figural or foliage design. No springers were used in the reconstruction, but chevron-decorated arches

[38]   Six bays of the Infirmary Cloister at Canterbury Cathedral still stand and are discussed below.

[39]   A useful recent survey of this material is Harrison (2006), to which the author is greatly indebted.

[40]   Lethaby (1925), 32–35.

[41]   Warwick Rodwell, private communication, 31 December 2012.

TABLE 4   LENGTHS OF ENGLISH ROMANESQUE CLOISTER WALKS

Church	Length of cloister walk (ft.)
Durham (1093)	115
Canterbury cathedral (1070s)	116
Ely (1081)	131
Peterborough (1118)	136
Westminster (c.1050)	143
Reading (1121)	145
St Albans (c. 1077)	148
Norwich (1096)	176
Bury St Edmunds (1081)	180
Winchester Cathedral (1079)	188

have been assembled entirely from voussoirs. Chevron arches and trefoil, foliage and figural capitals with varied supports are all found at Reading too.

What has not been established with certainty is the date of the cloister in the Westminster reconstruction. It is not the original cloister of the Confessor's abbey; the forms of the capitals and the sophisticated chevron decoration make that impossible. Attempts have been made to date the cloister on the basis of a capital discovered in 1807 but subsequently lost (figure 115).[42] This shows Abbot Gilbert Crispin (c. 1085–1117) and King William Rufus (1087–1100) under an inscription crediting them with work at the church. It has sometimes been assumed from this that the cloister must date from the period 1087–1100 during which both held office, but again stylistic considerations make this early date difficult to accept.[43] The forms of both the chevron decoration, carved frontally (i.e. with the points projecting) on the face and the soffit of the arch, and the foliage of some of the capitals suggest a date after c. 1130–40 and slightly later than the cloister at Reading. The iconography of the capital can be explained if it is assumed that the inscription commemorated Gilbert Crispin's and William Rufus's work elsewhere in the abbey,

[42]   The capital was discovered in 1807, when a wall between two taverns on Union Street was taken down, and was obtained by the antiquarian William Capon at that time. He later sold it to Sir Gregory Page Turner, but not before he had made drawings of it. The capital was lost, but the drawings remained in the hands of John Britton, and were published in Brayley (1834), 87–88 and Brayley and Britton (1836), 415, 445–46.

[43]   R. Gem in Wilson et al. (1986), 17–18.

remain, and the lower parts of the supporting pillars,) it has not been considered necessary to engrave.

In the first Compartment is the King, holding with upraised arms a long roll, or charter; on one side is the Abbot, distinguished by his crosier; and on the other, an attendant monk with a book. One arm of the King's seat represents the head and neck of a dog. On the abacus is WILLELMO SECVN—, and two broken letters. It is remarkable that the W is actually formed by a double V.

In the second Compartment is the Abbot, in the

centre, bearing the charter in his left hand, and in his right holding what appears to be a key. On each side is an attendant monk, one of whom seems to be considering the extended roll. The remaining inscription is —V. SVBABBE. GISLEB—.

The third Compartment represents the Abbot as standing before a kind of reading desk, held by an attendant, on which are the open scriptures, with the words EGO SUM on the dexter page. Behind the Abbot is another figure, partly mutilated, who is, also, holding a book. The letters remaining on the abacus appear to read thus,—E. CLAVSTR$\bar{V}$. ET RELL,—but the two last, from their broken state, are perhaps questionable.

To what particular grant, or instrument, these sculptures refer is unknown. Very few charters were given by William the Second; and neither Dugdale, nor any other writer that we have sedulously inspected for the purpose of ascertainment, mentions any grant made by him to the monks of Westminster. Were the manuscripts yet preserved in the muniment room of the Abbey church carefully examined, this regretted *desideratum* might probably be supplied.   B.

———————

WARDROBE ACCOUNTS.

THE utility and value of Wardrobe Accounts, in illustrating the manners and customs of our ancestors, and in furnishing historical data, are so generally ac-

115   AN ILLUSTRATED ACCOUNT OF THE DISCOVERY OF THE WESTMINSTER ABBEY CLOISTER CAPITAL WAS PUBLISHED IN BRAYLEY (1834).

or even that it recorded work in the cloister initiated by Gilbert using funds originally given by William.

2 CANTERBURY CATHEDRAL PRIORY

Canterbury offers a good deal of evidence about the appearance of English twelfth-century cloisters, in the form of the partially surviving Infirmary Cloister, evidence from the Waterworks plan, and speculations about the form of the Great Cloister based on fragments.

Six bays of the east walk of a twelfth-century Infirmary Cloister still stand, usually dated to the time of Prior Wibert (1152/53–67) (figure 116).[44] The bays alternate in their supports between heavy, monolithic, cylindrical calc-sinter shafts with scallop capitals, and slender twin shafts of Purbeck marble decorated with spiral or chevron designs and carrying waterleaf capitals.[45] Above impost level the arcade is now and was probably originally completely plain.[46]

The present Great Cloister of Canterbury Cathedral belongs to Prior Chillenden's rebuilding of c. 1395–1414, but there is some evidence of what was there before. The first post-Conquest Archbishop, Lanfranc (1070–89), began work on the monastic buildings after he had rebuilt the church he found in ruins on his arrival in 1070, building a spacious cloister to accommodate an expected increase in the number of monks. Whether Lanfranc's cloister was replaced before Prior Chillenden's rebuilding is largely a matter of speculation. Prior Wibert (1152/53–1167) is often assumed to have done it, and much else besides, but his *obits* actually credit him only with the installation of a hydraulic system. Likewise the chronicler Gervase, who described the rebuilding of the choir after the 1174 fire, is silent on any work on the cloister. Thus, despite the wealth of documentation associated with the various rebuildings of Canterbury Cathedral, we cannot be sure whether or not the cloister was replaced between the end of the eleventh century and the end of the fourteenth.

This is not the same as saying that we have no evidence of any rebuilding. In fact there are three sets of relevant information to consider. The first is the drawing produced c. 1165 which shows the hydraulic

[44] Tatton-Brown (2006), 91–93; Woodman (1981), 79–80. Kahn (1991), 179 states that the dating is 'relatively secure', but is then undecided whether to place it in Theobald's archiepiscopate (1139–61) or around the time of the 1174 fire.

[45] One support is of four Purbeck shafts. The identification of the other stone as calc-sinter was demonstrated by Christopher Wilson in Fergusson (2011), 156–60. These shafts were labelled 'jasper' by Woodman (1981), 80, and more recently 'onyx' or 'onyx marble'. The crucial difference between the two last-named was explained by Worssam (1995b), 27.

[46] Tatton-Brown (2006), 99. The loose fragments of arches richly decorated with chevron, lozenges and foliage, attributed by Kahn (1991), 135–36 to the Infirmary Cloister, are more likely to have graced the Great Cloister.

116 IN THE INFIRMARY CLOISTER ARCADE AT CANTERBURY CATHEDRAL, PAIRED AND SINGLE SHAFTS ALTERNATE.

system installed by Prior Wibert (plate XXXVIII).[47] This also shows the main cloister on the same site as the present cloister – the north side of the nave. Its arcades, like Reading's, are carried entirely on shafts with no piers, even at the angles. The drawing is schematic, of course, and it would be a mistake to treat it as if it were a detailed representation of the cloister which actually existed, but it is still valuable in showing how a cloister arcade was visualised in mid-twelfth-century England – as a light, skeletal structure supported on slender shafts. We also have two sets of fragments, each of which has, at some time, been associated with the cloister that Chillenden took down.

The so-called Canterbury screen fragments, displayed in the crypt of Canterbury Cathedral, are a group of high-quality relief sculptures and

---

[47] The plan is now bound into the back of the Eadwine Psalter (Cambridge, Trinity College R.17.1., fols 284v–285r. See Tatton-Brown (2006), 92–102; Woodman (1992), passim.

carved architectural fragments, most of which were excavated during repairs to the west alley of Prior Chillenden's cloister between 1968 and 1972.[48] Opinion is divided over the original provenance of these fragments. In 1976 Zarnecki proposed that they were the remains of the choir screen erected by William the Englishman in 1180 to separate the monks from the laity in the nave.[49] In fact, as West pointed out in his timely and thoughtful analysis of the problem, first aired at the British Archaeological Association's Canterbury Conference in 2009, the chronicler Gervase did not mention a screen at all, only a wall that went around the choir and presbytery. In effect there were no twelfth-century screen fragments available to Chillenden for his rebuilding work at the end of the fifteenth century. Nevertheless it was in Chillenden's cloister that most of the fragments were found, and it is safe to assume that they did indeed originate from a structure that he demolished and re-used as building material. Despite the lack of evidence for any major rebuilding of the Great Cloister between Lanfranc's work and Chillenden's, it has thus been argued that these fragments were from unrecorded work there by Prior Wibert in the mid-twelfth century.[50] A third hypothesis, argued by West, is that the stones came from Wibert's lavatorium – close enough to the find-site to be conveniently re-used, and corresponding, in their geometry, to an octagonal structure.[51]

These stones are only relevant to us if we are convinced that they were from a cloister more or less contemporary with Reading's, and our best evidence is the form of the fragments themselves. I should say at the outset that they do not immediately suggest an original location in a cloister arcade. At Reading we have the capitals, bases, springers and voussoirs which were the component parts of such an arcade: the jigsaw is seriously depleted, but we can have no doubt that there was a picture of a cloister on the box. The Canterbury fragments include none of these essential pieces. Instead, we have sections of string-course, three beast-head label-stops

---

[48]   The dispute over the original provenance of these stones has been recently analysed in West (2013). An account of the discovery of the fragments, one of which was unearthed as early as the eighteenth century, was given by Kahn (1991), 145–46.

[49]   Zarnecki (1976), 91. He elaborated his ideas in Zarnecki, in London (1984), 195–98. Kahn (1991), 145–71 gives the fullest and most convincing published account of this hypothesis.

[50]   Woodman (1981), 83–84 presents this hypothesis as fact with no argument to support it. Prior Chillenden's rebuilding was so comprehensive that the stones could theoretically have come from almost anywhere. For the suggestion that they formed part of a tomb, constructed on the lines of Hubert Walter's tomb of c. 1205 in the south choir aisle of the cathedral, see Saxl (1954), 26–27. West (2013), 171 is sceptical of the notion that the fragments were from a cloister rebuilt, wholly or in part, by Wibert.

[51]   West (2013), 171–73.

(one of which is still attached to part of a label decorated with foliage and billet), several small annulets with similar carving, and a series of half-length relief figures in quatrefoils and heads or busts in roundels, whose shape implies an original position in the spandrels of an arcade.

The main comparative evidence suggesting a cloister setting for these fragments comes from the Cathedral of Aix-en-Provence (see figure 103). Here, grotesque heads in roundels are carved in the spandrels of the arcade, and it must be admitted that the shape of these blocks is very similar to those preserved at Canterbury. At Aix, too, fragments of a foliage string-course survive at the top of the arcade wall. The comparison with Aix is a compelling one, but the case for a cloister provenance for all the fragments is seriously weakened by other considerations. If they were indeed from the cloister we would be forced to assume that only the upper part of the arcade wall had been found. We would also be at a loss to explain the annulets, for which surviving cloisters provide no obvious parallels.

Tatton Brown offers a different set of fragments held in the stone store for our consideration as components of the Great Cloister, and again he sees Prior Wibert as its builder.[52] These include a springer, long voussoirs with chevron ornament, a spurred double base, and several spiral-carved shaft fragments, all in Purbeck marble. These can be stylistically connected with similar voussoirs re-used as building material in the Deanery Garden, and Tatton Brown has published his reconstruction of the Great Cloister as a more elaborate version of the Infirmary Cloister, with arcades carried on paired shafts and quadruple shafts at the angles. These support foliate double-capitals that carry arches decorated with chevron on their faces and soffits.[53]

3 HYDE ABBEY, WINCHESTER

The remains of the early twelfth-century cloister of Hyde Abbey, Winchester, amount to just five capitals and a springer excavated from the ruins and now preserved in the church of St Bartholomew in Hyde.[54] The capitals are all single and carved on all four faces, while the springer is carved on both faces, indicating that the arcade from which they came was carried on single shafts (plates XXXIX, XLIX). The capitals are carved with a rich variety of beasts, inhabited foliage and Byzantine blossom, and while there are comparisons to be made with the Reading cloister sculp-

---

[52] Tatton-Brown (2006), 97–101. The store is at Broad Oak Farm, Sturry (Kent).
[53] Ibid., figs 8 and 9.
[54] Cave (1945), 79; Zarnecki in London (1984), 172–73; Winchester (2010), 10–11. Dugdale reported that 'many capitals of columns, heads and other ornaments, which have been dug out of the ruins of Hyde, are to be seen in different parts of the city (Dugdale Monasticon 2, 432).

ture, the degree of undercutting points to these works being later than Reading rather than earlier. The geometry of the single springer suggests an arch span of approximately 900 mm, similar to that of the Reading arcades. Dating the Hyde Abbey capitals is not straightforward. The monastery was the successor of the New Minster, which stood alongside the cathedral, or Old Minster, until 1109 when overcrowding on the site led to a move to Hyde Mead, just outside the city walls on the north side. While the new house was ready to take the relics of Alfred the Great, by the following year it seems inconceivable that the cloister could have been built so quickly. King Henry I was involved in the decision to move, and made generous grants to the abbey, so that it is not surprising to find the successors of his Reading sculptors working there. When this took place is uncertain, but it must have been before 1141 when the city was fired in the course of the Anarchy, and the abbey destroyed.[55] Zarnecki has suggested 1125–30, while Franklin prefers a slightly earlier date, around 1120, and Barbara Yorke a slightly broader range of 1125–35.[56]

4   NORWICH CATHEDRAL

The twelfth-century cloister of Norwich Cathedral Priory was gradually replaced by the present Gothic cloister between 1279 and 1430, stone from the old cloister being reused as building material in the new.[57] A number of carved double capitals came to light during conservation work in 1900, and to date a total of fourteen double capitals along with five capitals from the nook-shafts of a doorway and a large number of carved voussoirs and jamb fragments have been excavated.[58] The double capitals show that the cloister arcade was carried on paired shafts, like the surviving French examples at Saint-Trophime at Arles (Bouches-du-Rhone) and Saint-Bertrand-de-Comminges (Haute-Garonne). These capitals have all been trimmed for reuse, but enough remains to show that in most cases a historiated or decorated block capital was twinned with a plain, undecorated cushion (figure 117). It can be assumed that the decorated capitals faced the cloister walk, while the plain cushions faced the garth.[59] The Norwich cloister is undated, and Zarnecki's estimate of c. 1130 on stylistic grounds sits ill with the documented foundation date of 1096. A dating some ten years earlier, as suggested by Franklin, seems preferable.[60]

---

[55] VCH Hampshire, 2 (1903), 116–22.
[56] Zarnecki in London (1984), 173; Franklin (1983), 58; Yorke in Winchester (2010), 11.
[57] Franklin (1983), 56–70.
[58] Ibid., 56.
[59] Zarnecki, in London (1984), 167.
[60] Franklin (1983), 67–68.

117   A DOUBLE CAPITAL FROM NORWICH CATHEDRAL CLOISTER HAS A PLAIN CUSHION
FACING THE GARTH AND A FIGURE TRAPPED IN FOLIAGE CARVED ON THE WALK-SIDE
CAPITAL.

5   GLASTONBURY

The spectacular cloister capitals of c. 1150 from Glastonbury Abbey, crisp-
ly carved in Blue Lias limestone, may have come from an arcade with alternating single and paired supports. Two of them were certainly double
capitals, as shown by the preservation of the adjoining neckings and parts
of the bells (plate XL).[61] In contrast, there is no fragment that can be in-
controvertibly shown to come from a single capital, in spite of Zarnecki's
assertion to the contrary.[62] It has therefore usually been assumed that the
entire cloister arcade was carried on paired shafts, as at Norwich Cathedral or Bridlington Priory rather than single ones, as at Reading Abbey,
but while the evidence in these cases is unimpeachable, at Glastonbury it
is not. The Glastonbury capitals and bases are generally in a very fragmentary state, and while a small piece of a double capital might be identified
by the junction of two bells and their neckings, a similarly small part of a
single capital could have no such diagnostic feature. In short there is no
fragment that comprises enough of the capital to identify it certainly as

[61]   Salisbury and South Wiltshire Museum no.206; Glastonbury Museum S.783. A
more detailed examination of the cloister at Glastonbury by the present author
will appear in a volume on Glastonbury Abbey excavations, edited by Roberta
Gilchrist and scheduled for publication by the Society of Antiquaries in 2015.
[62]   London (1984), 184–85.

single. It is thus entirely possible that Glastonbury had a system of alternating single and twin shafts, as in the contemporary Infirmary cloister at Christ Church, Canterbury. At Canterbury the fat single shafts with a diameter of 0.20–0.23m were of calc-sinter imported from Germany, while the slimmer paired shafts (diameter 0.12m) were of Purbeck. At Glastonbury, fragments of eight shafts survive, but in only four cases is there enough to estimate the diameter. Three of these have diameters between 0.140m and 0.142m, while the fourth is significantly fatter at 0.180m. This evidence is by no means conclusive; the fatter shaft may have come from a doorway or other feature, but it does keep alive the possibility that the cloister arcades had alternating single and double supports.

6   BRIDLINGTON

Inside the former Priory Church of St Mary, Bridlington (Yorkshire) there is a reconstruction of the twelfth-century cloister arcade from the Augustinian priory (figure 118). This cloister can be dated on stylistic grounds to c. 1160–80.[63] The reconstruction was supervised by John Bilson and dates from 1911–13.[64] It consists of two lengths of arcading, one of two bays and the other of three, with paired octagonal shafts carrying double capitals with integral impost blocks, and arches decorated with various types of chevron on both face and soffit. There is a label carved with a deeply undercut foliage scroll and adorned with label stops in the form of human heads. Most of the shafts are modern replacements, and Thurlby has pointed out that the original arrangement would have included some cylindrical shafts, since the neckings of some of the capitals are round in plan.[65]

This brief summary of the available evidence about English twelfth-century cloisters is enough to show that there was considerable variation in the form of the cloister arcade. Westminster, Reading, the Canterbury Waterworks drawing and Hyde Abbey had arcades carried on single shafts. Bridlington, Norwich Cathedral Priory and possibly the Great Cloister of Canterbury Cathedral had paired shafts, while Canterbury's Infirmary cloister and possibly the Glastonbury cloister used alternating systems of single and paired supports. What the fragments cannot usually disclose is the extent to which piers were used in place of shafts at the angles of the arcade and elsewhere. Piers were not used at Reading and they are not

[63]   Franklin (1989), 44–61; Thurlby (1989), 33–43. Both authors attempt to associate the start of work on the cloister with the priorate of Robert the Scribe (c.1147–54/59), on the grounds that Leland saw his tombstone in the cloister, but the argument is by no means conclusive.

[64]   Bilson (1911); Bilson (1913).

[65]   Thurlby (1989), 33–34.

118 A RECONSTRUCTION OF THE CLOISTER OF BRIDLINGTON PRIORY IS INSTALLED
INSIDE THE PRIORY CHURCH OF ST MARY.

shown on the Canterbury Waterworks drawing, but there is no evidence
concerning the other sites discussed.

To judge from the surviving fragments, the Reading cloister was very
lavishly carved. Comparisons with the more or less contemporary Benedictine houses from which fragments survive – Westminster, Norwich,
Hyde Abbey and Glastonbury, for example – are hampered by the paucity
of survivals from these houses compared to Reading. In particular, the
voussoirs and springers which would have shown us the form of the arch
decoration are very scarce. From Westminster a number of voussoirs with
an elaborate decoration of frontal chevrons on face and soffit have survived and were used in the reconstruction. From Norwich there are twenty-five voussoirs with related forms of foliage decoration, but Franklin has
demonstrated that they form too large an arch to be from the cloister, and
they may have formed the arches of a multi-order doorway.[66] None of the other English cloisters under consideration has yielded voussoirs or springers in
sufficient numbers to allow a reconstruction of the arcade arches.

SURVIVING CLOISTERS IN FRANCE

For both of these issues – the use of piers in alternation with columns, and
the form of the arch decoration – evidence may be found in France. Far

[66] Norwich (1980), 23–26.

119   THE CLOISTER OF DAOULAS (FINISTÈRE) WAS REBUILT IN 1875, AND SINCE THEN
THIS NEW RECONSTRUCTION HAS BEEN MADE.

more twelfth-century cloisters have survived there, especially in the south
where the warmer climate has made replacement with glazed arcades un-
necessary. There are a few standing examples of arcades carried entirely
on shafts, and one of the most interesting is Daoulas (Finistère), whose rebuilt cloister arcade is carried on alternating single and paired shafts with
quadruple shafts at the angles.[67] Daoulas, like Reading, had some chevron
decoration in the arches. It dates from the foundation of a College of Augustinian canons in 1167, and might represent a late and distant echo of a
typically English form of cloister (figure 119).

Elsewhere in France, the available evidence points to widespread use
of piers, either at the angles only, as at Lavaudieu (Haute-Loire) or Saint-
Michel-de-Cuxa (Pyrénées-Orientales), or more commonly as an element in an alternating system of supports. Typical is a group of abbeys in
Provence, including Ganagobie (Alpes-de-Haute-Provence) and Vaison
and Senanque (both Vaucluse), where the rhythm of the arcading along
the walks is broken by the introduction of piers at regular intervals. These
piers form a giant order of enclosing arches visible on the garth side only
(figure 120).

[67]   Levot (1877). For the 1875 reconstruction, see ills after p. 144.

120   HEAVY PIERS WERE INCORPORATED IN THE DESIGN OF THE CLOISTER OF NOTRE-
DAME-DE-NAZARETH, VAISON (VAUCLUSE).

When we turn to the decoration of the arcade arches in French cloisters, an interesting picture emerges. In many cases the arches were left
uncarved both inside and out, as at Lavaudieu. Where the arches were
carved, the carving on the walk side was invariably more elaborate than
that on the garth. At Elne (Pyrénées-Orientales), the arches on the walk
side have rosettes carved in a hollow moulding, while on the garth they
are plain with a hollow chamfered label. In the cathedral of Saint-Trophime at Arles, the garth-side arches are completely plain, while on the
walk side the decoration varies from plain on the north walk to a complex
moulded profile with spandrel figures on the east. This hierarchy of walk
decoration, suggested in my reconstruction of Reading, also occurs at the
cathedral of Aix-en-Provence. On the garth side, all four ranges have plain
arches with rosettes in the spandrels and a hollow chamfered string course
above. On the walk side, the string course is carved with foliage decoration and the arches themselves are moulded. This moulding is the extent
of the arch decoration on the north and west walks, while on the south
walk the mouldings are enriched with a pattern of flat, stylised leaves. On
these three walks there are roundels in the spandrels on the walk side,
decorated with a variety of floral and geometric ornament. A much richer
form of decoration is reserved for the east walk. The spandrel roundels are

decorated with human and animal heads, and the arches themselves are carved with frontal chevron on face and soffit.

CONCLUSIONS

Although it has proved possible to reconstruct the appearance of the cloister of Reading Abbey in detail, it cannot be claimed that it looked like any other cloister we can name. In its design and decoration, Reading Abbey cloister is more similar to the cloister at Westminster Abbey than anything else, but the present state of research into Westminster does not permit any firmer conclusion. What seems indisputable is that more is now known about the design of the Reading cloister than about any other early twelfth-century cloister in England, and that it differed significantly from its French contemporaries.

First, it was visually lighter and more skeletal, being supported entirely on shafts with no piers in its construction, even at the angles. The evidence of the Canterbury waterworks drawing and the Cistercian cloister at Rievaulx both suggest that this might have been a common approach to cloister design in this country. In his study of Norwich Castle, Heslop has made the point that blind arcading was used to produce the visual effect of continuity and lightness on the exteriors of both the castle keep and the north transept of Norwich Cathedral, and that this use of overall arcading as a unifying feature was a characteristic of English design.[68] This appears to be true of cloister design too: none of the French examples except Daoulas, which is both late and marginal, approach the simple uniformity of Reading. Second, the alternating system of shaft and capital types corresponds to a particularly English approach to aesthetics. Third, the arcade was lavishly carved on the walk side: more so than any of the surviving French examples. This carving appears to have been almost entirely decorative: there is no extended narrative scheme of the type found at Moissac, La Daurade in Toulouse or Saint-Trophime at Arles. This issue will be examined in the next chapter from the viewpoint of iconography, but is worth stressing here that the surface richness of the Reading cloister arcade is very much in line with what has come to be seen as a characteristically English approach to architectural articulation.

[68]   Heslop (1994), 63.

THE SCULPTURE OF THE CLOISTER

8

INTRODUCTION

Since 22 June 1916, when Charles Keyser read the paper presenting his discoveries at Sonning, Shiplake and Windsor to the assembled Fellows of the Society of Antiquaries, the chief claim of Reading Abbey to the attention of art historians has been the sculpture of the cloister.[1] In this chapter the story begins with the stone used by the sculptors. Next, the collection of capitals, bases, springers and voussoirs surviving from the cloister will be described in turn, before attention is turned to the figural and foliage styles characteristic of the workshop, and the iconographic elements that can be identified. The chapter will conclude with an attempt to place the sculpture in a context of workshop and patronage.

STONE

Jurassic limestone from Caen in Normandy was used for all the capitals and voussoirs of Reading Abbey cloister, while most of the double spring-ers, both of the large corner springers, and the two column bases were carved from stone quarried at Taynton, in the Windrush Valley in Ox-fordshire, approximately 100km from Reading.[2] The two stones are super-ficially similar in appearance, but Caen stone has a finer and more even grain without large fossils or shell detritus, whereas Taynton is distinctly shelly, with harder bands that stand out on weathered surfaces.[3] The use of

[1] Keyser (1916) – although, as described in the Introduction, they did not take much notice of it until Zarnecki's work in the 1940s and 1950s.

[2] Worssam (1995a). Five of the double springers are of Caen stone, the remainder of Taynton.

[3] Ibid.

stone from several quarries was by no means abnormal for major building projects, perhaps because a single quarry could not cope with the demand.[4] Both Caen and Taynton were well-established sources for English buildings by the 1120s.[5] Caen stone was imported for William I's foundation of Battle Abbey in 1067, while the quarries at Taynton had been in use for some time, certainly since the eleventh century.[6] Stone from both quarries could be brought to the site by water, although the distances involved would make the Caen stone much more expensive than Taynton stone, especially since the journey involved Channel crossings which were hazardous and subject to delays. The use of Caen stone at Reading implies that money was no problem, but there must also have been a specific reason for its use. Either it was perceived by the patron or the sculptors to be superior to the local product, or the quarries were larger and better organised than those in England. It is possible too that Henry chose it for Reading simply because his father had used it at Battle.[7]

The Taynton stone seems to have been first used as the ashlar facing for the church.[8] It was also used for various stones in Reading Museum whose original location within the monastery is not known: an elaborately carved colonnette, the head of an arch, possibly from a blind arcade, and a beast-head corbel. It may be that the discovery that it made an acceptable and cheaper substitute for carved work was made later in the campaign. Since, as we shall see, the same sculptural workshop carved stones from both sources, the carving was almost certainly done on-site in Reading, and any work at the quarries must have been confined to rough shaping.

[4] Documentary information is only available from the later Middle Ages. At Eton College in the 1440s, stone was brought from the nearby quarries of Taynton (Oxon) and Merstham (Surrey), but also from three quarries in Kent, two in Yorkshire, and Caen in Normandy (Parsons (1991), 21–22).

[5] During the first half of the twelfth century, Caen stone was used for sculpture at many major sites including St Augustine's Abbey in Canterbury, Westminster Abbey, Norwich Cathedral and Castle, and Wolvesey Palace, Winchester (London (1984), 156, 158, 167, 175, 183; Heslop (1994), 12). The Taynton quarries are mentioned in the Domesday Survey.

[6] Parsons (1991), 10–11.

[7] William I arranged for stone from Caen to be imported for the building of Battle, but when a quarry was discovered near the abbey site, this stone was used instead (Lehmann-Brockhaus (1955–60), 1, 67 (no. 249). Something similar might have happened at Reading.

[8] Slade (1975–76), 46.

SCULPTURAL ELEMENTS

CAPITALS

As noted in the previous chapter, Reading Museum holds ten trefoil capitals, ten block capitals and a triple corner capital from the cloister, and there is another block capital on display in the chancel of St James's Church. An unusual technical feature of all of these capitals is that they are carved from the same block as their imposts, whereas normal practice was to carve capital and impost from two separate blocks of stone. The method used at Reading is both very unusual and extremely wasteful of both stone and labour: approximately forty per cent of the stone is cut away and wasted simply in roughing out the shape of the capital from the block. Furthermore, the stone for the capitals was imported from Caen, and it would seem unnecessarily extravagant to ship a cargo, almost half of which was destined to be discarded on arrival – especially since, as Salzman has calculated, for journeys longer than 12 miles the cost of transport was greater than the cost of the stone.[9] It is thus possible that the initial roughing-out of the capitals took place at the quarry in Normandy, and that the Reading workshop travelled to Caen to do it accurately. Whether this was done or not, it is certain that money was no object to the patron,[10] who was prepared to pay handsomely either to ensure that capital face and impost designs were correctly matched, or to avoid an intrusive mortar bed, or simply to employ a chosen workshop which habitually followed that practice. Integral imposts are commonly found on capitals made for small-scale objects, like altars, tombs and especially piscinas, where carving a separate capital and impost block would be very awkward, and its use at Reading raises the possibility that the carvers were trained in this tradition.

Larger-scale capitals with integral impost blocks are uncommon but not unknown. The method was famously used in the twelfth-century cloister of Sainte-Marie-de-Lombez (Gers), now demolished, from which capitals survive in the V&A and other museums.[11] In England, odd examples may be seen in Evesham Museum and at Bridlington and St Albans,[12] as well as on the south doorway of St Mary's Cholsey,

[9] Salzman (1967), 119.
[10] A point made by Zarnecki in London (1984), 167.
[11] V&A accessions A58–1935 and A59–1935. Related capitals are in the Musée des Augustins, Toulouse, the National Gallery of Canada in Ottawa, the Musées Royaux in Brussels, the Cloisters in New York and the Pitcairn Collection, Bryn Athyn (PA). For the V & A capitals, see Williamson (1983); Mesplé (1958), 177–84; P. Barnet in New York (1982), 53–54.
[12] The Evesham capital is a plain scalloped respond capital with a hollow-chamfered impost. The examples from Bridlington and St Albans are illustrated in Kahn

a former possession of Reading. But the most suggestive comparison is with two damaged capitals from the Cluniac priory at Bermondsey, now in the parish church (figure 121).[13] Both are carved from Caen stone, are of the trefoil type and measure approximately 14" (0.36m) square, which makes them closely comparable with the Reading trefoil capitals in size and probably in function. A third capital of this type is known from a drawing by Buckler.[14] The best match for this technical peculiarity is therefore at another English Cluniac site, and the similarities are close enough to suggest a direct connection. This is not to imply that there was anything like a 'Cluniac style' in England, but simply that the links between the monks at Bermondsey and Reading were close enough for them to share a workshop. Unfortunately it is not possible to be certain of the direction of travel of the workshop. Bermondsey was founded in 1082, but it was not until 1089 that four monks arrived from La Charité-sur-Loire. In the interim some building must have taken place, because the Domesday Survey recorded a new and handsome church on the site in 1086.[15] Although the monastic *annales* record gifts of money and lands throughout the twelfth century, none of these are explicitly connected with any building programme. As one writer puts it, 'the whole period is in fact an almost total blank in the architectural history of the priory'.[16] It must be accepted that the capitals under discussion cannot belong to the first building campaign, and their dating relative to Reading must be based on stylistic considerations.

TREFOIL CAPITALS

The ten trefoil capitals in Reading Museum all have uncarved impost blocks and octagonal neckings, and all are similar in shape, although no two are identical (figure 100a-j). The trefoil capital is a variation of the cushion capital in which the shields have a trilobed instead of a semicircular form. All the Reading trefoil capitals are of this form except for 1992.100, whose shields have an angular, stepped form (figure 100h). The shields are all recessed by one or more steps, and the angles below the shields are decorated with ribbed or fluted stylised leaf forms. Again, 1992.100 stands out from the rest because its leaves extend vertically downwards rather than following the shape of the bell, giving it a squared-off appearance. Apart

(1991), plates 166–67. Both are late-twelfth-century variants of the multi-scallop capital with pleating on the shields.

[13]   Lockett (1971), 46. The capitals were said to have been dug up 'near the church which formerly stood nearby'.

[14]   Martin (1926), 192–228, fig. 14C.

[15]   Literally *Nova et pulchra ecclesia*. Lockett (1971), 46. See also *Annales Bermundeseia*, 426.

[16]   Martin (1926), 209.

121   TWO
CAPITALS FROM
BERMONDSEY
PRIORY ARE
PRESERVED IN THE
PARISH CHURCH
OF ST MARY,
BERMONDSEY.

from the leaf decoration, most of the trefoil capitals are carved with rows of beading, either around the shield, or in a line above it, or around the necking, or on the ribs of some of the leaves. 1992.100 is again unique in having no beading at all.

Simpler forms of trefoil capital may be seen in Anselm's crypt at Canterbury Cathedral (1096–1100). In one case, the basic form of the capital is a simple cushion and the scalloping is simply a decoration of the shield, but another of the Canterbury capitals has trefoil-shaped shields, and consequently the form of the bell is more complex. It is this type, enriched with beading and foliage motifs, that forms the basis of the rich and varied series of trefoil capitals found at Reading. As noted in chapter seven, trefoil capitals are among the cloister fragments from Westminster Abbey, dateable c. 1120, just before Reading. As at Reading these are varied in form, but several have such typical Reading features as recessed shields framed by narrow rolls and foliage decoration in the lower angles of the bell (figure 122).

122   A TREFOIL
CAPITAL FROM
THE CLOISTER OF
WESTMINSTER
ABBEY.

The three Bermondsey trefoil capitals also exhibit similarities of decoration (figure 121).[17] All have recessed shields, like the Reading trefoil capitals, but they also have chamfered borders to the recess, a feature not found at Reading. Just as at Reading, all three Bermondsey capitals differ slightly in their treatment of the shield. One exhibits the common form

[17]   Royal Commission on Historical Monuments, *London*, V, 1930, 3 and plate 18; Martin (1926), 221, fig. 14C; Lockett (1971), 46.

XXVI   THE POSITIONS OF THE RESPONDS BETWEEN THE BAYS OF THE SOUTH TRANSEPT
INTERIOR WEST WALL STAND OUT SHARPLY IN THIS VIEW FROM THE SOUTH EAST.

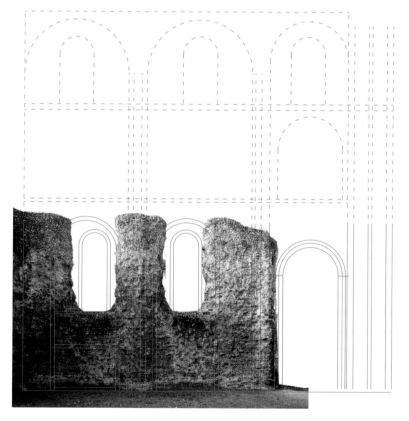

XXVII   THE GIANT ORDER ARRANGEMENT OF THE INTERIOR WEST WALL OF THE
SOUTH TRANSEPT SUPERIMPOSED ON THE STANDING REMAINS.

XXVIII   A VIEW IN THE SOUTH CHANCEL AISLE SHOWS THE JUNCTION BETWEEN THE AISLE WALL AND THE SOUTH TRANSEPT INNER CHAPEL.

XXIX   SOME OF THE COURSED ASHLAR OF THE VAULT WEB IS STILL IN PLACE IN THE
SOUTH TRANSEPT INNER CHAPEL.

XXX   THIS VIEW INTO THE SOUTH NAVE AISLE LOOKING EAST SHOWS THE SW CROSSING PIER
BASE ON THE LEFT AND THE AISLE WALL WITH THE CLOISTER DOORWAY ON THE RIGHT.

XXXI   THE SOUTH TRANSEPT INNER CHAPEL IS DEEPER THAN ITS COMPANION TO THE SOUTH. THIS AP-
PEARS TO BE AN ORIGINAL ARRANGEMENT, AND IT MIGHT HAVE BEEN INTENDED TO HOUSE THE HAND OF ST
JAMES.

XXXII   THE GIANT ORDER IN THE NORTH NAVE ARCADE OF ROMSEY ABBEY (HANTS) IS USUALLY DATED C.
1140, SLIGHTLY AFTER READING.

XXXIII   THE WALL AT THE EAST END OF THE FORBURY GARDENS INCORPORATES MANY
CARVED STONES FROM THE ABBEY SITE.

XXXIV   THE CORONATION OF THE VIRGIN CAPITAL (READING MUSEUM 1992.95) HAS NO IMPOST BLOCK ANY
LONGER, AND HAS SERIOUS LOSSES ELSEWHERE.

XXXV THE DORMITORY DOORWAY IS TOWARDS THE SOUTHERN END OF THE EAST
RANGE OF THE CLOISTER. BEYOND IT, FURTHER SOUTH, IS THE SCAR MARKING THE END
OF THE EAST WALK.

XXXVI THE EXTERNAL WALL ARCADE OF ANSELM'S CHOIR AT CANTERBURY CATHEDRAL USES AN
ALTERNATING SYSTEM IN BOTH SHAFTS AND CAPITAL TYPES.

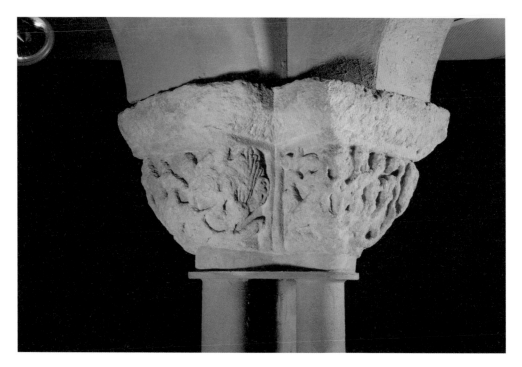

XXXVII   THE TREATMENT OF THE ANGLES OF THE CLOISTER ARCADE IS SHOWN BY THIS TRIPLE CAPITAL.
THE FACE SHOWN WOULD HAVE BEEN TOWARDS THE GARTH.

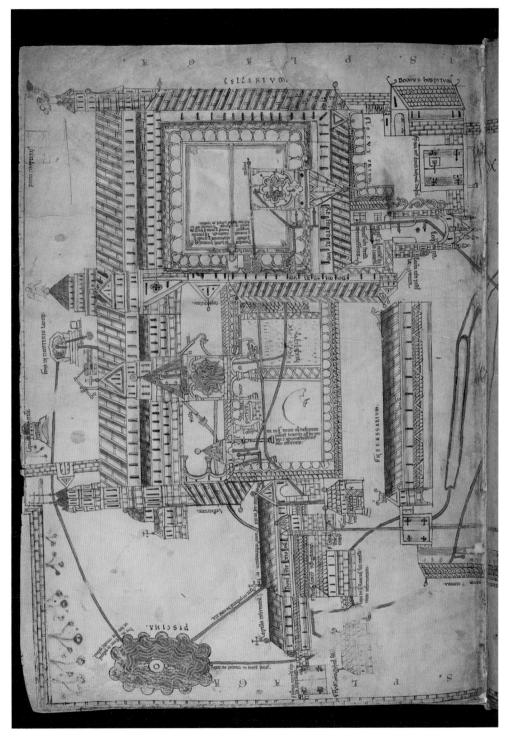

XXXVIII   THE CANTERBURY CATHEDRAL WATERWORKS DRAWING IN THE EADWINE PSALTER SHOWS THE
MAIN CLOISTER ON THE RIGHT, WITH BROAD BAYS CARRIED ON SINGLE SHAFTS.

XXXIX   THE SPRINGER FROM THE CLOISTER OF HYDE ABBEY, WINCHESTER, WAS DESIGNED TO CARRY
ADJACENT ARCHES CARVED WITH DIFFERENT DESIGNS.

OPPOSITE, TOP: XL   A FRAGMENT OF A DOUBLE CAPITAL FROM BISHOP HENRY OF BLOIS' CLOISTER AT
GLASTONBURY ABBEY SHOWS THE JUNCTION OF THE NECKINGS AND BELLS OF TWO APPARENTLY SIMILARLY
CARVED CAPITALS.

OPPOSITE, BOTTOM: XLI   THE RESET TYMPANUM AT ST PETER'S, CHARNEY BASSETT (BERKSHIRE) HAS
U-SHAPED LEAVES ON THE FRAME AROUND THE MAIN FIELD.

XLII   THE WINGED FIGURES ON CAPITAL 1992.118 ARE OFTEN DESCRIBED AS ANGELS BUT THEIR LONG
BEARDS AND THE ATTRIBUTES THEY CARRY MAKE THIS UNLIKELY.

XLIII   ONE OF THE CAPITALS ON THE WEST DOORWAY OF LEOMINSTER PRIORY IS
CARVED WITH CONFRONTED LIONS.

XLIV ONE OF THE MOST ASSURED OF THE READING CLOISTER CAPITALS IS CARVED
WITH MIRROR-PAIRED DRAGONS ON EACH FACE.

XLV THE BEAKHEAD ON THE WEST DOORWAYS OF LINCOLN CATHEDRAL, PART OF BISHOP ALEXANDER'S
CAMPAIGN OF 1141–45, HAS INVENTIVELY CARVED TONGUES LYING ACROSS THE ANGLE ROLLS. THIS SHOWS
A DETAIL OF THE NORTH DOORWAY OF THE WEST FACADE.

XLVI   ON THE SOUTH DOORWAY OF ST SWITHUN'S, QUENINGTON, BEADED BEAKER-CLASPS ALTER-
NATE WITH BIRD BEAKHEADS.

XLVII   THE SOUTH DOORWAY OF DALMENY CHURCH (LOTHIAN) IS THE BEST SURVIVING COMPARISON FOR THE BULBOUS VOUSSOIRS OF THE READING CLOISTER, BUT ANY WORKSHOP CONNECTION BETWEEN THEM IS UNLIKELY IN THE EXTREME.

XLVIII   THE PREENING BIRD DESIGN CARVED ON A READING CORNER SPRINGER (FIGURE 139) ALSO APPEARS ON A CAPITAL FROM GOULT PRIORY.

XLIX   A CAPITAL FROM HYDE ABBEY, WINCHESTER, IS DECORATED WITH A SIMILAR GRIFFIN TO THOSE ON THE READING NOOK-SHAFT.

L   IN A WELL-PRESERVED CAPITAL AT GOULT PRIORY, A HUNTER IS SEEN TO BE SPEARING A LION THAT IS ATTACKING A STAG.

with three curved cusps, similar to Reading Museum 1992.107 (figure 100i). The second surviving Bermondsey capital has a curious key-like variant of the trefoil shield unlike anything from Reading. The Buckler drawing shows a shield with a curved lower cusp and a squared-off top, like Reading Museum 1992.100 but without the steps.

Unlike the Reading trefoil capitals, but like the figural and foliage capitals from the cloister, the Bermondsey capitals have designs carved on their impost chamfers: in one case, a stepped triangle design, and on the other surviving capital and the Buckler drawing, a repeated pattern of a fluted leaf with scalloped edges curved into a U-shape. Neither design finds any exact parallel with the surviving Reading capital imposts, but comparisons may be found for the U-shaped leaves among the Reading-related sculpture at Charney Bassett, Avington and Quenington (plates XLI and XLVI). Finally, the lower angles of the bells of the Bermondsey capitals are carved, not with simple leaf designs as at Reading, but with quadrupeds or dragons. It seems likely in view of their formal and technical similarities that the Bermondsey and Reading capitals came out of the same workshop, and it is difficult to resist the conclusion that the Bermondsey capitals represent a later stage of experimentation with the trefoil form, especially in the use of animal motifs at the angles, the adventurous key-type variant of the shield itself, and the use of chamfered mouldings.

Also worth considering are three trefoil capitals from Winchester Cathedral, now in the tribune (figure 123). Like the Westminster Abbey trefoil capitals, they are carved without their impost blocks, and their size (approximately 0.30m square at the top and 0.29m high), and the fact that they are carved on all four faces, both suggest that they may have come from a cloister arcade. All three have shields recessed with chamfers, like the Bermondsey examples. One has the simple triple-cusped shields, while the other two have curved lower cusps with a straight T-bar at the top – a form found at both Westminster Abbey and Bermondsey. The Winchester capitals have clearly defined conical bells with simple vegetal motifs in the angles. These rise from neckings carved with single-strand cable. In general appearance they are very clearly articulated, the sculptural decoration giving the impression of ornament applied to a simple architectural member, and in this they resemble the Westminster Abbey cloister capitals. There is no historical evidence to assist us with the dates of these capitals. They are much too advanced to belong to Walkelin's campaign of 1079–98.[18]

18   Gem (1983), 1–12.

123   A TREFOIL CAPITAL AT WINCHESTER CATHEDRAL HAS DEEPLY RECESSED SHIELDS
AND PINE-CONE DECORATION.

BLOCK CAPITALS

The eleven known Reading block capitals, ten single capitals and one triple, all have circular neckings, confirming that they were carried on cylindrical shafts, and integral chamfered impost blocks with decoration on
the chamfers (figure 124a-k). Impost chamfers are generally carved on all
four faces, but Reading Museum capitals 1992.114 and 1992.118 have one
chamfer left undecorated, presumably the one intended to face the garth.
Two of the block capitals are so badly damaged that they have no imposts
remaining at all, which throws some doubt on their status as cloister arcade capitals (1992.70 and 1992.95); but their other measurements, their
provenance and the fact that they are carved on all faces makes it extremely likely that they were.[19] The repertoire of motifs includes foliage, often
with reeded or beaded stems and furled-leaf or spiral terminals; grotesque
masks carved at angles or on capital faces; the decorative five-lobed Byzantine blossom, so-called; dragons; and animal and human figures. There
is some variation in the decoration of the neckings, with plain rolls, horizontal grooves, guilloche, foliage, beading, and single and double cable

[19]   For full descriptions including dimensions, see the relevant entries in CRSBI.

124 A TO K. THE ELEVEN KNOWN BLOCK CAPITALS FROM READING ABBEY CLOISTER VARY WIDELY IN THEIR DECORATION BUT ARE PRODUCTS OF A SINGLE WORKSHOP.
ABOVE LEFT: A   READING MUSEUM 1977.100. ABOVE RIGHT: B   READING MUSEUM 1992.70.

ABOVE LEFT: C   READING MUSEUM 1992.76. ABOVE RIGHT: D   READING MUSEUM 1992.78.
BELOW LEFT: E   READING MUSEUM 1992.95. BELOW RIGHT: F   READING MUSEUM 1992.106.

124 CONTINUED. ABOVE: G   READING MUSEUM 1992.108.

ABOVE LEFT: H   READING MUSEUM 1992.112. ABOVE RIGHT: I   READING MUSEUM 1992.114.
BELOW LEFT: J   READING MUSEUM 1992.118. BELOW RIGHT: K   READING, ST JAMES'S RC CHURCH.

TABLE 5   BLOCK CLOISTER CAPITALS

Reference	Type	Provenance	Notes
1977–100	Single	Avebury	The dragon fight capital. Guilloche necking. Knotwork on impost
1992–70	Single	Twyford	Confronted lion capital, badly damaged. Plain necking, no surviving impost
1992–76 (Keyser 7)	Single	Sonning	Foliage and angle masks. Grooved necking, two rows of leaves on impost
1992–78 (Keyser 3)	Single	Sonning	Foliage and angle masks. Roll necking, 2 rows of foliate sawtooth on impost
1992–95 (CL 1)	Single	Borough Marsh	Coronation of the Virgin. Single cable necking, no surviving impost
1992–106 (Keyser 10)	Single	Sonning	Inhabited foliage (lower part lost). Beaded necking, 4 designs on impost
1992–108 (CL 3)	Triple	Borough Marsh	Triple capital with figure in mandorla and foliage. Necking lost, triangular leaves on impost
1992–112 (Keyser 9)	Single	Sonning	Foliage and angle and face masks. Worn foliate necking, triangular leaves on impost
1992–114 (Keyser 6)	Single	Sonning	Symmetrical dragons. Double cable necking, upright leaves on 3 faces of impost, 4th face uncarved
1992–118 (Keyser 8)	Single	Sonning	Angels and foliage. Double cable necking; beaded guilloche on 3 faces of impost, 4th face uncarved
St James, Reading	Single	unknown	Capital with foliage. Plain roll necking, 2 rows sawtooth on impost

all appearing. It has been considered useful to include a table describing these capitals (Table 5).

There seems at first sight to be considerable variation in the design and execution of the sculpture. The style of capital 1992.112, with its messy jumble of foliage and very approximate symmetry, appears very different from the bold, calligraphic design and assuring handling of 1992.76, 1992.78 and the St James's Church capital, or the rhythmic simplicity of 1992.106, with its heavy reliance on Byzantine blossom, shared by 1992.118 and 1992.108. But a careful examination of the foliage capitals very quickly demonstrates that the same motifs were used throughout, albeit on slightly different scales and with varying degrees of symmetry and assuredness.

Several of the block capitals include figures in foliage. Two opposing faces of capital 1992.118 (figure 124j) are carved with grooved figure-of-eight scrolls filled with large Byzantine blossoms like that seen on capital 1992.106. A third face also has a figure-of-eight scroll, beaded in this case, but here the two rings are linked by a small central mask and occupied by a pair of lions running away from one another, their heads turned back to bite at stems of loose foliage. The most significant decoration is reserved for the fourth face, probably that facing the cloister walk (plate XLII). It is carved with a pair of nimbed and winged figures in beaded mandorlas, the left one raising two fingers of his right hand in blessing and carrying a book, and the right one holding a crosier in his right hand. Zarnecki made the point that if they are to be read as angels, the two figures should not be in mandorlas – a type of framing reserved for Christ alone. But examples abound of mandorla-like frames surrounding figures that are not Christ.[20] It must be added that they should not be carrying books and liturgical objects either. If they are to be interpreted in any precise way, it can only be as a pair of saints, one with writings and the other a bishop or an abbot, shown winged on account of their heavenly status. Their lower bodies are worn, but the drapery on their shoulders is depicted by a series of parallel grooves. The hair is also shown in straight parallel grooves, like some of the masks on 1992.76, 1992.78 and 1992.112. The eyes are large, bulbous and almond-shaped with grooved lids. The opposite face of this capital is

[20]   London (1984), 168. The commonest occupants of a mandorla apart from Christ are the Virgin, either as Virgin and Child (as on the tympanum of Fownhope church) or alone in Assumption scenes, and Daniel, protected by a mandorla in the lions' den, as seen on capitals at Vézelay, Autun and St Porchaire de Poitiers. The c. 1100 sarcophagus of Doña Sancha in Jaca depicts the soul of the dead as a naked figure in a mandorla borne by two angels (see Simon (1979)).

carved with a pair of addorsed running lions, their heads turned back to bite the scrolls of foliage in which they are framed.[21]

The triple capital, 1992.108, is carved on its prominent central face with a half-length human figure, badly worn, within a frame formed of two long, curving fluted leaves with scalloped outer edges (figure 124g). Despite the mandorla-like shape of the framing elements, there is nothing in this worn figure to suggest that it is a saint or an angel; indeed, its pose suggests an orant.

Four capitals remain to be discussed, labelled here the confronted lion capital (1992.70), the Coronation of the Virgin capital (1992.95), the dragon fight capital (1977.100), and the symmetrical dragon capital (1992.114).

THE CONFRONTED LION CAPITAL

Among the fragments unearthed by Zarnecki at Borough Marsh was a badly worn capital (now Reading Museum 1992.70), lacking its impost and most of its plain necking, carved on each face with a lion in deep relief (figure 124b). The lions on adjacent faces are alternately confronted and addorsed, and where they are confronted they share a single head at the angle. These two twin-bodied lions are devouring prey of some kind, but the condition of the capital makes it impossible to guess what this might be. Each lion has a mane of two rows of fluting, and a beaded tail which passes down between its legs and up over its body. In one case, a large brush-like terminal to the tail has survived. The carving appears crude, but this might be a consequence of advanced wear. What is clear is that the relief is much deeper on this capital than on any of the others, so that the beasts appear to structure the capital, with the projecting heads and hindquarters acting as volutes. This design is rare in England, but comparisons may be made with capitals carved in the 1140s by the Herefordshire School sculptors, e.g. at Leominster Priory (plate XLIII) and Shobdon.[22] The Leominster capital is also deeply carved and the lions' legs are treated in the same way, but it lacks both the shared heads and the prey. Also of interest is the mid-twelfth-century font in St Mary's, Stafford, whose decoration includes a band of four walking lions, alternately confronted and addorsed, and below this on the plinth, four grotesque heads, each with two bodies. A clue to the interpretation of the font, and perhaps the Reading capital too, takes the form of an inscription above the lions reading

[21]   Zarnecki (London (1984), 168) calls them 'rampant, dog-like creatures', but their manes identify them as lions, while heraldically they should be described as courant regardant rather than rampant.

[22]   Shobdon arches, right arch, 2nd order right capital. The lions are barely distinguishable now, but are clearly shown in Lewis's drawing (reproduced in Thurlby (1999), fig. 133.

DISCRETVS NON ES SI NON FVGIS ECCE LEONES (You are not wise if you do not flee. Behold the lions). While we struggle to find convincing English parallels, the position is different in France, where this subject is commonplace and widespread.[23]

THE CORONATION OF THE VIRGIN CAPITAL

The Coronation of the Virgin capital (1992.95) is by any reckoning the most significant of Zarnecki's discoveries at Borough Marsh, despite its damaged condition.[24] The entire upper part of the capital, including, presumably, an impost, is lost. At worst, on the back face of the capital, only 0.07m of the bell survives above the necking. No carving survives in this area or, in fact, on approximately one third of the surface of the bell. The necking shows a heavy cable moulding.

The front face shows the Coronation of the Virgin (plate XXXIV, figure 125a). She is seated towards the left of a long bench-like throne facing forwards, her body turned slightly towards the centre and her straight legs angled diagonally inwards. Her hands appear to be clutched together on her lap, and she may be holding some object under her right arm. She wears a robe with a hood wrapped around her head, framing her face and falling in a loop of fabric on the left. To the right is Christ. The lower half of his body is lost, so it is not clear whether he is seated or standing, although since the arcaded back of the throne reappears to the right of his body, he must be assumed to be sitting on it. He is carved on a much larger scale than Mary. Only the lower half of his head survives, from which all trace of features is eroded away. With his right arm, bent at the elbow, he reaches to the top of Mary's head, but the hand and the crown it once held are lost. He holds a book in his left hand and wears a waist-length tunic over a robe with keyhole braid at the neck. The tunic is articulated with plate drapery, but the folds of the robe below this, as well as Mary's robe, are simply shown as parallel grooves. The state of wear must contribute to the crude appearance of these figures, but neither Christ nor Mary is convincingly seated; Mary's head is disproportionately large, and Christ's broad torso is out of scale with his short and slender arms. To the left of the scene is a fictive pier with accurately depicted nook-shafts to either side, these being shown with bases and cushion capitals (figure 125b). A single impost covers the pier and both capitals, and the beginnings of arches with triple-roll mouldings frame the scenes to left and right. To the left of this pier an angel, doubtless the angel of the Annunciation, advances left

23   Comparable examples may be seen at Plaimpied (Cher), Chauvigny (Vienne), Allichamps (Haute Marne), Sigogne (Charente) and Saint-Côme-du-Mont (Manche).
24   Zarnecki (1949), 524; Zarnecki (1950b) passim; London (1984), 159. See also Heslop (2005).

125 A TO D. THE CORONATION OF THE VIRGIN CAPITAL IS BADLY DAMAGED, BUT PARTS OF THREE SCENES ARE
VISIBLE.
ABOVE LEFT: A   CORONATION OF THE VIRGIN. ABOVE RIGHT: B   PIER DIVIDING THE CORONATION AND
ANNUNCIATION SCENES.
BELOW LEFT: C   ANNUNCIATION. BELOW RIGHT: D   FACE OPPOSITE THE CORONATION SHOWING A
DIAGONAL STAFF.

in the direction of a badly worn mass which was presumably the standing
Virgin (figure 125c). Most of one of the angel's wings survives, decorated
with two rows of cusping at the top and long feathers below. His drapery
resembles the Virgin's in the Coronation scene. The only other feature
worth mentioning is a straight, slanting fillet of stone on the face opposite
the Coronation, which could conceivably be the remains of a staff (figure
125d).

The relief is deep, with recessed fields on each face bounded by the
architectural forms on the angles. There is none of the vitality of the
men entangled in foliage of 1992.106 or the energetic tongue-pullers of
1977.100 in the stiff, doll-like forms of Christ, the Virgin and the Angel of
the Annunciation. A comparison could be made between the plate-dra-
pery on Christ's tunic and that on the angels in mandorlas of 1992.118

126   THE CORONATION OF THE VIRGIN TYMPANUM AT ST SWITHUN'S, QUENINGTON (GLOUCS) IS A VASTLY
EXPANDED VERSION OF THE INTIMATE SCENE ON THE READING CAPITAL.

(which also has a cable necking), but it is not a particularly close one, and differences in the treatment of the angels' wings render common authorship of the two capitals extremely unlikely. Its figure style differs from the other capitals carved with human figures, and given the importance of its subject matter it is tempting to suggest that it was entrusted to the head of the workshop.

This capital has attracted more attention than any other from Reading, owing to its precocious iconography. The same subject appears on the south doorway tympanum of Quenington Church, Gloucestershire (figure 126), but the treatment is very different. At Quenington, Christ is shown crowning the Virgin on his right, the two sharing a plain, backless bench. Christ is centrally placed on the tympanum, and his centrality is emphasised by a vertical band rising from the lower edge of the tympanum, on which his feet rest. This main group is surrounded by the symbols of the four evangelists. On the far left of the composition is a six-winged seraph, and balancing him on the right is a complex architectural structure decorated with arcading and topped by a dome with a cross. At the foot of the building is a crescent moon, and the half-length figure to the right of Christ could therefore represent the sun. Surrounding the entire composition is a triple row of chevron, doubtless intended to evoke the heavenly setting. The tympanum thus conflates the Coronation of the Virgin with an apocalyptic vision of Christ in Majesty.

The treatment of the subject is symmetrical and hieratic, with all the figures facing forwards, and in this it could hardly be more different from the intimacy of the Reading capital, which has only two figures, both off-centre and turning towards one another while seated on a high-backed throne decorated with arcading. Nevertheless, two key iconographic features are common to both: the shared seat and the crowning of the Virgin by Christ himself. Quenington is less than fifty miles from Reading, and Zarnecki has suggested that the provincial carver responsible for the tympanum copied a Reading model: perhaps not this capital, but another tympanum, now lost, which would have been appropriate in an abbey church dedicated to the Virgin. In this version of events, the lost Reading tympanum could have shown the conflated scene, including the apocalyptic elements, or perhaps formed one element of a multiple portal showing both subjects. If this is so, it seems probable that the tympanum of the north doorway of Quenington church, showing the Harrowing of Hell, was also copied from a Reading tympanum.

The subject of the Coronation of the Virgin became enormously popular in French facade sculpture in the twelfth and thirteenth centuries, where it was treated in three different ways. The earliest composition, found at Senlis c. 1170, and copied at Mantes c. 1180 and Laon c. 1200 shows Christ and the Virgin sharing a throne but seated some distance apart. Both wear crowns and the Virgin also carries a sceptre and a book. Since no act of crowning is taking place, the composition has sometimes been called the Triumph of the Virgin. It is arguable, but by no means certain, that the tympanum of Senlis was copied from a stained glass window, now lost, which Abbot Suger of Saint-Denis gave to the cathedral of Notre-Dame in Paris. In fact the earliest surviving example of this particular composition is not in French sculpture but in an Italian mosaic executed between 1140 and 1148 in the apse of Sta Maria in Trastevere, Rome.

A second version of the subject is a true coronation, but the Virgin is crowned by an angel rather than by Christ. This appears twice at Notre-Dame in Paris: on the west portal, c. 1210–20, and on the Porte Rouge, c. 1260, as well as at Longpont and Amiens, c. 1230. It was not until the middle of the thirteenth century that the type of coronation shown on the Reading capital, where Christ himself crowns the Virgin, first appeared in French sculpture. Among the earliest examples are the gable of the central west portal at Reims Cathedral, c. 1245–55, and the north transept portal of Saint-Thibault-en-Auxois (Côte d'Or, c. 1240–50). The latter in particular is compositionally very close to the Reading capital, but it is difficult to visualise any kind of direct relationship on account of the hundred-year time gap between them.

The Coronation of the Virgin capital is so badly damaged that its original size cannot be accurately assessed; nevertheless, those dimensions which can be measured match the other cloister capitals, including the diameter of the lower bearing surface, which, at 0.17m, matches the column diameter of the cloister arcades. Zarnecki has suggested that the carving of the capital was never completed,[25] but its condition is equally consistent with severe damage to a completed capital, and the fact that it was found among material from the cloister in the excavation at Borough Marsh suggests that it was originally situated in the east or south walk of the cloister (see chapter seven). Of all the Reading sculpture, this is the only piece to depict an identifiable religious narrative and for this reason it is likely that it occupied a prominent position, possibly opposite the chapter house entrance on the east walk.

THE SYMMETRICAL DRAGON CAPITAL

This capital, 1992.114, is certainly the most striking of the entire ensemble, as well as being the most accurately symmetrical of all the figural or foliage capitals (plate XLIV). Its four faces are identically carved with pairs of dragons biting their own forefeet. Their tails form precise tapering spirals, and there is a pleasing tension between these centrifugal curves and the acute centripetal lines of their wings. A similarly rhythmic treatment appears on the faces of 1992.76, but the effect is nothing like so dynamic. On 1992.114 the dragons' tails end in furled leaves and their wings in small, tight spirals, both of types found on no other capitals. The dragons themselves, with their slender necks and tails, heavy bodies and long wings are nothing like the snake-like beasts of capital 1977.100 or springer 1992.109, and their birdlike heads are of an entirely different type. These differences could simply result from copying a different model for the design, but the surface decoration of 1992.114 also includes features found on no other piece of sculpture. The wings are hatched with fine parallel grooves. Some of the dragons' bodies have a line of beading along the tail and a beaded collar, while others have bodies that are either plain or inscribed with a simple double groove, and a collar decorated with small drilled holes. The drilled decoration and fine grooving do not appear on other capitals. Capitals at many sites bear general similarities to this design, but the closest parallels are to be found in southern Normandy, at Lonlay (Orne) and the Priory of Saint-Michel at La Lande-de-Goult near Domfront, where Henry I had major holdings before he became king

[25] London (1984), 159.

127   THE SYMMETRICAL DRAGON DESIGN APPEARS ON A CAPITAL OF THE WEST
DOORWAY OF THE FORMER PRIORY OF LA LANDE-DE-GOULT (ORNE).

(figure 127).[26] These capitals share the detail of the dragons biting their
own legs, and also include drilled decoration.

THE DRAGON FIGHT CAPITAL

A capital which has attracted a good deal of iconographic speculation is
the dragon fight capital, 1977.100 (figures 128a-d).[27] At first glance, each
of its four faces appears to have the same composition. Two dragons are
shown back to back with their tails interlacing amid a good deal of foliage. Their heads, which occupy the upper angles of each face, are turned
to face one another. Emerging from, or seated on, each dragon's tail is a
small human figure pulling the dragon's tongue. The two figures on each
face thus sit back to back. The scenes differ in the extent to which the little
men have pulled out their dragon's tongue. On each face the tongues have
been pulled out by a different amount, so that the four faces can be read
as a series, in which the final scene shows the figures leaning back so far

[26] Baylé (1991), 86–93.
[27] The capital was taken to Avebury Manor, Wiltshire, from a garden in Reading,
and examined by Zarnecki in 1959. His identification of it as a Reading Abbey
cloister capital was based on the stone, the dimensions and the carving style. After
lengthy negotiations it was purchased by Reading Museum for the sum of £6,250
(including a grant of £1,000 from the National Art Collections Fund) in 1971.

128 A TO D. THE FOUR FACES OF THE DRAGON FIGHT CAPITAL SHOW THE PROGRESSIVE DISEMBOWELLING OF
A PAIR OF DRAGONS BY TWO MEN.

in their efforts that they too have crossed and are now facing one another,
while the two tongues, with guts and organs attached, are pulled out so far
that they cross each other.

An imaginative attempt has been made to identify this capital with an
episode in the Norse *Saga of Hrolf Kraki*, in which the champion Bothvar
killed a dragon and made the cowardly Hott drink its blood and eat its
heart to gain courage. The dead dragon was then made to appear alive,
and Hott pretended to kill it himself, subsequently being acclaimed as a
champion himself.[28] It is extremely difficult to reconcile this story with the
scenes shown on the capital, and it is much more likely that the intention

---

28   Ettlinger (1975–76), passim.

was to depict the struggle between good and evil in a picturesque way.

VOUSSOIRS

The forms of the voussoirs and their distribution have already been sketched out in chapter seven. Here we shall concentrate on the motifs with which they are decorated: beakheads, foliage, bosses and chevron.

BEAKHEADS

Beakhead ornament is a method of decorating arches with carved heads of birds, beasts or human beings, but the term is not used for every arch decorated with heads, and it will be as well to understand precisely how it is used. Clapham defined the beakhead as 'an ornament taking the form of the head of a bird, beast or monster, the beak or jaw of which appears to grip the moulding across which it is carved'.[29] This adequately describes the bird beakheads at Reading, but not those at Mesland (Loire-et-Cher) where fantastic human heads are carved with their beards lying across the angle-roll, or those on the west doorways at Lincoln where

129   BEAKHEAD IS USED IN THE DECORATION OF THE CHANCEL ARCH OF THE CHURCH OF ST MARK AND ST LUKE, AVINGTON (BERKSHIRE). THE EAST FACE HAS BIRDS AND THE WEST FACE BEASTS.

the angle-roll is overlapped by the elaborately decorated tongues of monstrous heads (plate XLV). A more useful general definition of the beakhead might be 'an ornament taking the form of the head of a bird, beast, human or monster, some part of which, usually the beak or jaw, is carved to overlap the moulding across which it is carved'.

Each of the Reading beakhead voussoirs is carved with a single beakhead, and two basic designs are used. In the first, a bird's head is carved with its beak gripping an angle roll (figure 104). This design gained enormous popularity throughout the country, both at major sites like Old Sarum, and in parish churches like SS Mark and Luke at Avington, a well-preserved twelfth-century church only some 20 miles from Reading, where its appearance on the chancel arch and vault ribs suggests copying of the abbey sculpture by local craftsmen (figure 129).

There is a good deal of variation in the second type of beakhead, which I have called beast-head and described in chapter seven (see figures 105 and 106). A simplified form of this decoration, taking the form of

---

[29]   Clapham (1934), 130.

130   THE SHUTTLECOCK FORM OF BEAST-HEAD ORNAMENT
APPEARS ON THE NORTH DOORWAY OF GREAT DURNFORD
(WILTSHIRE).

shuttlecock-like motifs and clearly copied from Reading, appears on the inner order of the doorway at Great Durnford, Wilts (figure 130).[30]

Although it is possible that the beakhead ornament has its roots in France, the evidence of surviving examples is that it was much more popular in England than anywhere else.[31] A motif similar in form to the beast-head ornament is found at an early date at Tavant (Indre et Loire) in southern Normandy. A doorway there has an order of voussoirs carved with a design of fir-cones within fluted leaves, similar to Great Durnford and to many of the Reading beast-heads, particularly voussoirs 1992.29 and 1992.37 (figures 105, 131, 132). The bird-head variant, however, is a predominantly English class of decoration, and although French examples exist they are far less common and generally later in date. Zarnecki has suggested that it was an adaptation of Anglo-Saxon biting birds from manuscript illumination to the decoration of an arch,[32] and it is true that there are conceptual similarities between the birds gripping initials in their beaks in a group of late tenth-century Canterbury manuscripts and the Reading bird-head voussoirs.[33] The difficulties with this kind of explanation are in accounting for the transmission of a late tenth-century manuscript motif into stone carving more

[30]   Zarnecki and Henry (1958), 22.
[31]   The standard works on beakhead are still Salmon (1946) and especially Zarnecki and Henry (1958). The latter authors list some 130 examples of beakhead arches in England compared with 23 in France (all north of the Loire) and very few elsewhere. For a more recent but simpler treatment, see Baxter (2004).
[32]   Zarnecki and Henry (1958), 25.
[33]   Zarnecki notes the Aldhelm, *De Laude Virginitatis* (Lambeth Palace 200, f. 70r), and Temple (1976), 55–63 describes another twenty or so manuscripts with this type of decoration.

than a century later, and without anything in the way of convincing intermediaries, but an ingenious way of tackling the problem has recently been suggested by Roger Stalley.[34] His material is Irish, at the churches of Dysert O'Dea, Clonfert and Clonmacnoise, and his parallels are with metalwork rather than manuscripts, but the visual connections are close and there are enough parallels with English material to suggest that a similar mechanism might have been at work here. Far more Irish than English medieval metalwork has survived, of course, so that a similar case could not be argued for England, but the possibility exists and should not be ignored.

Of course there is no pressing need to opt for a single explanation, and a different line of enquiry for beakheads in general might be by way of the treatment of arches rather than the tracking of motifs. The crucial monument here may be the keep of Norwich Castle, started by William II, but probably substantially built for Henry I in the first two decades of the twelfth century.[35] The main doorway was originally of three orders,[36] the innermost being

131   THE WEST DOORWAY OF SAINT-NICOLAS DE TAVANT (INDRE ET LOIRE) SHOWS AN EARLY FORM OF THE BEAST-HEAD ORNAMENT. THIS DOORWAY ALSO HAS BOSSED ORNAMENT SIMILAR TO THAT AT READING.

decorated with a simplified proto-beakhead design, ingeniously christened 'beaker moulding' or 'beaker clasp' by Heslop, both in the archivolt and on the jambs.[37] In the archivolt this consists of a series of relief panels carved

---

[34]   Stalley (2012), 111–27.

[35]   Heslop (1994), 8.

[36]   A plain continuous order was later inserted inside the original inner order to reduce the size of the doorway. Only the right-hand jamb survives in anything like its original state: the left jamb has been rebuilt in brick.

[37]   Heslop (1994), 34, 70.

132   THE CHARACTERISTIC PINE CONE MOTIF
OCCURS ON THIS BEAST-HEAD VOUSSOIR
READING.

with figural, foliage and interlace motifs, which are linked to the angle roll on the inner edge of the order by a series of tapered and chamfered stone bridges, like drinking beakers (figure 133). These beaker clasps continue down the jambs of this order, where the relief panels are replaced by a design of concentric semicircular cusps.[38] There are both direct and indirect links with the Reading cloister sculpture. Each of the beakhead voussoirs at Reading is carved with cusping on the outer edge of its front face, producing a cusped border to the archivolt similar in appearance to the Norwich Castle jambs. Even closer parallels with the Norwich doorway, however, are found in two churches which are clearly dependent on Reading for their sculptural decoration. The south doorway of Avington church (figure 134), has a simple form of the beaker moulding, without chamfers or cusping, carved on the jambs,[39] and in the south doorway of Quenington church (Gloucs), beaker-clasps decorated with beading alternate with bird beakheads in the arch (plate XLVI). Both of these examples are versions of motifs copied from Reading Abbey by local sculptors.

The beaker moulding was widely used at Norwich Castle for decorating window arches and blind arcading on all four main facades. The motif produces alternations of light and shadow across the arches which are effective in conveying a feeling of richness and solidity, and which echo similar effects produced by the corbel tables and battlements. In this view of the development of beakhead ornament, the figural carving of the beakheads is an embellishment of a motif whose original purpose was to provide texture through the alternation of light and shadow, in much the same way as the chevron ornament with which it is often combined.

Reading is usually credited with the earliest appearance of bird beakheads in England, although its primacy over Roger of Salisbury's Old

[38]   Each voussoir of the archivolt contains one relief panel, one stone bridge and a section of angle roll. On the jamb, however, the bridges do not line up with the cusping in any regular way.

[39]   Pevsner (1960), 75 describes the decoration as beakhead 'planned, but not carried out.'

133   THE PLAIN BEAKER CLASP MOTIF CONSISTS OF TAPERED POLYGONAL BRIDGES
RESTING ON THE INNER ANGLE ROLL OF THE 2ND ORDER OF THE KEEP DOORWAY OF
NORWICH CASTLE.

Sarum is difficult to establish with any certainty.[40] In practice it is perhaps
not important: both sites are closely associated with Henry I and his immediate circle.

FOLIAGE VOUSSOIRS

Each of these arch voussoirs except the keystones carries only half a design, and is cut away deeply into the plane of the arch at one side only
(see figure 109). The foliage carving contains similar elements to those
seen on the block capitals: reeded stems with spiral or furled leaf terminals and the five-lobed Byzantine blossom. It sometimes issues from the
masks of lions, or composite human heads, or is inhabited by biting birds
or diminutive human figures. When the arch was assembled it presented
a series of bulbous projections, like large balls with figural and foliage designs on the surface. In fact the geometry of the voussoirs tells us that each
of these arches was made up of only five voussoirs resting on the springers,
giving the appearance of just five 'balls' per arch – one for each springer,

[40]   Stalley (1971), 77–78; King (1996); London (1984), 174.

134   BEAKER CLASPS ARE FOUND ON THE EAST JAMB OF THE
SOUTH DOORWAY OF AVINGTON CHURCH, BERKSHIRE.

one for the keystone, and one each for the pairs of voussoirs on either side of it.[41] It is possible that the half-voussoirs of each bulbous projection were mirrors of each other but, if that is so, no mirror-pairs have survived. There is some evidence to support this idea, however. First, the keystones are clearly symmetrical (although the symmetry is only approximate) – see the foliage voussoir 1992.46 and the similar example set at the apex of the Forbury arch, and especially voussoir 1992.30, with symmetrical foliage scrolls issuing from a pair of lion masks side-by-side (figures 135 and 136). Next, the fragmentary voussoir 1992.18 (figure 137) is carved with the left half of a lion mask, with a single stem of reeded foliage issuing from it and terminating in a furled leaf with a fluted surface and scalloped edge. The adjacent voussoir must surely have mirrored it, completing the lion mask design.

I know of no other Romanesque examples of arch designs carried on pairs of projecting voussoirs, and in fact even arches with single voussoirs which project in this way are uncommon. Zarnecki has described the south doorway of Dalmeny church (West Lothian) as 'perhaps a distant echo of them, although made of single stones,'[42] and the comparison is a striking one. At Dalmeny, however, dating from the 1140s, projecting corbel-like voussoirs carved with heads alternate in the arch with flat voussoirs bearing a variety of animal and interlace designs (plate XLVII). The designs are quite different, but the overall effect shows that the designers had something similar in mind.

[41]   Arches of only five voussoirs are by no means unusual. They are found in the cloisters of Senanque (Vaucluse), Aix-en-Provence (Bouches-du-Rhône), Ganagobie (Alpes-de-Haute-Provence) and elsewhere.
[42]   Zarnecki in London (1984), 171.

BOSSED VOUSSOIRS

Five of the Reading voussoirs are decorated with pairs of bosses, roughly hemispherical in form, projecting from the chamfered face of the arch (see figure 110). The bosses are carved with a variety of decorative motifs: spiral grooves, concentric scalloped rings or daisy-like or star-shaped flowers with fluted petals. This kind of decoration is relatively common, but it is interesting to find it at sites which have independent links with Reading, like Avington and Quenington. The work of the Reading sculptors was copied at these sites, but Reading-type bosses also appear at Norwich Castle,[43] in conjunction with the beaker ornament, and at Tavant,[44] alongside the proto beast-head vegetal ornament described above (see figure 131). In these two cases the bosses add weight to the argument that these sites were part of the workshop background of the Reading sculptors.

135   THE KEYSTONE OF A FOLIAGE ARCH FROM READING ABBEY CLOISTER.

CHEVRON VOUSSOIRS

Chevron was probably the commonest form of ornament employed by twelfth-century sculptors. It has been noted in chapter seven that only one chevron voussoir comparable in size with the other cloister voussoirs has found its way into the museum, and its provenance is unknown so that it would not be possible to relate it to the sculpture we know to be from the cloister were it not that its distinctive design (four rows of beaded lateral chevron with hollows between) is identical to that on the corner springer, 1992.99 (figures 111, 93).

SPRINGERS

Keyser discovered 14 double springers at Shiplake House, and more were unearthed in the Borough Marsh excavation, including the two corner springers. Another double springer came to the museum in 1982 from

---

43   At Norwich, the bosses decorate the label of the keep doorway. Any decoration they had is now completely worn away.

44   The doorway at Tavant is carved on its label with bosses bearing geometrical designs, as at Reading.

136   THIS CLOISTER KEYSTONE IS CARVED WITH A
SYMMETRICAL DESIGN OF FOLIAGE AND LION MASKS.

David Verey, the Gloucestershire historian (now accessioned as 1992.75, see figure 96). In addition a fragmentary double springer (1992.67) has no known provenance and might easily have been mistaken for a voussoir in the past. This brings the total to 28. The structure of the springers and their relationship with the four types of arch ornament have been discussed in chapter seven, but it remains here to point out that apart from the beakhead ornament, which is most common of all, the springers are carved with chevron, foliage, dragons, birds and large rosettes of interlace. Of the double springers the most striking is 1992.81 (figure 138). It comes from an arch made up of the foliage-ornamented half-voussoirs described above, as is clear from the extent to which the design is cut back into the plane of the arch. It is carved with a symmetrical composition of two large confronted birds, their wings spread and their long necks turned back to preen their own flight feathers. They have small heads, long beaks and heavy fanned tails that droop downwards, and a good deal of trouble has been taken to represent the textures of different types of plumage. The heavy corner springer, 1992.99, is carved with different designs on two of its faces, and the implications of this for the architecture of the cloister have been discussed in the previous chapter (figures 93, 112). The right face of the springer is badly worn. It certainly contains a foliage design in the form of a Y-shaped Romanesque tree, and under each of the two branches is a figure. They might possibly represent a hunter, on the left, shooting at a deer with a bow, but the state of wear is so advanced as to make this highly speculative. The left face is in a much better state, and shows a bird standing in right profile among tangled foliage with its head bent down to grip its own throat in its hawk-like beak (figure 139). It has an oval eye, and plumage indicated by a pattern of tiny gouges, except on the wing and tail, which have parallel grooves. Both clawed feet are shown, one resting on a small boss, the other on a stem of the foliage.[45] As in the case of the symmetrical dragon capital, there is a very close parallel for this motif among Henry's possessions near Domfront, again on a capital at Goult priory church near Domfront (plate XLVIII). Zarnecki describes the Reading bird's action as 'preening its breast', but raises, and rejects, the possibility that it might represent the pelican, a type of Christ's crucifixion in the *Physiologus* and later Bestiaries, which pierces its own breast to revive the chicks it has killed in a fit of rage three days previously.[46]

NOOK SHAFT

There is no known provenance for the colonnette 1992.79 (figure 140 a to d). It was already in Reading Museum in 1916, before Charles Keyser's discoveries were made.[47] It is cylindrical, and carved in deep relief around approximately one half of its diameter, indicating its original function as a nook-shaft. Its subject matter and carving style also connect it with the cloister sculpture. It is carved with two vertical rows of medallions enclosed by beaded straps, each row consisting of a central medallion with a half-medallion above and below,

137   THE MIRROR SYMMETRY OF THE PAIRED VOUSSOIRS MAKING UP THE FOLIAGE ARCHES OF THE CLOISTER IS IMPLIED BY THIS VOUSSOIR CARVED WITH HALF OF A LION MASK.

which would have been completed on the next section of shaft. Each medallion is linked to its neighbours above, below or alongside by a short, double-beaded strap. The triangular fields between the medallions and the edges of the uncarved area, and the diamond-shaped fields between medallions are occupied by star-shaped flowers, lengths of stem with paired, spiralling leaves, or three-petalled Byzantine blossom.

Each medallion encloses a beast in undercut relief, although only the two complete medallions display a complete beast. These are a pair of confronted griffins (188b, 188d) while the half-medallions contain an unidentified quadruped, perhaps a crocodile (188b, top), an owl (188b, bottom), a two-headed creature that might be an amphisbaena (188d, bottom) and what could be Samson and the lion (188d, top). This last

---

[45]   London (1984), 170.

[46]   Ibid. For the pelican, see Baxter (1998), 40.

[47]   Keyser (1916), 242, fig. 18.

138   THIS DOUBLE SPRINGER WITH CONFRONTED BIRDS CONTAINS THE REMAINS OF A
BOSS, SUGGESTING THAT IT ORIGINALLY SUPPORTED ONE OF THE ARCHES AT THE EAST
END OF THE SOUTH RANGE.

composition is badly worn, but a man's legs and a lion's may be clearly
distinguished; the mane is clearly shown, and what can be seen of the
lion's head is turned back. Contemporary colonnettes carved with a
similar degree of detail and shafts with beasts in medallions are found
on the Prior's doorway at Ely Cathedral, but no good comparison can be
made with this one. A much closer parallel is with one of the Hyde Abbey
(Winchester) capitals showing a similar griffin in a beaded medallion
(plate XLIX).[48]

[48]   London (1984), 172 (128a face 1).

FOLIAGE STYLES

Much of the foliage decoration of
the cloister is descended from the
so-called Winchester acanthus, a
persistent and widespread form
of stylised foliage decoration that
actually has very little to do with
acanthus, either the botanical variety or the classical foliage form
found on Corinthian capitals.[49]
Zarnecki has traced the Winchester acanthus from manuscripts
of around the year 1000, like the
Arenberg Gospels (New York,
Pierpont Morgan Lib. 869), to
capitals both in England, at Bibury
(Gloucestershire), Steyning (Sussex) and Canterbury Cathedral,
and at various continental locations (Fécamp, Saint-Bertin, and
Maastricht).[50] The problem with
this kind of analysis is that while
it serves to emphasise the ubiq-
uity of a motif in time and space,
its comprehensive approach practically rules out any possibility
of identifying craftsmen, workshops, or believable mechanisms
of transmission. What we can
do, however, is to look for closer
parallels nearer to hand, and the

139   A DETAIL OF THE CORNER SPRINGER SHOWN IN FIGURES
93 AND 112 SHOWS THE BIRD BITING ITS OWN BREAST.

most striking are to be found in the capitals from Westminster Hall, Norwich Cathedral and Hyde Abbey, Winchester, sites already associated with
Reading's cloister architecture in chapter seven. At Reading, Norwich and
Hyde Abbey, the typical hooked and furled leaf terminals are augmented
by the so-called Byzantine blossom; a widespread form of decoration that
appeared and grew more elaborate during the first quarter of the twelfth
century in English artistic production in all media. Whether the Byzantine blossom has any connection with Byzantium is a matter for dispute.
In discussing the motif in English manuscripts, Kauffmann presented it

---

[49]   West (1993), passim.
[50]   Zarnecki (1955), 1–4. Jeffrey West adds to this list the tiny fragment of an impost
       from Peterborough (London (1984a), 130–31).

ABOVE AND OPPOSITE: 140 A TO D. THE NOOK-SHAFT CARVED WITH BEASTS IN MEDALLIONS IN READING MUSEUM.

as an English development, culminating in the luxuriant forms painted in the Bury Bible, but avoided any mention of Byzantium (although he did find other Byzantine features in that manuscript).[51] In stone sculpture it appeared in various parts of the country during the same period.[52]

[51]   Kauffmann (1975), 26, 89. He describes them as 'large luxuriant plant formations that extend in all directions like the tentacles of a fleshy octopus'.
[52]   Early examples are known at Winchester, Ely, Norwich, Northampton and Durham; see Franklin (1983), 58.

THE ARTISTIC BACKGROUND OF THE READING COURT STYLE

It is unusual to write of a court style at this early date, but it must be clear from what has gone before that the sculptural parallels to be made with the Reading cloister workshop are all associated with the patronage of Henry I. Before he became king in 1100 he was already the patron of works in his domains around Domfront in southern Normandy, where a workshop of sculptors was carving high-quality work in Caen stone that was quite different from that found elsewhere in Normandy, but which bears a remarkable similarity to later Reading work (figures 127, 131, plate XLVIII). As Henry's patronage in England began to take shape, elements from the Normandy workshop in the form of men or their designs were brought over to augment what was already here: the traditional use of Caen stone,

141   ONE OF THE NORWICH CASTLE KEEP DOORWAY CAPITALS SHOWS A HUNTER WITH
TWO BEASTS ATTACKING ONE ANOTHER.

and the Winchester acanthus forms and trefoil capitals of Westminster
Abbey. The similarities between the cloister designs of Reading and Westminster have already been noted, along with the Windsor Castle work
of 1107–10, and the royal works at Norwich Castle must also be added
to this network of connections. The beaker clasp moulding connects this
sculpture to the development of the beakhead ornament, seen in its early
stages at Tavant with which the Reading beast-head form of the motif is
connected, but a more direct connection with Henry I's work in southern
Normandy appears on a capital on the Norwich keep doorway showing a
hunting scene, a man spearing a lion that attacks an ungulate – also from
the Goult repertoire and much better preserved at Goult than at Norwich
(figure 141 and plate L).

ICONOGRAPHIC THEMES

To a sensitive medieval Christian the cloister sculpture of Reading Abbey
was a terrifying sight, made more vivid by the colouring applied to the
sculpture. Most obviously the beakhead that decorated more than a quarter of the arches presented an alternation of predatory biting birds and
grotesque beasts. The message of the foliate and figural arches and many
of the capitals was a more subtle one. First, a large proportion of the arcade

was covered in tangled foliage, either issuing from the mouths of lions or inhabited by them; we are reminded of the warning found on the Stafford font to beware of the lions.[53] Dragons and more predatory birds also live in this perilous forest, and at critical points little human figures are trapped within the coils of foliage (figure 142). Tangled foliage was widely used in the twelfth century as a metaphor for hell, or for the snares and temptations of the world. This is most obviously the case for the Herefordshire School of sculpture, where the hell from which Christ pulls Adam on the Eardisley font is shown, not as flames but as foliage (figure 143).[54] In the Herefordshire School carvings the treacherous foliage is sometimes relieved by indications of a possibility of salvation, as exemplified by the tympanum at Billesley (Warwickshire) where a warrior pursued by a serpent and a dragon through tangled foliage makes his way towards a dove.[55] In this case, the semiotic weight of the

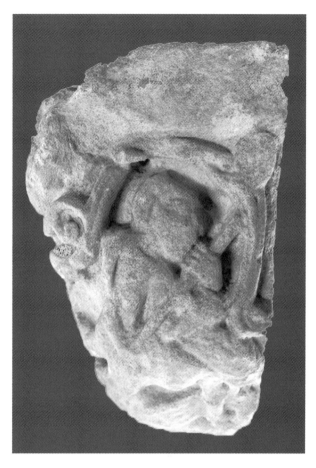

142   A TINY HUMAN SOUL IS ENTANGLED IN FOLIAGE ON THIS VOUSSOIR FROM READING CLOISTER.

image is reinforced by the positioning of the two creatures on the positive (dove) and negative (dragon) sides of the tympanum.[56] At Reading the few unambiguously positive subjects – the nimbed saints on capital 1992.118 (figure 166) and the Virgin scenes on 1992.95 (figure 168) – might perform the same functions.

[53]   While single lions may represent Christ, lions in quantity are invariably dangerous.
[54]   Zarnecki and Baxter, 'St Mary Magdalene, Eardisley, Hereforshire, Berkshire'. CRSBI.
[55]   London (1984), 177; Morris (1983).
[56]   The dove on the left, which would be Christ's right hand in a Last Judgement and the side where paradise is shown; and the dragon on the right, corresponding to Christ's left hand and hell.

143   ON THE FONT AT ST MARY MAGDALENE, EARDISLEY (HEREFORDSHIRE), CHRIST PULLS ADAM FROM A
HELL REPRESENTED AS A TANGLE OF FOLIAGE.

THE CLOISTER, ST BERNARD AND THE *REPREHENSIO*

Almost every treatment of cloister iconography takes as its starting point
Bernard of Clairvaux's well-known diatribe from his *Apologia ad Guillelmum* about monstrous and secular imagery in a cloister,[57] and in most cases he is psychoanalysed far beyond the words he actually wrote. We should
remind ourselves, therefore, that the specific subjects he singled out for
complaint were apes, lions, centaurs, composite human/animal creatures,
tigers, soldiers and hunting scenes. He was especially critical of composite
forms, combining parts of different animals, and of creatures with either
extra heads or extra bodies.[58] With this in mind we can be sure that the
cloister of Reading Abbey was not a place where Bernard would have felt
at home, and as it was the major Cluniac foundation of its date in England
this is hardly surprising. In fact, a polemic written in opposition to the

[57]   Bernard of Clairvaux, 3, 106.
[58]   Rudolph (1988) provides a reasonable analysis of the text.

Abbot of Clairvaux's *Apologia* was circulating in England very soon after Bernard's production of his revised text in 1125–26.[59] The text is known in only one late twelfth-century copy that belonged to the Augustinians of St Mary Overy, Southwark, and is generally called the *Reprehensio,* from the first word of the title given in the index at the beginning of the mixed volume in which it is bound.[60] The *Reprehensio* is a systematic response to Bernard's denunciation of traditional monasticism, and especially the Cluniac observance, but although it is 12,000 words long, it is an incomplete copy, addressing less than half of Bernard's points and ending in the middle of a sentence. That might not matter so much to us were it not that what survives deals only with matters of diet and dress; the sections that doubtless answered the Abbot of Clairvaux's criticisms of the church and the liturgy are wanting.

A further problem is that there is no indication of the author beyond what can be deduced from the contents themselves. Dom Wilmart, who published the text, was confident that the likeliest author was Hugh of Amiens, writing as Abbot of Reading, and that the work must date from no earlier than 1127–28.[61] This opinion was enthusiastically supported by C. H. Talbot,[62] although both scholars were at pains to point out that, in the present state of our knowledge, it was impossible to be absolutely certain. From internal evidence it is clear that the author was a Cluniac who was in England at the relevant time; that he was in a position of authority in a monastery, and most probably an abbot; that his background lay in France, because he displayed a detailed knowledge of the monks of Savigny, Tiron and the Cistercian order that would be impossible for one brought up in England; and finally that he was a man of great authority and learning who was not awed by the Abbot of Clairvaux but who treated his writings with 'the amused condescension of a master dealing with a wayward pupil'.[63] Without disputing any of these conclusions, the most recent writer on Hugh of Amiens, Ryan P. Freeburn, doubts Hugh's authorship of the *Reprehensio* on literary grounds. Hugh produced a good deal of written work that can be used for comparative purposes, and in general the *Reprehensio* matches neither his writing style, nor his use of Latin, nor even, in some cases, his known views on moral issues.[64]

Freeburn does not entirely rule Hugh out, however, and is at a loss to find an alternative candidate. He excludes the two most prominent

---

[59] Oxford, Bodleian Library MS Ashmole 1285, fols 198–238, published in Wilmart (1934), 309–44. An early draft was sent to William of Saint Thierry for comment, and the final text was toned down somewhat; see Talbot (1956), 77.

[60] *Reprehensio libelli abbatis Clare Vallis quem ipse edidit generalliter contra monacos.*

[61] Wilmart (1934), 306–09.

[62] Talbot (1956), passim.

[63] Ibid., 77.

[64] Freeburn (2011), 96–98, 239–44.

Cluniacs of the period, Henry of Blois, then Abbot of Glastonbury, and Henry of Poitou, Abbot of Peterborough, but offers Anscher, Prior of Lewes (1126–30) and Hugh of Amiens' successor as Abbot of Reading (1130–35) as a new possibility.[65] It seems very likely, therefore, that the *Reprehensio* was produced at Reading, and while the fragment that remains to us wants the crucial section on cloister iconography, it is clear enough that someone in authority there was concerned to position himself and his monastery in opposition to Bernard of Clairvaux. The arguments that could have been adduced are well known. The monstrous and demonic imagery was to be read as a metaphor for the traps of the devil with which the world was filled. This was imagery aimed specifically at monks – at Reading, men who had led a full and active life before entering the monastery in their maturity, and needed reminders of what the world was really like lest they should lapse into wistful reminiscence of illusory pleasures.[66]

Reading Abbey was the biggest of big commissions: the king's own abbey and mausoleum. Workshops of sculptors that the king had used before – in his Norman possessions and in the royal projects at Westminster, Windsor and Norwich – were brought in to produce a spectacular building on a scale to rival almost anything in the country. At Reading Henry would have two hundred monks to pray for his soul using the elaborate liturgy of Cluny, and above all with a cloister inhabited by a wealth of grotesque and monstrous imaginings that could almost be read as a manifesto of the opposition to Bernard of Clairvaux's Cistercian aesthetic of austerity.

[65] Ibid., 241–44.
[66] The Reading foundation charter specifically excludes child oblation.

AFTERWORD

King Henry I's decision to build a monastery at Reading that would eventually house his body and provide a locus for the eternal salvation he hoped to achieve was governed by the views he held about the kind of worship God required. At the beginning of the twelfth century, when work began, there were two conflicting views about this. The Cistercians held that God was best served by an apostolic model of austerity and simplicity, in plain buildings and with simple liturgies, said not sung. In contrast, for the Cluniacs and their Benedictine sympathisers, God deserved no less than the best that man could offer: the most elaborate liturgy administered using the richest vessels of gold and precious stones and sung in settings of surpassing beauty, inside the finest churches adorned with sculpture, painting and rich furnishings. God should be treated like the king he was, and it is unsurprising that this model should be attractive to a king like Henry.

This theology is manifest in all we know about Henry's abbey; from the Foundation Charter to the establishment of the abbey with monks from the Cluniac mother house, to the details of its architecture and sculpture that we have been at such pains to uncover. The collection of high-class relics, begun by Henry and his daughter the Empress Matilda, was responsible for a church plan designed with pilgrims in mind, and Henry's own body, interred before the High Altar, acted almost like a relic itself, attracting other royal and aristocratic burials throughout the Middle Ages. The Abbey Church, one of the largest in the country, was architecturally daring with its giant order elevation and lavishly decorated with carvings and paint; while the cloister, the part of the building complex we know most about, was practically a manifesto, carved by the court workshop, of Cluniac monstrosity.

Henry's vision of what a monastery should be resonated throughout the medieval period: what he had envisaged as the court of the King of Heaven continued to be a place of royal resort until the Reformation and even beyond it. King Henry himself might not still be there; the evidence is by no means clear. This author for one fervently hopes that his bones have not been disturbed, and never will be: we might not agree with his theology, but we cannot doubt his sincerity or deny his wishes the respect they deserved.

APPENDIX A
READING ABBEY RELIC LISTS

1 THE RELIC LIST IN BL EGERTON 3031

Rubrics, in red in the manuscript, are shown in **bold** here. Implied words, uncertain readings and words not recognised by the editor are [bracketed thus]. Additions by a later scribe are in *italics*.

	He sunt reliquie que continentur in ecclesia sancte Marie de Radingia	These are the relics held in the church of St Mary of Reading
	De ligno domini	**Of the Tree of the Lord**
1	Crux quedam que de Constantinop' allata et deaurata in vi capitibus; auro quod oblatum fuit ihu xpo.	A cross that came from Constantinople, gilt in six main parts with gold that was offered to Christ
2	Item crux quae de latin urbem allata est undique gemmate.	Also a cross that came from Rome, jewelled all over
3	Item de ligno crucis cum tribus granis thurifero quod oblatum fuisse puero Ihesu creditur cum abi de eodem thure.	Also wood from the cross with three grains of incense, which is believed to come from the incense offered to the child Jesus
4	Item de ligno domini in magna cruce	Also wood from the cross in a great cross
5	Item de ligno domini crux que fuit de capella ducis saxonie.	Also a cross from the chapel of the Duke of Saxony, with wood from the cross

6	Item de ligno domini in vi locis & de loco ubi crux fixa stetit.	Also wood from the cross in six places, and [earth] from the place where the cross was fixed
7	Preputium domini vel illud quod ab umbilico pueri Iesu precisum est creditur esse cum cruce de ligno domini in textu quem imperator Constantinopolitanus misit Henrico regi Anglorum primo.	The foreskin of the Lord, or part of the umbilical cord, with wood from the cross that the Emperor of Constantinople sent to King Henry I
8	De caliga domini.	[Relic] of the Lord's sandal
9	De petra et de terra Bethleem ubi Christe natus est.	Stone and earth from Bethlehem where Christ was born
10	De presepio domini in quattuor locis.	From the stable of the Lord, in four places
11	De cunabulo Criste in duobus locis.	From the cradle of the Lord, in two places
12	De aquae in qua dominus apud Bethleem balneatus est ac deinde ipsa aqua conversa est in manna usque in hodiernum diem.	Water in which the Lord was bathed in Bethlehem, and now that water is turned into manna.[1]
13	Lapides de c(i) pra et de loco desertu ubi dominus jejunavit.	Stones from the wilderness where the Lord fasted
14	De petra ubi christus supersedit.	Stone where Christ sat
15	De petra ubi oravit ad patrem in duobus locis.	Stone from the place where he prayed to the father, in two places
16	De stipite ubi dominus ligatus fuit et verberat.	Some of the column where the Lord was tied and beaten
17	De loco ubi factus est sudae domini sicut guttae sanguinis.	From the place where the sweat of the Lord fell as drops of blood
18	De pane cene	Bread from the Last Supper
19	De quinque panibus.	Bread from the five loaves

---

[1] Any miraculous fluid or dust associated with relics.

20	Lapis de monte calvarie super quem cecidit sanguis de latere dominum.	Stone from Mount Calvary where fell blood from the Lord's side
21	Item sanguis et aquae de latere domini et de terra ubi ablutus sunt.	Also blood and water from the Lord's side and earth where they dripped
22	De panno que facies domini operta fuit in passione.	Some of the cloth with which the Lord's face was wiped in the Passion
23	De monte et loco calvarie in quinque locis.	From the mountain and Calvary in five places
24	De sepulcro domini in decem locis.	Fragments from the sepulchre of the Lord in ten places
25	De sindone munda.	From Christ's shroud
26	De oleo quod angelus illuminavit in pascha.	Oil that the angel burns at Easter.[2]
27	De petra de qua ascendit dominus.	Stone from the place where Christ ascended
28	Cristallus cum balsamo.	Crystal with balsam.[3]
	Reliquie de domina nostra Sancta Maria	**Relics of Our Lady St Mary**
29	Capillus sancte Marie ut putantur	A hair of St Mary, reputedly
30	De terra ubi nata fuit beata virgo maria	Earth from the place where the Blessed Virgin Mary was born
31	De vestimentu eius in quattuor locis	From her clothes in four places
32	De lecto eius in duobus locis	From her bed, in two places
33	De zona eius.	From her girdle
34	De sepulcro eius in viii locis	From her tomb, in eight places
	De patriarchis & prophetas	**Of the patriarchs and prophets**
35	Reliquie sanctorum patriarcharum Abraham, Ysaac & Iacob	Relics of the holy patriarch Abraham, Isaac and Jacob

[2] For an account of the Holy Fire; the spontaneous burning of oil in the lamps hanging over Christ's tomb on Holy Saturday in the church of the Holy Sepulchre in Jerusalem, see Meinardus (1961), *passim*

[3] Presumably the balsam prepared by the holy women to anoint Christ's body (Luke 23, 56).

36	De ylice in Mambre	From the oak tree of Mambre[4]
37	De loco ubi iacob dormiendo vidit angelos ascendente et descendente	From the place where Jacob saw angels ascending and descending in a dream.[5]
38	De virga Moysi	From the staff of Moses
39	De virga Aaron	From the staff of Aaron
40	De silice quem percussit Moyses	From the rock that Moses struck[6]
41	De ruto quem vidit Moyses	From the bush that Moses saw[7]
42	Manna de monte Synay	Manna from Mount Sinai[8]
43	De sancto Johanne Baptista in tribus locis	Relics of St John the Baptist in three places
44	Item de sepulchro eius	Also from his sepulchre
45	De sancto zacharia propheta	Relic of the holy prophet Zechariah
46	Reliqe Helysei et Danieli prophetarum	Relics of the prophets Elijah and Daniel
47	De sancta Anna matre sancte Marie	Relic of St Anne, mother of St Mary
48	Item de sepulcro eius	Also from her sepulchre
49	De sancto Lazaro	Relic of St Lazarus
50	De sepulcro eius in quinquibus locis	From his sepulchre in five places
51	Reliquie de sancta Martha	Relics of St Martha
52	Tres dentes sancti Symeonis	Three teeth of St Simeon
53	Item de ossibus eius	Also of his bones
	De Apostolis	**Of the apostles**
54	Reliquie sancti Petri apostoli et de cruce eius	Relics of St Peter the apostle and his cross
55	Manna de sepulcro sancti Johannis evangeliste	Manna from the sepulchre of St John the Evangelist

4 See Gen. 18,1; Gen. 23, 17–20.
5 Gen. 28, 11–12.
6 Exod. 17, 6.
7 Exod. 3, 2.
8 Exod. 16, 12–15.

56	Manus sancti Iacobi cum carne et ossibus	The hand of St James with flesh and bones
57	Pannus in quo involuta fuit manus sancti Iacobi	A cloth in which the hand of St James was wrapped
58	Item de panno in quo voluta fuit manus sancti Iacobi	Also some cloth in which the hand of St James was wrapped
59	De costa sancti Andree apostoli	From a rib of St Andrew the apostle
60	Item de eodem in duobus loci et de cruce eius	Also relics of him in two places, and of his cross
61	De sancto Philippo apostolo unum os *et caput eius*	From St Philip the apostle, a bone *and his head*
62	De sancto Iacobo iusto in duobus locis.	[Relic] of St James the Just, in two places[9]
63	De sancto Mathio apostolo et evangelista in duobus locis	[Relic] of St Matthew the apostle and evangelist in two places
64	De pallio sancti Thome apostoli	From the pallium of St Thomas the apostle
65	Dens sancti Luce evangeliste, sed nescitur ubi sit *nisi fuerit Leominstre*	Tooth of St Luke the Evangelist but its location is not known *unless it is in Leominster*
	Iohannis rex Anglie dedit nobis caput Philippi apostoli venerandum. Et nobis nundinas ipso die concedit habere	*King John of England gave us the venerated head of Philip the apostle, and granted us a fair on the same day*

	De Martiribus	**Of the martyrs**
66	De sancto Stephano prothomartyre in quinque locis	[Relic] of St Stephen protomartyr in five places
67	Costa cuiusdam Innocentis	The rib of one of the Innocents
68	Item de Innocentibus in tribus locis	Also [relics] from the Innocents in three places
69	De corpore at sanguine sancti Laurentii cum carbonibus	From the body and blood of St Lawrence with coals

9   St James the Just, 1st Bishop of Jerusalem, is usually identified with James the Less and James the brother of the Lord.

70	Item de sancto Laurentio in duobus loci	Also [relic] of St Lawrence in two places
71	De sancto Vincentio levita in duobus locus	[Relic] of St Vincent the deacon in two places
72	Brachium sancti Pancratii martyris	The arm of St Pancras the martyr
73	Item de ossibus eius in duobus locis	Also [relic] of his bones in two places
74	Brachium sancti Quintini martyris cum iunctura digiti eiusdem	The arm of St Quentin the martyr with joints of his fingers
75	De brachio sancti Georgii martyris et de ossibus eius in duobus locis	From the arm of St George the martyr and his bones in two places
76	Oleum de archa unguenti Cosme et Damiani	Oil from the medicine chest of SS Cosmas and Damian
77	Item de sancto Cosma	Also [relic] of St Cosmas
78	De sancto Fabiano et Sebastiano	[Relic] of SS Fabian and Sebastian
79	Item de sancto Fabiano	Also [relic] of St Fabian
80	De sancto Marco et Marcelliano	[Relic] of SS Marcus and Marcellinus
81	De ossibus Crispini et Crispiniam	Bones of Crispin and Crispinian
82	De ossibus sanctorum Nerei et Achillei	Bones of SS Nereus and Achilleus
83	De reliquiis sanctorum Gervasii et Prothasii	Relics of SS Gervasius and Protasius
84	De vestibus sancti Mauricii et de ossibus eius in duobus locis	From the clothes of St Maurice and his bones in two places
85	De ossibus Sergii et Bachi	Bones of SS Sergius and Bacchus
86	De reliquis sancti luciam sociorumque eius	Relics of St Lucian and his companions[10]

---

[10]   St Lucian of Beauvais and his companions, SS Maximian and Julian.

87	De sancto Servatio et Remaclo	[Relic] of St Servatius and St Remaclus[11]
88	De sancto Christoforo	[Relic] of St Christopher
89	De sancto Hermete	[Relic] of St Hermes
90	De sancto Eutropio	[Relic] of St Eutrope
91	De sancto Albano duo ossa	Two bones of St Alban
92	Item relique de eodem et de pallio unde involutum fuit caput eius	Also relics of him, and of the cloak that his head was wrapped in
93	De pallio sancti Edmundi regis et martyri	From the cloak of St Edmund, king and martyr
94	De sancto Oswaldo regi et martyri in duobus locis	From St Oswald, king and martyr in two places
95	De capite sancti Edwardi regis et martyri in duobus locis	From the head of St Edward, king and martyr in two places
96	Item quoddam magnus os de ipso	Also a large bone from him
97	Item alibi de eodem. Alibi unus dens ipsius alibi de camisia ipsius	Again the same thing. Also his tooth and a piece of his shirt
98	Maxilla sanctii Aethelmodi martyris cum octo dentibus. Alibi unus dens ipsius	Upper jawbone of St Aethelmod with eight teeth. Elsewhere another tooth.
99	Dens sancti Reginaldi martiris	Tooth of St Reginald the martyr[12]
100	De sancto Blasio duo ossa	Two bones of St Blaise
101	De sancto Eustachio	[Relic] of St Eustace
102	De sancto Benigno	[Relic] of St Benigne

[11] St Servatius (d. 384) and St Remaclus (d. 663) were both bishops of Maastricht, although obviously not associated in their lifetimes, and martyrdom does not feature in either of their legends. Their relics are presumed, therefore, to have come from the Mosan region, possibly Stavelot, where St Remaclus was abbot after he retired from the see of Maastricht.

[12] Bethell raises the possibility that this refers to Reynald of Chatillon, executed by Saladin in 1187. This seems unlikely, as Bethell himself admits, but it is difficult to find other possible candidates.

103	De capite sancti Demetrii fratris sancti Dionisii martiris	From the head of St Demetrius, brother of St Dionysius the martyr
104	De oleo sancti Demetrii	Oil of St Demetrius
105	De sancto Ignatio	[Relic] of St Ignatius
106	De sancto Urbano in duobus locis	[Relic] of St Urban in two places
107	De sancto Theodoro in duobus locis	[Relic] of St Theodore in two place
108	De sancto Iuliano	[Relic] of St Julian
109	De sancto Calixto	[Relic] of St Callixtus
110	De sancto Leodegario in duobus locis	[Relic] of St Leodegar in two places
111	De sancto Saturnino	[Relic] of St Saturninus
112	De sancto Agapito	[Relic] of St Agapitus
113	De sancto Salvio	[Relic] of St Salvius
114	De sancto Arnulfo	[Relic] of St Arnulf[13]
115	Articulus digiti sancti Venerandi levite et martiris.	Finger joint of St Venerandus, deacon and martyr[14]
116	De fauce sancti Maximi episcopi et martiris	From the throat of St Maximus, bishop and martyr.[15]
117	De ossa canole sancti Fredmundi Constantiniensis episcopi et martyris.	From the collar-bone of St Fredmundus, bishop of Constantinople and martyr[16]
118	De ossibus sancti Longini martiris	Bones of St Longinus the martyr
119	De sanguine et cerebro sancti Thome archiepiscopi et martiris in duobus locis	Blood and brain from St Thomas, the archbishop and martyr, in two places[17]

[13] There are several saints of this name but only one suffered martyrdom: Arnulf, Archbishop of Mainz (Arnold von Selenhofen), who was murdered by an angry mob in 1160.

[14] Venerandus was the brother of bishop Maximus (see next note) and his deacon.

[15] Maximus, Bishop of Evreux, who died c. 384 together with his brother Venerandus.

[16] No bishop, archbishop or patriarch of Constantinople of this name (or anything like it) is known.

[17] i.e. Thomas Becket.

120	De cilitio eius in tribus locis	From his hair-shirt in three places
121	De cuculla eius de staminia de sotulari de caligula de lecto de [inmit] eius in duobus locis	From his cowl, his shirt, his slipper, his shoe, his bed and his [amice] in two places
122	Item unus pilus de capite eius et rochetum eius.	Also a hair from his head and his [surplice][18]
123	Item marmor super quod cecedit dum occidetur	Also the marble where he fell when he was killed
124	Item de reliquiis eius in duobus locis et de panno intincto sanguine et cerebro eius	Also his relics in two places, and cloth stained with his blood and brains
125	De sancto Alphego archiepiscopo et martyre in duobus locis	[Relic] of St Alphege, archbishop and martyr in two places
126	Sotular sancti Willielmi martyre intinctus sanguine eius et de arbore in qua suspensus fuit	The shoe of St William the martyr stained with his blood, and part of the tree from which he was hanged
127	Minimus digitus sancti Amphiboli martyre	Little finger of St Amphibalus the martyr
128	De sancto Nestore	[Relic] of St Nestor
129	De sancto Procopio	[Relic] of St Procopius
130	De sancto Theonosto	[Relic] of St Theonost
131	De sancto Exuperio	[Relic] of St Exuperius
132	De sancto Valentino	[Relic] of St Valentine
133	Pannus intinctus sanguine sancti Roberti martyris	Cloth stained with the blood of St Robert the martyr
	De confessionibus	**Of the Confessors**
134	Anulus sancti Nichodemi	Ring of St Nicodemus
135	De sancto Constantino imperatore unum os	A bone of the emperor Constantine
136	Dens sancti Nicholai	Tooth of St Nicholas

---

[18] The manuscript appears to read *rokerum*, an uncommon word for a rock, which would be meaningless in this context. I have therefore suggested *rochetum*, a rochet or vestment similar to a surplice.

137	Item de reliquiis eius	Also relics of him
138	Dens sancti Machuti	Tooth of St Machutus[19]
139	Dens sancti Walteri confessori et abbatis de Ponte Ysare	Tooth of St Walter, confessor and abbot of Pontoise[20]
140	De sancto Ieronimo	[Relic] of St Jerome
141	De sancto Exaudio archiepiscopo	[Relic] of St Exaudius the archbishop
142	De sancto Branwalatore	[Relic] of St Branwalator
143	De sancto Walarico	[Relic] of St Walric[21]
144	De sancto Flavio archiepiscopo	[Relic] of St Flavius, archbishop
145	De brachio sancti Germani autisiodorentis episcopi et de vestimentis eis	[Relics] of the arm of St Germanus, bishop of Auxerre and his vestments
146	De costa & carne sancti Rumpharii episcopi	From the rib and flesh of St Rumpharius the bishop[22]
147	De sancto Sansone	[Relic] of St Samson
148	De sancto Laudo	[Relic] of St Lauto[23]
149	De sancto Petro & et pallio quo involutum fuit corpus eius	[Relic] of St Petrus and the pallium that his body was wrapped in
150	De capillis sancti Bernardi	Hair of St Bernard
151	De tunica sancti Malachie archiepiscopi	From the tunic of St Malachy the archbishop[24]
152	Reliquie sancti Melchiadis confessori	Relics of St Miltiades the confessor[25]
153	De sancto Laudonio	[Relic] of St Lauto

---

[19]   Another name of St Malo or Maclou, a follower of St Brendan the Navigator.
[20]   Walter of Pontoise, c. 1030–99, was canonized in 1153.
[21]   Also known as St Valery. Founder of the abbey of Leuconay, and died in 622.
[22]   Bishop of Coutances, died c. 586.
[23]   Bishop of Coutances, 528–68, better known as Saint-Lô, but also as St Lautonius; see item 154.
[24]   St Malachy (1094–1148), Archbishop of Armagh from 1132–36.
[25]   Pope Miltiades, 311–14.

154	De sepulcro sancti Edwardi regis et confessori	From the sepulchre of St Edward, king and confessor
155	De sancto Birstano	[Relic] of St Birstan[26]
156	Item de reliquiis eius	More relics of him
157	De sancto Birino in duobus locis	[Relic] of St Birinus in two places
158	De sancto Swithuno in duobus locis	[Relic] of St Swithun in two places
159	De ossibus sancti Hedde episcopi	Bones of St Hedda, bishop[27]
160	De Birro sancti Brandam	[Relic] of St Brendan of Birr
161	Reliquie de sancto Antonio	Relics of St Antony
162	De sancto Egidio	[Relic] of St Giles
163	De sancto Leonardo in duobus locis	[Relic] of St Leonard in two places
164	De sancto Lupo	[Relic] of St Lupus
165	De sancto Lanfranco	[Relic] of St Lanfranc[28]
166	Reliquie sancti Phiacri	Relics of St Fiacre[29]
167	Reliquie sancti Pharaonis	Relics of St Faro[30]
168	De sancto Botulfo	[Relic] of St Botolph
169	De sancto Audomaro	[Relic] of St Audemar[31]
170	De sancto Ermolao	[Relic] of St Hermolaos
171	De sancto Iohanne Eleymone	[Relic] of St John the Almsgiver
172	De sancto Auxentio	[Relic] of St Auxentius
173	De sancto Mardario	[Relic] of St Mardarius
174	De sancto Curico Alexandrino	[Relic] of St Cyril of Alexandria

[26] Birstan (c. 870–934), Bishop of Winchester 931–34.
[27] Hedda, Bishop of Dorchester then Winchester, 676–705.
[28] Lanfranc, Archbishop of Canterbury 1067–89.
[29] St Fiacre (d. 670), a hermit educated in Ireland but settled in the diocese of Meaux where he was befriended by the bishop, St Faro.
[30] St Faro, Bishop of Meaux c. 626–75.
[31] St Audemar, Abbot of Saint-Gall (720–59).

175	De sancto Gerotheo archiepiscopo	[Relic] of St Gero, archbishop[32]
176	De sancto Philotheo archiepiscopo	[Relic] of St Philotheus, archbishop[33]
177	De vestimenti sancti Dunstani	Vestments of St Dunstan
178	Duo panni de pannis sancti Cuthberti qui maior est et pulchior annius decem cum eo inventus est incorruptus. Alius qui minor est annis cccc & xviii similiter in postra translatione incorruptus sicut nunc cernitur inventus est	Two fragments of the vestments of St Cuthbert, of which the larger and more beautiful was with his incorrupt body for ten years. The other, smaller, was found as it is now seen when the incorrupt body was translated after 418 years.
179	De costa sancti David episcopi	From a rib of St David the bishop
180	Item unum os de eo	Also one of his bones
181	De sepulcro sancti Auberti Abrincencsis episcopi	[Relic] of the sepulchre of St Aubert, bishop of Avranches[34]
182	Stola sancti Nicholai	The stole of St Nicholas
183	Quiddam magnum os & due coste sancti Hemme primi abbatis Leominstri monasterii	A certain large bone and two ribs of St Hemma, first abbot of the monastery of Leominster
184	Item de reliquiis eius	Also some of his relics
	De virginibus	**Of the Virgins**
185	De costa sancte Marie Magdalene et de vestimento eius	[Relics] of a rib of St Mary Magdalene and of her clothing
186	Item de reliquiis eius in duobus locis	Also relics of her in two places
187	De sancta Helena matre Constantinii imperatoris	[Relic] of St Helena, mother of the emperor Constantine

---

[32]   Probably Archbishop Gero of Cologne (969–76)

[33]   A mysterious figure, perhaps no more than a mistranslation, and clearly not the Philotheus who was martyred in Samosata c. 300, along with Hipparchus, as he was a magistrate and neither an archbishop nor a confessor saint.

[34]   St Aubert, Bishop of Avranches (d. 720).

188	De sancta Felicitate matre vii filiorum martyrum in quattuor locis	[Relic] of St Felicity, mother of seven sons who were all martyred, in four places
189	Manus sancte Anastasie	A hand of St Anastasia
190	Item de reliquiis eius	Also relics of her
191	De sancta Cecilia	[Relic] of St Cecilia
192	De vestimento eius in duobus locis	[Relics] of her clothes in two places
193	De pulvere corporis eius	Dust of her body
194	Item de [cuta]^{35} ei et de reliquiis eius in duobus locis	Also her rib (?) and relics of her in two places
195	De sancta Margarita	[Relic] of St Margaret
196	Item de reliquiis eius in tribus locis	Also relics of her in three places
197	De capite sancte Brigide	[Relic] of the head of St Brigid
198	De maxilla eius	[Relic] of her upper jaw
199	De vestimentis eius	[Relics] of her clothes
200	De costa eius. De capillis eius	Her rib, her hair
201	De capite sancte Fidis. Item de reliquiis eius	[Relic] of the head of St Faith, also relics of her
202	De capite sancte Frideswide	[Relic] of the head of St Frideswide
203	Item de ossibus eius	Also of her bones
204	De capillis sancte Marie Egyptiace	Hair of St Mary of Egypt
205	Pulvis de corpore sancte Edburge virgine	Dust of the body of St Edburga the virgin
206	De pulvere ossuum sancte Eufemie virgine et martiris	From the dust of the bones of St Euphemia, virgin and martyr
207	De costa sancte Agnetis	From the rib of St Agnes
208	Item de eadem	Also from her
209	De costa sancte Milburge virginis	From the rib of St Milburga, virgin

---

[35] Perhaps costa (rib), or cutis (skin).

210	Item de eadem in duobus locis	Also from her, in two places
211	De peplo sancte Barbare virginis et de reliquiis eius	From the robe of St Barbara, virgin, and [other] relics of her
212	Item de peplo ei sanguine infecto	Also from her robe, stained with blood
213	De sancta Columba virgine	[Relic] of St Columba, virgin
214	De sancta Ursula qui fuit princeria xi m̄ virginum	[Relic] of St Ursula who was a princess, and her eleven thousand handmaidens[36]
215	De sancta Cristina	[Relic] of St Christina
216	De sancta Basilissa	[Relic] of St Basilissa
217	De sancta Concordia martyris nutriae sancti Ypoliti martiris	[Relic] of St Concordia the martyr, nurse of St Hippolytus the martyr
218	De sancta Ciriaca de qua in passione sancte Laurentii legitur	[Relic] of St Cyriaca of whom we read in the passion of St Lawrence[37]
219	De sancta Katerina	[Relic] of St Catherine
220	Item de oleo eius	Also her oil
221	Item pannus cum cotona infusus oleo eius	Also cotton cloth infused with her oil
222	Reliquie sancte Aldegundis regine	Relics of St Aldegundis
223	Quoddam magnum os sancte Aelfgive regine avie sancti Edwardi regis et martiris	A large bone of St Aelftgyfu, the queen, grandmother of St Edward, king and martyr
224	De sancta Alueva virgine	[Relic] of St Alueva[38]
225	Reliquie sancte Nimphe virginis	Relics of St Nymphe the virgin
226	Reliquie sancte Yrenee virginis	Relics of St Irene the virgin

[36] The text has *xi m̄ virginum* which can be read as either 11,000 virgins (which is normal), or 11 martyr virgins (which is arguable).
[37] St Lawrence was buried in the Cemetery of St Cyriaca in Rome.
[38] Bethell (1972), 66 suggests Aethelgyfu

227	Reliquie sancte Vite martyris quod Ysoi dicitur grece	Relics of St Vita the martyr, whom the Greeks call Ysoi
228	Duo magno ossa de sancta Willa virginis et martyris	Two large bones of St Willa, virgin and martyr
229	Reliquie sancte Tecle virginis	Relics of St Tecla the virgin
230	De sepulcro sancte Lucie virginis et martyris	From the sepulchre of St Lucy, virgin and martyr
	Multe etiam alie reliquie quarum scripta	Also many more relics than are noted here
	Dux aquitanie dedit puerum regi henrico fundatori monastrii rading'	*The Duke of Aquitaine gave a [statue of the holy] child to Henry the founder of the Monastery of Reading*

2 DR LONDON'S LIST, 18 SEPTEMBER 1538 (WRIGHT (1843), 226–27)

THE INVENTORYE OFF THE RELICS OFF THE HOWSSE OFF REDYNG

Inprimis, two peces off the holye crosse.
Item, saynt James hande.
Item, saynt Phelype stole.[39]
Item a bone off Marye Magdalene with other moo.
Item, saynt Anastasius is hande, with other moo.
Item, a pece off saynte Pancrates arme.
Item, a bone off saynt Quyntyns arme.
Item, a bone off saynt Davyde is arme.
Item, a bone off Marye Salomes arme.
Item, a bone off saynt Edwarde the Martyre is arme.
Item, a bone of saynt Hierome, with other moo.
Item, bones off saynt Stephyn, with other moo.
Item, a bone off saynte Blase, with other moo.
Item, a bone off saynt Osmonde, with other moo.
Item, a pece off saynt Ursula stole.[40]
Item, a chowbone of saynt Ethelmold.

---

[39] i.e. skull.
[40] i.e. skull.

Item, bones off saynt Leodigarye and of S. Herenei.
Item, bones off saynt Margarett.
Item, bones off saynt Arnal.
Item, a bone off saynt Agas, with other moo.
Item, a bone off S. Androwe, and ij peces of his crosse.
Item, a bone off S. Fredyswyde.
Item, a bone of saynt Anne.
With many othere.
Ther be a multitude of small bonys, laces, stonys, and ermys, wiche wolde occupie iiij schetes of papyr to make particularly an inventory of every part therof. They be all at your lordeschips commaundement.

VERSES FOR PROPHETS AND APOSTLES
RECORDED IN LAMBETH PALACE MS 371

Venit de celis testis de lege fidelis	*moyses*
Rex veniet fortis qui solvet vincula mortis	*David*
Virgo deum pariet: mater sine semine fiet	*Ysaias*
Qui deus est magnus ad nos mittetur ut agnus	*Jeremias*
Qui dubitas, veniet venturus nec mora fiet	*Ezechiel*
Sanctus sanctorum descendet ab arce polorum	*Daniel*
Missus de celis Christus venit. esto fidelis	*Oseas*
De celis numen veniet de lumine lumen	*amos*
Gentes docturum Christum scitote futurum	*abacuc*
Ex utero matris nascetur gloria patris	*Jonas*
De stella solem cerne de virgine prolem	*baptista*
Petrus ego celi portas reserabo fideli	*Petrus*
Qui fueram Saulus modo dicor nomine Paulus	*paulus*
Vexor morte crucis que dat michi gaudia lucis	*andreas*
Plus me dilexit qui me sub pectore vexit	*Johannes*
Occubui gladio Christi sic hostia fio	*Jacobus*
Patrem nescivi patrem vidui cupivi	*Philippus*
Terre prostratus vivus sum decoriatus	*bartholomeus*
De templo st(r)atus vivo super astra beatus	*Jacobus minor*
Truncatus capite merui michi gaudia vite	*matheus*
Lancea me stravit que me super astra locavit	*Thomas*
Sternimur a turbis iudas simonque per urbis	*Judas et*
Compita. sic morimur sic Christi iure petimur	*simon*
Pro iuda positus eius sum sede potitus	*mathius*

INVENTORY OF ITEMS RECEIVED BY KING JOHN FROM ALAN MARCELL, 18 DECEMBER 1204

Rex etc. omnibus etc. Sciatis quod die Lune proxima ante Natale Domini anno regno nostril vjto apud Rading' per manum fratris Alani preceptoris Novi Templi London' et fratris Rogeri elemosinarii recipimus,

Coronam nostrum auream factam apud London'.

Mantell' de samitto vermeill' frettatum cum saphiris et kathmath', et perlis cum uno firmaculo an' insuto.

Dalmaticam de eodem samitto urlatam de orfreis, et cum lapidibus.

Tunicam de diaspro albo.

Unum Pannum serricum quadratum ad sedem regiam.

Sandalia et soculares de predicto samitto. bondatos de orfreis

Baldredum de eodem samitto cum kathmath' et aliis lapidibus

Et cyrotecas albas cum uno saphiro et una amatista

Et gladium qui factus fuit ad coronationem nostrum cum scabberg' de orfreis.

Item duas zonas cum esmall' et iiijor margaritis (?) cum membris aureis et unam magnam cum granatis, et saphiris et perlis

Item unum firmaculum cum rubis.

Unum firmaculum cum smaragdinibus et rubis quod Episcopus Norewic' dedit nobis.

Unum firmaculum cum saphiris de opere London'

Item unum firmaculum cum saphiris

Item unum firmaculum cum iiijor smaragdinibus ett iiijor baleis

Item unum firmaculum cum ix bonis saphiris

Item unum firmaculum cum ij saphiris ij smaragdinibus et ij baleis

Item unum firmaculum cum iij smaragdinibus iij saphiri et ij baleis

Item unum firmaculum cum iiij smaragdinibus iiij saphiri et iiij baleis et j turkesiis in hardillone

Item unum firmaculum cum ij saphiris et I topac' et cum grossis perlis et minutis saphiris.

Item unum firmaculum cum saphiris quod camerarius nobis dedit.

Item unum firmaculum cum iiij baleis et iiij smaragdinibus

Item unum firmaculum cum iij smaragdinibus et iij saphiris et j turkeis' et minutis perlis et parvis rubis

Item unum baculum cum x saphiris grossis

Item unum baculum cum xxiij diamant'

Item unum baculum cum lx smaragdinibus

Item unum baculum cum lvij smaragdinibus

Item unum baculum cum vij topac' bonis et j lapide qui ignoratur

Item unum baculum cum ix turkeis'

Item unum baculum cum xiiij saphiris bonis in caston'

Item ij magna pectin aur' cum diversibus lapidibus ponderantes ij marc' vj unc' et dimid'

Et ideo volumus quod magister Templi et fratres Templi de omnibus superscriptis quieti sint; et in hujus rei testimonium etc. Teste G fil' Petri com' Essex apud Rading' xviij die Dec. (Rot. Pat. 6 Joh).

BIBLIOGRAPHY

Abbey Quarter

Reading Borough Council, *Revealing the Abbey Quarter.*

Reviving Reading's Historic Heart, Outline Conservation Statement, November 2011.

Abou-el-Haj (1983)

B. Abou-el-Haj, 'Bury St Edmunds Abbey between 1070 and 1124: a history of property, privilege, and monastic art production', *Art History*, 6/1 (1983), 1–29.

Adam Usk

C. Given-Wilson (ed. and trans.), *The Chronicle of Adam Usk 1377–1421*, Oxford 1997.

Albury (1881)

F. W. Albury, 'Reading Abbey, its History and Architecture and the Reading Abbey Stone', *Berkshire Archaeological and Architectural Society Transactions*, 1880–81, 65–90.

Allen and Vosper (1999)

M. Allen and M. R. Vosper, 'An Edward III Class 15d Penny of Reading', *The British Numismatic Journal*, 69 (1999), 214.

Anglo-Saxon Chronicle

G. N. Garmonsway (trans. and ed.), *The Anglo-Saxon Chronicle*, London 1953 (new ed. 1972).

Annales Bermundeseia

H. R. Luard (ed.), *Annales Monastici*. Rolls Series 36, vol. 3 (1865).

Annales Monastici

H. R. Luard (ed.), *Annales Monastici*. Rolls Series 36, 5 vols (1864–69).

Annales Radingenses

F. Liebermann (ed.), *Ungedruckte anglo-normannische Geschichtsquellen*, Strassburg, 1879, 9–12.

Annales Radingenses Posteriores

C. W. Previté-Orton (ed), 'Annales Radingenses Posteriores, 1135–1264', *English Historical Review* 37(1922), 400–03.

Annales Ricardi secundi

H. T. Riley (ed.), 'Annales Ricardi secundi et Henrici quarti, regum Angliae', in

Johannis de Trokelowe et Henrici de Blaneforde ... chronica et annales, pt 3 of *Chronica monasterii S. Albani*, Rolls Series, 28 (1866), 155–420.

Annales Sancti Disibodi

G. H. Pertz (ed.), *Monumenta Germaniae Historica*, 17, 4–30.

Annales de Waverleia

H. R. Luard (ed.), *Annales Monastici*. Rolls Series 36, vol. 2 (1865).

Annales Wintonia.

H. R. Luard (ed.), *Annales Monastici*. Rolls Series 2 (1865).

Anon. Chron.

V. H. Galbraith (ed.), *The Anonimalle chronicle, 1333 to 1381, from a MS. written at St Mary's Abbey, York*, Manchester 1927.

Arnold of Lübeck, Chronica

MGH (SS rer. Germ.), vol. 14.

Astill (2002)

G. Astill, 'Windsor in the Context of Medieval Berkshire', L. Keen and E. Scarff (eds), *Windsor: Medieval Archaeology, Art and Architecture of the Thames Valley* (British Archaeological Association Conference Transactions 25), Windsor 2002, 1–14.

Aston (1973)

M. Aston, 'English Ruins and English History: The Dissolution and the Sense of the Past'. *Journal of the Warburg and Courtauld Institutes* 36 (1973), 231–55.

Barfield (1888)

S. Barfield, 'Lord Fingall's Cartulary of Reading Abbey', *English Historical Review*, 3 (1888), 113–25.

Barker (1986)

J. R. V. Barker, *The Tournament in England, 1100–1400*, London 1986.

Barlow (1962)

F. Barlow (ed.), *The Life of King Edward who rests at Westminster. Attributed to a monk of St Bertin*, London 1962.

Barron 1898

O. Barron, *The Visitation of Berkshire in 1532 by Thomas Benolte*, London 1898.

Baxter (1998)

R. Baxter, *Bestiaries and their Users in the Middle Ages*, Stroud 1998.

Baxter (2004)

R. Baxter, 'Beakhead ornament and the Corpus of Romanesque Sculpture', *Historic Churches*, 11 (2004), 8–10.

Baxter and Harrison (2002)

R. Baxter and S. Harrison, 'The Decoration of the Cloister at Reading Abbey', L. Keen and E. Scarff (eds), *Windsor: Medieval Archaeology, Art and Architecture of the Thames Valley* (British Archaeological Association Conference Transactions 25), Windsor 2002, 302–12.

Baylé (1991)

M. Baylé, *Les Origines et les Premiers Développements de la Sculpture Romane en Normandie*, Caen 1991.

Bayley (1830)

J. Bayley, *The history and antiquities of the Tower of London, with memoirs of royal and distinguished persons, deduced from records, state-papers, and manuscripts, and from other original and authentic source*, London, 2nd ed., 1830.

Beani (1885)

G. Beani, *Memorie Storiche di S Iacopo Apostolo il Maggiore*, Pistoia 1885.

Bell and Dale (2011)

A. R. Bell and R. S. Dale, 'The Medieval Pilgrimage Business', *Enterprise and Society*, 12 (2011), 601–27.

Benedict of Peterborough

W. Stubbs (ed.), *Gesta regis Henrici secundi benedicti abbatis : the chronicle of the reigns of Henry II and Richard I, A. D. 1169–1192*. Vol. 1, London 1867.

Benet's Chronicle

G. L. and M. A. Harris (eds), 'John Benet's Chronicle for the years 1400 to 1462', *Camden Fourth Series*, 9 (1972), 151–233.

Bennett et al (2012)

C. Bennett, N. J. Morgan, J. Cheshire, H. T. Küpper and G. Plumb, *Stained Glass of Lincoln Cathedral*, London 2012.

Bent (1963)

I. Bent, 'The English Chapel Royal before 1300', *Proceedings of the Royal Musical Association*, 90, 1, 1963–64, 77–95.

Bernard of Clairvaux

J. Leclercq *et al.*, *Sancti Bernardi Opera*, 8 vols, Rome 1957–77.

Bethell (1972)

D. Bethell, 'The making of a twelfth-century relic collection', *Studies in Church History*, 8 (1972), 61–72.

Bettley and Pevsner (2007)

J. Bettley and N. Pevsner, *The Buildings of England: Essex*, New Haven and London 2007.

Biddle (1985)

M. Biddle, 'Seasonal Festivals and Residence: Winchester, Westminster and Gloucester in the Tenth to Twelfth Centuries', *Anglo-Norman Studies*, 8 (1985), 51–72.

Biddle (1993)

M. Biddle 'Early Renaissance at Winchester' in J. Crook (ed.) *Winchester Cathedral, Nine Hundred Years 1093–1993*, Chichester 1993, 257–304.

Biddle and Kjølbe-Biddle (1980)

Biddle and Kjølbe-Biddle, 'England's Premier Abbey: the Medieval Chapter House of St Alban's Abbey and its Excavation in 1978', *Excavation. The Magazine of the University of Pennsylvania Museum of Archaeology and Anthropology*, 22.2, Winter 1980, 17–32.

Bilson (1911)

J. Bilson, 'Fragments of a Cloister Arcade', *Yorkshire Archaeological Journal*, 21 (1911), 174–75.

Bilson (1913)

J. Bilson, 'Bridlington Priory Church: The Cloister Arcade', *Yorkshire Archaeological Journal*, 22 (1913), 238–39.

Bindoff (1982)

S. T. Bindoff, *The House of Commons 1509–1558*, London 1982.

Binski (1995)

P. Binski, *Westminster Abbey and the Plantagenets. Kingship and the Representation of Power 1200–1400*, New Haven and London 1995.

Boase (1953)
T. S. R. Boase, *English Art 1100–1216*, Oxford 1953.
Boehm (1997)
B. D. Boehm, 'Body-Part Reliquaries: The State of Research', *Gesta*, 36 (1997), 8–19.
Bond (1905)
F. Bond, *Gothic Architecture in England*, London 1905.
Bony (1958)
J. Bony, 'The Resistance to Chartres in Early Thirteenth-Century Architecture', *Journal of the British Archaeological Association* (ser. 3), XX-XXI (1957–1958), 35–52.
Bony (1976)
J. Bony, 'Diagonality and Centrality in Early Rib-Vaulted Architectures', *Gesta*, 15 (1976), 15–25.
Brayley (1834)
E. W. Brayley (ed), *The Graphic and historical illustrator: an original miscellany of literary, antiquarian, and topographical information*, London 1834.
Brayley and Britton (1836)
E. W. Brayley and J. Britton, *The history of the ancient palace and late Houses of Parliament at Westminster*, London 1836.
Breck (1918)
J. B. Breck, 'A Reliquary of Saint Thomas Becket Made for John of Salisbury', *Bulletin of the Metropolitan Museum of Art,* 13 (October 1918), 220–24.
Brooke (1976)
G. C. Brooke, *English Coins from the seventh century to the present day*, London 1976.
Brooke (1993)
C. Brooke, 'Bishop Walkelin and his Inheritance', in J. Crook (ed.) *Winchester Cathedral, Nine Hundred Years 1093–1993*, Chichester 1993, 1–12.
Brown (2003)
S. Brown, *'Our Magnificent Fabrick': York Minster, An Architectural History c. 1220–1500*, Swindon 2003.
Bruce (1841)
J. Bruce (ed.), *Original Letters and Other Documents relating to the Benefactions of William Laud, Archbishop of Canterbury, to the County of Berks*, London 1841.
Buckler (1823)
J. Buckler, *Notes on the Architecture of Reading Abbey,* British Library MSS Add. 36400A and B.
Bynum and Gerson (1997)
C. W. Bynum and P. Gerson, 'Body-Part Reliquaries and Body Parts in the Middle Ages,' *Gesta*, 36 (1997), 3–7.
Camden Britannia
W. Camden, *Britannia siue Florentissimorum regnorum, Angliae, Scotiae, Hiberniae, et insularum adiacentium ex intima antiquitate chorographica descriptio*, London 1586.
Campbell and Steer (1988)
L. Campbell and F. Steer, *A Catalogue of Manuscripts in the College of Arms Collections,* 1, London 1988.

Capes (1909)

W. W. Capes (ed.), Registrum Ricardi de Swinfield, episcopi Herefordensis, AD MCCLXXXIII-MCCCXVII, *Cantilupe Soc. and Canterbury and York Society*, 6 (1909), 124–5.

Capgrave

F. C. Hingeston (ed.), *The Chronicle of England by John Capgrave*, London 1858.

Carpenter and Kanter 2009

D. Carpenter and J. Kanter, 'Henry III and Windsor' (Fine of the Month: November 2009, accessed November 2011). Henry III Fine Rolls Project (www.finerollshenry3.org.uk/home.html).

Cave (1945)

C. J. P. Cave, 'Capitals from the cloister of Hyde Abbey', *Antiquaries Journal*, 25 (1945), 79.

CCR

Calendar of Close Rolls.

CFR

Calendar of Fine Rolls.

Cheney (1936)

C. R. Cheney, 'A Monastic Letter of Fraternity to Eleanor of Aquitaine', *English Historical Review*, 51.203 (1936), 488–93.

Chibnall (1991)

M. Chibnall, *The Empress Matilda: Queen Consort, Queen Mother and Lady of the English*, Oxford 1991, 1993 edition.

Chron. Angliae

E. M. Thompson (ed.), *Chronicon Angliae 1328–1388 of St Albans*, Rolls Series 64 (1874).

Chron. Knighton

J. R. Lumby (ed.), *Chronicon Henrici Knighton, vel Cnitthon, monachi Leycestrensis*, 2 vols, Rolls Series 92 (1889–95).

Chron. London

C. L. Kingsford (ed.), *Chronicles of London*, Oxford 1905.

Chron. Maj.

H. R. Luard (ed.), *Matthaei Parisiensis, Monachi Sancti Albani, Chronica Majora*, 7 vols, London, Rolls Series (1872–83).

Clanchy (1979)

M. T. Clanchy, *From Memory to Written Record, England 1066–1307*, London 1979.

Clapham (1934)

A. W. Clapham, *English Romanesque Architecture after the Conquest*, Oxford 1934.

Clapham (1952)

A. W. Clapham, 'The Form of the Early Choir of Tewkesbury and its Significance', *Archaeological Journal*, 106, Supplement for the year 1949 (1952), 10–15.

Clarendon (1717)

E. Hyde, Earl of Clarendon, *The History of the Rebellion and Civil Wars in England, begun in 1641*, 7 vols, Oxford 1717. New edition, 8 vols, Oxford 1826.

Clarke (1824)

W. N. Clarke, *Parochial Topography of the Hundred of Wanting*, Oxford 1824.

CLR Henry III

Calendar of the Liberate Rolls of the Reign of Henry III Preserved in the Public Record Office, 6 vols, London 1910- 64.

Coates (1802)

C. Coates, *The History And Antiquities Of Reading*, London 1802.

Coates (1999)

A. Coates, *English Medieval Books. The Reading Abbey Collections from Foundation to Dispersal*, Oxford Historical Monographs 1999.

Collinson and Craig (1998)

P. Collinson and J. Craig, *The Reformation in English Towns 1500–1640*, London 1998.

Colvin (1963–82)

H. Colvin (ed.), *The History of the King's Works*, 6 vols plus plans, London 1963–82.

Cooper King (1887)

C. Cooper King, *A History of Berkshire*, London 1887.

CPR

Calendar of Patent Rolls.

Craib (1923)

T. Craib, *The Itinerary of King Henry III, 1216–72*, edited and annotated by S. Brindle and S. Priestley. Undated limited edition supplied by S. Brindle.

Crook (1994)

J. Crook, '"A Worthy Antiquity": the movement of King Cnut's bones in Winchester Cathedral', in A. Rumble (ed.), *The Reign of Cnut: King of England, Denmark and Norway*, London 1994, 165–92.

Crosby (1987).

S. M. Crosby, *The Royal Abbey of Saint-Denis from its Beginnings to the Death of Suger, 475–1151*, New Haven and London, 1987.

Crouch 2000

D. Crouch, *The Reign of King Stephen*, Harlow 2000.

CRSBI

Corpus of Romanesque Sculpture in Britain and Ireland. Website at www.crsbi.ac.uk

Crump

J. J. Crump, *The Itinerary of King John Project* <http://purl.org/neolography/JohnItinerary> [consulted 5 August 2015].

CSP (Domestic)

Calendar of State Papers, Domestic Series.

CSP (Scotland)

Calendar of State Papers, Scotland.

CSP (Spain)

Calendar of State Papers, Spain.

CSP (Venice)

Calendar of State Papers Relating to English Affairs in the Archives of Venice, 38 vols, 1864–1947.

Devon (1837)

F. Devon, *Issues of the Exchequer; being a collection of payments made out of his majesty's revenue from King Henry III to King Henry VI inclusive*, London 1837.

Dickinson (1970)

P. Dickinson, *Hinchingbrooke House*, Huntingdon 1970.

Doble (1947)

G. H. Doble, 'The Leominster Relic List', *Transactions of the Woolhope Naturalists' Field Club*, 31 (1942–7), 58–65.

Domesday Survey

A. Williams and G. H. Martin (eds), *Domesday Book. A Complete Translation.* London 1992 (2003 edition).

Doran (1835)

J. Doran, *The History and Antiquities of the Town and Borough of Reading in Berkshire*, Reading and London 1835.

Dormer (1923)

E. W. Dormer, *Gray of Reading: a sixteenth-century controversialist and ballad-writer*, London 1923.

Dormer (1937)

E. W. Dormer, 'The Stream called the Hallowed Brook at Reading', *Berkshire Archaeological Journal*, 41 (1937), 73–81.

Draper (1987)

P. Draper, 'Architecture and Liturgy' in J. Alexander and P. Binski (eds), *Age of Chivalry: Art in Plantagenet England 1200–1400*, London 1987, 83–91.

Duffin (1988)

R. W. Duffin, 'The Sumer Canon: A New Revision', *Speculum* 63 (1988), 1–21.

Dugdale Monasticon

W. Dugdale, *Monasticon Anglicanum: a History of the Abbies and other Monasteries, Hospitals, Frieries, and Cathedral and Collegiate Churches, with their Dependencies, in England and Wales*, 6 vols in 8 parts, London 1817–30.

Edwards (1983)

R. Edwards, *The Itinerary of King Richard III 1483–1485*, London 1983.

Elizabeth of York Privy Purse Expenses

N. H. Nicholas, *Privy Purse Expenses of Elizabeth of York: Wardrobe Accounts of Edward IV*, London 1830.

Englefield (1782)

H. Englefield, 'Observations on Reading Abbey', *Archaeologia* 6 (1782), 61–66.

Ettlinger (1976)

E. Ettlinger, 'A Romanesque Capital from Reading Abbey in the Reading Museum and Art Gallery', *Berkshire Archaeological Journal*, 68 (1975–76), 71–75.

Excerpta Historica

S. Bentley (ed.), *Excerpta Historica, or, Illustrations of English History*, London 1831.

Exch. K.R. Ch Gds

TNA Exchequer Records, King's Remembrancer, Church Goods.

Eyton 1878

R. W. Eyton, *Court, Household and Itinerary of Henry II*, London 1878.

Farley (2009)

D. Farley, *An Irreverent Curiosity: In Search of the Church's Strangest Relic in Italy's Oddest Town*, New York 2009.

Fasham and Stewart (1991)

P. J. Fasham and I. J. Stewart, 'Excavations at Reading Abbey, 1985–86', *Berkshire Archaeological Journal*, 73 (1986–90), 89–103.

Fergusson (2011)

P. Fergusson, *Canterbury Cathedral Priory in the Age of Becket*, New Haven and London 2011.

Fernie (1976)

E. C. Fernie, 'The ground plan of Norwich Cathedral and the square root of two', *Journal of the British Archaeological Association*, 129 (1976), 77–86.

Fernie (1987)

E. C. Fernie, 'Reconstructing Edward's Abbey at Westminster', in N. Stratford (ed.), *Romanesque and Gothic: Essays for George Zarnecki*, 2 vols, Woodbridge 1987, 1, 63–67.

Fernie (1993)

E. C. Fernie, *An Architectural History of Norwich Cathedral*, Oxford 1993.

Fernie (2000)

E. C. Fernie, *The Architecture of Norman England*, Oxford 2000.

Fletcher (1984)

E. Fletcher, *Saint James's Catapult: The Life and Times of Diego Gelmírez of Santiago de Compostela*, Oxford 1984.

Flood (1924)

W. H. G. Flood, 'The Beginnings of the Chapel Royal: An Unwritten Page of English Musical History', *Music and Letters*, 5.1 (Jan. 1924), 85–90.

Flor. Hist.

H. R. Luard (ed.), *Flores Historiarum*, 3 vols, Rolls Series 95, 1890.

Flowers of History

C. D. Yonge (trans.), *The Flowers of History especially such as relate to the Affairs of Britain from the beginning of the world to the year 1307, collected by Matthew of Westminster* (English translation of *Flores Historiarum*), 2 vols, London 1853.

Forester (1853)

T. Forester (ed. and trans.), *The Chronicle of Henry of Huntingdon comprising the History of England from the Invasion of Julius Caesar to the Accession of Henry II*, London 1853.

Foxe

G. Townsend and S. R. Cattley (ed.), *The Acts and Monuments of John Foxe: A New and Complete Edition*, 8 vols, London 1837–41.

Franklin (1983)

J. A. Franklin, 'The Romanesque Cloister Sculpture at Norwich Cathedral Priory', F. H. Thompson (ed.), *Studies in Medieval Sculpture*, Society of Antiquaries Occasional Paper NS 3, London 1983, 56–70.

Franklin (1989)

J. A. Franklin, 'Bridlington Priory: an Augustinian Church and Cloister in the Twelfth Century', in C. Wilson (ed.), *Medieval Art and Architecture in the East Riding of Yorkshire* (British Archaeological Association Conference Transactions 9), Leeds, 1989, 44–61.

Freeburn (2011)

R. P. Freeburn, *Hugh of Amiens and the Twelfth-Century Renaissance*, Farnham 2011.

Freeman (1882)

E. A. Freeman, *The Reign of William Rufus*, Oxford 1882.

Friedmann (1884)

P. Friedmann, *Anne Boleyn; a Chapter of English History*, 2 vols, London 1884.

Froissart

T. Johnes (trans.), *The Chronicles of England, France, Spain and the adjoining countries by Sir John Froissart*, 2 vols, London 1839.

Gachard (1874–82)

L. P. Gachard (ed.), *Collection des Voyages des Souverains des Pays-Bas*, 4 vols, Brussels 1874–82.

Gaimster and Gilchrist (2003)

D. Gaimster and R. Gilchrist (eds), *The Archaeology of Reformation,1480–1580* (Society for Post-medieval Archaeology Monograph 1), Leeds 2003.

Gairdner (1861–63)

J. Gairdner (ed.), *Letters and papers illustrative of the reigns of Richard III and Henry VII*, 2 vols, London 1861, 1863.

Gams (1956)

P. B. Gams, *Kirchengeschichte von Spanien*, 2 vols, Graz 1956 (reprint of the Regensburg 1862 edition).

Gardner (1937)

A. Gardner, *A Handbook of English Medieval Sculpture*, Cambridge 1935, 2nd edn 1937.

Garry (1893)

F. N. A. and A. G. Garry (eds), *The Churchwardens' Accounts of the Parish of St Mary's, Reading, Berks, 1550–1662*, Reading 1893.

Geary (1978)

P. J. Geary, *Furta Sacra. Thefts of Relics in the Central Middle Ages*, Princeton 1978, revised ed. 1990.

G. E. C. (1910–59)

G. E. C. [G. E. Cockayne], *The Complete Peerage*, 2nd edn, 13 vols in 14 parts, London, 1910–59.

Gem (1983)

R. Gem, 'The Romanesque Cathedral of Winchester: Patron and Design in the Eleventh Century', *Medieval Art and Architecture at Winchester Cathedral* (British Archaeological Association Conference Transactions for 1980), Leeds 1983, 1–12.

Gesta Abbatum S. Albani

H. T. Riley (ed.), *Gesta abbatum monasterii Sancti Albani,*

a Thoma Walsingham, regnante Ricardo Secundo, ejusdem ecclesiæ præcentore, compilata, Rolls Serie 28, 3 vols, London 1867–69.

Gesta Normannorum Ducum

E. M. C. van Houts (ed.), *The Gesta Normannorum Ducum of William of Jumieges, Orderic Vitalis and Robert of Torigni*, Oxford 1995, vol. 2.

Gesta Stephani

K. R. Potter and R. H. C. Davis (eds), *Gesta Stephani*, Oxford 1976.

Giles (1889)

J. A. Giles (trans.), *Matthew Paris's English History from the year 1235 to 1273*, 3 vols, London 1853–89.

Gilyard-Beer (1970)
R. Gilyard-Beer, 'The Eastern Arm of the Abbey Church at Bury St. Edmund's', *Proc. Suffolk Institute of Archaeology and Natural History*, 31/3 (1970), 256–62.

Given-Wilson and Curteis (1984)
C. Given-Wilson and A. Curteis, *The Royal Bastards of Medieval England*, London 1984.

Glass (1987)
Dorothy F. Glass, 'Pseudo-Augustine, Prophets, and Pulpits in Campania', *Dumbarton Oaks Papers*, 41 (1987), 215–226.

GMF
S. Letters, *Online Gazetteer of Markets and Fairs in England Wales to 1516* (http://www.history.ac.uk/cmh/gaz/gazweb2.html).

Golding 1985
B. Golding, 'Burials and benefactions: an aspect of monastic patronage in thirteenth-century England', in W. M. Ormrod (ed.), *England in the thirteenth century: proceedings of the 1984 Harlaxton symposium*, Nottingham 1985, 64–75.

Gough (1900)
H. Gough, *Itinerary of King Edward the First throughout his Reign, A.D. 1272–1307*, 2 vols, Paisley and London 1900.

Gransden (1973)
A. Gransden, *The Customary of the Benedictine Abbey of Bury St. Edmunds in Suffolk*, London 1973.

Green (1986)
J. A. Green, *The Government of England under Henry I*, Cambridge 1986.

Greenaway (1971)
D. E. Greenaway (ed.), *Fasti Ecclesiae Anglicanae 1066–1300*, vol. 2, *Monastic Cathedrals (Northern and Southern Provinces)*, London 1971.

Grierson (1951)
P. Grierson, 'Oboli de Musc', *English Historical Review*, 66.258 (1951), 75–81.

Griffiths (1981)
R. A. Griffiths, *The Reign of King Henry VI: the exercise of royal authority, 1422–1461*, Berkeley and Los Angeles 1981.

Grisar (1908)
H. Grisar, *Die römische Kapelle Sancta sanctorum und ihr Schatz*, Freiburg im Breisgau 1908.

Guilding (1891)
J. M. Guilding, 'Henry the First's Tomb in Reading Abbey', *Berkshire Archaeological and Architectural Society Quarterly Journal*, 1 (1889–91), 95–99.

Guilding (1892–96)
J. M. Guilding (ed.), *Reading Records, Diary of the Corporation*, 4 vols, London 1892–96.

Gunn (2009)
S. Gunn, 'Prince Arthur's preparation for Kingship', S. Gunn and L. Monckton (eds), *Arthur Tudor, Prince of Wales: Life, Death and Commemoration*, London 2009, 7–19.

Hahn (1997)
C. Hahn, 'The Voices of the Saints: Speaking Reliquaries', *Gesta*, 36 (1997), 20–31.

Hallam (1981)

E. M. Hallam, 'The Burial Places of English Kings', *History Today*, July 1981, 44–47.

Hallam (1982)

E. M. Hallam, 'Royal burial and the cult of kingship in France and England, 1060–1330', *Journal of Medieval History*, 8 (1982), 360.

Hallam (1984)

E. M. Hallam, *The itinerary of Edward II and his household, 1307–1328*, List and Index Society Publications, vol. 211 (1984).

Halsey (1985)

R. Halsey, 'Tewkesbury Abbey: some recent observations', in *Medieval Art and Architecture at Gloucester and Tewkesbury* (British Archaeological Association Conference Transactions 7), Leeds 1985, 16–35.

Halsey (1990)

R. Halsey, 'The Twelfth-Century Church of St Frideswide's Priory', in J. Blair (ed.), *Saint Frideswide's Monastery at Oxford*, Gloucester 1990, 115–67.

Hare (1999)

J. N. Hare, *The Dissolution of the Monasteries in Hampshire*, Hampshire CC 1999.

Harrison (2006)

S. Harrison, 'Benedictine and Augustinian Cloister Arcades of the Twelfth and Thirteenth Centuries in England, Wales and Scotland', *Journal of the British Archaeological Association*, 159 (2006), 105–30.

Harvey (1993)

B. Harvey, *Living and Dying in England 1100–1540: The Monastic Experience*, Oxford 1993, 1995 ed.

Hasted (1797–1801)

E. Hasted, *The History and Topographical Survey of the County of Kent*, 12 vols, Canterbury 1797–1801.

Hatherley and Cantor (1980)

J. M. Hatherley and L. M. Cantor, 'The Medieval Parks of Berkshire', *Berkshire Archaeological Journal*, 70 (1979–80), 67–80.

Hawkes (1991)

J. Hawkes, 'Excavations on the Site of Reading Abbey Stables, 1983', *Berkshire Archaeological Journal*, 73 (1986–90), 66–87.

Hayward (2005)

M. Hayward, 'Gift Giving at the Court of Henry VIII: The 1539 New Year's Gift Roll in Context', *Antiquaries Journal* 85 (2005), 125–75.

HBC

E. B. Fryde, D. E. Greenway, S. Porter and I. Roy (ed.), *Handbook of British Chronology*, 3rd ed. London 1986.

Héliot (1956)

P. Héliot, 'La nef et le clocher de l'ancienne cathedrale de Cambrai', *Wallraf-Richartz-Jahrbuch*, 18 (1956), 91–110.

Hell and Hell (1966)

V. Hell and H. Hell, *The great pilgrimage of the middle ages. The road to St James of Compostela*, London 1966 (translated from the German edition, Tübingen 1964).

Henry (1990)

A. Henry, *The Eton Roundels: Eton College, MS 177 ('Figurae bibliorum')*, Aldershot 1990.

Henry of Huntingdon
D. Greenway (trans. and ed.), *Henry of Huntingdon, The History of the English People 1000–1154*, Oxford 1996 (2002 edition).

Henry VIII Privy Purse Expenses
N. H. Nicolas (ed.), *The Privy Purse Expences of King Henry the Eighth*, London 1827.

Herwaarden (1980)
J. van Herwaarden, 'The Origins of the Cult of St James of Compostela', *Journal of Medieval History*, 6 (1980), 1–35.

Heslop (1986)
T. A. Heslop, '"Brief in words but heavy in the weight of its mysteries"', *Art History*, 9.1 (1986), 1–11.

Heslop (1994)
T. A. Heslop, *Norwich Castle Keep, Romanesque Architecture and Social Context*. Norwich, 1994.

Heslop (2005)
T. A. Heslop, 'The English Origins of the Coronation of the Virgin', *Burlington Magazine*, 147 (2005), 790–97.

Hicks (2002)
M. A. Hicks, *Warwick the Kingmaker*, London 2002.

Hillaby (1995)
J. Hillaby, 'Leominster and Hereford: The Origins of the Diocese', in D. Whitehead (ed.), *Medieval Art, Architecture and Archaeology at Hereford* (British Archaeological Association Conference Transactions 15), Leeds 1995, 1–14.

Historia Compostellana
E. Flórez (ed.), *Historia Compostellana*, Madrid, 1765.

Hohler (1978)
C. Hohler, 'Reflections on some MSS containing 13th-century Polyphony', *Journal of the Plainsong and Medieval Music Society*, 1 (1978), 2–38.

Hope (1906)
W. St J. Hope, 'The Making of Place House', *Archaeological Journal*, 63 (1906), 231–43.

Hope (1913)
W. St J. Hope, *Windsor Castle: an architectural history*, 3 vols, London 1913.

Hope (1917)
W. St J. Hope, 'Quire Screens in English Churches, with special reference to the Twelfth-Century Quire Screen formerly in the Cathedral Church of Ely', *Archaeologia*, 68 (1917), 43–110.

Horn (1963)
W. Horn, 'The Great Tithe Barn of Cholsey, Berkshire', *Journal of the Society of Architectural Historians*, 22.1 (1963), 13–23.

Horrox and Hammond (1979–83)
R. Horrox and P. W. Hammond (eds), *British Library Harleian Manuscript 433*, 4 vols, London 1979–83.

Hoving (1965)
T. P. F. Hoving, 'A Newly Discovered Reliquary of St. Thomas Becket', *Gesta*, 4 (Spring 1965), 28–30.

Howard (1987)

M. Howard, *The Early Tudor Country House: Architecture and Politics, 1490–1550*, London 1987.

Howard (2003)

M. Howard, 'Recycling the Monastic Fabric: Beyond the Act of Dissolution', in Gaimster and Gilchrist (2003), 221–34.

Howard Accounts

J. P. Collier (ed.), *Household Books of John, Duke of Norfolk and Thomas, Earl of Surrey, 1481–90*, London 1844.

Hurry (1901)

J. B. Hurry, *Reading Abbey*, London 1901.

Hurry (1906a)

J. B. Hurry, *The Rise and Fall of Reading Abbey*, London 1906.

Hurry (1906b)

J. B. Hurry, 'Reading Abbey', *Journal of the British Archaeological Association*, NS 12 (1906), 40–42.

Hurry (1914)

J. B. Hurry, *Sumer is icumen in*, London 1914.

Hurry (1915)

J. B. Hurry, 'The Shrine of St James at Reading Abbey', *The Antiquary*, 51 (1915), 382–86.

Hurry (1919)

J. B. Hurry, *The Trial by Combat of Henry de Essex and Robert de Montfort at Reading Abbey*, London 1919.

Hurry (1930)

J. B. Hurry, *The Woad Plant and its Dye*, Oxford 1930 (published posthumously).

Ives (1983)

E. W. Ives, *The Common Lawyers of pre-Reformation England*, Cambridge 1983.

James and Jenkins (1932)

M. R. James and C. Jenkins, *A Descriptive Catalogue of the MSS in the Library of Lambeth Palace*, Cambridge 1932.

Jocelin of Brakelond

H. E. Butler (ed. and trans.), *Cronica Jocelini de Brakelonda de rebus gestis Samsonis Abbatis Monasterii Sancti Edmundi*, London 1949 (repr. 1962).

John of Reading

J. Tait (ed.), *Chronica Johannis de Reading et anonymi Cantuarensis 1346–1367*, Manchester 1914.

John of Salisbury

M. Chibnall (ed.) *The Historia Pontificalis of John of Salisbury*, Oxford 1986.

John of Wallingford

J. Stevenson (ed.), *The Church Historians of England*, vol. 2, part 2, London 1854, 523–64.

John of Worcester

P. McGurk (ed.), *The Chronicle of John of Worcester*, 3 vols, Oxford 1998.

Joranson (1938)

E. Joranson, 'The Palestine pilgrimage of Henry the Lion', in J. L. Cate and E. N. Anderson (ed.), *Medieval and historiographical essays in honor of James Westfall Thompson*, Chicago 1938, 146–225.

Juvenis (1786)

Juvenis, 'Body lately found at Reading not that of HenryI', *Gentleman's Magazine* 56 (1786), 11–13.

Kahn (1991)

D. Kahn, *Canterbury Cathedral and its Romanesque Sculpture*, London 1991.

Kauffmann (1975)

C. M. Kauffmann, *Romanesque Manuscripts 1066–1190*, A Survey of MSS Illuminated in the British Isles, ed. J. Alexander, vol. 3, London 1975.

Keefe (1981)

T. K. Keefe, 'King Henry II and the Earls: The Pipe Roll Evidence', *Albion: A Quarterly Journal Concerned with British Studies*, 13.3 (Autumn 1981), 191–222.

Kemp (1968)

B. Kemp, 'The Monastic Dean of Leominster', *English Historical Review*, 83 (1968), 505–15.

Kemp (1970)

B. Kemp, 'The Miracles of the Hand of St James', *Berkshire Archaeological Journal*, 65 (1970), 1–20.

Kemp (1986)

B. Kemp (ed.), *Reading Abbey Cartularies*, 2 vols, London (Camden Fourth Series, vols 31 (1986) and 33 (1987)).

Kemp (1988)

B. Kemp, 'The Seals of Reading Abbey', *Reading Medieval Studies*, 14 (1988), 139–162.

Ker (1964)

N. R. Ker, *Medieval Libraries of Great Britain. A list of surviving books*, 2nd edn, London 1964.

Kerry (1883)

C. Kerry, *History of the Municipal Church of St Lawrence, Reading*, Reading 1883.

Keyser (1916)

C. E. Keyser, 'Norman capitals from Sonning, Berks., and sculptured stones at Shiplake and Windsor Castle, probably brought from Reading abbey', *Proceedings of the Society of Antiquaries of London*, 2nd series, 28 (1915–16), 234–45.

Kidson (1962)

P. Kidson in P. Kidson and P. Murray, *A History of English Architecture*, London 1962.

King (1996)

J. F. King, 'Sources, Iconography and Context of the Old Sarum Master's Sculpture', L. Keen and T. Cocke (eds), *Salisbury Cathedral, Medieval Art and Architecture* (British Archaeological Association Conference Transactions 17), Leeds 1996, 79–84.

King (2000)

E. King, 'Stephen of Blois, Count of Mortain and Boulogne', *English Historical Review*, 115.461 (April 2000), 271–96.

Klein (2004)

H. A. Klein, 'Eastern Objects and Western Desires: Relics and Reliquaries between Byzantium and the West', *Dumbarton Oaks Papers*, 58 (2004), 283–314.

Knowles (1938)

D. Knowles, 'The Canterbury Election of 1205–6', *English Historical Review*, 53.210 (April 1938), 211–20.

Knowles (1959)

D. Knowles, *The religious orders in England*, 3, The Tudor Age, Cambridge 1959 (reprinted 1971).

Knowles and Hadcock (1974)

D. Knowles and R. N. Hadcock, *Medieval religious houses, England and Wales*, 2nd edn, London 1971.

Lancs Inquests

W. Farrer (ed.), *Lancashire Inquests, Extents, and Feudal Aids: A.D. 1205-A.D. 1307; Part II. A.D. 1310-A.D. 1333; Part III. A.D. 1313-A.D. 1355*, Lancashire and Cheshire Record Society, vols 48, 54, 70 (1903–15).

Landon (1935)

L. Landon, *The itinerary of King Richard I: with studies on certain matters of interest connected with his reign*, London 1935.

L and P Henry VIII

Letters and Papers Foreign and Domestic of the Reign of Henry VIII, 21 vols, 1st edn, London 1862–1910, or 2nd edn, London 1920–32.

Lasko (1972)

P. Lasko, *Ars Sacra 800–1200*. Pelican History of Art, Harmondsworth 1972.

Lawrence (2008)

M. Lawrence, 'Secular Patronage and Religious Devotion: The Despensers and St Mary's Abbey, Tewkesbury', N. Saul (ed.), *Fourteenth Century England*, V (2008), 78–93.

Lehmann-Brockhaus (1955–1960)

O. Lehmann-Brockhaus, *Lateinische Schriftquellen zur Kunst in England, Wales und Schottland vom Jahre 901 bis zum Jahre 1307*, 5 vols, Munich 1955–1960.

Leland Collectanea

T. Hearne (ed.), *Joannis Lelandii Antiquarii de Rebus Britannicis Collectanea cum Thomae Hearnii Prefatione Notis …* , 6 vols, London 1770–74.

Leland Itineraries

L. T. Smith (ed.), *The Itinerary of John Leland in or about the years 1535–1543*, 5 vols, London 1906–10.

Leo de Rozmital

De Leonis a Rosmital nobilis Bohemi itinere per partes Germaniae, Belgii, Britanniae, Franciae, Hispaniae, Portugalliae atque Italiae, annis MCCCCLXV–VII, Stuttgart 1843.

Lethaby (1925)

W. R. Lethaby, *Westminster Abbey re-examined*, London 1925.

Levot (1877)

P. Levot, 'Daoulas et son abbaye', *Bulletin de la Société archéologique du Finistère*, 2nd series, 3 (1875–76), Brest 1877, 113 –190.

Leyser (1975)

K. Leyser, 'Frederick Barbarossa, Henry II and the Hand of St James', *English Historical Review* 90 (1975), 481–506.

Liber Eliensis

E. O. Blake (ed.), *Liber Eliensis*, Camden Society, 3rd series, 92, 1962.

Lockett (1971)

R. B. Lockett, 'A Catalogue of Romanesque Sculpture from the Cluniac Houses in England', *Journal of the British Archaeological Association*, 3rd series, 34 (1971), 43–61

London (1984)

English Romanesque Art 1066–1200. Exhibition catalogue, Arts Council of Great Britain, Hayward Gallery, London 1984.

London (1984a)

The Golden Age of Anglo Saxon Art 966–1066. Exhibition catalogue, British Museum, London 1984.

London (1987)

Age of Chivalry. Art in Plantagenet England 1200–1400, Exhibition catalogue, Royal Academy of Arts, London 1987.

Lysons (1806–22)

D. and S. Lysons, *Magna Britannia*, 6 vols, London 1806–22.

McAleer (1983)

J. P. McAleer, 'The Romanesque Choir of Tewkesbury Abbey and the Problem of the "Colossal Order"', *Art Bulletin*, 65 (1983), 535–58.

McCulloch (1981)

F. McCulloch, 'Saints Alban and Amphibalus in the Works of Matthew Paris: Dublin, Trinity College MS 177', *Speculum* 56.4 (1981), 761–85.

McFarlane (1972)

K. B. McFarlane, *Lancastrian kings and Lollard knights*, Oxford 1972.

Man (1816)

J. Man, *The history and antiquities, ancient and modern, of the borough of Reading: in the county of Berks*, Reading 1816.

Martin (1926)

A. R. Martin, 'On the Topography of the Cluniac Abbey of St Saviour at Bermondsey', *Journal of the British Archaeological Association*, 32 (1926), 192–228.

Martin (1998)

J. Martin, 'Leadership and Priorities in Reading during the Reformation', in Collinson and Craig (1998), 113–129.

Mason (1988)

E. Mason, 'Fact and fiction in the English crusading tradition: the earls of Warwick in the twelfth century', *Journal of Medieval History*, 14 (1988), 81–95.

Massé (1900)

H. J. L. J. Massé, *Bell's Cathedrals: The Abbey Church of Tewkesbury with some Account of the Priory Church of Deerhurst Gloucestershire*, London 1900.

Meinardus (1961)

O. Meinardus, 'The Ceremony of the Holy Fire in the Middle Ages and To-Day', *Bulletin de la société d'archeologie copte*, 16 (1961–62), 243–52.

Mesplé (1958)

P. Mesplé, 'Chapiteaux du cloitre de Lombez au Musée des Augustins de Toulouse et au Victoria and Albert Museum de Londres', *La Revue des Arts*, 8 (1958), 177–84.

Meyer (1891)

P. Meyer (ed. and trans.), *L'Histoire de Guillaume le Marechal Comte de Striguil et de Pembroke*, 3 vols, Paris 1891–1901.

MGH (SS)

Monumenta Germaniae Historica, Scriptores in folio (SS), 38 vols, Hanover 1826–2000.

MGH (SS rer. Germ.)

Monumenta Germaniae Historica, Scriptores rerum Germanicarum in usum scholarum separatim editi, 75 vols, Hanover 1871–2002.

Molyneux (2008)

N. A. D. Molyneux, 'Kenilworth Castle in 1563', *English Heritage Historical Review*, 3 (2008), 46–61.

Morgan (1982)

N. J. Morgan, *Early Gothic Manuscripts*, I, 1190–1250, London 1982.

Morris (1983)

R. K. Morris, 'The Herefordshire School: Recent Discoveries', in F. H. Thompson (ed.), *Studies in Medieval Sculpture*, London 1983, 198–201.

Morris (2009)

R. K. Morris, '"I was Never More in Love with an Olde Howse nor Never Newe Worke Could be Better Bestowed": The Earl of Leicester's Remodelling of Kenilworth Castle for Queen Elizabeth I', *Antiquaries Journal*, 89 (2009), 241–306.

Mortimer (1994)

R. Mortimer, *Angevin England 115 –1258*, Oxford 1994 (paperback edition 1996).

Mowat (1919)

R. B. Mowat, *Henry V*, Boston 1919.

Müller (1907)

A. V. Müller, *Die hochheilige Vorhaut, im Kult und in der Theologie der Papstkirche*, Berlin 1907.

Nares (1817)

R. Nares, 'Observations on the Discovery of Part of a Sarcophagus at Reading Abbey, in Berkshire, supposed to have contained the Remains of King Henry I', in a Letter from the Rev. Robert Nares, B.D. F.R.S. and S.A. to Henry Ellis, Esq. F.R.S. Secretary, *Archaeologia, 18* (1817), 272–74.

Navascués (1948)

J. M. de Navascués, 'La dedicación de la Iglesia de Santa Maria y de todas las Virgines de Mérida', *Archivo español de arqueología*, 21 (1948), 309–59.

New York (1982)

Radiance and Reflection: Medieval Art from the Raymond Pitcairn Collection, Exhibition Catalogue, New York, Metropolitan Museum (Cloisters), 1982.

Nichols (1823)

J. G. Nichols, *The Progresses and Public Processions of Queen Elizabeth*, 3 vols, London 1823.

Nichols (1828)

J. G. Nichols, *The Progresses, Processions and Magnificent Festivities of King James the First*, 4 vols, London 1828.

Nichols (1857)

J. G. Nichols (ed.), *Literary Remains of King Edward the Sixth*, 2 vols, London 1857.

Norwich (1980)

Medieval Sculpture from Norwich Cathedral, Exhibition catalogue, Norwich, Sainsbury Centre for Visual Arts, University of East Anglia, 1980.

Ordericus Vitalis

M. Chibnall (ed.), *The Ecclesiastical History of Ordericus Vitalis,* 6 vols, Oxford, 1969–80.

Ormrod (1989)

W. M. Ormrod, 'The Personal Religion of Edward III', *Speculum,* 64 (1989), 849–77.

Oxford DNB

Oxford Dictionary of National Biography, Oxford University Press, 2004.

Paris (1981)

Les Fastes du Gothique. Le Siècle de Charles V, Exhibition catalogue, Paris, Galeries nationales du Grand Palais, 9 October 1981–1 February 1982.

Paris (1998)

L'Art au temps des rois maudits, Philippe le Bel et ses fils 1285–1328, Exhibition catalogue, Paris, Galeries nationales du Grand Palais, 17 March–29 June 1998.

Parker (1902)

J. H. Parker, *An Introduction to the Study of Gothic Architecture,* Oxford 1849 (14th ed. 1902, reprinted Wakefield 1978).

Parry (1839)

C. H. Parry, *The Parliament and Councils of England, chronologically arranged, from the reign of William I. to the Revolution in 1688,* London 1839.

Parsons (1991)

D. Parsons, 'Stone', in J. Blair and N. Ramsay (eds), *English Medieval Industries,* London 1991.

Paul (1960)

J. E. Paul, 'The Last Abbots of Reading and Colchester', *Bulletin of the Institute of Historical Research,* 33 (1960), 115–21.

Pettigrew (1860)

T. J. Pettigrew, 'On Reading and its Antiquities', *Journal of the British Archaeological Association,* 16 (1860), 177–200.

Philp (1968)

B. Philp, *Excavations at Faversham 1965: The Royal Abbey, Roman Villa and Belgic Farmstead,* Crawley 1968.

Pigott (1785)

F. Pigott, 'Skeleton of King Henry the First discovered at Reading', *Gentleman's Magazine,* 15 (1785), 881.

Postles (1996)

D. Postles, 'Monastic Burials of Non-Patronal Lay Benefactors', *The Journal of Ecclesiastical History,* 47 (1996), 620–37.

Preston (1935)

A. E. Preston, 'The Demolition of Reading Abbey', *Berkshire Archaeological Journal,* 39 (1935), 107–44.

Prior (1900)

E. S. Prior, *A History of Gothic Architecture in England,* London 1900.

Prior and Gardner (1912)

E. S. Prior and A. Gardner, *An Account of Medieval Figure-Sculpture in England,* Cambridge 1912.

Pritchard (1913)

C. F. Pritchard, *Reading Charters, Acts and Orders 1253 – 1911*, Reading 1913.

Privy Council

Sir H. Nicolas, *Proceedings and ordinances of the Privy Council of England*, 7 vols, London 1834–37.

Prynne (1659)

W. Prynne, *Parliamentary Writs (The First Part of a Brief Register, Kalendar and Survey of the several Kinds, Forms of all Parliamentary Writs*, London 1659.

Ralph of Diceto

W. Stubbs (ed.), *Radulfi de Diceto decani Lundoniensis opera historica*, Rolls Series 68, 2 vols, London 1876.

Ramm *et al.* (1977)

H. G. Ramm, D. W. Black, E. C. Rouse, F. Wormald, C. Oman, A. E. A. Werner and G. A. C. Summers, 'The Tombs of Archbishop Walter de Gray (1216–55) and Godfrey de Ludham (1258–65) in York Minster, and their contents', *Archaeologia*, 103 (1977), 101–47.

Reading Corp. MSS

W. D. Macray (ed.), 'The Manuscripts of Reading Corporation', *Historical Manuscripts Commission Eleventh Report, Appendix, Part VII*, London 1888.

Reeve (2008)

M. M. Reeve, *Thirteenth-Century Wall Painting of Salisbury Cathedral: Art, Liturgy, and Reform*, London 2008.

Regesta Regum

Regesta regum Anglo-Normannorum 1066–1154, 4 vols, Oxford 1913–1968, vol. 1, H. W. C. Davis (ed.), Oxford, 1913; vol. 2, C. Johnson and H.A. Cronne (ed.) Oxford, 1956; vols. 3 and 4, H. A. Cronne and R. H. C. Davis (ed.) Oxford, 1968.

Remensnyder (1996)

A. G. Remensnyder, 'Legendary Treasure at Conques: Reliquaries and Imaginative Memory', *Speculum* 71 (1996), 884–906.

Rickman (1881)

T. Rickman, *An Attempt to Discriminate the Styles of Architecture in England from the Conquest to the Reformation*. 7th ed. London, 1881.

Robert de Torigni

L. Delisle (ed.), *Chronique de Robert de Torigni, Abbe du Mont Saint-Michel*, vol. 1, Rouen 1872.

Robertini (1994)

L. Robertini (ed.), *Liber miraculorum sancte Fidis*. Spoleto 1994.

Robinson (1998)

W. R. B. Robinson, 'Princess Mary's Itinerary in the Marches of Wales 1525–1527: a Provisional Record', *Historical Research*, 71 (1998), 232–52.

Röhrig (1955)

F. Röhrig, *Der Verduner Altar*, Klosterneuburg 1955.

Rot. Chartarum

T. D. Hardy (ed.), *Rotuli Chartarum In Turri Londinensi Asservati*, Vol. 1. Pars 1. Ab anno MCXCIX ad annum MCCXVI. London 1837.

Rot. Cur. Reg.

F. Palgrave (ed.), *Rotuli Curae Regis.. 6 Richard I – 1 John*, 2 vols, London 1835.

Rot. Litt. Patt. King John.

T. D. Hardy (ed.), *Rotuli Litterarum Patentium*, vol. 1, pars 1, London 1835.

Rot. Parl.

Rotuli Parliamentorum: ut et petitiones et placita in parliamento, 6 vols, London 1783.

Rudolph (1988)

C. Rudolph, 'Bernard of Clairvaux's Apologia as a Description of Cluny, and the Controversy over Monastic Art', *Gesta*, 27.1/2 (1988), 125–32.

Rylands (1907)

W. H. Rylands (ed.), *Visitations of Berkshire, 1532, 1566, 1623 and 1665–66.* London (Harleian Society Publications), 2 vols, 1907–08.

Rymer

T. Rymer, *Foedera, conventiones, literae et cujuscunque generis acta publica inter reges Angliae et alios quosvis imperatores, reges, pontifices ...* , 10 vols, The Hague, 1739–45.

Safford (1974–77)

E. W. Safford, *Itinerary of Edward I*, 3 parts. List and Index Society Publications vols 103 (1974), 132 (1976), 135 (1977).

Salmon (1946)

J. Salmon, 'Beakhead ornament in Norman Architecture', *Yorkshire Archaeological Journal* 36 (1946), 349–57.

Salzman (1967)

L. F. Salzman, *Building in England, down to 1540: a Documentary History*, revised ed., Oxford, 1967.

Saul (1997)

N. Saul, 'Richard II, York, and the Evidence of the King's Itinerary', in J. L. Gillespie, *The Age of Richard II*, London 1997, 71–92.

Sawyer (1968)

P. H. Sawyer, *Anglo-Saxon Charters: an Annotated List and Bibliography*, London 1968. Available online at The Electronic Sawyer (www.trin.cam.ac.uk/chartwww/esawyer.99/esawyer2.html)

Saxl (1954)

F. Saxl, *English Sculptures of the Twelfth Century*, London 1954.

Scantlebury (1943)

R. E. Scantlebury, *The Story of Reading Abbey and The Catholic Church in Reading*, Reading 1943.

Scofield (1923)

C. L. Scofield, *The life and reign of Edward the fourth King of England and of France and Lord of Ireland*, 2 vols 1923.

Seabourne (2007)

G. Seabourne, 'Eleanor of Brittany and her treatment by King John and Henry III', *Nottingham Medieval Studies*, 51 (2007), 73–110.

Searle (1980)

E. Searle, 'Women and the Legitimisation of Succession at the Norman Conquest', *California Institute of Technology, Pasadena Social Science Working Paper 328*, July 1980.

Shell (1997)

M. Shell, 'The Holy Foreskin: or, Money, Relics, and Judeo-Christianity' in J. and

D. Boyarin (ed.), *Jews and Other Differences: the New Jewish Cultural Studies*, Minneapolis 1997, 345–59.

Sheingorn (1995)

P. Sheingorn, *The Book of Sainte Foy*, Philadelphia 1995.

Shenton (2007)

C. Shenton, *The itinerary of Edward III and his household, 1327–1345* . List and Index Society Publications vol. 318 (2007).

Short (1973)

I. Short (ed.), *The Anglo-Norman Pseudo-Turpin Chronicle of William de Briane*. Anglo-Norman Text Society. Oxford 1973.

Simon (1979)

D. L. Simon, 'Le Sarcophage de Doña Sancha à Jaca,' *Cahiers de Saint-Michel de Cuxa*, 10 (1979), 107–124.

Skelton (1951)

R. A. Skelton, 'Tudor town plans in John Speed's *Theatre*', *Archaeological Journal*, 108 (1951), 109–20.

Slade (1970)

C. F. Slade, "Paving Tiles at Reading Abbey", *Berkshire Archaeological Journal*, 64 (1970), 9.

Slade (1972)

C. F. Slade, "Excavations at Reading Abbey 1964–67." *Berkshire Archaeological Journal*, 66 (1971–72), 65–116.

Slade (1975–76)

C. F. Slade, "Excavations at Reading Abbey 1971–73." *Berkshire Archaeological Journal*, 68 (1975–76), 29–70.

Slade (2001)

C. F. Slade, *The Town of Reading and its Abbey*, Reading 2001.

Speed (1610)

J. Speed, *The Theatre of the Empire of Great Britaine*, London 1610–11, reprinted as J. Speed and N. Nicolson (introduction), *The Counties of Britain: A Tudor Atlas*, London 1989.

Spencer (1990)

B. Spencer, *Salisbury and South Wiltshire Museum Medieval Catalogue. Part 2, Pilgrim souvenirs and secular badges*. Salisbury 1990.

Stafford (2000)

P. Stafford, '*Cherchez la femme*. Queens, Queens' Lands and Nunneries: Missing Links in the Foundation of Reading Abbey', *History* 85, 277 (2000), 4–27.

Stalley (1971)

R. Stalley, 'A Twelfth-Century Patron of Architecture. A study of the buildings erected by Roger, Bishop of Salisbury 1102–1139', *Journal of the British Archaeological Association* 34 (1971), 62–83.

Stalley (2012)

R. Stalley, 'Diffusion, Imitation and Evolution: The Uncertain Origins of 'Beakhead' ornament', J. A. Franklin, T. A. Heslop and C. Stevenson (ed.), *Architecture and Interpretation. Essays for Eric Fernie*, Woodbridge 2012, 111–27.

Stenton (1951)

D. M. Stenton, *English Society in the Early Middle Ages (1066–1307)*, Harmondsworth 1951 (4th edition 1965).

Stone (1955)

L. Stone, *Sculpture in Britain. The Middle Ages,* Pelican History of Art, Harmondsworth 1955.

Storey (1957)

R. L. Storey, 'The Wardens of the Marches of England towards Scotland, 1377–1489', *English Historical Review,* 285 (1957), 593–615.

Stoughton (1862)

J. Stoughton, *Windsor: A History and Description of the Castle and the Town,* London 1862.

Stratford (1978)

N. Stratford, 'Notes on the Norman Chapterhouse at Worcester', *Medieval Art and Architecture at Worcester Cathedral* (British Archaeological Association Conference Transactions 1), 51–70.

Studd (2000)

R. Studd, *An Itinerary of the Lord Edward, 1254–72,* List and Index Society Publications vol. 284 (2000).

Swarzenski 1954

H. Swarzenski, *Monuments of Romanesque Art. The Art of Church Treasures in North-Western Europe.* London 1954, 1974 ed.

Symeonis Monachi Opera

Simeon of Durham. *Symeonis Monachi Opera Omnia.* ed. by T. Arnold. Rolls Series 75, 2 vols. London 1882–1885.

Talbot (1956)

C. H. Talbot, 'The Date and Author of the Riposte', in G. Constable and J. Kritzeck (ed.), *Petrus Venerabilis (1156–1956): studies and texts commemorating the eighth centenary of his death,* Rome 1956, 72–80.

Taralon (1989)

D. Taralon, 'Le «reliquaire de Pépin» du trésor de Conques', Mémoire de maîtrise d'histoire de l'art, Université de Paris-Sorbonne IV, 1989.

Tatton Brown (2006)

T. Tatton Brown, 'The Two Mid-Twelfth-Century Cloister Arcades at Canterbury Cathedral Priory', *Journal of the British Archaeological Association,* 159 (2006), 91–104.

Taylor (1890)

J. Okey Taylor, 'Reading Abbey', *Quarterly Journal of the Berks Archaeological and Architectural Society,* 1.7 (Oct. 1890), 156–60.

Taylor (1997)

B. Taylor, 'The Hand of St James', *Berkshire Archaeological Journal* 75 (1994–97), 97–102.

Temple (1976)

E. Temple, *Anglo-Saxon Manuscripts, 900–1066.* London 1976.

Tewkesbury Chronicle

W. Dugdale, *Monasticon Anglicanum,* 2, London 1819, 59–65.

Thiébaut (1975)

J. Thiébaut, 'La cathédrale disparue de Cambrai et sa place dans l'évolution de l'architecture du Nord de la France', PhD thesis, Lille 1975.

Thirion (1988)

J. Thirion, 'Le Cloitre de Saint-Sauveur d'Aix', *Congres Archéologique de France,* 143rd session (1985), Paris 1988, 65–90.

Thompson (1902)

E. M. Thompson, *Customary of the Benedictine Monasteries of St Augustine, Canterbury and St Peter, Westminster,* 2 vols, London 1902, 1904.

Thompson (2002)

K. Thompson, 'Queen Adeliza and the Lotharingian Connection', *Sussex Archaeological Collections* 140 (2002), 57–64.

Thompson (2003)

K. Thompson, 'Affairs of State: the illegitimate children of Henry I', *Journal of Medieval History* 29, 2 (2003), 129–51.

Thurlby (1989)

M. Thurlby, "Observations on the Twelfth-Century Sculpture from Bridlington Priory", in C. Wilson (ed.), *Medieval Art and Architecture in the East Riding of Yorkshire.* (British Archaeological Association Conference Transactions 9), Leeds 1989, 33–43.

Thurlby and Baxter (2002)

M. Thurlby and R. Baxter, "The Romanesque Abbey Church at Reading", L. Keen and E. Scarff (ed.), *Windsor: Medieval Archaeology, Art and Architecture of the Thames Valley* (British Archaeological Association Conference Transactions 25), 282–301.

Thurley (1991)

S. Thurley, 'English Royal Palaces 1450–1550', PhD thesis, Courtauld Institute of Art, University of London 1992.

Tighe and Davies (1858)

R. R. Tighe and J. E. Davies, *Annals of Windsor, being a History of the Castle and Town with Some Account of Eton and Places Adjacent,* 2 vols, London 1858.

TNA

The National Archives.

Tout (1920)

T. F. Tout, *Chapters in the Administrative History of Mediaeval England: The Wardrobe, The Chambers and the Small Seals,* 6 vols, Manchester 1920–33.

Tracy (2009)

C. Tracy, 'The 14th-Century Canons' Stalls in the Collegiate Church of St Mary, Astley, Warwickshire', *Journal of the British Archaeological Association,* 162 (2009), 88–124.

Usher (1972)

G. A. Usher, 'The Career of a Political Bishop: Adam de Orleton (c. 1279–1345), *Transactions of the Royal Historical Society (Fifth Series),* vol. 22 (1972), 33–47.

VCH Berkshire 2 (1907)

W. Page and P. H. Ditchfield (eds), *The Victoria History of the County of Berkshire,* 2 (1907).

VCH Berkshire 3 (1923)

W. Page and P. H. Ditchfield (eds), *The Victoria History of the County of Berkshire,* 3 (1923).

VCH Hampshire 2 (1903)

H. A. Doubleday and W. Page (eds), *The Victoria History of the County of Hampshire,* 2 (1903).

VCH Hampshire 3 (1908)

H. A. Doubleday and W. Page (eds), *The Victoria History of the County of Hampshire,* 3 (1908).

VCH Somerset 2 (1911)
W. Page (ed.), *The Victoria History of the County of Somerset*, 2 (1911).
VCH Hertfordshire 3 (1912)
W. Page (ed.), *The Victoria History of the County of Hertford*, 3 (1912).
VCH Sussex 2 (1907)
W. Page (ed.), *The Victoria History of the County of Sussex*, 2 (1907).
Vince, Fasham and Hawkes (1979)
A. G. Vince, P. J. Fasham and J. W. Hawkes, 'Excavations at Reading Abbey 1979 and 1981', *Berkshire Archaeological Journal*, 71 (1982), 33–55.
Vita Oswaldi
Vita Oswaldi archiepiscopi eboracensis, in J. Raine (ed.), *The Historians of the Church of York and its Archbishops*, vol. 1, London 1879, 399–475.
Walpole letters
P. Cunningham (ed.), *The Letters of Horace Walpole Earl of Orford*, 9 vols, Edinburgh 1906.
Webb (1965)
G. Webb, *Architecture in Britain. The Middle Ages*, Pelican History of Art, Harmondsworth 1965.
Webb (2000)
D. Webb, *Pilgrimage in Medieval England*, Hambledon and London, 2000.
Wedgwood and Holt (1936)
J. C. Wedgwood and A. D. Holt, *History of Parliament : Biographies of the Members of the Commons House 1439–1509*, London 1936.
Weir (2001)
A. Weir, *Henry VIII. King and Court,* London 2001.
West (1993)
J. West, 'Acanthus ornament in late Anglo-Saxon and Romanesque England', in *L'acanthe dans la sculpture monumentale de l'Antiquité à la Renaissance*, Mémoires de la section d'archéologie et d'histoire de l'art IV, Histoire de l'art VI, Paris 1993, 247–268.
West (2013)
J. West, 'The Romanesque Screen at Canterbury Cathedral Reconsidered', in A. Bovey (ed.), *Medieval Art, Architecture and Archaeology at Canterbury* (British Archaeological Association Conference Transactions, 35), Leeds 2013, 167–79.
Westminster Chronicle
L. C. Hector and B. F. Harvey (eds), *The Westminster Chronicle 1381–94,* Oxford 1982.
Whittingham (1951)
A. B. Whittingham, 'Bury St. Edmund's Abbey: The Plan Design, and Development of the Church and Monastic Buildings', *Archaeological Journal*, 108 (1951), 160–89.
Wilkins (1979)
N. Wilkins, *Music in the Age of Chaucer,* Cambridge 1979.
William of Malmesbury
J. Stevenson (ed.), *The Church Historians of England, Vol. III, part I, containing the History of the Kings of England and of his Own Times by William of Malmesbury,* trans. (1815) J. Sharpe, London 1854.

William of Malmesbury GR

R. A. B. Mynors, completed by R. M. Thomson and M. Winterbottom (eds), *William of Malmesbury, Gesta Regum Anglorum*, 2 vols, Oxford 1998–1999.

William of Malmesbury GP

N. E. S. A. Hamilton (ed.), *Willelmi Malmesbiriensis monachi De gestis pontificum anglorum Libri Quinque*, London 1870.

William of Malmesbury HN

E. King (ed.), K. R. Potter (trans.), *Historia Novella: the contemporary history*, Oxford 1998.

William of Newburgh

William of Newburgh, *Historia rerum Anglicarum*, ed. R. Howlett, in *Chronicles of the reigns of Stephen, Henry II, and Richard I*, Rolls Series 82, 4 vols, London 1884–89.

Williamson (1983)

P. Williamson, *Catalogue of Romanesque Sculpture, Victoria and Albert Museum*, London 1983.

Willis (1845)

R. Willis, *The Architectural History of Canterbury Cathedral*, London 1845.

Wilmart (1934)

A. Wilmart, 'Une Riposte de l'Ancien Monachisme au Manifeste de Saint Bernard', *Revue Bénédictine*, 46 (1934), 296–344.

Wilson *et al.* (1986)

C. Wilson, P. Tudor-Craig, J. Physick and R. Gem, *The New Bell's Cathedral Guides: Westminster Abbey*, London 1986.

Wilson (1990)

C. Wilson, *The Gothic Cathedral*, London 1990

Winchcombe Annals

R. R. Darlington, 'Winchcombe Annals 1049–1181', in P. M. Barnes and C. F. Slade (eds), *A Medieval Miscellany for Doris Mary Stenton*, London 1962, 111–37.

Winchester (2010)

Treasures of Hyde Abbey, Exhibition catalogue, Winchester City Council, 2010.

Wolffe (1981)

B. Wolffe, *Henry VI*, New Haven and London 1981 (2001 edn).

Woodman (1981)

F. Woodman, *The Architectural History of Canterbury Cathedral*, London and Boston 1981.

Woodman (1992)

F. Woodman, 'The Waterworks Drawings of the Eadwine Psalter', M. Gibson, T. A. Heslop and R. W. Pfaff (eds), *The Eadwine Psalter, Text, Image and Monastic Culture in Twelfth-Century Canterbury*, London 1992, 168–77.

Woodward (1861–69)

B. B. Woodward, *A General History of Hampshire or the County of Southampton including the Isle of Wight*, 3 vols, London 1861–69.

Worssam (1995a)

B. C. Worssam, *First Report on the Identification of Carved Stones from Reading Abbey*, Report to Reading Museum, 25 July 1995.

Worssam (1995b)

B. C. Worssam, 'A Guide to the Building Stones of Rochester Cathedral', *Friends of Rochester Cathedral, Report for 1993/4*, 23–24.

Wright (1843)

T. Wright (ed.), *Three Chapters of Letters relating to the Suppression of the Monasteries*, Camden series 26, London 1843.

Wyatville (1841)

J. Wyatville, *Illustrations of Windsor Castle* (to which is prefixed *An Essay on the History and Antiquities of Windsor Castle* by A. Poynter), ed. H. Ashton, London 1841.

Wylie (1884)

J. H. Wylie, *History of England under Henry the Fourth*, 4 vols, London 1884.

Yarrow (2006)

S. Yarrow, *Saints and their Communities: Miracle Stories in Twelfth-Century England*, Oxford 2006.

Zarnecki (1949)

G. Zarnecki, 'The Buried Sculpture of Reading Abbey: Chapters of an Archaeological "Detective Story"', *Illustrated London News*, April 16 1949, 524–25.

Zarnecki (1950a).

G. Zarnecki, *Regional Schools of English Sculpture in the Twelfth Century: the Southern School and the Herefordshire School*, unpublished thesis, University of London, 1950.

Zarnecki (1950b)

G. Zarnecki, 'The Coronation of the Virgin on a Capital from Reading Abbey', *Journal of the Warburg and Courtauld Institutes*, 13 (1950), 1–12.

Zarnecki (1951)

G. Zarnecki, *English Romanesque Sculpture 1066–1140*, London, 1951.

Zarnecki (1955)

G. Zarnecki, 'The Winchester Acanthus in Romanesque Sculpture', *Wallraf-Richartz Jahrbuch*, 17 (1955), 1–4.

Zarnecki (1966)

G. Zarnecki, '1066 and Architectural Sculpture', *Proceedings of the British Academy*, 1966, 87–102.

Zarnecki (1976)

G. Zarnecki, 'English 12th-century sculpture and its resistance to St Denis', F. Emmison and R. Stephens (eds), *Tribute to an antiquary: essays presented to Marc Fitch,* London 1976, 83–92.

Zarnecki and Henry (1958)

G. Zarnecki and F. Henry, 'Romanesque Arches decorated with Human and Animal Heads', *Journal of the British Archaeological Association*, 20–21 (1957–58), 1–35.

INDEX